WARNING: THIS BOOK CANNOT BE RETURNED
ONCE THE DISK SEAL HAS BEEN BROKEN.

THE CD HAS BEEN REMOVED. THE CD HAS BEEN REMOVED. THE CD HAS BEEN REMOVED. THE CD HAS BEEN REMOVED. THE CD HAS BEEN REMOVED.

An Introduction to

Digital Signal Processing
with Mathcad®

A Mathcad Electronic Book

Robert O. Harger
University of Maryland

 PWS Publishing Company
I(T)P **An International Thomson Publishing Company**

Boston • Albany • Bonn • Cincinnati • London • Madrid • Melbourne • Mexico City
New York • Paris • San Francisco • Singapore • Tokyo • Toronto • Washington

PWS Publishing Company
20 Park Plaza, Boston, MA 02116-4324

International Thomson Publishing
The trademark ITP is used under license.

For more information, contact:

PWS Publishing Company
20 Park Plaza
Boston, MA 02116-4324

Sponsoring Editor: Bill Barter
Technology/Developmental Editor:
Leslie Bondaryk
Assistant Technology Editor:
Susan Garland
Assistant Editor: Suzanne Jeans
Editorial Assistant: Tricia Kelly
Market Development Manager:
Nathan Wilbur
Production Editor: Pamela Rockwell
Manufacturing Manager:
Andrew Christensen
Text and Cover Printer: Malloy Lithographing, Inc.

International Thomson Publishing Europe
Berkshire House 168–173
High Holborn
London WC1V 7AA
England

Thomas Nelson Australia
102 Dodds Street
South Melbourne, 3205
Victoria, Australia

Nelson Canada
1120 Birchmount Road
Scarborough, Ontario
Canada M1K 5G4

International Thomson Editores
Campos Eliseos 385, Piso 7
Col. Polanco
11560 Mexico C.F., Mexico

International Thomson Publishing GmbH
Königswinterer Strasse 418
53227 Bonn, Germany

International Thomson Publishing Asia
221 Henderson Road
#05–10 Henderson Building
Singapore 0315

Printed and bound in the United States of America.

98 99 01 02—10 9 8 7 6 5 4 3 2 1

International Thomson Publishing Japan
Hirakawacho Kyowa Building, 31
2-2-1 Hirakawacho
Chiyoda-ku, Tokyo 102
Japan

Table of Contents

Sampling

IIR Filters

Spectral Density Estimation

Image Processing

Adaptive Filtering

Radar Data Processing

31 Radar Processing

Radar model for range estimation; signal processing theory; linear FM (chirp) pulse modulation; digital signal processing

32 Imaging Radar

Synthetic aperture radar; digital signal processing and simulation; the SAR image of a two-scale scene

A Mathcad Tutorial

Regions; text regions; mathematics regions; graphical regions: plots; programming; more help

Bibliography

Index

About Mathcad Electronic Books

Mathcad Electronic Books are described in the *Mathcad User's Guide*. We point out here five special features that facilitate their use.

The Electronic Book Controls Palette

A Mathcad Electronic Book is a sequence of Mathcad documents. Each document corresponds to a section of a traditional book. To enable flexible access to these sections, there is a **Controls Palette** at the upper left of the Mathcad applications window. It consists of seven buttons that allow direct access to the Table of Contents, the Index, the preceding and succeeding sections, the previously accessed section and the previous and next page in the accessed section.

Hyperlinks

Hyperlinks from a text region of a document to another document are indicated by the presence of **underlined and boldfaced text**. If you **click once** on a hyperlinked region, you will see a **message** at the bottom of the application window. (Try it!) The message will tell you what **action** will happen if you activate the hyperlink: e.g., "Go to Chapter 13". To execute the action, **double-click** on the region. The associated message will often indicate a page of the linked section. After double-clicking on the linked region, you can then use **Go to Page...** under the **Edit** menu to get to the page of the linked section.

 The **hyperlink icon** shown at the left will result in a special **Book Popup Window**. It is used in this book to provide amplifying remarks to exercises, problems and projects. The **Book Popup Window** contains a special Mathcad document that can only be copied to the clipboard.

Special Pasting Action

Mathcad documents are made up of regions containing text, mathematics or graphics. A region can be easily copied from the Electronic Book to a user-created document by dragging. Multiple regions may be more easily copied using the Windows Clipboard.

The Full-Text Search

Every word in an Electronic Book can be located using the Full-Text Search feature, which is accessed by choosing **Search Book** in the **Books** menu.

Annotation

While the original Electronic Book is always accessible, the user can make, highlight, save and delete changes for a personal copy. This feature is accessed by choosing **Annotate Book** in the **Books** menu.

Preface

This interactive book is an introduction to the analysis, modeling, design and simulation of digital signal processing systems directly on a digital computer using the high-level mathematical language Mathcad. The use of a high-level mathematical language, with symbolic, numeric, graphic and text capabilities, enables relatively easy implementation of all the topics covered in an introductory course in digital signal processing systems. Interactivity, "what if" trial-and-error solutions and graphic visualization are powerful learning methods.

A Mathcad document has a worksheet interface familiar to scientists and engineers. The syntax is relatively easy to learn and a productive facility can be obtained in a few hours. A brief Mathcad tutorial is included at the end of the book to help you get started. The active document is itself a self-checking report, easily distributed electronically.

This book is a set of hyperlinked Mathcad documents. Each document is completely interactive and composed of text, mathematics and graphics regions that can be edited and copied into new documents created by the user.

Such an environment naturally enforces some of the reality of digital signal processing (DSP) systems. A successfully implemented model is an efficiently produced prototype to guide implementation in the lower-level mathematical languages of real DSP systems.

Introduction

Digital signal processing (DSP) is an area of ever-increasing importance and interest. Its diverse applications include systems that transmit and store information - for example, digital communication systems such as wireless networks; systems that process data - for example, radar and sonar systems; and personal entertainment systems - for example, the digital compact cassette. Spurred by the ever-increasing power of microchip digital computers and the availability of high-level software for analysis and design, DSP has rapidly matured into a distinct subject based on numerical computation algorithms. Software systems are used in all stages of digital system design, from algorithm design to manufacturing. Mathematical software such as Mathcad is an economical and powerful tool for DSP algorithm conception, understanding and design.

Our primary objective in this book is to introduce the reader to digital signal processing on the computer. A secondary objective is to move reasonably rapidly to interesting, motivating applications of DSP. Collaterally, the reader will attain a facility with Mathcad, a high-level mathematical programming language. A background that would be helpful to the reader is a previous exposure to the concepts of linear systems and the use of a computer with a Windows operating system. However, much of the material is developed from basic ideas.

Contents

A linear system that is defined by the finite convolution sum, with a finite length impulse response (FIR), has many applications, including imaging and adaptive systems, and is a natural starting point for discussion of DSP systems. The natural frequency decomposition, in which many filter and system concepts are phrased and best understood, is given by the discrete Fourier transform (DFT). The DFT is implemented via what is arguably the most important algorithm in DSP, the fast Fourier transform (FFT). Then signal modeling, generation, filtering and simulation can be discussed with the FFT at hand as a built-in function in Mathcad. Chapters 1 through 4 cover this basic DSP material.

An introduction to digital image processing is accessible at this point and is given in Chapter 27. Chapter 5 applies these basic concepts to the practically important problem of processing long signals.

The frequency decomposition appropriate for arbitrarily long signals is the discrete-time Fourier transform (DTFT), a theoretical construct described in Chapters 6 and 7. The DTFT is introduced as a limiting case of the DFT. The DTFT has periodicity 2π in the frequency (ω) and is, in the cases of interest here, a rational function of $\exp(i\omega)$. The poles and zeros are of considerable interest as they provide insight into the nature of a linear system and even yield a crude design technique. The poles and zeros generally are not of the form $\exp(i\omega_k)$; in other words, they may lie elsewhere in the complex (z) plane. If one replaces $\exp(i\omega)$ with z in the DTFT, the resulting form is called the z transform (ZT). As numerical algorithms are used in DSP systems, the algebraic DTFTs and ZTs needed here are computed knowing the sum of a geometric series and using the symbolic mathematics capability of Mathcad.

FIR filters can have a linear phase characteristic, which is of considerable practical importance. A nonlinear phase characteristic causes, for example, the dispersion of pulses which can cause intersymbol interference and hence errors in digital communication systems. This class of FIR filters is described in Chapters 8 and 9.

Chapters 10 through 14 describe several FIR filter design techniques. The frequency sampling method, discussed in Chapter 10, also helps to clarify the nature of FIR filters. An application of this filter design method in a sophisticated communication system that generates a "single-sideband waveform" is discussed at length in Chapter 11. The classical window design methods are covered in Chapter 12. Chapter 13 discusses design with an optimal window and demonstrates the power of high-level software in DSP design. Here the relation to the Kaiser approximation is pointed out. The equiripple approximation, a popular design criterion for a filter's frequency response, is given an accessible treatment in Chapter 14. Advanced algorithms that compute such filters are a standard feature of DSP design software.

In many applications the ultimate source of digital signals is a sequence of samples of an analog signal. Chapter 15 addresses the critical relation between the two types of signals and explores related topics such as aliasing, reconstruction, truncation and spectral estimation. Finally, because the ability to change sample rates of digital signals is necessary, Chapters 16 and 17 treat the interpolation and decimation operations whose effects are most readily understood by associating the digital signal with a real or virtual analog signal.

A linear difference equation is a natural, efficient computational algorithm, and its implementation can be a preferred realization of a DSP system. When it has an autoregressive part, its impulse response will generally be of infinite length. Hence such filters are called infinite impulse response (IIR) filters, and the complications of stability, or summability, of sequences arises. Chapters 18 through 20 discuss these complications and demonstrate that the DTFT, necessarily a rational function of $\exp(i\omega)$, provides the needed theoretical tool for frequency domain analysis of these systems. Its extension to the ZT gives the pole-zero portrait of an IIR filter and leads to the geometric view, which provides insight into simple design methods.

Chapter 21 introduces a classical design method for IIR filters: mapping an analog filter design into a digital filter design with the bilinear transformation. The design of digital filters of the Butterworth and Chebyshev families is discussed in Chapters 22 and 23, respectively. The digital filter is directly designed for a specified squared-magnitude frequency response.

Chapters 24 through 26 introduce spectral density estimation. The spectral density can be a defining characterization of a digital signal for DSP. We require some background on random sequences, which is provided in Chapter 24, and statistical estimation, which is provided in Chapter 25. Chapter 26 discusses the common periodogram estimator and a modification of it to provide a computationally effective spectral density estimator.

Chapter 27 introduces digital images and their processing with simple FIR filters. The large computational demands of image processing are immediately evident. Chapter 28 introduces two-dimensional FIR filter design by the frequency sampling method.

Chapter 29 discusses the increasingly important topic of adaptive filtering. Such filters are useful when the data characterization is unknown or temporally varying. System identification and noise cancellation with the LMS algorithm are discussed. Then Chapter 30 considers a sophisticated application, the important problem of adaptive filtering, or equalization, for digital communication through bandlimited channels.

Radar signal processing was historically one of the first and most technologically demanding applications for DSP. Chapter 31 discusses the classic range-finding radar and illustrates the use of symbolic mathematics in a system analysis. Chapter 32 discusses imaging synthetic aperture radar, which is itself a sampling system. Its data rate is so great that DSP has only gradually replaced analog processing.

The reader should select and order the material in this book according to his or her own needs and interest. Interdependencies of the sections are sketched below for reference. Column flow on the left indicates a sequence through the basic ideas of DSP. This material can be augmented at various points. Notice, for example, that a basic introduction to image processing (in Chapter 27) can be taken up near the outset. Important augmentations to the basic material are Chapters 8 and 9, which provide additional material on FIR filters with linear phase, and Chapters 10 and 12, which discuss simple but useful design methods. Following the discussion of FIR filters and FIR design via the frequency sampling method, the reader may refer to Chapter 28 for information on the design of image-processing filters. Alternatively, the reader could progress to Chapter 29 for a discussion of adaptive filtering, or to Chapter 30, which explores digital communication, a key DSP application.

Section Dependencies

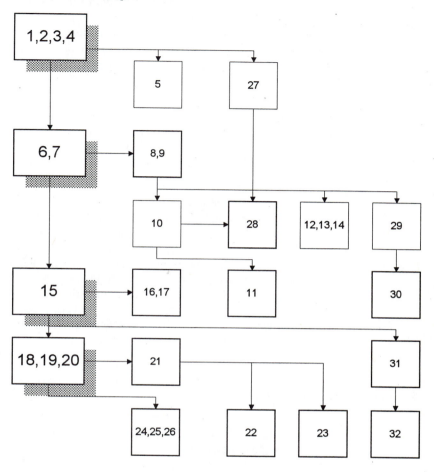

Suggestions on Use

The book has been written in an informal style to invite active involvement. Theorem - proof style has been deliberately avoided, but assertions are supported appropriately, with references given. Definitions are indicated with boldface. Examples are often used to aid in introducing new ideas.

Three types of specific interactivity are suggested: exercises, problems and projects, in order of increasing difficulty. Exercises are an integral part of the development of the material and generally request interactivity, such as changing a parameter and noting the result. Most of these are meant to be done as a chapter is studied.

Problems may suggest supplementary work and may require construction of a proof or a Mathcad document, perhaps after consulting a reference. The projects are meant to show the application of the material and, especially here, the reader should follow his or her own interest. They range in difficulty from straightforward design projects to those worthy of a final course project.

Each chapter is a Mathcad document that can be rapidly computed to enable efficient trial-and-error learning. Each also contains more than enough material for a learning unit corresponding to a one-hour-and-fifteen-minute interactive session.

After diligent interaction with the core material of this book, the reader will have developed a working familiarity with the basic ideas of digital signal processing and the principal methods of digital filter design. This interactive study also introduces the important DSP applications of digital image processing, spectral density estimation, adaptive filtering, radar data processing and digital communications. The reader will also have developed an independent skill with a high-level mathematical programming language with which he or she may efficiently develop realistic DSP models, algorithms, designs and simulations.

Acknowledgements

I would like to thank the students who have helped me develop the book and its use in a computer classroom over many semesters at the University of Maryland. Some of their suggestions are cited in the book. I also thank the editors at PWS Publishing for supplying the core of the tutorial chapter and for their guidance, patience and endurance in this novel venture. I and the publisher also wish to thank the following reviewers: Guoxiang Gu, Louisiana State University, Yu Hen Hu, University of Wisconsin, Kurt Kosbar, University of Missouri - Rolla, Bisi Oladipupo, Hampton University and Ravi Warrier, GMI Engineering and Management Institute.

1 Digital Signals

We begin our study of DSP systems with a discussion of models for their signals. A signal will be defined as a sequence whose index corresponds to a time instant. A sequence is represented in a computer by an indexed array using a programming language. We show how this is done in Mathcad and go on to implement basic operations on signals.

Digital Signals as Sequences

A **digital signal** is a real- or complex- valued function of an integer variable n, in other words, a **sequence**. The index n usually will be interpreted as **discrete time**. Typical mathematical notations for a sequence include $\{s_n\}$, $\{s\}$ and s. The value of the sequence at time n is denoted s_n.

A digital computer can store a sequence of only finite length, commonly denoted N. For digital signals of length N, the index n conventionally takes on the values $\{0,1,...,N-1\}$. A sequence of finite length is also denoted as $\{s_n, n=0,...,N-1\}$. We fit N to the problem and the computer. Ns up to the order of 100s will suffice very well for our introduction to digital signal processing with Mathcad.

To implement a finite-length sequence in Mathcad we define its **length**, N, the **discrete-time index**, n, and the mathematical form of s_n. We define an **array** that represents the digital signal; for example, an **exponential sequence** could be implemented this way:

$$N := 64 \qquad n := 0 .. N - 1 \qquad a := 0.1 \qquad s_n := e^{-a \cdot n}$$

(The mechanical steps to enter these expressions - and most others in this chapter - are given in the chapter entitled "A Mathcad Tutorial".) In Mathcad, n is termed a **range variable** and it must take on nonnegative values. Note that such declarations are computed automatically by Mathcad for every declared n.

As we begin to see, Mathcad mathematical expressions are very similar in appearance to conventional mathematical notation. As we become more familiar with Mathcad, we will begin to state mathematical problems directly in its language. The great advantage is that these expressions are interactive.

A sequence's **plot** is very helpful in understanding the sequence and any processing operations upon it.

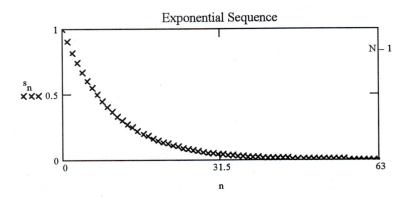

In Mathcad, there are various **formatting** and other options available for plotting. For sequences, we may or may not wish to use the default straight-line interpolation of the values. This is a matter to be decided in each instance.

■ **EXERCISE 1.1** Choose other definitions for {s_n} and observe their plots. Explore the plotting options in Mathcad. For example, click on the plot and select, from the menu bar, **XY Plot** then **Format...** and change the Trace type. ¤

An important means of generating a signal sequence for digital signal processing is by **sampling** an analog signal to obtain a digital signal. This operation is called **analog to digital conversion (ADC).**

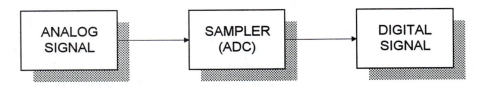

An **analog signal** is a real- or complex- valued function of a real variable t. Here t will be interpreted as **continuous time**. In Mathcad, we will use a **function** definition for an analog signal. For example, an **exponential** analog signal can be entered as

$$a := 0.05 \qquad sa(t) := e^{-a \cdot t}$$

We can plot an analog signal over a finite range at discrete points chosen at a density sufficient to create an apparently smooth curve. In Mathcad, the function's values are connected, or **interpolated**, with straight-line segments by default.

$$t := 0, 0.1 .. 100$$

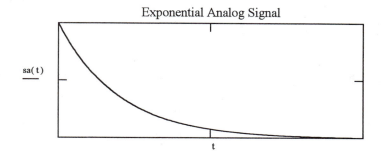

Exponential Analog Signal

$sa(t)$

t

■ **EXERCISE 1.2** Choose other functions with which you are familiar for analog signals and observe their plots. ¤

The correspondence between an analog signal sa(t) and a digital signal {sd_n}, related by ADC with a **sampling period** T_s, is

$$T_s := 1 \qquad sd_n := sa(n \cdot T_s)$$

A digital sequence so derived is called a **sample sequence**.

■ **EXERCISE 1.3** Plot sd_n for various choices of T_s and note how inferable the sampled analog signal is. (You can create space below this line by clicking the cursor there and pressing Control and F9 together.) ¤

Even when the digital signal is not actually created by the sampling process, it is often convenient to imagine it so in order to interpret various operations upon sequences. At the same time, it is important to develop a facility for thinking and working directly with the digital signals as sequences.

Examples of Digital Signals

Example 1.1 _____

The (discrete-time) **unit impulse at time nd**, conventionally denoted $\delta_{n,nd}$, is a fundamental sequence in digital signal processing. It is defined to be one when n=nd and is zero otherwise. It is implemented in Mathcad with the **built-in function** δ**(n,nd)**. (Note the very similar notation.) Its plot is shown below.

$$nd1 := 8 \qquad sl_n := \delta(nd1, n)$$

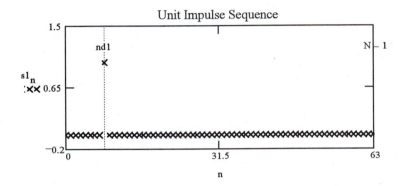

A **unit impulse** is understood to be a unit impulse at time zero. We will later see that a digital filter's output for a unit impulse sequence input completely defines the digital filter. ‡

Example 1.2 _____

We next define a **sinusoidal sequence**. A sinusoidal sequence is of the form $\cos(\omega n + \theta)$ with **frequency** ω and **phase** θ. Notice immediately that, for an integer k, $\cos((\omega + 2\pi k)n + \theta) = \cos(\omega n + \theta)$ because the cosine function has period 2π. Therefore, the frequencies $\{\omega + k2\pi,\ k=0, +/-1,...\}$ are *indistinguishable*. They are said to be **aliases**. We will see that it is convenient to express the frequency in a particular form.

$$k := 4 \qquad \omega := \frac{2 \cdot \pi}{N} \cdot k \qquad sc_n := \cos\left(\omega \cdot n + \frac{\pi}{4}\right)$$

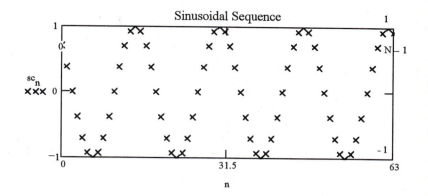

Sinusoidal Sequence

The plot does appear to be samples of the familiar sine wave. ‡

 EXERCISE 1.4 Graph the above sinusoidal sequence for other choices of k. Note especially when k is replaced by k+N. Is it always obvious that the sequence is sinusoidal? For what values of k is the fluctuation rate highest? Lowest? Intermediate? (These values may be a surprise to you!) ¤

A sequence $\{s_n\}$ is said to have **period** N if $s_{n+N}=s_n$. Whereas every sinusoidal function is periodic, only special sinusoidal sequences are periodic. For example, suppose there exits an integer N such that

$$\cos(\omega\cdot(n+N)+\theta)=\cos(\omega\cdot n+\theta)$$

Then, as the cosine function has period 2π, it follows that necessarily

$$\omega\cdot N=k\cdot 2\cdot\pi$$

where k is an integer. That is, a sinusoidal sequence is periodic if and only if its frequency is a rational multiple of 2π.

$$\omega=\frac{k}{N}\cdot 2\cdot\pi$$

PROBLEM 1.1 Show that k in [0,N-1] gives all the possible sinusoidal sequences of period N. ‡

Note that the sine sequence $\sin(\omega n+\theta)$ is included in the above considerations - replace θ by $\theta+\pi/2$. Also, as the **complex exponential** $\exp(i(\omega n+\theta))=\cos(\omega n+\theta)+i\sin(\omega n+\theta)$, these comments on periodicity apply to it. If the sinusoidal sequence of frequency ω is a sample sequence obtained from a sinusoidal analog signal of frequency ν, then we have the relation

$$\omega = T_s \cdot \nu$$

But, as ω is not distinguishable from its aliases, we see that all the analog frequencies $\{\nu+k\,2\pi/Ts, k=0,+/-1,...\}$ are indistinguishable, i.e., **aliases**. The **sampling frequency** is $\omega_s = 2\pi/T_s$. We shall study this aliasing phenomenon for general analog signals in **Chapter 15**.

PROBLEM 1.2

Show that, if a sinusoidal analog signal of frequency $\nu=2\pi/T$ is sampled with period T_s, then the resulting digital signal is periodic if and only if T_s/T is a rational number. ‡

Example 1.3

We generalize Example 1.2 to a sum of sinusoids.

$N := 64$ $n := 0..N-1$

frequencies: $k := 0..\dfrac{N}{2}$ $\omega_k := \dfrac{2\cdot\pi}{N}\cdot k$

weights: $c_k := \text{if}\left(k \leq \dfrac{N}{8}, k, 0\right)$

signal: $s3_n := \sum_k c_k \cdot \cos(\omega_k \cdot n)$

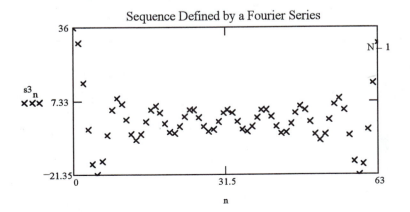

Sequence Defined by a Fourier Series

This is an example of a Fourier series representation. More general examples will be central to much of our discussion of DSP. ‡

■ **EXERCISE 1.5** Choose other sets of weights and phases and observe the resulting sequences. ¤

In DSP, models that employ **random sequences** are of great utility. We want to enrich our models to be able to include degrading random effects such as noise. Mathematical and scientific software applications are generally capable of generating at least a random variable uniformly distributed over (0,1) with repeated calls yielding a sequence of approximately independent random variables. Mathcad's built-in function **rnd(a)** generates a sample of a random variable uniformly distributed over (0,a). With suitable transformations, we can then generate more complicated random models. Also, Mathcad has built-in functions for generating many types of random variables.

Example 1.4 _____

We can generate a sequence of independent **normal random variables** $\{no_k\}$, of mean μ and standard deviation σ, using the built-in random number generator rnorm(N,μ,σ), which models the commonly encountered **thermal noise** sample sequence. It is convenient to denote the variance, which is the square of σ, by var.

mean: $\mu := 0$ **standard deviation:** $\sigma := 1$ **variance:** $var := \sigma^2$

normal random sequence: $no := rnorm(N, 0, 1)$

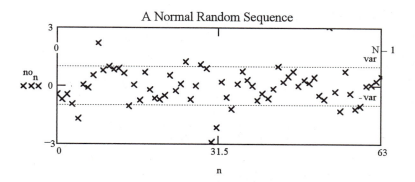

A Normal Random Sequence

You may recall that, with probability greater than 0.99, the values of such a random sequence will lie in the range (-3σ,+3σ). ‡

EXERCISE 1.6 Click on the statement defining σ and repeatedly press F9 to generate a new set of normal random variables independent of each other and the earlier sets. ¤

Basic Operations on Sequences

We may regard an N-length sequence as a **vector** in an N-dimensional linear vector space. Importantly, this allows us to apply our knowledge of the algebra of such spaces and to take advantage of the powerful numerical algorithms already developed for this subject, available in DSP and scientific application software. There are a variety of such linear algebra functions, called **operators,** available in Mathcad. We define and implement some of the basic operations here.

Addition/Subtraction of Sequences

By this we mean the element-by-element addition/subtraction of same-indexed members of the sequences to form a new sequence.

$$\text{sum}_n := s_n + sc_n \qquad \text{sum} := s + sc \qquad \text{sum} := \overrightarrow{(s + sc)}$$

In Mathcad, the definition is explicitly implemented in the first form. In the second form, Mathcad "understands" the intent. The third form uses Mathcad's **vectorize** operation, which performs the indicated algebraic operation element by element and is computationally faster; the subject arrays must be of the same size.

Multiplication of Sequences

By this we mean the element-by-element multiplication of same-indexed members of the sequences to form a new sequence.

$$sp_n := s_n \cdot sc_n \qquad sp := \overrightarrow{(s \cdot sc)}$$

In Mathcad, the first form implements the definition and the second form employs the vectorize operation.

Multiplication of a Sequence by a Scalar

By this we mean the multiplication of every member, or element, of a sequence by a scalar.

$$sm_n := \pi \cdot s_n \qquad sm := \pi \cdot s$$

In Mathcad, the first form implements the definition and the second form is understood.

Scalar/Inner Product of Sequences

This operation produces a scalar.

$$ip := \sum_n s_n \cdot \overline{sc_n} \qquad\qquad ip := s \cdot \overline{sc}$$

The first form implements the definition; the second form is understood by Mathcad. The overbar denotes complex conjugate. Recall that, supposing sc to be a unit-length basis vector, the inner product is the coordinate of s on sc. (We define length next.) Also, supposing both s and sc to be unit-length vectors, their inner product is the cosine of the angle between them. These geometrical concepts will be very valuable to us in understanding the Fourier series representations we will encounter later.

Norm of a Vector

This scalar gives the **length**, or **norm**, of a vector; its square has the interpretation of the **energy** of the sequence. (It is not to be confused with the length or number of elements in the sequence.)

$$\text{norm1} := \sqrt{\sum_n \left(|s_n| \right)^2} \qquad \text{norm2} := \sqrt{\overline{s \cdot s}} \qquad \text{norm} := |s|$$

The definition is implemented in the first form and alternatively defined in terms of the inner product in the second form. The third form is Mathcad's efficient implementation.

EXERCISE 1.7 Verify the asserted equivalence of the various Mathcad implementations of the basic operations on sequences. You can do this by comparing sets of numbers with graphs and also, if N is not too large, by using Mathcad's **table** display for an array. For example, forming differences and inspecting for zeros is an effective procedure. (You can create space below this line by clicking the cursor there and pressing Control and F9 together.) ¤

Basic DSP Operations on Digital Signals

Array of Sequences

In digital signal processing we are often concerned with multiple data sequences, or **records**. It is convenient and conventional to store these records as columns in a matrix array. Given such an array, an individual record can be accessed as a specific column. Mathcad has a simple way to do this. We illustrate with a simple example composed of M records of length N of a pulse with M different delays.

$$M := 16 \qquad\qquad m := 0 .. M - 1 \qquad\qquad nd_m := m^{1.4}$$

$$sm_{n,m} := \exp\left[-\frac{\left(n - 8 - nd_m\right)^2}{32} \right]$$

A **surface plot** visually summarizes all the data records.

Data Records

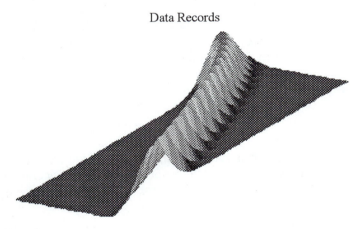

sm

![] **EXERCISE 1.8** Click on the surface plot and choose **Surface Plot** from the menu. Experiment with the formatting options. Note that a **contour plot** is available. ¤

In Mathcad, the columns of a matrix can be specified as a vector by using the **array superscript**. We can demonstrate this by accessing a particular record in the matrix sm and plotting it.

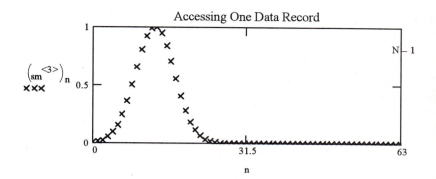

Accessing One Data Record

Forming and Assembling Subsequences

It is often necessary in digital signal processing to form subsequences, or **blocks,** of a sequence. For example, when processing long sequences, it may not be possible to load into the computer the entire sequence. In that case, operations may be performed on the individual blocks, and the processed blocks may be reassembled in a prescribed manner to form a new, or processed, long sequence. (See **Chapter 5**.)

Example 1.5 _____

We give a simple example of forming and reassembling blocks of a given sequence. We define a sinusoidal sequence of length N and form J disjunct blocks from it, each labeled by an index j and each of length M=N/J. These subsequences then form the columns of an M-by-N matrix sb.

long sequence:	$N := 128$	$n := 0 .. N - 1$	$v := \dfrac{2 \cdot \pi}{N} \cdot 4$	$s_n := \cos(v \cdot n)$

block indexing:	$J := 4$	$j := 0 .. J - 1$	$M := \dfrac{N}{J}$	$m := 0 .. M - 1$

arrayed blocks:

$$sb_{m,j} := s_{m + j \cdot M}$$

We can reassemble the N-length sequence from the subsequences, or blocks.

reassembly:

$$sr_{m + j \cdot M} := sb_{m,j} \qquad ‡$$

EXERCISE 1.9 Verify that the scheme given in Example 1.5 actually forms disjunct blocks and that they are correctly reassembled. You may want to use a more distinctive signal and you may wish to create plots that are helpfully laid out. ¤

**PROBLEM
1.3**   Which element of $sb_{m,j}$ is s_n? In other words, give (m,j) in terms of n and M. ‡

Extension of Sequences

We often must consider a sequence for indices outside the range for which it has been defined. For example, the translation of a sequence may be of interest. Indeed, a translation of a sequence is used in defining the operation of a digital filter, as we discuss in Chapter 2. There are two natural and useful ways to extend the definition of a sequence to a greater range of indices. We will call them aperiodic and periodic extensions. Also, sometimes we just want to extend a finite length sequence to a longer length by adding zeros: this will be called zero padding. Usually we append zeros but sometimes we prepend zeros; we will even find reason to insert zeros in more complicated ways.

Zero Padding Extension

Example 1.6 _____

We extend an M-length sequence $\{s_n\}$ to an N-length sequence $\{se_n\}$ (N>M) by appending zeros to it.

**original
sequence:** $M := \dfrac{N}{4}$ $m := 0..M - 1$ $s_m := \cos\left(\dfrac{2\cdot\pi}{M}\cdot 2\cdot m\right)$

**extended
sequence,
first form:** $se_n := \mathrm{if}(n<M, s_n, 0)$

**extended
sequence,
second form:** $se_n := (n<M)\cdot s_n$

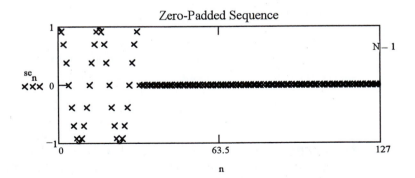

Zero-Padded Sequence

This is an example of the **zero padding** operation. ‡

In Example 1.6, we gave two ways to implement the zero padding operation. The first form used Mathcad's **conditional if function** to explicitly implement the definition. Here, we explicitly ask for s_n only for the n for which it is defined. The second form used the **Boolean operator < in the Boolean expression (n<M)**, which takes on the value 1 when the condition is true and the value 0 when the condition is false. Here, we implicitly ask for s_n only for the n for which it is defined. We will make frequent use of these functions.

■ **EXERCISE 1.10** In the above plot, graph the sequence

$$\text{Boole}_n := (n<M)$$

Now write se as the product of two sequences. ¤

■ **EXERCISE 1.11** Modify Example 1.6 to prepend the zeros - that is, add the zeros at the beginning of the sequence. ¤

Aperiodic Extension and Translation

We can extend the definition of a finite-length sequence by prepending and appending an unlimited number of zeros. We call this the **aperiodic extension** of the sequence and denote it $\{se_n\}$ or $\{se\}$. For example, the aperiodic extension of the M-length sequence $\{s_n, n=0,...,M-1\}$ is zero for any index not in the set [0,M-1] and can be usefully implemented in Mathcad in two ways. If we only need the aperiodic extension for nonnegative indices, then we can implement it with an array.

**aperiodic extension,
array form:** $se_n = (n<0)\cdot(n \geq M)\cdot s_n$

If we want to use the aperiodic extension with negative indices, then in Mathcad we must use the expedient of a function.

**aperiodic extension,
function form:** $se(n) = (n<0)\cdot(n \geq M)\cdot s_n$

Now we can define an **aperiodic translation** of the finite sequence $\{s_n\}$ to be a translate of the aperiodic extension $\{se_n\}$. Since the latter is defined for all indices, there is no difficulty in defining its translate, by nt, as $\{se_{n-nt}\}$. It can be implemented in Mathcad in either array or function form as follows.

aperiodic translation, array form:	$set_n = (n - nt \geq 0) \cdot (n - nt < M) \cdot s_{n-nt}$

aperiodic translation, function form:	$set(n) \equiv se(n - nt)$

For nt>0, the translation is called a **delay**. For nt<0, the translation is called an **advance**.

Example 1.7 _____

We illustrate the aperiodic extension and aperiodic translation.

original sequence:	$M := \dfrac{N}{4} \qquad m := 0..\, M-1 \qquad s_m := \cos\!\left(\dfrac{2 \cdot \pi}{M} \cdot 2 \cdot m\right)$

aperiodic extension, function form:	$se(n) := (n \geq 0) \cdot (n < M) \cdot s_n$

translation:	$nt := -24$

aperiodic translation, function form:	$set(n) := se(n - nt)$

$\eta := -64, -63 .. 64$

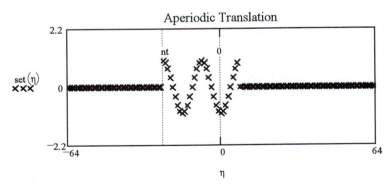

We plot the aperiodically translated sequence over a finite set of indices, of course. ‡

> **EXERCISE 1.12** Choose other values of nt, both positive and negative, in Example 1.7. In particular, choose nt=0 to see the aperiodic extension itself. ¤

Periodic Extension and Translation

Let n be any integer and N a nonnegative integer. Then, for some integer k, we can always write n=m+k*N, where m is in [0,N-1]. We denote such an m by **pod(n,N)**. Mathcad, like most mathematical programming languages, has a built-in function **mod(n,N)** defined as {remainder of n/N}. Thus mod(n,N) is in (-(N-1),N-1) and has the sign of n. We can use this built-in function to implement our desired function in Mathcad as follows.

$$\text{pod}(n,N) := \text{mod}(N + \text{mod}(n,N), N)$$

To see that this is the desired function, first note that when n is not negative, mod(n,N) is in [0,N-1]. Then adding N and again taking mod(.,N) does not change the result. Note also that when n is negative, mod(n,N) is negative and in [-(N-1),-1]. Then adding N has a result in [1,N-1], which is unchanged when mod(.,N) is taken.

EXERCISE 1.13 Experiment with the pod(n,N) function for several n and N. ¤

We may now define the **periodic extension of period N**, denoted {xp_n} or {xp}, of a sequence {x_n, n=0,...,N-1} of finite length N as {$x_{\text{pod}(n,N)}$, n=...,-1,0,1,...}. The periodic extension is implemented by an array or a function as follows.

periodic extension, array form:
$$sp_m \equiv s_{\text{pod}(n,N)}$$

periodic extension, function form:
$$sp(n) \equiv s_{\text{pod}(n,N)}$$

Regarding the use of these expressions, the same remarks apply as for the aperiodic extension.

Now we can define a **periodic translation** of the finite sequence {s_n} to be a translate of the periodic extension {sp_n}. Since the latter is defined for all indices, there is no difficulty in defining its translate, by nt, as {sp_{n-nt}}. It can be implemented in Mathcad either explicitly or implicitly as follows.

aperiodic translation, array form:
$$spt_n \equiv s_{\text{pod}(n-nt,N)}$$

aperiodic translation, function form:
$$spt(n) \equiv sp(n-nt)$$

Example 1.8

We illustrate the periodic extension and periodic translation. We take the sequence {s_m, m=0,...,M-1} of Example 1.7, zero pad it to length N and then find the periodic extension of period N. This is a typical operation.

zero-padded sequence:

$$s_n := (n>0)\cdot(n<M)\cdot s_n$$

periodic extension, function form:

$$sp(n) := s_{pod(n,N)}$$

translation:

$$nt := -24$$

periodic translation, function form:

$$spt(n) := sp(n - nt)$$

$$\eta := -\frac{3}{2}\cdot N, -\frac{3}{2}\cdot N + 1 .. \frac{3}{2}\cdot N$$

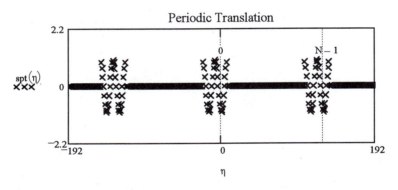

We plot the periodically translated sequence over a finite set of indices, of course. ‡

EXERCISE 1.14 Choose other values of nt, both positive and negative, in Example 1.8. In particular, choose nt=0 to see the periodic extension itself. ¤

Conventionally, a sequence with period N is plotted only for the index set [0,N-1]. This can be a confusing plot to interpret. We repeat Example 1.8 to study this.

Example 1.9

We illustrate the periodic extension and periodic translation. We take the sequence $\{s_m, m=0,...,M-1\}$ of Example 1.8, zero pad it to length N and then find the periodic extension of period N. But we examine the periodic translation only over one period, N in [0,N-1], and so we may use an array implementation of it.

**zero-padded
sequence:**

$$s_n := (n>0)\cdot(n<M)\cdot s_n$$

translation:

$$nt := -24$$

**periodic translation,
array form:**

$$spt_n := s_{pod(n-nt,N)}$$

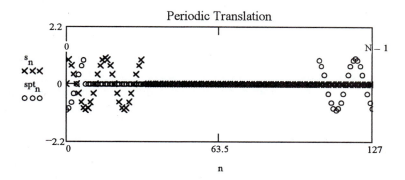

There is seemingly a **cyclic**, or wrap-around, effect. But, again, keeping the entire periodic sequence in mind, this phenomenon occurs only because we are viewing the periodic sequence over one fixed period, namely, [0,N-1]. ‡

▓ **EXERCISE 1.15** Choose other values of nt, both positive and negative, in Example 1.9. Experiment until you feel comfortable with this conventional plot. ¤

Causal Operations

We have considered a number of operations on sequences thus far. Some of these operations produce a new sequence, the output, from a given sequence, the input. A very simple example is multiplying a sequence by a scalar. The most important such operation for us is digital filtering, taken up in the next chapter. Sometimes we want the digital filter to have a property called causality, roughly meaning that in computing the output at time n, only values of the input for times n or less are used.

While the meaning of causality is intuitively clear, being precise about it is a little involved. One reason is that we are concerned with finite-length sequences. Operations can involve input and output sequences of different lengths. It is helpful to start the discussion now so that when we discuss causality for digital filters we will be better prepared.

Given a sequence $\{x\}$, the **future of $\{x\}$ at time n** is the subsequence $\{x_\eta, \eta=n+1, n+2, ..., x_n$ defined$\}$. The future of $\{x\}$ at time n may be the empty sequence because $\{x\}$ is not defined there.

Example 1.10

Consider the finite sequence $\{x_n, n=0,...,N-1\}$.

(a) The future of x_n at time n<0 is the sequence $\{x_n, n=0,...,N-1\}$.

(b) The future of x_n at time n=0 is the sequence $\{x_n, n=1,...,N-1\}$.

(c) The future of x_n at time n=N-2 is the sequence $\{x_n, n=N-1\}$.

(d) The future of x_n at time n>N-2 is the empty sequence. ‡

An operation on an input sequence $\{x\}$ to produce an output sequence $\{y\}$ is called **causal** if, at time n, y_n is computed from $\{x\}$ independently of the future of $\{x\}$ at time n.

Multiplying a sequence by a scalar c is a simple causal operation: $y_n=cx_n$, independently of the future of $\{x\}$ at time n.

The aperiodic extension of the sequence $\{x_n, n=0,...,N-1\}$ is clearly a causal operation. For any n, xe_n is either x_n or zero, depending on whether or not n is in [0,N-1], independently of the future of $\{x\}$ at time n.

The periodic extension $\{xp\}$ of the sequence $\{x_n, n=0,...,N-1\}$ is clearly *not* a causal operation. For any n<0, xp_n is $x_{pod(n,N)}$, which is in the future ($\{x_n, n=0,...,N-1\}$) of $\{x\}$ at time n<0.

PROBLEM 1.4   Show that the concatenation of two causal operations is a causal operation. ‡

Reading and Writing Data Files

Mathcad reads and writes ASCII text files containing numerical data, giving us the ability to import and export data files with other applications. For example, experimental data could be imported into Mathcad, processed and then displayed and/or exported. Here we illustrate one method of writing and reading one type of data file, an **unstructured file**, that is useful for data in sequence, or vector, form.

$$\text{WRITE}(\text{cosine}) := s_n$$

Writes the cosine sequence of Example 1.8 to data file cosine.dat

$$s_{\text{check}_n} := \text{READ}(\text{cosine})$$

Reads the contents of the file cosine.dat into the sequence s_{check}

$$s_{17} - s_{\text{check}_{17}} = 0$$

Verify that $s = s_{check}$

The Mathcad *User's Guide* should be referred to for details. For example, the **Associate Filename...** under the **File** menu is useful in handling data files in other directories.

PROBLEM 1.5

Whereas **READ** and **WRITE** are useful for data in vector form, **READPRN** and **WRITEPRN** are useful for data in matrix form. The **structured file** time_alt.prn is data recorded from a rocket launch. It is composed of 30 (time,altitude) pairs. When read with READPRN, a 30-by-2 matrix results, with the first column being the set of times and the second column being the corresponding measured altitudes. Read the file, extract the columns as time and altitude vectors and plot the altitude versus time. ‡

Project 1.1

In a new Mathcad document, create and edit text, equation and graphics regions. Copy sample regions from this document into your document. Illustrate the concepts discussed in this section with your own examples. ‡

Project 1.2

We implement a simulation of a digital communication system. This should demonstrate that, with a bit of creativity, we already can do significant work!

 (a) Create a new Mathcad document and define an analog pulse train, a periodic repetition of a basic pulse. Use a function definition to implement the basic pulse and use Mathcad's ability to sum functions to implement the pulse train. (You will have to choose workable parameters.) Plot the analog signal.

(b) Now choose, independently for each pulse, an amplitude to be randomly +1 or -1. Such an amplitude sequence represents the encoding of a sequence of binary symbols into a waveform that can be transmitted through a communication channel. Plot this communication signal.

(c) The communication channel will add thermal noise to the communication signal. It will be easiest to add this feature to our model a little later.

(d) We wish to implement a receiver to estimate each binary symbol from the signal-plus-noise sequence. The receiver will do three operations.

(i) The first operation is sampling the received analog waveform: Implement this. (You will have to choose the sample period. You should have several samples per pulse.)

It is at this point that we can add the thermal noise due to the communication channel: Add a sequence of independent, normal random variables of zero mean and variance var. Plot this signal-plus-noise sequence.

(ii) The second operation reduces the effect of the noise. We average the samples over one pulse to produce one sample, which will have a variance reduced by the number of samples averaged. This operation combines digital filtering, which we discuss next (**Chapter 2**), and sample decimation, which we take up later (**Chapter 17**). Plot this processed sequence.

(iii) The third operation is to make a decision for each symbol: "Was a +1 or a -1 amplitude transmitted?" This can be done with a comparison to a threshold. Plot the original and the estimated binary symbol sequences. ‡

References

Jackson (1996), Sec. 2.1
Oppenheim and Schafer (1989), Sec. 2.1
Proakis and Manolakis (1996), Secs. 1.3, 2.1

2 Digital (FIR) Filters

To introduce the idea of filtering, we discuss its common application to noise smoothing. Consider a data sequence $\{x_n\}$ which is the sum of a signal $\{s_n\}$ that varies little over a time duration L and a noise $\{no_n\}$ that varies independently. Suppose that each value x_n is replaced by y_n, which is the average of L contiguously indexed values, including x_n. Recall that averaging L independent noise samples reduces their variance by 1/L. Therefore, we have smoothed the noise while changing the signal little. Such a filter is called a moving average. We consider this application in detail in Example 2.10.

We note some important attributes of this filter. Notice that the operation of averaging is linear in that the signal and noise sequences are averaged separately. Of course, we are averaging a finite number of data values. Such a filter is said to have a finite impulse response, denoted FIR. If the L values averaged at time n are $\{x_n, x_{n-1},..., x_{n-L+1}\}$, then the present and past values are used and the filter is called causal. We will usually make this assumption. But note that if the data is in memory - e.g., a digital image - there is no compelling reason to assume causality. Notice also that near the ends of the data sequence special provision must be made: L data values are not available. We could modify the form of the moving average but this would destroy its unchanging, or invariant, form, which enables the powerful Fourier analysis that is central to our discussions. So instead, we extend the data sequence. For instance, we could supply the missing values as zeros.

We now turn to a more general treatment of FIR filters. Given a finite-length digital signal $\{x_n, n=0,...,J-1\}$, a new discrete-time signal $\{y_n, n=0,...,N-1\}$ is formed as follows. At each time n, y_n is formed as a weighted sum of the values $\{x_m, m=n,...,n-M\}$, the weighting given by a finite-length sequence $\{h_n, n=0,...,M\}$. We begin to implement this computation in Example 2.1.

Example 2.1

We define a simple signal and filter weights.

signal: $J := 24$ $j := 0 .. J - 1$ $x1_j := 1$

weights: $M := 8$ $m := 0 .. M - 1$ $h1_m := \dfrac{1}{M}$

Now we attempt to compute the filter output.

new signal: $N := 64$ $n := 0 .. N - 1$

$$yl_n := \sum_{m=0}^{M-1} h1_m \cdot x1_{n-m} \quad \blacksquare \qquad\qquad \ddagger \qquad (2.1)$$

⬛ **EXERCISE 2.1** Toggle (2.1) to the active state and note the error message that appears. Then toggle (2.1) inactive. (In Mathcad, an equation may be toggled between active and inactive states. Click on the declaration sign (:=) and choose **Toggle Equation** from the **Math** menu.) ¤

If we toggle equation (2.1) to the active state, Mathcad gives us an error message "index out of bounds". This is because $x1_{n-m}$ is not defined for (n-m) not in [0,J-1]: We must supply a definition. Mathcad has shown us that we do not yet have a well-defined mathematical form. This illustrates one use of mathematical software - to help define a mathematical statement or problem.

Recall that in Chapter 1 we mentioned two ways to extend the sequence $\{x_j\}$. First, we can extend the definition of x by the aperiodic extension. Second, we can extend the definition of x by periodic extension. Although the first choice may seem natural and the second choice awkward, we will see that the second choice in fact arises as a matter of course when we later learn how to compute the convolution using an alternative algorithm that can require much less computation than (2.1). We will thus be concerned with both extensions, resulting in, respectively, an aperiodic convolution and a periodic convolution. In digital signal processing, we are often concerned with arranging matters so that the latter produces the former. This is a task requiring some art, which we will spend some time on later.

Given that we complete the definition of (2.1), it is called a **convolution sum** or, more briefly, a **convolution**. In the context of DSP, the convolution defines the operation of a **filter**, and $\{x_n\}$ and $\{y_n\}$ are called, respectively, the **input sequence** and the **output sequence**. The sequence of weights $\{h_n\}$, for reasons that we will soon discover, is called the **impulse response (IR)** of the filter. Because $\{h_n\}$ is of finite length, the filter is said to be a **finite impulse response (FIR) filter**.

Aperiodic Convolution

We can complete a definition of (2.1) with the understanding that the finite input sequence $\{x_n\}$ is replaced by its aperiodic extension $\{xe_n\}$. A mathematically more elegant and symmetric definition replaces *both* finite sequences $\{h_n\}$ and $\{x_n\}$ by their aperiodic extensions.

$$ye_n = \sum_m he_m \cdot xe_{n-m} \qquad (2.2)$$

We will soon see that $\{ye_n\}$ is the aperiodic extension of a finite sequence $\{y_n\}$. We will call both $\{ye_n\}$ and $\{y_n\}$ the **aperiodic convolution** of $\{h_n\}$ and $\{x_n\}$. The aperiodic convolution is the traditional definition of **digital filtering**.

Example 2.2 _____

We now modify Example 2.1 to compute the aperiodic convolution of $\{h\}$ and $\{x\}$. Note that we do not need the explicit aperiodic extension $\{he\}$ of $\{h\}$ since only the subsequence $\{h\}$ of it is actually used. Note carefully that we can use the aperiodic extension of $\{x\}$ in array form inside the convolution sum.

signal: $\qquad J := 24 \qquad j := 0 .. J - 1 \qquad x2_j := 1$

weights: $\qquad M := 8 \qquad m := 0 .. M - 1 \qquad h2_m := \dfrac{1}{M}$

aperiodic extension, array form:

$$((n \geq 0) \cdot (n \leq J - 1)) \cdot x2_n$$

We would like to examine the aperiodic convolution for arbitrary index, so we implement it with a function definition.

aperiodic convolution:

$$y2e(n) := \sum_{m=0}^{M-1} h2_m \cdot ((n - m \geq 0) \cdot (n - m \leq J - 1)) \cdot x2_{n-m}$$

(2.3)

We plot the sequence $\{y2e_n\}$ over a finite range.

$$\eta := -N, -N + 1 .. N$$

‡

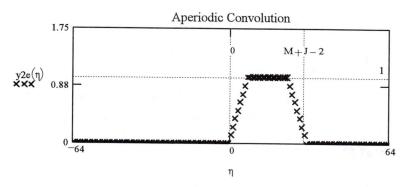

Aperiodic Convolution

EXERCISE 2.2 Choose other values for the parameters J,M,N, and recompute and plot the aperiodic convolution. Note carefully the index set on which its nonzero values occur. ¤

Note that we can compute the output ye_n for an arbitrary set of indices n using (2.3). But clearly there is a crucial set that includes the nonzero values of $\{ye_n\}$, namely, [0,M+J-2]. (See the plot.) Call this subsequence $\{y_n\} = \{ye_n, n=0,...,M+J-2\}$. Then $\{ye_n\}$ is clearly the aperiodic extension of $\{y_n\}$.

EXERCISE 2.3 In Example 2.2, we saw that we need only compute ye_n for n=0,...,N-1, with N=M+J-1, to determine the aperiodic convolution $\{y\}$. Then we can use the right side of (2.3) to define y_n. Do so and plot it. ¤

PROBLEM 2.1
Show that the aperiodic convolution (2.2) is a **commutative** operation on h and x. That is,

$$ye_n = \sum_m he_m \cdot xe_{n-m} = \sum_m xe_m \cdot he_{n-m} \qquad\qquad \ddagger \qquad (2.4)$$

The commutative property in (2.4) resulted from our symmetric definition of the aperiodic convolution. Both sums are finite, with the finite limits of the first form set by $\{h_n\}$ and the finite limits of the second form set by $\{x_n\}$. In actual computation, the sequence with argument m need not be implemented as aperiodically extended.

▨ **EXERCISE 2.4** Write down the finite limits of both sums for the running examples of $\{h_n\}$ and $\{x_n\}$. ¤

We now review our definition of the aperiodic convolution (2.2), which is perhaps a bit more complicated than we anticipated when we tried (2.1). To compute the aperiodic convolution of two finite-length sequences {h} and {x}, we convolve their aperiodic extensions {he} and {xe}, producing an aperiodically extended sequence {ye}. We may then extract the aperiodically extended sequence {y} from {ye}.

PROBLEM 2.2
Show that the aperiodic convolution {ye} of an M1-length sequence and an M2-length sequence is the aperiodic extension of a sequence {y} of length M1+M2-1. ‡

The assertion of Problem 2.2 is important because it tells us how to choose the set of indices to compute all of {y} with (2.3).

Example 2.3 _____
We compute the aperiodic convolution {y} of two finite-length sequences {h} and {x}.

signal: $\qquad J := 18 \qquad j := 0..J-1 \qquad x3_j := \cos\left(\dfrac{2\cdot\pi}{J}\cdot 2\cdot j\right)$

weights: $\qquad M := 12 \quad m := 0..M-1 \quad h3_m := e^{-\frac{m}{M}}$

We see that {x3} is of length J and {h3} is of length M. Therefore, their aperiodic convolution {y3} has length M+J-1. We know from Problem 2.2 and Example 2.2 that we compute {y3} entirely by computing (2.2) for n in [0, M+J-2]. As these indices are nonnegative, we can define {y3} by a sequence.

sufficient index set:	$N := M + J - 1 \qquad n := 0 .. N - 1$

aperiodic convolution:	$y3_n := \displaystyle\sum_{m=0}^{M-1} h3_m \cdot ((n - m \geq 0) \cdot (n - m \leq J - 1)) \cdot x3_{n-m}$

(2.5)

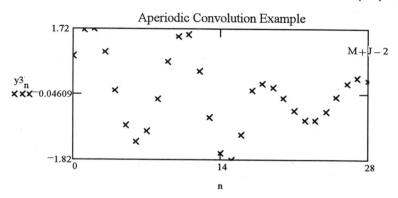

This example is typical of aperiodic convolution computations that we will be making. Thus its implementation should be well understood. ‡

EXERCISE 2.5 Using Example 2.3, try an N larger than M+J-1 to observe a subsequence of the aperiodically extended sequence {y3e}. In eq. (2.5), replace the sequence value $y3_n$ with a function value y3e(n) and plot the aperiodically extended sequence {y3e_n} for η in, say, [-(M+J), 2(M+J)]. This allows us to safely conclude that all of {y3}, the aperiodic convolution of {h3} and {x3}, has been computed. ¤

Impulse Response

Example 2.4 _____

We consider the special input {x4_n} of length 1 and of value 1. It is a unit impulse sequence at time zero, albeit of length 1. We compute the output {y4} for the filter with weights {h4}={h3}. Since the length of {x4} is 1 and the length of {h4} is M, the length of {y4} is M also.

signal:	$J := 1 \qquad j := 0 .. J - 1 \qquad x4_j := \delta(j, 0)$

weights:	$h4 := h3$

sufficient index set:	$N := M + J - 1 \qquad n := 0 .. N - 1$

$$\text{aperiodic convolution:} \quad y4_n := \sum_{m=0}^{M-1} h4_m \cdot ((n-m \geq 0) \cdot (n - m \leq J - 1)) \cdot x4_{n-m}$$

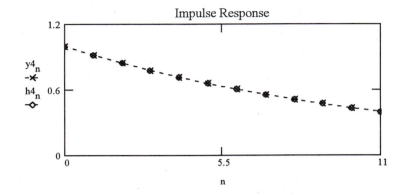

Impulse Response

We see that {y4}, the output (or response) of the filter for a unit impulse input, is the weight sequence {h4}. So we see why the weight sequence - in this example {h4} - is called the impulse response (IR) of the filter. ‡

Causality

By definition, the computation of the aperiodic convolution ye_n at time n does not involve the future of the aperiodically extended sequence input sequence {xe} at time n. Eq. (2.2) shows this clearly. This is therefore a causal operation on the aperiodically extended input sequence {xe}.

Property 2.1a The aperiodic convolution {ye} of {he} and {xe} is a causal operation on {xe}.

PROBLEM 2.3 Show that the aperiodic convolution {ye} of {he} and {xe} is a causal operation on {he}. ‡

Because the aperiodic extension of a sequence is a causal operation (**Chapter 1**) and since extracting {y} from {ye} is clearly a causal operation, we have the following property.

Property 2.1b The aperiodic convolution {y} of {h} and {x} is a causal operation on {x}.

Invariance

Given that the output $\{ye_n\}$ results from input $\{xe_n\}$, consider the output $\{yye_n\}$ that results from the translated input $\{xet_n\} = \{xe_{n-nt}\}$.

$$yye_n = \sum_m he_m \cdot xe_{(n-m)-nt} = \sum_m he_m \cdot xe_{(n-nt)-m} = ye_{n-nt}$$

We say that translating the input simply translates the output. This property of the aperiodic convolution is called **invariance**. We have established the following property.

Property 2.2 The aperiodic convolution $\{ye\}$ of $\{he\}$ and $\{xe\}$ is an invariant operation on $\{xe\}$.

Example 2.5 _____

We give a demonstration of this invariance property.

input: $\qquad\qquad J := 16 \qquad j := 0..J-1 \qquad x5_j := \cos\left(\dfrac{2 \cdot \pi}{J} \cdot 2 \cdot j\right)$

aperiodically extended input: $\qquad x5e(n) := (n \geq 0) \cdot (n \leq J-1) \cdot x5_n$

translation: $\qquad\qquad nt := 20$

translated input: $\qquad\qquad x5et(n) := x5e(n-nt)$

filter FIR: $\qquad\qquad M := 8 \qquad m := 0..M-1 \qquad h5_m := e^{-\frac{m}{M}}$

output for translated input: $\qquad yye(n) := \displaystyle\sum_{m=0}^{M-1} h5_m \cdot x5et(n-m)$

output for untranslated input: $y5e(n) := \displaystyle\sum_{m=0}^{M-1} h5_m \cdot ((n-m \geq 0) \cdot (n-m \leq J-1)) \cdot x5_{n-m}$

translated output for untranslated input: $\qquad y5et(n) := y5e(n-nt)$

We plot yye and y5et.

$\eta := -32..64$

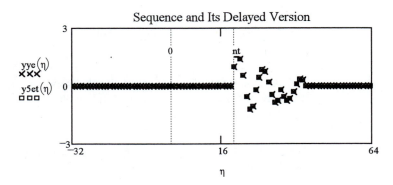

Clearly {yye} and {y5et} are the same sequence. ‡

■ **EXERCISE 2.6** Try other values of nt and observe the plot. ¤

Linearity

Given a filter defined by the sequence {h} and (2.2), consider an input that is the sum of two inputs, {xse}={xae}+{xbe}. The corresponding output is

$$yse_n = \sum_m h_m \cdot \left(xae_{n-m} + xbe_{n-m}\right) = \sum_m h_m \cdot xae_{n-m} + \sum_m h_m \cdot xbe_{n-m}$$

where we have exploited the linearity of the sum. But we recognize this to be the sum of the outputs {yae} and {ybe} for the inputs {xae} and {xbe}, respectively. This property is called the **linearity** of the aperiodic convolution.

Example 2.6 _____
We give an example demonstrating the linearity property.

extended input xae: $\quad J := 14 \qquad j := 0..J-1 \qquad xae(j) := (j \ge 0) \cdot (j < J) \cdot e^{-\frac{j}{J}}$

extended input xbe: $\quad nt := 20 \qquad xbe(n) := xae(n - nt)$

extended summed input xse:	$xse(n) := xae(n) + xbe(n)$

FIR:	$M := 10$	$m := 0 .. M - 1$	$h_m := \dfrac{1}{M}$

output for summed inputs:

$$yse(n) := \sum_{m=0}^{M-1} h_m \cdot xse(n-m)$$

summed outputs of separate inputs:

$$ysse(n) := \sum_{m=0}^{M-1} h_m \cdot xae(n-m) + \sum_{m=0}^{M-1} h_m \cdot xbe(n-m)$$

We plot {ysse} and {yse}, expecting them to be the same sequence.

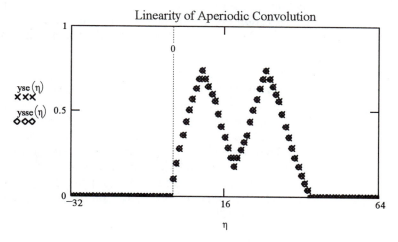

Linearity of Aperiodic Convolution

The outputs {y5e} and {y6e} are clearly the same. ‡

We have established the following property.

Property 2.3 The aperiodic convolution is linear.

PROBLEM 2.4

Construct one or more examples that illustrate the properties of linearity, invariance and causality of the FIR filter defined by the aperiodic convolution (2.2). ‡

An FIR filter is also called a **moving average**, **MA**, filter because its operation on the input sequence is to form, at each time n, a weighted average of a finite set of input values. If the weights are equal, the filter will be called a **simple MA** filter.

Periodic Convolution

We can alternatively complete the definition of (2.1) with the understanding that the finite sequence $\{x_n\}$ is replaced by its periodic extension $\{xp_n\}$ with period N. A mathematically more elegant and symmetric definition replaces *both* finite sequences $\{h_n\}$ and $\{x_n\}$ by their periodic extensions $\{hp_n\}$ and $\{xp_n\}$ with common period N.

$$yp_n = \sum_{m=0}^{N-1} hp_m \cdot xp_{n-m} \tag{2.6}$$

We will soon see that $\{yp_n\}$ is the periodic extension, of period N, of a finite sequence $\{y_n\}$. We call both $\{yp_n\}$ and $\{y_n\}$ the **periodic convolution** of $\{h_n\}$ and $\{x_n\}$. The periodic convolution is important in digital filtering because it can be a more efficient computation than the aperiodic convolution.

It is obvious that the aperiodic convolution $\{ye_n\}$ of (2.2) and the periodic convolution $\{yp_n\}$ of (2.6) *cannot* be the same! An aperiodic sequence cannot equal a periodic sequence (with finite period). But it *can* be true that they are extensions of the *same* finite sequence $\{y_n\}$. Then we say that the aperiodic and periodic convolutions **agree**. When $\{y_n\}$ is the desired computation, the periodic convolution is then an attractive alternative computation to the aperiodic convolution. This makes the periodic convolution important in DSP.

▓ **EXERCISE 2.7** Show that (2.6) defines a sequence with period N. ¤

Example 2.7 _____

We compute the periodic convolution, of period N, of the two finite sequences considered in Example 2.2.

signal:	$J := 24$	$j := 0 .. J - 1$	$x7_j := 1$
weights:	$M := 8$	$m := 0 .. M - 1$	$h7_m := \dfrac{1}{M}$

The choice of period N is arbitrary, provided N>=J. However, if we want the aperiodic and periodic convolutions to agree, we will see that we need N>=J+M-1, the length of the aperiodic convolution.

period: $\qquad$ $N := J + M + 10$ $\qquad$ $n := 0 .. N - 1$

So that {x7} and {h7} will have the same period we extend them to be of common length N by zero padding (**Chapter 1**).

zero padding: $\qquad$ $x7_n := \mathrm{if}\big(n<J, x7_n, 0\big)$ $\quad$ $h7_n := \mathrm{if}\big(n<M, h7_n, 0\big)$

Now we implement the periodic extensions {xp} and {hp}.

$$\mathrm{pod}(n, N) := \mathrm{mod}(N + \mathrm{mod}(n, N), N)$$

explicit periodic extensions: $\quad$ $x7p(n) := x7_{\mathrm{pod}(n,N)}$ $\qquad\qquad$ $h7p(n) := h7_{\mathrm{pod}(n,N)}$

We would like to examine the periodic convolution for arbitrary index, so we implement it with a function definition.

periodic convolution: $\quad$ $y7p(n) := \displaystyle\sum_{m=0}^{M-1} h7p(m) \cdot x7p(n-m)$ $\qquad\qquad$ (2.7)

We plot the sequence {y7p$_n$} over a finite range.

$$\eta := -2 \cdot N, -2 \cdot N + 1 .. 2 \cdot N$$

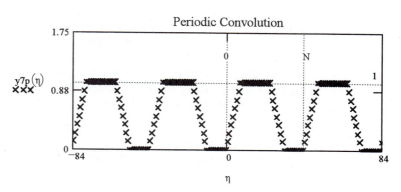

The period N of the periodic convolution is clearly evidenced. ‡

■ **EXERCISE 2.8** Change the plot marker N to M+J-2 and note that the range n=0,...,M+J-2 is the set of nonzero values in one period. Choose other values for N and carefully note the plot. It may well appear confusing for some N. (What N?) Restore N to a value greater than M+J-1. ¤

When N>=J+M-1, the subsequence $\{y7_n\}= \{y7p_n, n=0,...,M+J-2\}$, when periodically extended with period N, clearly yields the periodic convolution $\{y7p_n\}$. Furthermore, $\{y7_n\}$ is the same sequence as the aperiodic convolution $\{y2_n\}$ of Example 2.2. In other words, for such N, the aperiodic and periodic convolutions *agree*.

■ **EXERCISE 2.9** Decrease N from 40 in Example 2.7 and note when the periodic convolution and the aperiodic convolution disagree. ¤

PROBLEM 2.5

Show that the periodic convolution (2.6) is a commutative operation in {hp} and {xp}. That is,

$$yp_n= \sum_{m=0}^{N-1} hp_m \cdot xp_{n-m} = \sum_{m=0}^{N-1} xp_m \cdot hp_{n-m} \qquad ‡$$

This commutative property resulted from our symmetric definition of the periodic convolution. Note that the sequence with argument m need not be implemented as periodically extended.

Let us now review our definition of the periodic convolution, of period N. To compute the periodic convolution of two finite-length sequences {h} and {x}, zero padded as necessary to a common length N, we replace them by their periodic extensions of period N, {hp} and {xp}, respectively. Then the convolution sums (2.6) produce a periodically extended sequence {yp}, of period N. We may then extract the periodically extended sequence {y} from {yp}.

Furthermore, we can get the aperiodic and periodic convolutions of two finite sequences of length J and M to agree by choosing N>=J+M-1.

Example 2.8

We compute the periodic convolution, of period N, of the two finite sequences considered in Example 2.3.

signal: $\qquad J := 18 \qquad j := 0..J-1 \qquad x8_j := \cos\left(\dfrac{2 \cdot \pi}{J} \cdot 2 \cdot j\right)$

weights: $\qquad M := 12 \qquad m := 0..M-1 \qquad h8_m := e^{-\frac{m}{M}}$

We will be interested in seeing the effect of various choices of N. We will compute just one period of the periodic convolution, for the conventionally chosen index set [0,...,N-1]. Therefore, we can implement the periodic convolution as a sequence.

period: $\qquad N := M + J - 1 \qquad\qquad n := 0..N-1$

We zero pad both to the common length N.

**zero
padding:** $\qquad x8_n := (n<N) \cdot x8_n \qquad\qquad h8_n := (n<M) \cdot h8_n$

**periodic
convolution:** $\qquad y8_n := \displaystyle\sum_{m=0}^{M-1} h8_m \cdot x8_{pod(n-m,N)}$ $\qquad\qquad$ (2.7)

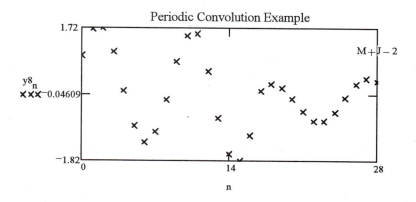

Periodic Convolution Example

We can verify that the periodic convolution {y8} and the aperiodic convolution {y3} agree. This example is typical of periodic convolution computations that we will be making. Thus its implementation should be well understood. ‡

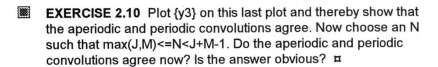

EXERCISE 2.10 Plot {y3} on this last plot and thereby show that the aperiodic and periodic convolutions agree. Now choose an N such that max(J,M)<=N<J+M-1. Do the aperiodic and periodic convolutions agree now? Is the answer obvious? ¤

Impulse Response

Example 2.9 _____

We consider a weight sequence {h9} that is of length M and a special input {x₉ₙ} of length 1 and of value 1. It is a unit impulse sequence at time zero, albeit of length 1. We compute the periodic convolution {y9} with period M.

weights: $M := 12 \quad m := 0..M-1 \quad h9_m := e^{-\frac{m}{M}}$

period: $N := M \quad n := 0..N-1$

zero-padded signal: $x9_n := \delta(n,0)$

periodic convolution: $y9_n := \sum_{m=0}^{M-1} h9_m \cdot x9_{pod(n-m,N)}$

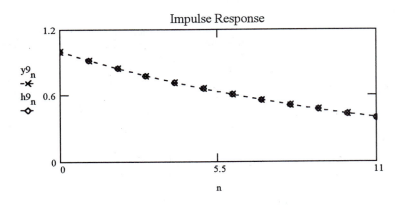

We see that this periodic convolution is the weight sequence. ‡

Causality

By definition, the computation of the periodic convolution yp_n at time n does not involve the future of the periodically extended sequence input sequence {xp} at time n. Eq. (2.6) shows this clearly. This is therefore a causal operation on the periodically extended input sequence {xp}.

Property 2.4a The periodic convolution {yp} of {hp} and {xp} is a causal operation on {xp}.

However, because periodic extension is not a causal operation (**Chapter 1**), the periodic convolution {yp} is *not* derived by a causal operation on {x}. This is obvious: a periodic function could not be causally related to a finite sequence.

There is a restricted sense in which we can say the periodic convolution is causally related to {x}. Suppose that the aperiodic and periodic convolutions agree. By this we mean that the same finite sequence {y} gives the aperiodic and periodic extensions describing the convolutions {ye} and {yp}. Then, since the aperiodic convolution is causally related to {x}, so must {y} be.

Property 2.4b If the aperiodic and periodic convolutions agree, then the sequence {y} of which they are extensions is the result of a causal operation on {x}.

Invariance

Given that the output {yp_n} results from input {xp_n}, consider the output {yyp_n} that results from the translated input {xpt_n}={xp_{n-nt}}.

$$yyp_n = \sum_m hp_m \cdot xp_{(n-m)-nt} = \sum_m hp_m \cdot xp_{(n-nt)-m} = yp_{n-nt}$$

We say that translating the input simply translates the output. This property of the periodic convolution is called **invariance**. We have established the following property.

Property 2.5 The periodic convolution {yp} of {hp} and {xp} is an invariant operation on {xp}.

Because a periodically translated sequence is conventionally plotted only for one period, n in [0,N-1], the plot may appear to be confusing (**Chapter 1**).

Linearity

Given a filter defined by the sequence {h} and (2.5), consider an input that is the sum of two inputs, {xsp}={xap}+{xbp}. The corresponding output is

$$ysp_n = \sum_m h_m \cdot \left(xap_{n-m} + xbp_{n-m} \right) = \sum_m h_m \cdot xap_{n-m} + \sum_m h_m \cdot xbp_{n-m}$$

where we have exploited the linearity of the sum. But we recognize this to be the sum of the outputs {yap} and {ybp} for the inputs {xap} and {xbp}, respectively. This property is called the **linearity** of the periodic convolution.

Property 2.6 The periodic convolution {yp} of {hp} and {xp} is a linear operation on {xp}.

Digital Signal Processing Applications

Data Smoothing

Example 2.10 _____

Suppose a data sequence is the sum of a slowly varying signal sequence and a rapidly varying noise sequence - as we informally discussed at the beginning of this chapter. The noise sequence is modeled by a sequence of uncorrelated, zero mean, normal random variables. We wish to design a data processor that will remove the effects of the noise as much as possible. The following thought leads us to consider a MA, or FIR, filter. The MA filter, of length M, averages M contiguous samples of the data. If the noise has a zero mean value sequence, then, if M is sufficiently large, an output noise sample will be, while random, quite close to its mean value of zero.

The limit on M will be determined by the need to have the output signal still follow the form of the input signal; that is, the signal sequence should be negligibly averaged.

The data is modeled as a random sequence. Thus we need to be able to compute a sample sequence of the data.

data length and index: $J := 256$ $j := 0 .. J - 1$

pulse signal: $s_j := (j > 50) \cdot (j < 150)$

noise: $var := 0.15$ $no := rnorm\left(J, 0, \sqrt{var}\right)$

data: $x_j := s_j + no_j$

FIR: $M := 8$ $m := 0 .. M - 1$ $h_m := \dfrac{1}{M}$

We will compute the output over the set of indices [0,J-1] since this includes the part of the output due to this signal. This can be verified with our implementation.

output index: $N := J$ $n := 0 .. N - 1$

We now filter the data - i.e., compute the aperiodic convolution (2.2).

filter output: $y_n := \displaystyle\sum_{m=0}^{M} h_m \cdot ((n - m \geq 0) \cdot (n - m \leq N - 1)) \cdot x_{n-m}$

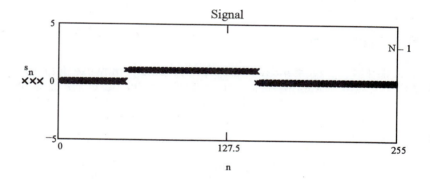

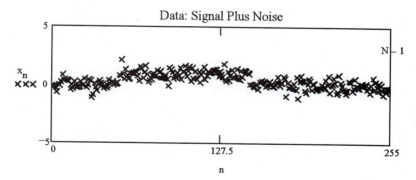

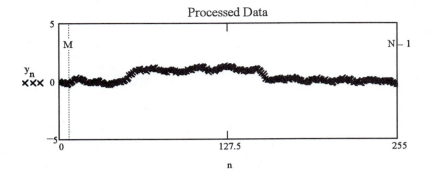

Processed Data

It is evident that the filter performs rather well. The reduction of the variability of the noise by the FIR/MA filter is called **smoothing**. ‡

EXERCISE 2.11 Vary the noise variance in Example 2.10 and note the plot. In particular, when the noise variance is zero, explain the shape of the output in terms of the MA filter. Study the effect of varying the parameter M in Example 2.3. Can you decide on a best M? ¤

Differentiation

PROBLEM 2.6

Numerical differentiation methods may use difference approximations to approximate the derivative of an analog signal. Three types are commonly employed. For an appropriate constant Ts, the sampling period, they are

backward difference:
$$fbd_n = \frac{f_n - f_{n-1}}{Ts}$$

forward difference:
$$ffd_n = \frac{f_{n+1} - f_n}{Ts}$$

central difference:
$$fcd_n = \frac{f_{n+1} - f_{n-1}}{Ts}$$

Put each of these difference operations in a form similar to (2.2), identify the FIR and determine whether the operation, or filter, is causal. ‡

Convolution Animation

We have used the convolution operation to define FIR filtering. Therefore, we should be certain that we understand this operation. Also, we will be using, in effect, the convolution in more complicated filtering schemes. The animation capability of Mathcad can be of assistance in clarifying the convolution. We give examples animating both the aperiodic and periodic convolutions.

Note that to create an animation - as described below - Mathcad must be in the automatic math calculation mode. If it is not, you can select **Math** then **Automatic Mode**.

Example 2.11

We will use the animation capability of Mathcad to create a movie of the aperiodic convolution operation. You can then play the movie, including advancing it step by step to observe the exact sequences involved in the convolution sum and the sum result, the filter output, at each time. You can also save the animation in an *.avi file. Note, however, that the animation files created can be rather large! A FRAME variable indexes, in this case, the output sequence for each time instant: A copy of the plot is made for each value of FRAME. The animation then displays the sequence of plots.

We first set up the plot that we wish to animate. We use functions instead of sequences so that we can make plots for negative time. We introduce the FRAME variable essentially as the index of the filter output sequence. However, we modify this sequence so that it graphs below the plot for times greater than the present time n. We use a simple moving average filter of length M+1 and a truncated exponential sequence of length J for the input.

MA FIR: $\qquad$ $M := 8$ $\qquad$ $h(m) := (m \geq 0) \cdot (m \leq M) \cdot \dfrac{1}{M+1}$

input sequence: $\qquad$ $J := 24$ $\qquad$ $x(j) := (j \geq 0) \cdot (j < J) \cdot e^{-\frac{j}{16}}$

convolution output index: $\qquad$ $n := -5, -4 .. 35$

output sequence from aperiodic convolution: $\qquad$ $y(n) := \displaystyle\sum_{m=0}^{M} h(m) \cdot x(n-m)$

animation/movie frame variable: $\qquad$ $F := FRAME$

animated, plotted output: $yplot(n, F) := if(n \le F, y(n), -10)$

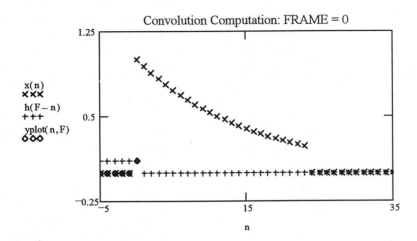

We will now carefully examine this example and animate it. ‡

EXERCISE 2.12 Enter a special value of F in the range -5 to 35 to the right of its declaration as FRAME and push F9 to recompute the plot. Carefully observe all the critical values of F. What do we mean by "critical value"? How many critical values are there? After you thoroughly understand this exercise, remove all declarations of F other than F:=FRAME. ¤

To create an animation of Exercise 2.12, select **Window**, then **Animation**, then **Create...** from the menu above, obtaining the Create Animation dialogue box to set up the animation parameters. Enclose the above plot by dragging the mouse across it. Then, in the dialogue box, set up the desired range of the FRAME variable. We choose FRAME to run from -5 to 35 for the animation. Then select **Animate**; the creation of the animation will take several seconds, depending on your computer. A **Playback** window will appear on the screen and you can play the animation and also step it through the frames. If desired, use **Save as...** to save the animation file for later playback. The resulting file size is 661 Kbytes.

EXERCISE 2.13 Playback the animation step by step, and repeat the analysis of Exercise 2.12. Change the input signal to a constant of the same length and repeat. ¤

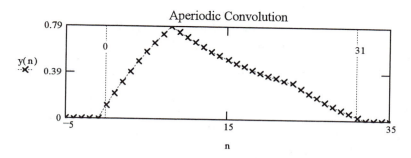

Aperiodic Convolution

$\boxtimes$ **EXERCISE 2.14** Exercise 2.12 asked about critical values. Identify them visually on this plot. Change the markers on the plot to verify your conclusions. (Click on the 0 marker, e.g, and then delete it: You will get a placeholder off the plot in which to insert a new marker value.) ¤

PROBLEM 2.7 Write down the mathematical sums that would be used to convolve the sequences of Example 2.12 over the significant range of the output index n. Use limits on the sums that include only nonzero products. These limits will change as the output index is changed.‡

Example 2.12

We will use the animation capability of Mathcad to create a movie of the periodic convolution operation. We follow Example 2.11 closely: We need to replace the aperiodic convolution (2.2) with the periodic convolution (2.6). Of greatest interest here is how the result depends on the choice of period N.

We first set up the plot that we wish to animate. We again use functions instead of sequences so that we can make plots for negative time. We plot the summand sequences at n=0 (this is informative) and the result of the periodic convolution, the output sequence. We will vary N, in effect, using the FRAME variable.

$$pod(n, N) := mod(N + mod(n, N), N)$$

MA FIR: $\qquad M := 8 \qquad h(m) := (m \geq 0) \cdot (m \leq M) \cdot \dfrac{1}{M+1}$

input sequence: $\qquad J := 24 \qquad x(j) := (j \geq 0) \cdot (j < J) \cdot e^{-\frac{j}{16}}$

longest period:	**convolution output index:**	**animation/movie-frame variable:**
$N := 36$	$n := -5, -4 .. N + 5$	$F := N - FRAME$

**animated, plotted
output sequence from
periodic convolution:**
$$\text{yplot}(n, F) := \sum_{m=0}^{M} h(m) \cdot x(\text{pod}(n - m, F))$$

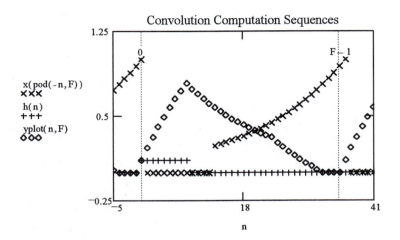

Convolution Computation Sequences

$x(\text{pod}(-n, F))$
×××

$h(n)$
+++

$\text{yplot}(n, F)$
◇◇◇

We will now carefully study this example and animate it. ‡

EXERCISE 2.15 Explain the difference between the convolution of Example 2.12 and that of Example 2.11. Slowly decrease N from 36 and note when, and for what n, the periodic convolution differs from the aperiodic convolution. Why does this happen? Explain in at least two ways, including by reference to the plot. ¤

We create an animation of Exercise 2.15. We choose FRAME to run from 0 to 20 for the animation. The resulting file size is 674 Kbytes.

EXERCISE 2.16 Playback the animation step by step, and repeat the analysis of Exercise 2.15. Change the input signal to a constant of the same length and repeat. ¤

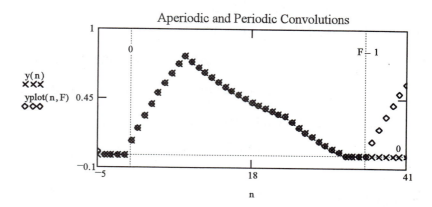

Aperiodic and Periodic Convolutions

 EXERCISE 2.17 Exercise 2.15 asked about the n for which the aperiodic and periodic convolutions agreed, given a particular choice of N=F. Identify them visually on this plot. Change the markers on the plot above to verify your conclusions. (Click on the 0 marker, e.g, and then delete it: You will get a placeholder off the plot in which to insert a new marker value.) ¤

PROBLEM 2.8 As a result of your experiments in Exercise 2.15, write down an expression for the values of n for which the aperiodic and periodic convolutions agree, as a function of the length parameters M+1 and J and the period N. ‡

We will take up these matters again in **Chapter 5**, where we want to apply an important fast computational algorithm for the periodic convolution. But first we must develop the frequency domain point of view of the convolution. We do this in Chapters 3 and 4.

Project 2.1

 Replace the constant signal of Example 2.10 with a sinusoidal signal. Study how the slow variability of the signal limits the ability of the filter to smooth the data. Can you find a "best" (define!) M for a given frequency of the sinusoid? ‡

Project 2.2

Replace the constant signal of Example 2.10 with a sinusoidal signal. Study how the slow variability of the signal limits the ability of the filter to smooth the data. Can you find a "best" (define!) M for a given frequency of the sinusoid? ‡

For each of the following simple FIR filters, describe its operation. One way to do this is to filter some trial input sequences - e.g., a set of sinusoids. A family such as described in **Example 1.2** is satisfactory for present purposes. We give the nonzero values of each FIR. The filters include low-, band- and high-pass filters.

(a) $M = 4$, $h_0 = h_1 = h_3 = h_4 = 0$, $h_2 = 1$

(b) $M = 4$, $h_0 = h_4 = 3/35$, $h_1 = h_3 = 12/35$, $h_2 = 17/35$

(c) $M = 4$, $h_0 = h_4 = -3/35$, $h_1 = h_3 = -12/35$, $h_2 = 18/35$

(d) $M = 4$, $h_0 = h_4 = 3/35$, $h_1 = h_3 = -12/35$, $h_2 = 52/35$

(e) $M = 4$, $h_0 = -8/35$, $h_1 = -13/35$, $h_2 = 6/35$, $h_3 = 12/35$,
$h_4 = 3/35$ ‡

Project 2.3

Using the rocket launch data in file time_alt.dat (see **Problem 1.6**), use central differences (see Problem 2.6) to approximate the velocity and acceleration. Plot the altitude, velocity and acceleration versus time. Comment on these results.
(a) How many stages does the rocket have?
(b) Explain the magnitude and sign of the acceleration curve in the various regions.
(c) Can you determine the acceleration scale?
(d) What is the maximum g-force on the rocket? ‡

Project 2.4

In Example 2.10 and Exercise 2.11, the question of a "best" M arose. Using a minimum mean-square error criterion, where the error is defined to be the input signal minus the output signal, find the best M. ‡

References

Jackson (1996), Sec. 2.2
Oppenheim and Schafer (1989), Sec.2.2
Proakis and Manolakis (1996), Sec. 2.3

3 Discrete Fourier Transform

We now begin to develop what we will call the frequency domain view of filtering. This is the use of Fourier analysis to greatly facilitate our understanding of the analysis, design and implementation of filters and of DSP systems in general. The linearity and invariance properties of the filter are essential for this development.

We will in this chapter begin to study the frequency domain view of the FIR filtering of a finite-length input sequence defined by the periodic convolution (2.5) with period N. There are good reasons for choosing this filtering problem for our basic discussion of filtering. The most important reason is that we are immediately led to the most important algorithm in DSP, the discrete Fourier transform (DFT). Also, we need only be concerned with finite sequences, so there are no mathematical problems about convergence to obscure the basic ideas. Of course, only finite-length sequences are actually encountered in DSP applications. Finally, we have already seen (**Chapter 2**) that we can arrange matters so that the periodic and aperiodic convolutions agree if in fact the latter is desired. Indeed, a preferred computational method computes the latter with the former!

The discrete Fourier transform is so central to DSP that we will spend this chapter discussing it. In **Chapter 4** that discussion is continued, establishing the frequency domain view of filtering. In **Chapter 5** we continue with exploitation of the DFT as an algorithm used in practical filtering.

Invariant Exponential Sequences

We start by making the significant discovery that the complex exponentials have a certain invariance property under the periodic convolution. Recall the form of the periodic convolution (**Chapter 2**):

$$y_n = \sum_{m=0}^{N-1} h_m \cdot x_{pod(n-m,N)} \tag{3.1}$$

Example 3.1

For simplicity, we assume an MA filter of uniform weights and length M+1<=N.

FIR: $\qquad M := 8 \qquad m := 0..M \qquad h_m := \dfrac{1}{M+1}$

Suppose that the input sequence is one of a family of complex exponential sequences $\{\{ec_{n,k}, n=0,...,N-1\}, k=0,...,N-1\}$ of frequencies $\{\omega_k=(2\pi)/N)k\}$. Since this complex exponential has period N in either n or k, we need only consider k in [0,N-1]. We can arrange all these imput sequences into a matrix array whose columns are the complex exponential sequences.

input sequence family:

$\qquad N := 32 \qquad n := 0..N-1 \qquad k := 0..N-1$

$$ec_{n,k} := \exp\left(i \cdot \frac{2\cdot\pi}{N} \cdot k \cdot n\right)$$

The corresponding set of output sequences $\{\{y_n, n=0,...,N-1\}, k=0,...,N-1\}$ are then computed by (3.1). We can compute them all with one statement, placing them in a matrix array whose columns are the separate output sequences.

output sequence family:

$$pod(n,N) := mod(N + mod(n,N), N)$$

$$y_{n,k} := \sum_m h_m \cdot ec_{pod(n-m,N),k}$$

We plot a pair of input-output sequences.

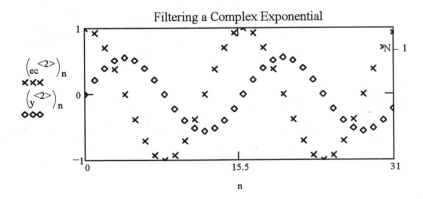

Filtering a Complex Exponential

Note that, by default, Mathcad will plot the real part of a complex sequence. ‡

EXERCISE 3.1 Compute the above plot for various values of k and examine it carefully. Can you observe an "invariance" property? ¤

In performing Exercise 3.1, we note that the output corresponding to each input also appears to be a complex exponential at the same frequency, but with a phase shift and amplitude change. We now prove it. Since the complex exponentials have period N, by definition $ec_{pod(n,N),k} = ec_{n,k}$. Therefore $ec_{pod(n-m,N),k} = ec_{n-m,k} = ec_{n,k} \, ec_{-m,k}$ and $ec_{-m,k} = \text{conjugate}(ec_{m,k})$. So the periodic convolution (3.1) is, in this case, alternatively expressed as

$$yc_n = \sum_{m=0}^{N-1} h_m \cdot ec_{pod(n-m,N)} = \left(\sum_m h_m \cdot \overline{ec_{m,k}} \right) \cdot ec_{n,k} \qquad (3.2)$$

Example 3.2

To check this important result, we can implement (3.2) and compare with the computation of Example 3.1 in a plot.

$$yc_{n,k} := \left(\sum_m h_m \cdot \overline{ec_{m,k}} \right) \cdot ec_{n,k}$$

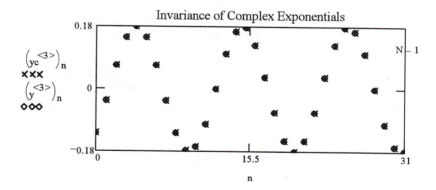

It is apparent that the sequences {y} and {yc} are the same. ‡

EXERCISE 3.2 Plot the real and imaginary parts of $\{y_n\}$ and $\{ya_n\}$ for various values of k. You should see agreement in every case. ¤

This is a remarkable result! Filtering a member of this family of complex exponentials just results in its multiplication by a complex scalar. We say that the members of this family are **invariant** under this filtering. The set of complex scalars is called the **N-periodic frequency response** of the filter. We will see that the impulse response sequence is recoverable from it. Hence this frequency response itself will completely define the FIR filter.

Note that, for any input that is in the form of a weighted sum of members of this family of complex exponentials, the filter output is easily computed by multiplying each term of said sum by the filter's frequency response at the corresponding frequency. The linearity of the filtering operation allows us to do this. In effect, the convolution operation is replaced by the much simpler operation of scalar multiplication.

It is therefore of great importance to know that *any* sequence of length N has a representation as a weighted sum of complex exponentials of this specific form. This possibility, in a different context, was first recognized by Fourier and therefore such a representation is called a Fourier series. Further, since the time of Gauss, it has been known how to efficiently compute such representations with an algorithm now called a fast Fourier transform (FFT). The existence of the FFT has made possible widespread digital signal processing applications. Specifically, the periodic convolution, implemented by using an FFT algorithm, can be a very efficient and practical computation (**Chapter 4**).

We shall now elaborate on this remarkable set of ideas that is central to the analysis, modeling, simulation and implementation of digital signal processing systems.

Fourier Series for Sequences

Given a sequence of length N, we can extend it to have period N. Then we may seek a Fourier series representation for the sequence. We may propose as a **basis** for such an expansion the family of complex exponentials $\{\{ec_{n,k} = \exp[i(2\pi/N)kn], n=0,...,N-1\}, k=0,...,N-1\}$. We have already observed that $\exp[i(2\pi/N)kn]$ has period N in k and that therefore there are only N unique such basis sequences. Then the proposed **Fourier series representation** of a sequence $\{x_n, n=0,...,N-1\}$ is of the form of a weighted sum of the basis sequences.

It is very helpful to think of N-length sequences as vectors in an N-dimensional vector space. For example, visualize a three-dimensional space, corresponding to N equal to 3, and recall how vectors could be represented in terms of the $(\mathbf{i},\mathbf{j},\mathbf{k})$ unit vectors. The complex exponential sequences are, as we soon show, an orthogonal set of vectors spanning the N-dimensional space. Then any vector in the space has a representation as a weighted sum of the basis vectors, with the set of weights $\{X_k, k=0,...,N-1\}$ given by the **projection** of the vector onto each of the basis vectors. Prior to proving this, we give an example.

Example 3.3

Consider a truncated exponential sequence for illustration.

$$a := 0.85 \qquad\qquad x_n := a^n$$

The set of weights is given by the inner, or scalar, products

$$X_k := x \cdot \overline{ec}^{<k>} \tag{3.3a}$$

and the Fourier series representation of the sequence is

$$xrep_n := \frac{1}{N} \sum_k X_k \cdot ec_{n,k} \tag{3.4a}$$

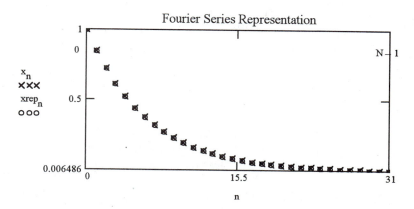

Fourier Series Representation

We see that in fact the sequence and its Fourier series representation are the same. ‡

EXERCISE 3.3 Define {x} by other sequences in Example 3.3. ¤

In a more general context the sequence $\{X_k, k=1,...,N-1\}$ computed by (3.3a), is called the **discrete Fourier transform (DFT)** of the sequence $\{x_n, n=0,...,N-1\}$ and (3.4a) is called the **inverse discrete Fourier transform (IDFT)**. We recopy them, writing out the complex exponentials.

discrete
Fourier transform:

$$X_k = \sum_{n=0}^{N-1} e^{-i \cdot \left(\frac{2 \cdot \pi}{N}\right) \cdot k \cdot n} \cdot x_n \qquad (3.3b)$$

inverse discrete
Fourier transform:

$$x_n = \frac{1}{N} \cdot \sum_{k=0}^{N-1} e^{i \cdot \left(\frac{2 \cdot \pi}{N}\right) \cdot k \cdot n} \cdot X_k \qquad (3.4b)$$

EXERCISE 3.4 Prove that the right side of (3.3b) has period N in k. Prove that the right side of (3.4b) has period N in n. ¤

The definitions (3.3b) and (3.4b) are standard in digital signal processing but are not the only possible choices. In fact, Mathcad uses a different definition and implements the DFT and IDFT with fast algorithms as the built-in functions **cfft(x)** and **icfft(X)**. We can get the forms we want with the following function definitions, *which we will always use from now on*:

$$\text{dft}(x) := \sqrt{N} \cdot \text{icfft}(x) \qquad\qquad \text{idft}(X) := \frac{1}{\sqrt{N}} \cdot \text{cfft}(X)$$

Note that we are implicitly taking advantage of a built-in fast algorithm.

The reason the 1/N appears in the IDFT is that, whereas the complex exponential sequences are orthogonal, they are not orthonormal. Their norm is sqrt(N) and so $\{\{ec_{n,k}/\text{sqrt}(N)\}\}$ is an orthonormal set of basis vectors. By convention in DSP, the DFT is defined with ec not normalized; to correct for this the 1/N factor appears in the IDFT.

EXERCISE 3.5 Compute several inner products and norms of the complex exponentials. For example,

$$ec^{<2>} \cdot \overline{ec^{<2>}} = \qquad\qquad ¤$$

We now prove that (3.4b) is the inverse of (3.3b). If so, then the DFT operation followed by the IDFT operation must be the identity operation. Thus, we substitute (3.3b) into the right side of (3.4b) and show that in fact the sequence $\{x_n, n=0,...,N-1\}$ is recovered. Thus we want to evaluate the double sum

$$xx_{nn} = \frac{1}{N} \cdot \left[\sum_k ec_{nn,k} \cdot \left(\sum_n \overline{ec_{n,k} \cdot x_n} \right) \right] \qquad (nn = (0..N-1))$$

and show that xx=x. After exchanging the order of summation to get

$$xx_{nn} = \sum_n x_n \cdot \left(\frac{1}{N} \cdot \sum_k ec_{nn,k} \cdot \overline{ec_{n,k}} \right) \tag{3.5}$$

we are led to evaluate the sum

$$S_{nn,n} = \frac{1}{N} \cdot \sum_k ec_{nn,k} \cdot \overline{ec_{n,k}} = \frac{1}{N} \cdot \sum_{k=0}^{N-1} \left[e^{-i \cdot \left(\frac{2 \cdot \pi}{N} \right) \cdot (nn-n)} \right]^k \tag{3.6}$$

We recognize the sum of a finite geometric series. First note that when pod(nn-n,N)=0, S=1. When pod(k-k1,N) is not zero, we have

$$S_{k,k1} = \frac{1 - \left[e^{i \cdot (nn-n) \cdot \left(\frac{2 \cdot \pi}{N} \right)} \right]^N}{1 - e^{i \cdot (nn-n) \cdot \left(\frac{2 \cdot \pi}{N} \right)}} \qquad (pod(k1-k,N) \text{ not zero })$$

But

$$\left[e^{i \cdot (nn-n) \cdot \left(\frac{2 \cdot \pi}{N} \right)} \right]^N = e^{i \cdot (nn-n) \cdot 2 \cdot \pi} = 1^{nn-n} = 1$$

and hence S is 0. Summarizing,

$$S_{nn,n} = \delta(pod(nn-n,N),0) \tag{3.7}$$

Now, substituting (3.7) into (3.5), we see that $xx_{nn}=x_{nn}$ as was to be proved.

Using the above discussion, show that

$$\sum_{k} ec_{nn,k} \cdot \overline{ec_{n,k}} = N \cdot \delta(pod((nn-n,N),0)$$

and hence that the family of complex exponentials is orthogonal and of norm sqrt(N). ‡

DFT Examples

The DFT is generally complex. We can plot its real and imaginary parts. When the DFT is an N-periodic frequency response, typically the magnitude and phase are plotted. Recall that the phase of a complex number is not defined when its magnitude is zero; it is convenient here to then take it as zero.

Example 3.4 _____

We compute and plot the magnitude and phase of the DFT of the unit impulse.

$$x_n := \delta(n,0) \quad X := dft(x) \quad Xmag := \overrightarrow{(|X|)} \quad Xph_k := \overrightarrow{\left(Xmag_k > 0\right) \cdot arg\left(X_k\right)}$$

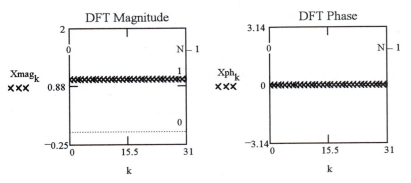

So, the DFT of the unit impulse is a sequence of constant value 1. ‡

Example 3.5 _____
We compute the DFT of a constant sequence.

$$x_n := \frac{1}{N} \quad X := dft(x) \quad Xmag := \overrightarrow{(|X|)} \quad Xph_k := \overrightarrow{\left(Xmag_k > 0\right) \cdot arg\left(X_k\right)}$$

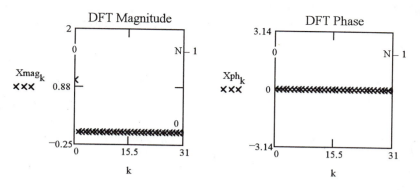

As we could have anticipated from Example 3.1 and the similarity of the DFT and the IDFT, the DFT of a constant sequence is an impulse sequence. ‡

Example 3.6

We compute the DFT of a finite, complex exponential sequence.

$$\omega := \frac{2 \cdot \pi}{N} \cdot 4 \qquad x_n := \exp(i \cdot \omega \cdot n)$$

$$X := dft(x) \qquad Xmag := \overrightarrow{(|X|)} \qquad Xph_k := \left(Xmag_k > 0\right) \cdot \overrightarrow{arg\left(X_k\right)}$$

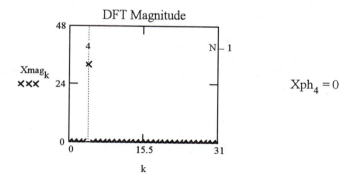

$$Xph_4 = 0$$

We see that a complex exponential of a suitably chosen frequency has an impulse sequence as its DFT. Actually, we could have anticipated this fact in view of the noted orthogonality of the basis sequences. ‡

EXERCISE 3.6 (a) For Example 3.6, give a "rule" for the location of the impulse. (b) Choose a frequency not of the form $(2\pi/N)k$ taken in Example 3.3 and note the phenomenon called **leakage** in the DSP jargon. ¤

Example 3.7 _____
We compute the DFT of a finite, sinusoidal sequence.

$$\omega := \frac{2 \cdot \pi}{N} \cdot 4 \qquad x_n := \cos(\omega \cdot n)$$

$$X := dft(x) \qquad Xmag := \overrightarrow{(|X|)} \qquad Xph_k := \overrightarrow{\left(Xmag_k > 0\right) \cdot arg\left(X_k\right)}$$

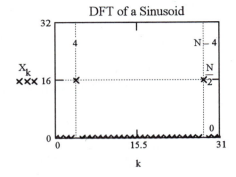

DFT of a Sinusoid

$Xph_4 = 0$

$Xph_{N-4} = 0$

Since, by Euler's formula, the cosine is expressible as a sum of two conjugate complex exponentials, we could have anticipated that the DFT would consist of the sum of two impulse sequences, one at n = 4 and one at n = -4. Because we use the conventional indexing from 0 to N-1, and because the DFT has period N, this second line appears at (-4+N). This is an important observation. ‡

■ **EXERCISE 3.7** In the declaration of ω in Example 3.7, replace the factor 4 with other integers. Comment on, for example, the plots for 4 and N-4, recalling the discussion of aliases in **Chapter 1**. ¤

Example 3.8 _____
We compute the DFT of a finite sequence of independent random variables, each uniformly distributed over [-1,1].

$$x_n := rnd(2) - 1 \qquad X := dft(x)$$

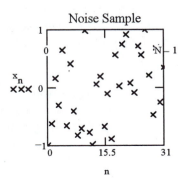

Noise Sample

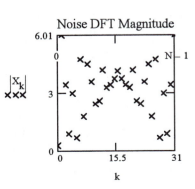

Noise DFT Magnitude

There is no readily understood structure, apparently. ‡

▦ **EXERCISE 3.8** Click on the declaration for {x} and repeatedly push F9 to recompute. Note the plots. ¤

Example 3.9

We further develop Example 3.8 by computing the **sample average** of the magnitudes of a number of DFTs of independently chosen random sequences. We form a matrix of such sequences: Each column is a random sequence and can be accessed with Mathcad's special exponent notation.

$$L := 64 \qquad l := 0..L - 1 \qquad x_{n,1} := rnd(2) - 1 \qquad X^{\langle l \rangle} := dft\left(x^{\langle l \rangle}\right)$$

sample average: $\qquad Sp_k := \frac{1}{L} \cdot \sum_l \left|\left(X^{\langle l \rangle}\right)_k\right|$

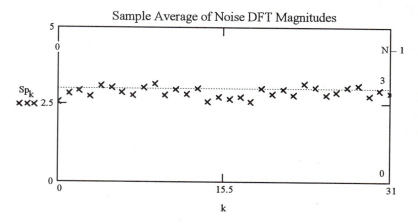

Notice that the sample average of the DFT magnitude of an uncorrelated sequence is approximately a constant (for L sufficiently large). Such a sequence is called **white**, in analogy to the magnitudes of the nearly equal components of ordinary, or white, light at each frequency. ‡

▦ **EXERCISE 3.9** Vary L in Example 3 and note the dependence on L of the variability about the constant. ¤

N-Periodic Frequency Response

We have seen that the N-periodic frequency response of an FIR filter is the DFT of its impulse response, extended as necessary by zero padding to a length N.

Example 3.10

The simple MA filter has an N-periodic frequency response easily computed by the DFT. Since it is complex, we plot the magnitude and phase, as is conventionally done.

$$M := 9 \qquad he_n := if\left(n<M, \frac{1}{M}, 0\right) \qquad H := dft(he)$$

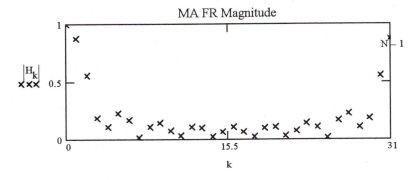

MA FR Magnitude

The phase of a complex number z=x+iy is defined when the magnitude z_m=sqrt(x^2+y^2) is not zero. Recall that the arctangent(y/x) determines an angle in [-π/2,π/2] and could be used to define the phase of the frequency response. However, knowing x and y allows us to determine the quadrant of z in the complex plane and hence the angle in [-π,π], which is more informative. This function is implemented as the **arg** built-in function in Mathcad and gives us a conventionally defined phase. However, a still more informative definition of the phase is obtained by recursively computing the phase differences between samples, as follows.

phase unwrapping algorithm: $\quad \theta_0 := arg\left(H_0\right) \qquad\qquad j := 1 .. N - 1$

$$\theta_j := \theta_{j-1} + arg\left(H_j \cdot \overline{H_{j-1}}\right)$$

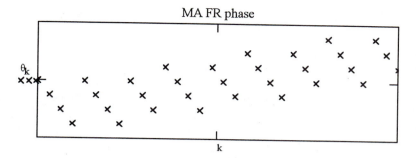
MA FR phase

This phase determination is called **phase unwrapping**. Note that we may have to improve its implementation to handle a zero sample value where arg( ) is not defined. If we know where the zeros occur, we can adjust the sample locations to miss the zeros. But it usually works as it stands. ‡

To better understand the nature of this phase function, we analytically compute the DFT. (Better, you can do it!) This is easy to do since it is a finite geometric series.

PROBLEM 3.2
Show that the DFT of the MA filter of length M and weights {1/M}, zero padded to length N, is

real factor:
$$T_k := \text{if}\left[k=0, 1, \frac{\sin\left[\left(\frac{2 \cdot \pi}{N}\right) \cdot \left(\frac{M}{2}\right) \cdot k\right]}{M \cdot \sin\left[\left(\frac{2 \cdot \pi}{N}\right) \cdot \left(\frac{1}{2}\right) \cdot k\right]} \right]$$

DFT:
$$Ha_k := \exp\left[-i \cdot \left(\frac{2 \cdot \pi}{N}\right) \cdot \left(\frac{M-1}{2}\right) \cdot k\right] \cdot T_k \qquad ‡$$

One might hastily conclude that the phase of {H_k} is

$$\phi_k := -\left(\frac{2 \cdot \pi}{N}\right) \cdot \left(\frac{M-1}{2}\right) \cdot k$$

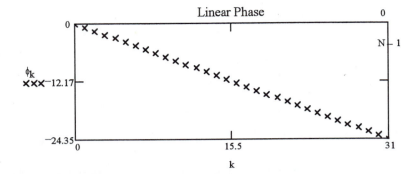

Linear Phase

However, we note that the sequence $\{T_k\}$ changes sign and so it is not a proper magnitude; the sign changes must be accounted for by the phase.

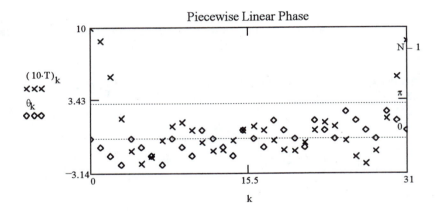

Piecewise Linear Phase

We see that $\{T_k\}$ itself changes sign (M-1) times. This change of sign must be accounted for by a jump of π in the phase of the frequency response. Examining the latter's plot, we see that there are exactly (M-1) jumps at the correct indices.

▨ **EXERCISE 3.10** Change the value of M and verify the conclusions just arrived at. ¤

DFT Symbolic Computation

The DFT is important as a numerical algorithm. However, it is useful to have a collection of typical DFTs in analytic form. Then, to check a specific implementation, for example, we can refer to the collection, often called a table.

We show how to compute the DFT of a typical generic sequence using Mathcad's symbolic mathematics capability. There is a certain art involved in using such software. Agreeable forms are sometimes obtained only after using the symbolic mathematical operations of simplify, factor, expand and collect.

Example 3.11 _____

We begin with a simple sequence: a geometric series whose sum we know. We write down a finite geometric series in a region of our Mathcad document:

$$\sum_{n=0}^{N-1} a^n$$

We click on and enclose this expression. Then we choose **Evaluate Symbolically** from the **Symbolic** menu and then **Simplify** from the **Symbolic** menu. After discarding intermediate forms, we get the result

$$\frac{\left(a^N - 1\right)}{(a - 1)}$$

which we know to be correct. ‡

▦ **EXERCISE 3.11** Duplicate the above steps. ¤

Example 3.12 _____

We can now compute the DFT of any exponential sequence $\{a^n\}$ in a similar manner. Note that $\exp[-(2\pi/N)kn] = \{\exp[-(2\pi/N)k]\}^n$.

IDFT: $\quad a^n$ $\qquad\qquad$ **DFT:** $\quad \dfrac{\left(a^N - 1\right)}{\left(a \cdot \exp\left(-2 \cdot i \cdot \dfrac{\pi}{N} \cdot k\right) - 1\right)}$

We can use the form to define a function.

$$F(k, a, N) := \frac{\left(a^N - 1\right)}{\left(a \cdot \exp\left(-2 \cdot i \cdot \frac{\pi}{N} \cdot k\right) - 1\right)}$$

(3.8)

Then we can assign values to the parameters and graph the DFT.

$$N := 32 \qquad\qquad k := 0 .. N - 1 \qquad\qquad a := 0.5$$

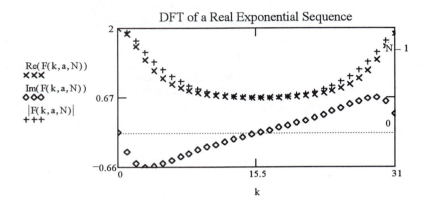

The particular case of a complex exponential is of special interest, as we have already noted. (The case of α an integer must be handled separately by returning to the original form.)

$$\alpha := 3.17 \qquad\qquad a := \exp\left[i \cdot \left(\frac{2 \cdot \pi}{N}\right) \cdot \alpha\right]$$

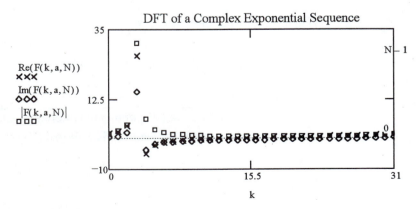

We know that a complex exponential with a frequency other than $(2\pi/N)k$, where k is an integer, cannot be orthogonal to any of the basis complex exponentials and so will have all nonzero DFT values, the projections. This is called leakage, as mentioned. ‡

EXERCISE 3.12 Choose other values of α and observe the plots. For example, vary α through the range (k,k+1), k an integer. ¤

Project 3.1

For each of the FIRs of **Project 2.2**, compute the N-periodic frequency response. Interpret each filter's operation and compare to your earlier conclusions. ‡

Project 3.2

The DFT is an important numerical algorithm. But it is useful for analysis and checking to have a collection of DFT-IDFT pairs. These can be derived by hand or by using Mathcad's symbolic mathematics capability. In itself it is useful to learn how to use symbolic mathematics software. Construct a table of DFTs. Some entries are suggested below and are sequences defined for n and k in [0,N-1].

IDFT	DFT
1	$\delta(k,0)$
$\delta(n)$	1
$\exp(i(2\pi/N)\kappa n)$, $\exp(i\alpha n)$	$N\,\delta(\kappa,k)$, (eq. 3.8)
$\cos((2\pi/N)\kappa n)$, $\cos(\alpha n)$	?
$\sin((2\pi/N)\kappa n)$, $\sin(\alpha n)$	?
a^n	(eq. 3.8)
$\Phi(n,0) - \Phi(n,M)$	(Exercise 3.7) ‡

Project 3.3

Analog communication systems are classified according to the modulation type that they employ. For example, commercial AM broadcasts a signal of the form

$$s(t) = (1 + \mu \cdot m(t)) \cdot A \cdot \cos\left(\omega_c \cdot t\right)$$

Here m(t) is the **modulation** - for example, voice. An important problem is determining the bandwidth occupied by analog communication signals. (One reason is that spectral occupancy is controlled by the law!) One way to determine this is to compute the Fourier transform (FT) of a model of the signal but this is not easy. We can construct discrete-time models that give us insight into this problem. We choose a convenient sequence length N and make up discrete-time models using sequences that are sinusoidal with frequencies of the form $(2\pi/N)k$, where k is an integer. We then compute the DFT. This particular choice for the frequencies gives a suggestive similarity between the DFT and the FT.

For simple modulations composed of one or a few sinusoids, compute the DFT for the common types of analog modulated waveforms: (i) broadcast AM and (ii) broadcast FM. You can refer to Gibson for the forms. ‡

References

Gibson (1993), Chaps. 5 and 6
Jackson (1996), Sec. 7.1
Oppenheim and Schafer (1989), Secs. 8.0, 8.6
Proakis and Manolakis (1996), Sec. 5.1

4 Discrete Fourier Transform Properties

The DFT has a number of properties that are useful in DSP applications. From the point of view of digital filtering, the most important property provides an alternative computation of the periodic convolution (**2.6**). When the DFT is implemented with a fast algorithm, the FFT, this leads to a fast algorithm for computing (2.6) that is very important to DSP. In practice, data sequences may be of very long length - even simple sounds are many thousands of samples long and direct implementation of (2.6) would not be practical. We discuss applications of this fast algorithm in **Chapter 5**.

Basic Properties

Example 4.1

To provide specific illustrations of the various properties, we define two sequences of length N and will discuss the DFT for N-length sequences.

sequence length and index: $\qquad N := 32 \qquad n := 0 .. N - 1$

DFT and index: $\qquad dft(v) := \sqrt{N} \cdot icfft(v) \qquad k := 0 .. N - 1$

IDFT: $\qquad idft(v) := \dfrac{1}{\sqrt{N}} \cdot cfft(v)$

first sequence, zero padded: $\qquad M1 := \dfrac{N}{4} \qquad f_n := if\left[n < M1, 1 + \dfrac{1}{N} \cdot (n - N), 0 \right]$

second sequence, zero padded: $\qquad M2 := \dfrac{N}{2} \qquad g_n := if\left[n < M2, \dfrac{1}{N} \cdot (N - n), 0 \right]$

DFTs: $\qquad F := dft(f) \qquad G := dft(g) \qquad \updownarrow$

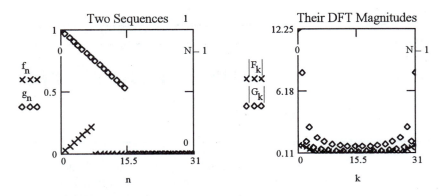

Two Sequences

Their DFT Magnitudes

Property 4.1: Periodicity The DFT and IDFT sequences have period N.

We have already noted that this periodicity in **Exercise 3.4** is a direct consequence of the period in either n or k of the sequences {exp[i(2π/N)nk]}. It is this property that allows the basic index set to be chosen arbitrarily, as long as the N unique values are included. Conventionally the set [0,...,N-1] is chosen. (A set symmetric about zero might seem more natural, but this can only be done for N odd.)

We make the periodic extensions in Mathcad as discussed in **Chapter 2**. We use the pod( ) function for implementation in Mathcad.

$$pod(n,N) := mod(N + mod(n,N),N)$$

It will be convenient for the illustrations to recall the orthogonal basis

$$ec_{n,k} := exp\left[i \cdot \left(\frac{2 \cdot \pi}{N}\right) \cdot k \cdot n\right] \qquad (n=0,...,N-1, \ k=0,...,N-1)$$

The DFT and, it follows, the IDFT, have a number of symmetries that can be useful in reducing the amount of required computation. We now discuss some of these for real sequences. Note that it is sensible to discuss a symmetry property about k=0 for a DFT: whereas it is computed explicitly for k=0,...,N-1, it is a periodic sequence of period N.

Property 4.2: Symmetries Assume that {f_n, n=0,...,N-1} is a real sequence with DFT {F_k}. Then {F_k} is Hermitian symmetric, i.e., $F_{-k}=F_k^*$, which may be expressed as $F_{N-k}=F_k^*$.

To prove this asserted property, simply express the complex conjugate, $F_k{}^*$, of the DFT F_k using the latter's **definition (3.3)** and thereby note that it is F_{-k}. But, by the periodicity of the DFT, $F_{-k}=F_{-k+N}$.

As an illustration, note that

$$\varepsilon_k := \overline{F_{pod(k,N)}} - F_{pod(N-k,N)} \qquad\qquad \varepsilon_3 = 0$$

is the 0 sequence.

▨ **EXERCISE 4.1** Let $\{FR_k\}$ and $\{FI_k\}$ be the real and imaginary parts of $\{F_k\}$, respectively. Then show that they are, respectively, even and odd sequences, conditions that are expressible as FR(N-k)=FR(k) and FI(N-k)=-FI(k), respectively. ¤

As an illustration, note that

$$\varepsilon_k := \mathrm{Re}\!\left(F_{pod(k,N)}\right) - \mathrm{Re}\!\left(F_{pod(N-k,N)}\right) \qquad\qquad \varepsilon_3 = 0$$

is the 0 sequence.

As a consequence of Property 4.2, it is only necessary to compute the DFT for k=0,...,floor(N/2) and then get the remaining values by a simple conjugation operation. (The Mathcad built-in function **floor(x)** is the greatest integer <= x.) Fast DFT algorithms can take advantage of this. For our purposes, though, such forms can introduce an impediment to understanding the basic ideas of the DFT (which already contain sufficient complications!) and we will not use them. Mathcad has, for real sequences, special fast algorithms for the DFT and its inverse, the built-in functions **fft** and **ifft**.

Property 4.3: Periodic time translation Given a sequence $\{f_k$, n=0,...,N-1\}, with DFT $\{F_k\}$, we extend it to have period N. Then, for any integer nd, the translated sequence $\{g_n=f_{n-nd}\}$ is defined over indices n in $\{0,...,N-1\}$ and we may compute its DFT $\{G_k\}$. We find that $G_k=\mathrm{conj}(ec_{nd,k})F_k$.

▨ **EXERCISE 4.2** Show that nd enters $\{G_k\}$ only as pod(nd,N). ¤

As an illustration, note that

$$\text{nd} := 37 \qquad g_n := f_{\text{pod}(n - nd, N)} \qquad G := dft(g) \qquad \varepsilon_k := G_k - \overline{ec_{\text{pod}(nd, N), k}} \cdot F_k$$

is the 0 sequence.

PROBLEM 4.1

Prove Property 4.3 ‡

Property 4.4: Periodic frequency translation Given a DFT {F_k, k=0,...,N-1}, with IDFT {f_n}, it has period N. Then, for any integer kd, the translated sequence {$G_k = F_{k-kd}$} is defined over indices k in {0,...,N-1} and we may compute its IDFT {g_n}. We find that $g_n = ec_{n,kd} f_n$.

▨ **EXERCISE 4.3** Show that kd enters {g_n} only as pod(kd,N). ¤

As an illustration note that

$$\text{kd} := 37 \qquad G_k := F_{\text{pod}(k - kd, N)} \qquad g := idft(G) \qquad \varepsilon_n := g_n - ec_{n, \text{pod}(kd, N)} \cdot f_n$$

is the 0 sequence.

PROBLEM 4.2

Prove Property 4.4. ‡

Property 4.5: Plancherel's Identity Given a sequence {f_n, n=0,...,N-1} with DFT {F_k, k=0,...,N-1},

$$\sum_n \left(|f_n| \right)^2 = \frac{1}{N} \cdot \sum_k \left(|F_k| \right)^2$$

We have defined the left side of this last relation as the squared norm of the sequence {f_n} regarded as a vector in an N-dimensional linear vector space. The sum on the right side is the squared norm of the DFT sequence {F_k}. These squared norms are therefore always related by a constant, fixed by N. If we had used the orthonormal sequences {$ec_{n,k}/sqrt(N)$} instead of the merely orthogonal {$ec_{n,k}$} in constructing the DFT and IDFT, then the 1/N would not appear in the statement of Plancherel's Identity. The DFT would then be a **unitary** transformation.

As an illustration, note that

$$\sum_{n}\left(\left|f_n\right|\right)^2 = 0.137 \qquad\qquad \frac{1}{N}\cdot\sum_{k}\left(\left|F_k\right|\right)^2 = 0.137$$

Property 4.6: Parseval's Identity Given sequences $\{f_n, n=0,...,N-1\}$ and $\{g_n, n=0,...,N-1\}$ with DFTs $\{F_k, k=0,...,N-1\}$ and $\{G_k, k=0,...,N-1\}$, respectively,

$$\sum_{n} f_n \cdot \overline{g_n} = \frac{1}{N}\cdot\sum_{k} F_k \cdot \overline{G_k} \qquad\qquad (4.1)$$

Parseval's Identity relates the inner products of two sequences and their DFTs by a constant fixed by N.

EXERCISE 4.4 Show that Property 4.5 is a corollary of Property 4.6. ¤

As an illustration, note that, with the present definitions of f and g,

$$\sum_{n} f_n \cdot \overline{g_n} = 0.056 + 0.016i \qquad\qquad \frac{1}{N}\cdot\sum_{k} F_k \cdot \overline{G_k} = 0.056 + 0.016i$$

To establish Property 4.6, substitute the Fourier representations (IDFTs) of the sequences $\{f_n\}$ and $\{g_n\}$ into the left side of (4.1) and interchange the order of the three summations so that the interior sum is of the form

$$\kappa = (0 .. N-1) \qquad\qquad S_{k,\kappa} = \frac{1}{N}\cdot\sum_{n} \overline{ec_{n,\kappa}}\cdot ec_{n,k}$$

We know from **Problem 3.1** that

$$S_{k,\kappa} = \delta(pod(k-\kappa, N), 0)$$

The remaining double sum now collapses to the desired single sum.

DFT and Periodic Convolution

An important use of the DFT in DSP is to provide a method of computing the periodic convolution that is an alternative to the direct computation **(2.6)** and that can be computationally more efficient. We establish this alternative computational method with the following property.

Property 4.7: IDFT of a product of DFTs Let $\{x_n, n=0,...,N-1\}$ and $\{h_n, n=0,...,N-1\}$ have DFTs $\{X_k\}$ and $\{H_k\}$, respectively. Let $\{Y_k=X_k\,H_k\}$. Then the IDFT of $\{Y_k\}$, $\{y_n, n=0,...,N-1\}$, is the periodic convolution of $\{x_n, n=0,...,N-1\}$ and $\{h_n, n=0,...,N-1\}$.

To establish this result, we use the definition **(3.4b)** of the IDFT to express $\{y_n, n=0,...,N-1\}$ in terms of $\{Y_k=X_k\,H_k\}$. Then we use the definition **(3.3b)** of the DFT to express $\{X_k\}$ and $\{H_k\}$ in terms of $\{x_n, n=0,...,N-1\}$ and $\{h_n, n=0,...,N-1\}$, respectively. We then interchange the order of the three summations to get the interior sum in the form

$$SS(m,j,n)=\frac{1}{N}\cdot\sum_{k}\exp\left[-i\cdot\frac{2\cdot\pi}{N}\cdot(m+j-n)\cdot k\right]$$

where $m=0,...,N-1$ and $j=0,...,N-1$. We have now encountered this sum several times and, from **(3.6)** and **(3.7)**, know it to be

$$SS(m,j,n)=\delta(pod(m+j-n,N),0)$$

PROBLEM 4.3   Show that, since j takes on values in $[0,...,N-1]$,

$$SS(m,j,n)=\delta(j-pod(n-m,N),0) \qquad \ddagger$$

We can now trivially sum over j and end up with the sum

$$y_n=\sum_{m}x_m\cdot h_{pod(n-m,N)}$$

which we recognize to be the periodic convolution, **(2.6)**, of the two sequences $\{x_n, n=0,...,N-1\}$ and $\{h_n, n=0,...,N-1\}$.

Property 4.7 gives us an alternative way of computing the periodic convolution; we call this the **frequency domain method**.

Example 4.2

We illustrate the frequency domain method of filtering and check it with the computation of (2.6) directly. We use the sequences of Example 4.1 but change to notation suggestive of the filtering application. We would like to be able to vary the period N here and so must redefine the DFT and IDFT functions here.

sequence length:
$$N := 32 \qquad n := 0 .. N - 1$$

DFT:
$$\mathrm{dft}(v) := \sqrt{N} \cdot \mathrm{icfft}(v)$$

IDFT:
$$\mathrm{idft}(v) := \frac{1}{\sqrt{N}} \cdot \mathrm{cfft}(v)$$

input signal and DFT:
$$x_n := \mathrm{if}\left[n<M2, \frac{1}{N} \cdot (N-n), 0 \right] \qquad X := \mathrm{dft}(x)$$

FIR and FR:
$$h_n := \mathrm{if}\left[n<M1, 1 + \frac{1}{N} \cdot (n-N), 0 \right] \qquad H := \mathrm{dft}(h)$$

output signal, direct computation:
$$y_n := \sum_{m=0}^{N-1} h_m \cdot x_{\mathrm{pod}(n-m,N)}$$

output signal, frequency domain method:
$$Y := \overrightarrow{(X \cdot H)} \qquad yy := \mathrm{idft}(Y)$$

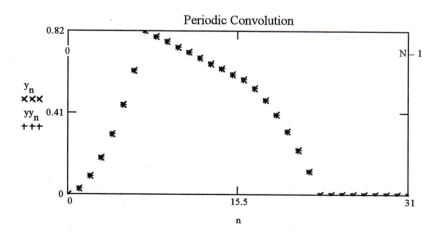

Periodic Convolution

As expected, the two methods of computation yield the same sequence. ‡

▦ **EXERCISE 4.5** Vary N in Example 4.2 Compare the computation times of the two methods of computing the periodic convolution. The value of N you have to choose to note a time difference depends on your computer. You can toggle declarations inactive to compute the methods one at a time. ¤

As Example 4.2 and Exercise 4.5 make clear, we now have an attractive alternative method of computing the output of a linear, invariant filtering operation defined as the periodic convolution. The procedure is as follows.

1. Given an FIR filter length of M1 and a data sequence length of M2, choose a DFT of size N. For example, if we want the periodic and aperiodic convolutions to agree, we choose N at least as large as M1+M2-1.

2. Compute the DFT of the FIR filter's impulse response. (This need only be done once, however many input sequences are processed.)

3. Compute the DFT of the input signal.

4. Multiply the two DFTs.

5. Compute the IDFT of the product.

When the DFT and IDFT algorithms are implemented by FFT and IFFT algorithms, this procedure can be much faster than the direct evaluation **(2.6)**. We summarize this procedure in the following flowchart.

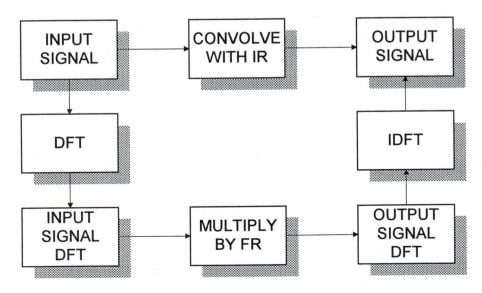

Example 4.3

We consider a simple filtering example that easily demonstrates a consequence of the periodic nature of the periodic convolution. We assume the LIV filter is simply a unit impulse at time nd.

Step 1: $nd := 4$ $\qquad$ $h_n := \delta(n, nd)$

Step 2: $x_n := \frac{1}{N} \cdot (N - n)$

Step 3: $H := dft(h)$ $\qquad$ $X := dft(x)$

Step 4: $Y := \overrightarrow{(X \cdot H)}$

Step 5: $y := idft(Y)$

We may also compute the periodic convolution from its definition (2.5).

$$yy_n := \sum_{m=0}^{N-1} h_m \cdot x_{pod(n-m, N)}$$

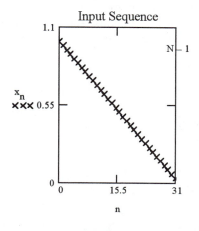

Input Sequence

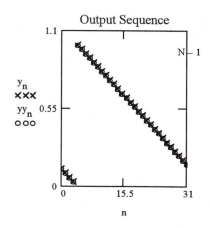

Output Sequence

We realize that the output sequence is just the periodically delayed input sequence. If you are confused by the plot of the output, a review of **Example 1.9** will be helpful. This plot again shows the cyclic artifact of periodic translation.

EXERCISE 4.6 Choose other values for the delay in Example 4.3 and note the resulting plots. ¤

Fast Fourier Transform

The fast Fourier transform (FFT) is implemented in a variety of forms and ways in lower-level languages such as Fortran and C. We use Mathcad to show how one may speed up the computation of the DFT when N is divisible by 2. Then we can rearrange the DFT computation so that only about one-half the required complex operations are required, a basic observation. A **complex operation** is a complex multiply and a complex add.

We will use an example with which we can time the computation of the forms.

$$N := 256 \qquad n := 0 .. N - 1 \qquad k := 0 .. N - 1$$

$$f_n := rnd(2) - 1 \qquad W(N) := \exp\left(-i \cdot \frac{2 \cdot \pi}{N}\right)$$

The definition of the DFT is

$$W1 := W(N) \qquad F_{def_k} := \sum_{n=0}^{N-1} W1^{n \cdot k} \cdot f_n$$

Assuming that the complex exponentials are available in negligible time, the number of complex operations required for this calculation is N^2. For each k, there are N complex multiply adds required and there are N values of k.

Now suppose we simply break the above sum into two sums, one over the even indices and the other over the odd indices. Each such sum will have N2 = N/2 terms.

$$N2 := \frac{N}{2}$$

$$F2_k := \sum_{n=0}^{N2-1} W(N)^{2 \cdot n2 \cdot k} \cdot f_{2 \cdot n2} + \sum_{n=0}^{N2-1} W(N)^{(2 \cdot n2 + 1) \cdot k} \cdot f_{2 \cdot n2 + 1}$$

Notice that a factor $W(N)^k$ can be brought outside the second summation. Also, note that $W(N)^2$ is $W(N/2)$. So we may write the last equation as

$$W2 := W1^2 \qquad F_{2_k} := \sum_{n=0}^{N2-1} W2^{n \cdot k} \cdot f_{2 \cdot n} + W1^k \cdot \sum_{n=0}^{N2-1} W2^{n \cdot k} \cdot f_{2 \cdot n + 1}$$

The number of complex operations required for each sum is now $(N/2)^2$. Also, N more are required to multiply by $W1^k$ and add. Thus $N^2/2 + N$ complex operations are required. For large N, the number of complex operations required to compute the DFT has been approximately halved by this simple device.

EXERCISE 4.7 You can choose N so that the computation times of F_{def} and F_2 may be easily compared. The value will depend on your computer speed. Make sure that this section has been entirely computed. (Select **Calculate Document** from the **Math** menu.) Then select the F_{def} equation and press F9, timing the computation. Similarly, select the F_2 equation, press F9 and time the computation. For example, for a DX486, 66 mHz cpu and N=256, the two computations times were 20 and 11 sec. Note that computations of the complex exponentials were included in the times: The number of such is nearly the same in both expressions, N^2 for F_{def} and $N^2 + N$ for F_2. ¤

If $N/2$ is also divisible by 2 then this process can be repeated. In fact, if N is a power of 2, say $N = M^2$, then the process can be iterated $M = \log_2(M)$ times. It can be shown that about $2N \log_2(N)$ complex operations will be required. If one makes certain simple modifications of the algorithm - namely (i) not multiplying by 1 and (ii) factoring out common multiplies by $W(N)$ - then about **(N/2)** **$\log_2(N)$** complex operations will be required.

EXERCISE 4.8 Make a comparison of N^2 and $(N/2) \log_2(N)$ for $N = 2^M$, M=1,2,...,12. ¤

It can be shown that if N is "highly composite" (that is, composed of the product of many integers) then considerable savings in computation may be made. Many mathematical applications, including Mathcad, have algorithms that can reduce the DFT computation for such N. It is good practice to choose such N when possible. In this book, almost always N is chosen as a power of 2. Such an algorithm is called a **fast Fourier transform (FFT)**.

We now use Mathcad's built-in function for the DFT/FFT and note the computation time in comparison to the above times: It is a fraction of a second!

$$F := \sqrt{N} \cdot \text{icfft}(f)$$

PROBLEM 4.4 Show that a fast algorithm for the DFT is, with simple changes, a fast algorithm for the IDFT. ‡

A Digital Signal Processing Application

Example 4.4 _____

We return to **Example 2.10** and now compute the periodic convolution using the frequency domain method of filtering. Also, having now defined the N-periodic frequency response, we will have an alternative, and powerful, explanation for the filter's action. We will choose a fairly long input sequence and will simultaneously do the computations for a family of FIR filters of varying lengths, defined as follows.

data length and index: $J := 256$ $\qquad$ $j := 0 .. J - 1$

pulse signal: $s_j := (j > 50) \cdot (j < 150)$

noise: $\text{var} := 0.15$ $\qquad$ $\text{no} := \text{rnorm}\left(J, 0, \sqrt{\text{var}}\right)$

input data: $x := s + \text{no}$

FIR family: $I := 3$ $\quad$ $i := 0 .. I - 1$ $\quad$ $M1_i := 2^{i+2}$ $\qquad$ $M1 = \begin{pmatrix} 4 \\ 8 \\ 16 \end{pmatrix}$

$$h_{(n,i)} := \text{if}\left(n < M1_i, \frac{1}{M1_i}, 0\right)$$

We will compute the output over the set of indices [0,J–1] since this includes the part of the output due to this signal. We will therefore take the period of the DFT as N=J.

DFT period: $N := J$ $\qquad$ $n := 0 .. N - 1$

The DFT and IDFT of N-length sequences are defined.

DFT: $\quad \mathrm{dft}(v) := \sqrt{N} \cdot \mathrm{icfft}(v)$ $\qquad$ **IDFT:** $\quad \mathrm{idft}(v) := \dfrac{1}{\sqrt{N}} \cdot \mathrm{cfft}(v)$

required DFTs: $\quad X := \mathrm{dft}(x) \qquad H^{<i>} := \mathrm{dft}\left(h^{<i>}\right)$

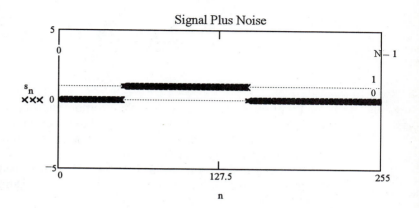

The family of FIRs and their N-periodic frequency responses are plotted.

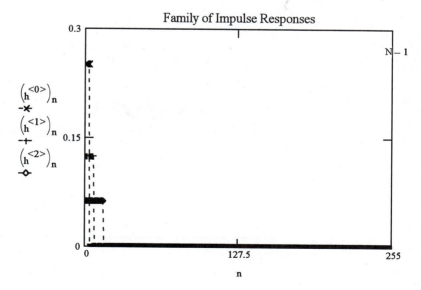

$$H^{<i>} := \mathrm{dft}\left(h^{<i>}\right)$$

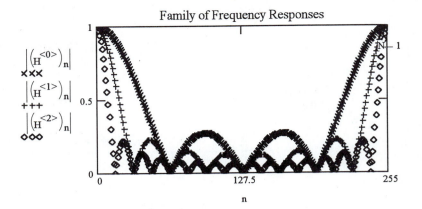

Family of Frequency Responses

$\left|\left(H^{<0>}\right)_n\right|$
×××

$\left|\left(H^{<1>}\right)_n\right|$
+++

$\left|\left(H^{<2>}\right)_n\right|$
◇◇◇

To interpret the action of this filter, remember that indices increasing from zero toward N/2, and decreasing from N-1 toward N/2, represent increasingly higher frequencies. Thus, as the FIR increases in length, the frequency response becomes increasingly concentrated toward low frequencies. Thus, the noise, which has on average a broad band of frequencies (recall **Examples 3.8** and **3.9**) is increasingly discarded.

We now compute outputs of the filters.

$$X := \mathrm{dft}(x) \qquad Y^{<i>} := \overrightarrow{\left(\overline{H^{<i>}} \cdot X\right)} \qquad y^{<i>} := \mathrm{idft}\left(Y^{<i>}\right)$$

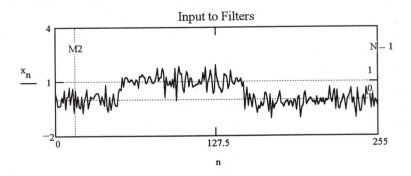

Input to Filters

$\dfrac{x_n}{1}$

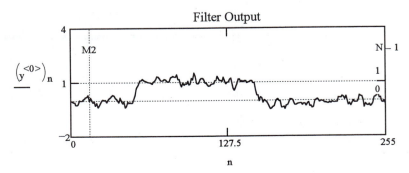

Filter Output

$\dfrac{\left(y^{<0>}\right)_n}{1}$

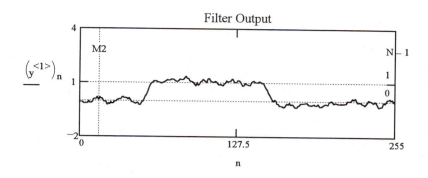

$$\left(y^{<1>}\right)_n$$

Filter Output

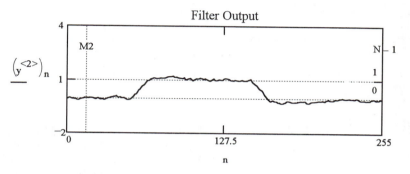

$$\left(y^{<2>}\right)_n$$

Filter Output

We may characterize these results, then, in one of two equivalent ways. First, we may observe that, as the FIR filter bandwidth becomes narrower, the rate of fluctuation of the filter output decreases (the output becomes smoother) because an increasingly large band of frequencies of the noise is filtered out.
Second, we may observe that, as the MA filter impulse response becomes longer, more (independent) random variates are being averaged and we would expect the output to tend toward the mean value sequence of x, which is {s}. ‡

 EXERCISE 4.9 Vary the noise variance in Example 4.4 and note the plot. In particular, when the noise variance is zero, explain the shape of the output in terms of the FR. Study the effect of choice of FIR length M. Can you decide on a best M? ¤

Project 4.1

In Example 4.4, let the signal vary - say, sinusoidally. Does a best filter length M exist? (You need to define "best".) ‡

Project 4.2

We study an FIR filter related to the FIR filter of **Example 3.10**. Its N-periodic frequency response (see **Problem 3.2**) has the phase $-(2\pi/N)((M-1)/2)k$ that can be, in view of Property 4.3, attributed to a time delay of a periodically extended FIR.

(a) Plot a few periods of the periodically extended FIR and its advance by $(M-1)/2$.

(b) Define an N-periodic frequency response to be that of **Example 3.10** except the factor $\exp[-i(2\pi/N)((M-1)/2)k]$ is replaced by unity. Compute and plot its IDFT, or N-periodic frequency response. Compare with your plot for (a). Carefully explain why we might call this filter noncausal.

(c) Define a signal

$$s_n = \left(n \geq \frac{N}{2} - \frac{M-1}{2} \right) \cdot \left(n \leq \frac{N}{2} + \frac{M-1}{2} \right)$$

The signal and filters are said to be matched (**Chapter 31**). Filter this signal with the causal FIR filter and with the noncausal FIR filter, using the DFT method of filtering. Plot the input and both outputs. Why might we prefer the noncausal FIR? (For example, consider an image processing application.) ‡

References

Jackson (1996), Secs. 7.1, 7.4
Oppenheim and Schafer (1989), Secs. 8.7, 9.1, 9.3
Proakis and Manolakis (1996), Secs. 5.2, 5.3, 6.1

5   Fast Convolution

We have seen that FIR filtering may be performed efficiently by the DFT method. In some applications, the data sequence length may be too long to be read entirely into the computer memory. And even if it could be read in, we might wish to make use of the output as soon as it can be computed. Because we want to exploit the computational advantage of the DFT method, we are led to consider whether we can process a long input in conveniently sized subsequences, or **blocks**, that would be processed by the DFT method, and then reassembled to get the desired filtered output. This is possible because the filter impulse response is of finite length. The desired output is the aperiodic convolution of the FIR with the data sequence. *In this chapter*, a value yp_n of the periodic convolution will be called *correct* if it agrees with the value ya_n of the aperiodic convolution.

Thus the following questions arise:
> How big should the blocks be?
> How should they be formed from the data sequence?
> What size DFT should be chosen?
> How should the processed blocks be reassembled?

We will discuss two solutions, the overlap-add and overlap-save methods, which are called **fast convolution** methods. To understand these methods, we will recall the nature of the periodic convolution, as the DFT method computes a periodic convolution.

Periodic Convolution for Unequal-Length FIR, Block and DFT

Consider an FIR $\{h_n, n=0,...,L-1\}$, a signal block $\{x_n, n=0,...,M-1\}$ and a DFT defined for sequences of length N. We wish to compare the periodic and aperiodic convolutions for a given set (L,M,N). We assume that the signal block length M is at least as large as the FIR length L because the filter should be "filled" at least once by the signal block for at least one correct output value. Also, we assume that N>=M because we want to fully utilize the signal block. Thus $\{h_n\}$ and $\{x_n\}$ are extended, if necessary, by zero padding to length N.

We will be going over again the discussions in **Chapter 2**, comparing the periodic and aperiodic convolutions. It may be helpful at this point to review the section Convolution Animation of **Chapter 2**, particularly your answers to Exercises 2.10 - 12 and Problem 2.8, whose solutions we will now find.

Example 5.1 _____

We define an example to be used for illustration.

DFT size:
$$N := 32 \quad n := 0..N-1 \qquad dft(v) := \sqrt{N} \cdot icfft(v)$$

FIR:
$$L := 8 \qquad h_n := if\left(n<L, \frac{1}{L}, 0\right) \qquad H := dft(h)$$

signal block:
$$M := 28 \qquad\qquad m := 0..N-1$$

$$x_n := if\left(n<M, \cos\left(\frac{2 \cdot \pi}{N} \cdot e \cdot n\right) + \cos\left(\frac{2 \cdot \pi}{N} \cdot \pi \cdot n\right), 0\right)$$

$$X := dft(x) \qquad\qquad pod(n, N) := mod(N + mod(n, N), N)$$

periodic convolution, direct method:
$$yp_n := \sum_m h_m \cdot x_{pod(n-m, N)}$$

aperiodic convolution, direct method:
$$ya_n := \sum_m h_m \cdot if\left[(n-m \geq 0) \cdot (n-m \leq N-1), x_{n-m}, 0\right]$$

periodic convolution, DFT method:
$$idft(v) := \frac{1}{\sqrt{N}} \cdot cfft(v) \qquad\qquad yq := idft\left(\overrightarrow{(H \cdot X)}\right)$$

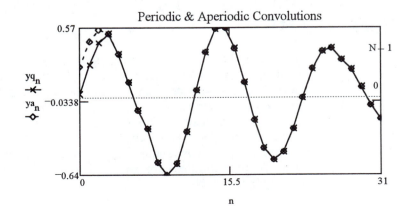

Periodic & Aperiodic Convolutions

We see that there is disagreement at the beginning of the computed sequences but agreement otherwise. ‡

EXERCISE 5.1 Try various values of (L,M,N) and observe when and where the aperiodic and periodic convolutions agree. ¤

To better understand this phenomenon, we plot the factors of the summand of the periodic convolution, first for n=0.

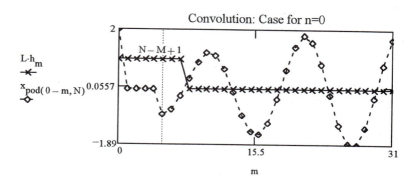

We see that if a periodic repetition of the signal falls into the basic interval [0,L-1] where $\{h_m\}$ has nonzero values, an incorrect value will result. The leftmost, possibly nonzero, point of this period is $-(M-1)+N$. If this point falls on or to the left of the last point of h_m, at L-1, then an incorrect value will be computed. In this case, we increase n until the first time there is no overlap of the periodic repetition with $\{h_m\}$, so that a correct value is computed.

EXERCISE 5.2 In the above plot, edit the changes $x_{pod(n-m,N)}$ for $x_{pod(0-m,N)}$ for values of n=1,...,M+L-N-1. Carefully observe the plots. When n=M+L-N-1, you will get the next plot. ¤

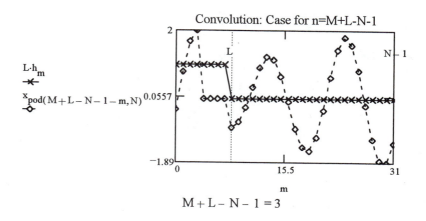

$$M + L - N - 1 = 3$$

We see that, at this point, the periodic repetition is not contributing to the convolution sum, which will therefore agree with the aperiodic convolution. Thus, as n increases, we will get correct values when n>=max{0, M+L-N-1}.

▣ **EXERCISE 5.3** Continuing Exercise 5.2, edit the change $x_{pod(n-m,N)}$ for $x_{pod(0-m,N)}$ for values of n =M+L-N-1,...,N-1. Carefully observe the plots. When n=N-1, you will get the plot below. ¤

At n=N-1, its maximum value, we have the following situation.

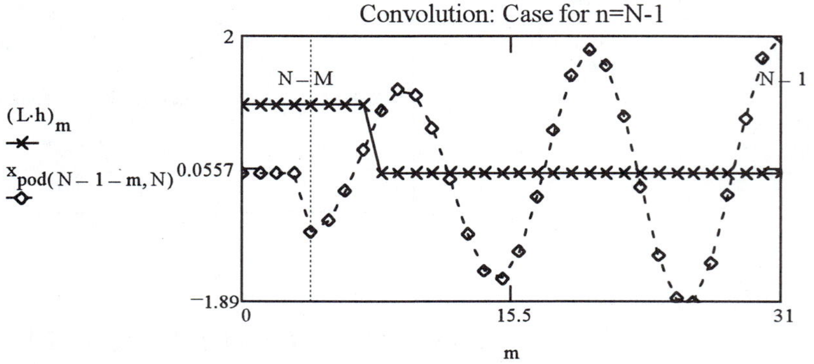

No periodic repetitions are falling in the basic summing interval [0,L-1] and so the value is correct. At this point, n=N-1, we have computed all N values of yp_n, which has period N. At n=N, we must again compute the value at n=0. Visualizing the period of x just off the plot to the left, increasing n from N-1 to N moves $x_{pod(n-m,N)}$ one step to the right, which recreates the plot shown above for n=0.

We have thus shown that the correct values are computed for

$$\max(0, M+L-N-1) \le n \le N-1 \qquad (5.1)$$

PROBLEM 5.1 Show that if M+L-2<N-1, then the values of the convolution for

$$M+L-2 \le n \le N-1$$

are a priori known to be zero. Modify the above example with an appropriate choice of L, M and N, and carefully repeat the graphical analysis. ‡

Thus, correct and not a priori known zero values are computed for

$$\max(0, M + L - N - 1) \leq n \leq \min(M + L - 2, N - 1) \qquad (5.2)$$

EXERCISE 5.4 Show that with the assumed ordering 0<L<=M<=N, the left member of the relations (5.2) is less than or equal to the right member. ¤

There are three cases of special interest to us. Note that the aperiodic convolution is of length M+L-1. These are established by simple substitution in (5.2). (Also, each case will be discussed later.)

1. M=L, N=M+D, 0<=D<=M-1. Then correct and not a priori known zero values are computed for

$$(M - D - 1 \leq n \leq M + D - 1) = N - 1 \qquad (5.3)$$

2. N=M. Then correct and not a priori known zero values are computed for

$$L - 1 \leq n \leq N - 1 \qquad (5.4)$$

3. N=M+L-1. Then correct and not a priori known zero values are computed for

$$0 \leq n \leq N - 1 \qquad (5.5)$$

PROBLEM 5.2 Verify the three inequalities in the above illustration. For each case, modify the above example with an appropriate choice of L, M and N, and carefully repeat the graphical analysis. ‡

Convolution Computation over a Restricted Range

It may happen that the aperiodic convolution is required only over a restricted range. In a signal design problem discussed below, the filter output is known to be of interest only over a small range of indices. Also, for estimating a covariance sequence (**Chapter 25**), its principal support is typically over a restricted range of indices. We assume that the two sequences to be convolved are of equal length: M=L. We take N=M + D where D is an integer in [0,M-1]. We have already seen (in case 1, eq. (5.3)) that the periodic convolution will be correct for n in [M-D-1,M+D-1]. It happens that this is the interval of most interest in filtering problems.

Example 5.2

We examine the **matched filtering (<u>Chapter 31</u>)** of a given sequence {x_n} where the filter impulse response is the signal reversed and zero padded to length N.

signal block:

$$MM := 120 \qquad mm := 0..MM-1 \qquad \kappa := 0.01$$

$$xx_{mm} := \cos\left[\kappa \cdot \left(\frac{MM}{2} - mm\right)^2\right]$$

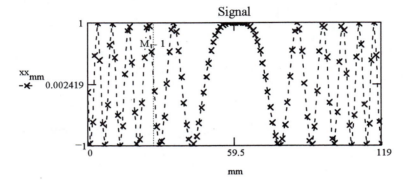

Signal

$$xx_{mm}$$
$$-\!\!\ast\!\!- \quad 0.002419$$

matched filter:

$$hh_{mm} := xx_{MM-mm-1}$$

parameter D:

$$DD := 8$$

zero padding to length N:

$$NN := MM + DD \qquad NN = 128 \qquad nn := 0..NN-1$$

$$xx_{nn} := if\left(nn < MM - 1, xx_{nn}, 0\right) \qquad XX := \sqrt{NN} \cdot icfft(xx)$$

$$hh_{nn} := if\left(nn < MM, hh_{nn}, 0\right) \qquad HH := \sqrt{NN} \cdot icfft(hh)$$

periodic convolution, direct form:

$$yyp_{nn} := \sum_{mm} hh_{mm} \cdot xx_{pod(nn-mm,NN)}$$

aperiodic convolution:

$$yya_{nn} := \sum_{mm} hh_{mm} \cdot \left[(nn-mm\geq 0)\cdot(nn-mm\leq NN-1)\cdot xx_{nn-mm}\right]$$

To speed up the calculation, we can use the alternate form

**periodic convolution,
DFT method:**

$$yydft := \frac{1}{\sqrt{NN}} \cdot cfft\left(\overrightarrow{(HH \cdot XX)}\right)$$

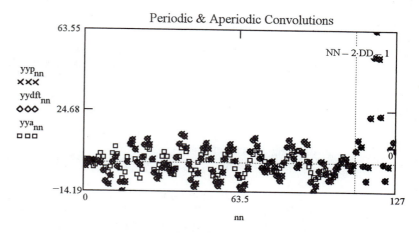

We expect the two computations to agree for 2DD+1 contiguous
indices including NN-1; we see that this is the case. ‡

EXERCISE 5.5 Vary DD and observe the results. ¤

A signal design problem is illustrated by Example 5.1. It can be
shown that, when white noise accompanies a signal, the maximum
SNR at the output of a filter is attained by the filter defined above.
The resolution (**Chapter 32**) of the output signal is especially
important. Two important parameters characterizing resolution are
(i) mainlobe width and (ii) the first sidelobe level. To examine these
parameters for any particular signal design one need only compute
the convolution over a restricted range, where it is correctly and
rapidly computed by the periodic convolution. We see from the
above plot that we have computed correctly all the values in the
mainlobe and beyond the first sidelobe.

The Overlap-Add Method

We now consider in detail the overlap-add method of filtering long
data sequences. We know that, for a filter length L and a data
block length of M, a DFT of length N=L+M-1 will compute a
periodic convolution in agreement with the aperiodic convolution -
which, of course, has length N=L+M-1. So, if we form
nonoverlapping, abutting M-length blocks from the input
sequence, we will have to somehow overlap and combine the
filterings of each block. We do this as follows.

Example 5.3

We write out the data sequence $\{x_n, n=0,...,NT\}$, formed into $J=NT/M$ blocks $\{\{x^j_n, n=0,...,M-1\}, j=0,...,J-1\}$. We illustrate this method with $(L,M,N) = (8,25,32)$.

$$NT := 75 \qquad nn := 0..\,NT - 1 \qquad N := 32 \qquad n := 0..\,N - 1$$

defining data:
$$x_{nn} := \cos\left(\frac{2\cdot\pi}{N}\cdot e\cdot nn\right) + \cos\left(\frac{2\cdot\pi}{N}\cdot\pi\cdot nn\right)$$

$$M := 25 \qquad J := \frac{NT}{M} \qquad J = 3 \qquad j := 0..\,J - 1$$

defining data blocks and zero padding:
$$xblk_{n,j} := if\left(n<M, x_{n+j\cdot M}, 0\right)$$

We can reconstruct the entire data record from the blocks with an explicit summation. The following elegant way, a modification of the method given in **Chapter 1**, is due to Richard Kuehnel.

reassembling:
$$w_{nn} := 0 \qquad w_{n+j\cdot M} := w_{n+j\cdot M} + xblk_{n,j} \qquad (5.6)$$

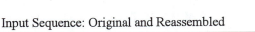

Input Sequence: Original and Reassembled

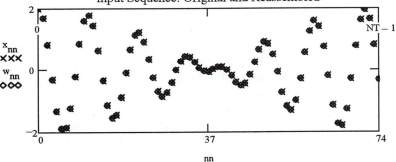

To understand (5.6), consider it first for $j=0$. It simply assigns the sequence $xblk_{n,0}$ to the first N positions of w, all the values of w_n having been initialized to zero. Next, when $j=1$, the right-hand side will, for $n=0,...,N-M-1$, add w_{n+M} to $xblk_{n,1}$ and assign the sum to w_{n+M}. For the remaining n, w_{n+M} is 0 and the values of $xblk_{n,1}$ are assigned to w_{n+M}. Thus the overlap is handled. Similarly for the remaining j. So, the reconstruction algorithm (5.6) builds up w_{nn} in this manner.

defining FIR filter and zero padding:
$$L := 8 \qquad h_n := if\left(n<L, \frac{1}{L}, 0\right)$$

Input Data Sequence

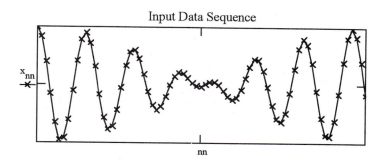

x_{nn}

nn

First Data Block

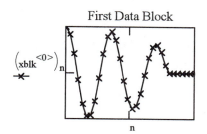

$\left(\text{xblk}^{<0>}\right)_n$

n

Second Data Block

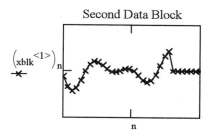

$\left(\text{xblk}^{<1>}\right)_n$

n

Third Data Block

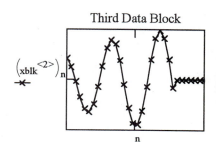

$\left(\text{xblk}^{<2>}\right)_n$

n

Now each separate data block is filtered using the DFT method.

$$\text{XBLK}^{<j>} := \text{dft}\left(\text{xblk}^{<j>}\right) \qquad\qquad H := \text{dft}(h)$$

$$\text{YBLK}^{<j>} := \left(\overline{\left(\overline{\text{XBLK}^{<j>}} \cdot \vec{H}\right)}\right)$$

$$\text{yblk}^{<j>} := \text{idft}\left(\text{YBLK}^{<j>}\right)$$

First Output Block

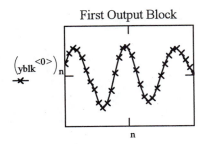

$$\left(\mathrm{yblk}^{<0>}\right)_n$$

n

Second Output Block

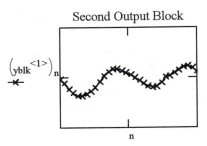

$$\left(\mathrm{yblk}^{<1>}\right)_n$$

n

Third Output Block

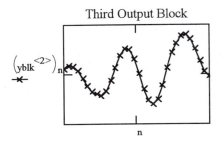

$$\left(\mathrm{yblk}^{<2>}\right)_n$$

n

We can reassemble the output blocks using the algorithm we have ready, (5.6).

$$y_{nn} := 0 \qquad\qquad y_{n+j\cdot M} := y_{n+j\cdot M} + \mathrm{yblk}_{n,j}$$

Filter Output by Overlap-Add Method

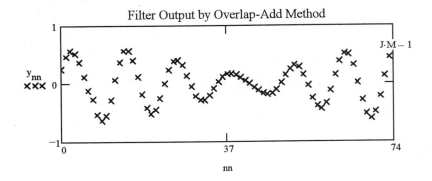

y_{nn}

nn

We check the result by computing the aperiodic convolution directly.

$$m := 0 .. L \qquad\qquad ya_{nn} := \sum_m h_m \cdot if\left(nn - m < 0, 0, x_{nn-m}\right)$$

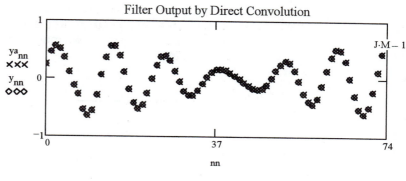

Filter Output by Direct Convolution

error: $\qquad\qquad \varepsilon_{nn} := y_{nn} - ya_{nn}$

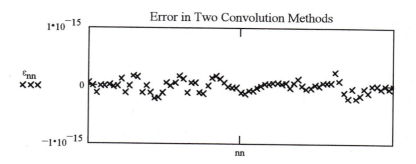

Error in Two Convolution Methods

Thus, within machine error, the computations agree and we have established an algorithm to perform the overlap-add method of fast convolution. ‡

EXERCISE 5.6 Choose at least one other signal and filter and carefully observe the computations. ¤

The Overlap-Save Method

For this method we choose a block size M>L and a DFT size N=M. So, as we observed above, the first L-1 values are incorrect and will be discarded. This means, referring to our beginning discussion in this chapter, that the first L-1 values of the data block were not used to produce correct results. Thus, the data blocks will have to be overlapped by L-1 indices. If we are worried about the initial values of the output, then we need to prefix the data with L-1 zeros. If we are processing a very long input, we may not care about a few initial values of the output.

Example 5.4 _____

$$M := 32 \qquad J := 3 \qquad j := 0..J-1 \qquad NT := J \cdot M$$

defining data: $\qquad NT = 96 \qquad nt := 0..NT-1$

$$x_{nt} := \cos\left(\frac{2 \cdot \pi}{N} \cdot \pi \cdot nt\right) + \cos\left(\frac{2 \cdot \pi}{N} \cdot e \cdot nt\right)$$

defining filter: $\qquad L := 8 \qquad N := M \qquad n := 0..N-1$

$$h_n := \text{if}\left(n<L, \frac{1}{L}, 0\right)$$

prefix zeros: $\qquad NP := NT + L - 1 \qquad nn := 0..NP-1$

$$xe_{nn} := \text{if}\left(nn<L-1, 0, x_{nn-L+1}\right)$$

defining data blocks: $\quad NML := N - L \qquad K := 0..NML-1$

$$xblk_{n,j} := xe_{n+j \cdot NML}$$

We reassemble the sequence from the blocks. Since the blocks were deliberately overlapped by L-1 samples, we take only the remaining part of the blocks and abut them. Note that the index K runs only over this partial block and that we discard the initial zero padding.

$$w_{nn} := 0 \qquad w_{K+j \cdot NML} := w_{K+j \cdot NML} + xblk_{K+L-1,j} \qquad (5.7)$$

Filter Input Data

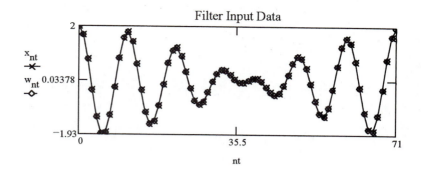

First Data Block

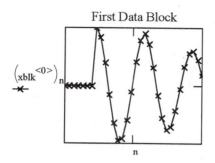

Second Data Block

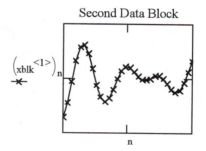

Third Data Block

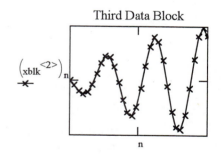

Now each separate data block is filtered using the DFT method.

$$XBLK^{<j>} := dft(xblk^{<j>})$$

$$YBLK^{<j>} := \left(\overline{\left(\overrightarrow{XBLK^{<j>} \cdot H}\right)}\right)$$

$$yblk^{<j>} := idft(YBLK^{<j>})$$

First Output Block

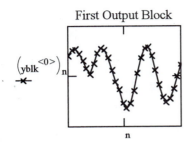

$\left(yblk^{<0>}\right)_n$

n

Second Output Block

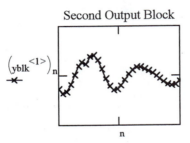

$\left(yblk^{<1>}\right)_n$

n

Third Output block

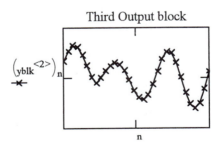

$\left(yblk^{<2>}\right)_n$

n

We now assemble the output, discarding the first L-1 incorrect values of each block. Our reconstruction algorithm (5.7) is already set to do this.

$$y_{nn} := 0 \qquad y_{K+j \cdot NML} := y_{K+j \cdot NML} + yblk_{K+L-1,j}$$

We also compute the aperiodic convolution for comparison and display the part of it we expect will agree with the periodic convolution.

$$1 := 0 .. L \qquad\qquad ya_{nt} := \sum_{l} h_l \cdot if\left(nt - l < 0, 0, x_{nt - l}\right)$$

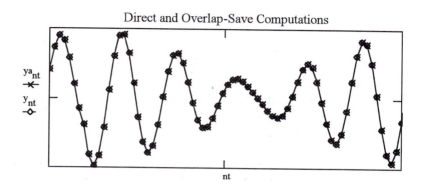

Direct and Overlap-Save Computations

Thus we have implemented the overlap-save method in Mathcad. ‡

■ **EXERCISE 5.7** Choose at least one other signal and filter and carefully observe the computations. ¤

The above discussion is illustrative of an important use of high-level mathematical software. A signal processing algorithm may be implemented, studied and understood relatively quickly. Then the algorithm may be translated into the much lower-level language that will be used in the actual application. This lower-level language is efficient computationally but quite a laborious and opaque algorithm development environment!

Project 5.1

Comparison of convolution computation methods. We have now discussed four methods of computing the discrete-time convolution - that is, the output of a digital filter. These are the direct method, the DFT/FFT method and the two fast convolution methods: overlap-add and overlap-save. Calling a complex multiply and a complex addition a **complex operation**, **CO**, compare the number of COs required for each method, without regard to memory requirements.

Suppose that we have available an FFT algorithm that requires $(N/2)\log_2 N$ COs to compute the DFT of an N-length sequence. Assume a data sequence of length N_g is to be filtered with an FIR filter of IR length L. We are especially interested in, and therefore assume, the case $N_g \gg L$. It is convenient to normalize the number of COs by $(N_g L)$, which therefore gives the number of COs required to compute each filter output value, normalized by the IR length. Then, e.g., the normalized COs for the direct method is 1. The other methods can have normalized COs less than or greater than 1. Note that the block size M is to be chosen in the fast convolution methods.

Your discussion should include a procedure for choosing the most efficient method and, as appropriate, the best block length. ‡

Project 5.2

Reconsider **Example 2.3** by implementing the overlap-save and overlap-add fast convolution methods. ‡

References

Jackson (1996), pp. 164 - 167
Oppenheim and Schafer (1989), Sec. 8.9
Proakis and Manolakis (1988), Sec. 5.3.2

6 Discrete-Time Fourier Transform

We have discussed filtering finite-length sequences with finite-length impulse response (FIR) filters. We have stressed the importance of the DFT method of computing the filtered output and compared the aperiodic and periodic convolutions. The filter was alternatively characterized by the N-periodic frequency response, which was the DFT, of length N, of the FIR.

DTFT as DFT Limit

In practice, the input sequence is commonly much longer than the FIR length. The latter may be of the order of a few tens whereas the former may be tens of thousands even for simple sound blocks. The frequency domain description of the filtering then involves, conceptually, an N-periodic frequency response computed with a DFT of much greater length (N) than the FIR length (M). In this case it is interesting to try letting N become indefinitely large. We shall see that the N-periodic frequency response has a well-defined limiting form, which is a natural description of the FIR filter for such applications.

Example 6.1

We will use the simple MA filter of length M to develop the idea.

DFT size and time index: $N := 64 \qquad n := 0 .. N - 1$

zero-padded FIR: $M := 8 \qquad h_n := (n<M) \cdot \dfrac{1}{M}$ (6.1)

We explicitly write out the N-periodic frequency response.

DFT index: $k := 0 .. N - 1$

DFT: $H_k := \displaystyle\sum_{m=0}^{M-1} \exp\left[-\left[i \cdot \left(\dfrac{2 \cdot \pi}{N}\right) \cdot k \cdot m\right]\right] \cdot h_m$ (6.2)

As N increases without bound, so too does the permitted range of k. However, the normalized variable

$$\omega_k := \frac{2 \cdot \pi}{N} \cdot k$$

always lies in $[0, 2\pi]$. So we plot the frequency response as a function of ω_k. ‡

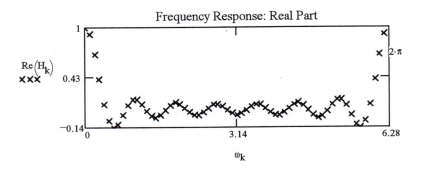

Frequency Response: Real Part

ω_k

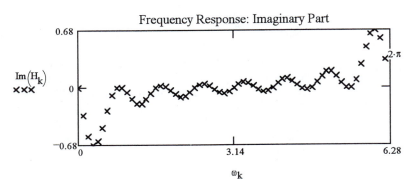

Frequency Response: Imaginary Part

ω_k

▨ **EXERCISE 6.1** Choose a sequence of increasing N in Example 6.1 and observe the apparent limit. (*Then reset N to 64.*) ¤

▨ **EXERCISE 6.2** Create an animation to solve Exercise 6.1 by modifying Example 6.1. Plot the magnitude of the FR, set

$$N = 2^{3 + FRAME}$$

and run FRAME from 0 to 7, say. (Remember to select **Automatic Mode** from the **Math** menu. Review the procedure to set up an animation in **Chapter 2**, if necessary.) ¤

As we increase N, it appears that the plots are an increasingly dense sampling of a continuous function defined over $[0,2\pi]$. This continuous function is obtained simply by replacing $\omega_k=(2\pi/N)k$ by the continuous variable ω in (6.2). It is

discrete-
time
Fourier
transform:
$$H1(\omega)= \sum_{m=0}^{M-1} e^{-i \cdot \omega \cdot m} \cdot h_m \qquad (6.3)$$

H1, defined by (6.3), is the **discrete-time Fourier transform, DTFT**, of the finite sequence $\{h_m, m=0,...,M-1\}$. In the DSP context, where the finite sequence is an (FIR) impulse response, $H1(\omega)$ is called the **frequency response (FR)**.

More generally, for any finite-length sequence $\{x_n\}$, we can define its DTFT as

discrete-
time
Fourier
transform:
$$X1(\omega)= \sum_{n=-\infty}^{\infty} e^{-i \cdot \omega \cdot n} \cdot xe_n \qquad (6.4)$$

where $\{xe\}$ is the aperiodic extension of $\{x\}$ (**Chapter 1**). The sum is over a finite number of terms, the limits set by $\{x\}$.

Properties

We note some basic attributes of the DTFT, which is well defined by the finite sum (6.3).

Property 6.1 $H1(\omega)$ depends on ω only as $\exp(i\omega)$ and may be written $H(\exp(i\omega))$.

We note that we can rewrite (6.3) as

$$H1(\omega)= \sum_{m=0}^{M-1} \left(e^{i \cdot \omega}\right)^{-m} \cdot h_m =H\left(e^{i \cdot \omega}\right) \qquad (6.5)$$

Property 6.2 The DTFT has period 2π and hence one may take ω in, e.g., $[-\pi,\pi]$.

We note that $\exp[i(\omega+2\pi)m]=\exp(i\omega m)[\exp(i2\pi)]^m$ and the second factor is 1.

EXERCISE 6.3 Plot (6.5) for ω in the range of several periods and note the evident 2π period. ¤

Property 6.3 The DTFT and all finite-order derivatives are continuous.

This property follows from that of $\{\exp(i\omega m), m=0,...,M-1\}$ and their finite, weighted sum.

PROBLEM 6.1

Show that the DTFT of $\{n^2 h_n\}$ is $-d^2 H1(\omega)/d\omega^2$. ‡

Property 6.4 H(z) is a rational function of z, with a pole of order (M-1) at z=0 and (M-1) zeros, which may be complex.

We note that

z transform:
$$H(z) = \sum_{m=0}^{M-1} h_m \cdot z^{-m} \tag{6.6}$$

which may be multiplied by z^{M-1}/z^{M-1} and written

$$H(z) = \frac{p(z)}{z^{M-1}} \qquad p(z) = \sum_{m=0}^{M-1} h_{M-1-m} \cdot z^{m} \tag{6.7}$$

H(z) is called the **z transform**, denoted **ZT**, and is defined by (6.4) with $\exp(i\omega n)$ replaced by z. In the DSP context, H(z) is called the **system function**. Since for FIR filters, the only pole is at the origin - see (6.7)- H(z) is an analytic function for all z not equal to 0. FIR filters are sometimes called, misleadingly, all-zero filters.

Given such a system function (ZT), the frequency response (DTFT) is easily obtained by setting z equal to $\exp(i\omega)$. Conversely, given a frequency response, we can obtain the system function by replacing $\exp(i\omega)$ by z; in this case, however, the dependence on $\exp(i\omega)$ of H1(ω) may not be explicit.

Property 6.5 The (M-1) zeros specify an FIR filter of length M. If complex, they occur in complex conjugate pairs for a real FIR.

For a real FIR filter, the polynomial p(z) has real coefficients, the IR weights themselves. If $\{z_\mu, \mu = 0,...,M-2\}$ are the roots of p(z) - it is of order (M-1) - then

$$\mu := 0..M-2 \qquad p(z) := \left[\prod_{\mu=0}^{M-2} (z - z_\mu) \right] \qquad (6.8)$$

In order for p(z) to have real coefficients, for any complex root z_μ its complex conjugate must also be a root.

Notice that, in view of Property 6.5, an FIR filter could be designed by placing zeros in the complex plane. We shall exploit this later **(Chapter 9)**.

▨ **EXERCISE 6.4** Compute the DTFT and the ZT of the simple MA filter defined by (6.1), using the known sum of a finite geometric series. ¤

Example 6.2 _____

The DTFT, or frequency response, of the simple MA filter (6.1) is

$$H1_{MA}(\omega, M) := e^{-i \cdot \left(\frac{M-1}{2} \cdot \omega\right)} \cdot if\left[\omega = 0, 1, \frac{\sin\left(\frac{M}{2} \cdot \omega\right)}{M \cdot \sin\left(\frac{1}{2} \cdot \omega\right)} \right] \qquad (6.9)$$

This may be obtained from the DFT of **Problem 3.2** by the substitution of ω for $(2\pi/N)k$. The ZT, or system function, is (Exercise 6.3)

$$H_{MA}(z) := \frac{z^M - 1}{M \cdot z^{M-1} \cdot (z - 1)}$$

The roots of the numerator polynomial of are the Mth roots of unity:

$$m := 0..M-1 \qquad z_m := e^{i \cdot \left(\frac{2\cdot\pi}{M} \cdot m\right)}$$

Since $z_0=1$, $z=1$ is in fact neither a pole nor a zero of $H_{MA}(z)$. Thus, the system function of the simple MA filter is

$$H_{MA}(z) := \frac{\left[\displaystyle\prod_{m=1}^{M-1} \left(z - z_m \right) \right]}{M \cdot z^{M-1}}$$

(6.10)

We can make a **pole-zero plot** of the singularities of the system function, which, with an amplitude scale or **gain**, completely defines the FIR filter.

$j := 1 .. M - 1$

Pole-Zero Plot of a Simple MA Filter

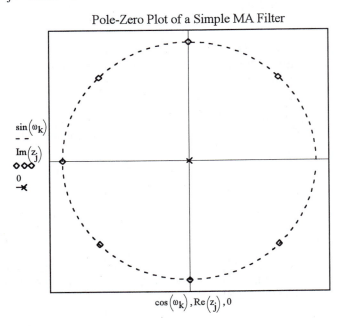

$\sin\left(\omega_k\right)$

$\mathrm{Im}\left(z_j\right)$

0

$\cos\left(\omega_k\right), \mathrm{Re}\left(z_j\right), 0$

The magnitude and phase of this filter are plotted next.

MA Filter FR Magnitude

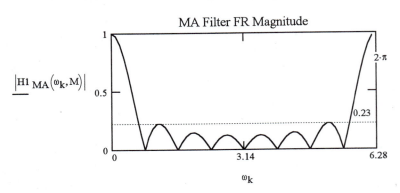

$\left| H1_{MA}\left(\omega_k, M\right) \right|$

ω_k

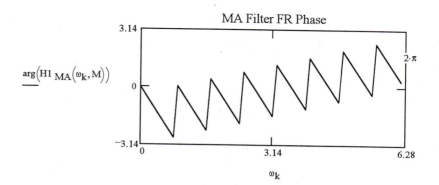

MA Filter FR Phase

$$\underline{\arg\left(H1_{MA}(\omega_k, M)\right)}$$

We notice the π jumps in phase at the frequencies where the factor of (6.9) involving the sines changes sign, which corresponds to frequencies where the magnitude is zero. ‡

PROBLEM 6.2 Advance two arguments against z = 0 being a zero of the system function, one directly from the observation that p(z) is of order M-1 and one directly from the definition of the system function. ‡

EXERCISE 6.5 Suppose a signal sequence is filtered by a simple MA filter of length M1=5, whose output is then filtered by a simple MA filter of length M2=7. The two filters are said to be in **cascade**. Show that the cascade combination is an FIR filter of length M1+M2-1=11 and find its (nonequal) weights. ¤

Example 6.3

Now we consider the cascade of two simple MA filters, one of length 5 and the other of length 7; the cascade is called a **5-by-7 filter**. We discussed this filter briefly in Exercise 6.5. Now we find its frequency response, which is the product of the individual frequency responses (**Chapter 7**).

$$H1_{5X7}(\omega) := H1_{MA}(\omega, 5) \cdot H1_{MA}(\omega, 7)$$

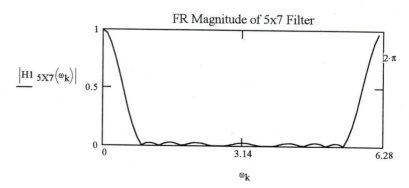

FR Magnitude of 5x7 Filter

$$\underline{\left|H1_{5X7}(\omega_k)\right|}$$

phase unwrapping algorithm:

$$\theta_0 := \arg\left(\text{H1}_{5X7}(\omega_0)\right)$$

$$\theta_k := \text{if}\left(k{=}0, \theta_0, \theta_{k-1} + \arg\left(\text{H1}_{5X7}(\omega_k) \cdot \overline{\text{H1}_{5X7}(\omega_{k-1})}\right)\right)$$

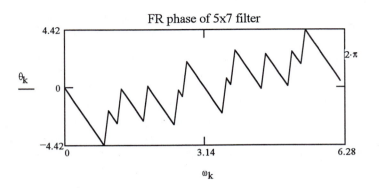

FR phase of 5x7 filter

We see that the phase of the frequency response contains 10 jumps of π at the locations of sign changes in the two real sin( )/sin( ) factors. Recall that, by definition, the magnitude of a complex number is real and nonnegative; thus the sign changes in these factors must be effected by π changes in the phase.

This filter's frequency response magnitude has a much lower gain outside its passband than the simple FIR filter. It is interesting to compare them, assuming equal lengths.

$$\omega\omega := 0, 0.025 .. 2\cdot\pi$$

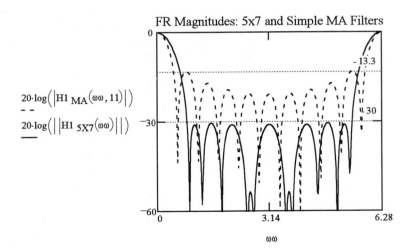

FR Magnitudes: 5x7 and Simple MA Filters

$20\cdot\log\left(\left|\text{H1}_{MA}(\omega\omega, 11)\right|\right)$

$20\cdot\log\left(\left|\left|\text{H1}_{5X7}(\omega\omega)\right|\right|\right)$

We see that the decreased gain outside the passband does result in a broader passband. This is a trade-off we shall see repeatedly. It is of interest to examine the IR of the 5-by-7 filter, which is the convolution of the FIRs of the MAs of length 5 and 7 (Exercise 6.5).

$$h57_n := \sum_{m=0}^{4} \frac{1}{5}\cdot\frac{1}{7}\cdot(n-m\geq0)\cdot(n-m<7)$$

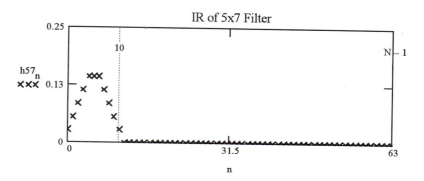

Compared to the simple MA filter, the 5-by-7 filter's IR has a **taper.** This is the feature that results in the lower gain outside the passband as well as the broader passband. We shall see such tapers in well-designed FIRs. ‡

DTFT/ZT Computation

Numerical Computation

By the very manner in which we introduced the DTFT for finite length sequences, it is clear that the DTFT may be approximated by its samples, spaced as densely as desired, in the following way. The finite-length sequence is zero padded to a length N as large as desired and its DFT computed. The DFT is $\{H_k = H1(\omega_k), \omega_k = (2\pi/N)k, k = 0,...,N-1\}$.

Example 6.4 _____

Now we consider the cascade of two simple MA filters, one of length 5 and the other of length 7; the cascade is called a 5-by-7 filter. We discussed this filter in Exercise 6.4 and Example 6.3, and we have the exact DTFT/FR $H1_{5X7}$ available. Now we find the N-length DFT of its zero-padded FIR {h57}, which is also available.

$$\mathrm{dft}(v) := \sqrt{N} \cdot \mathrm{icfft}(v) \qquad\qquad \mathrm{HDFT} := \mathrm{dft}(h57)$$

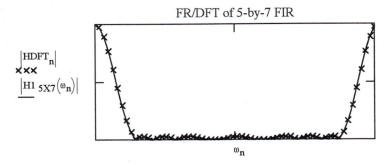

FR/DFT of 5-by-7 FIR

$$\begin{array}{l} |\mathrm{HDFT}_n| \\ \times\times\times \\ |\mathrm{H1}\ _{5X7}(\omega_n)| \\ \underline{} \end{array}$$

ω_n

As we expect, the agreement is exact at the sample points. ‡

Symbolic Computation

Nonnumerical computations of the DTFT are useful in analysis and modeling. We can always make an informative numerical computation and plot for any sequence. But a nonnumerical form may exist in tractable form. We can compute it using the symbolic engine. Also, we can find a DTFT by looking it up in tabulations. One may more likely find tables of the ZT. Of course, replacing z by exp(iω) gives the DTFT. Mathcad can symbolically compute the ZT and we give an example.

Example 6.5 _____

We consider again the simple MA filter. We have the exact ZT, $H_{MA}(z)$, available in (6.10) for arbitrary M. We wish to verify this result using the symbolic engine of Mathcad. Part of the art of using a symbolic engine is to enter a form the engine can use. After a little experimentation, we arrive at the following functional form for the FIR of a simple MA filter of length 3.

$$\frac{1}{3} \cdot (\Phi(n) - \Phi(n-3))$$

We enclose an instance of the variable n and select **Transforms** then **Z Transform** from the **Symbolic** menu. We get the following result.

$$\frac{1}{3} \cdot \frac{\left(z^2 + z + 1\right)}{z^2}$$

Is this correct? That is, does it agree with (6.10)? We can use the symbolic engine to help. We enter the latter form with M=3.

$$\frac{z^3 - 1}{3 \cdot z^2 \cdot (z - 1)}$$

Now we enclose the entire form and select **Simplify** from the **Symbolic** menu. We get the following form.

$$\frac{1}{3} \cdot \frac{\left(z^2 + z + 1\right)}{z^2}$$

Thus our analytic computation (6.10) agrees with the symbolic engine's computation in the case of M=3. ‡

EXERCISE 6.6 Repeat the above symbolic computations for another value of M. Try the symbolic engine on the general MA FIR

$$\frac{1}{M} \cdot (\Phi(n) - \Phi(n - M))$$

What is the result? Is it useful? ¤

Remark It is important to note that if we have available the frequency response H1(ω) - defined as the DTFT of the FIR, of length M - we can obtain any N-periodic frequency response - defined as the DFT - simply by sampling the frequency response at the points $\{\omega_k=(2\pi/N)k, k=0,...,N-1\}$, N>=M. Conversely, if we have available the N-periodic frequency response of an FIR filter (of length M<=N), the DTFT is the continuous function of a variable ω replacing $(2\pi/N)k$ in the DFT.

FIR Design Specification

Since it is usually true in practice that the FIR filter length M is short relative to the data length N and that the latter may vary in specific applications of the filter, it is common practice to specify the FIR filter by a frequency response defined as the DTFT. The usual design procedures approximate a desired DTFT/FR. We shall discuss such design at great length later in the book.

Inverse DTFT

Now consider the IDFT as N becomes arbitrarily large. Recall that (**Chapter 3**) the DFT is

$$H_k = \sum_{m=0}^{N-1} \exp\left[-\left[i \cdot \left(\frac{2 \cdot \pi}{N}\right) \cdot k \cdot m\right]\right] \cdot h_m$$

We write out the IDFT (**Chapter 3**) explicitly:

$$h_n = \frac{1}{N} \cdot \sum_{k=0}^{N-1} \exp\left[i \cdot \left(\frac{2 \cdot \pi}{N}\right) \cdot k \cdot n\right] \cdot H_k \tag{6.11}$$

Suppose that in the right side of (6.11) we take H_k to be the samples of the DTFT, $H1(\omega_k)$, where $\omega_k = (2\pi/N)k$, k=0,...,N-1. Then we get the form

$$g_n = \frac{1}{2 \cdot \pi} \cdot \sum_{k=0}^{N-1} \exp\left(i \cdot \omega_k \cdot n\right) \cdot H1\left(\omega_k\right) \cdot \left(\frac{2 \cdot \pi}{N}\right)$$

We recognize the Riemann sum approximating the Riemann integral

$$g_n := \frac{1}{2 \cdot \pi} \cdot \int_0^{2 \cdot \pi} e^{i \cdot \omega \cdot n} \cdot H1(\omega) \, d\omega \tag{6.12}$$

We have made (6.12) inactive because its numerical evaluation by Mathcad, using the Romberg numerical algorithm, takes a very long time. We will soon find a much quicker way.

EXERCISE 6.7 Toggle (6.12) active and note the computation time. (*Then toggle it inactive!*) How useful is such a numerical algorithm likely to be in a DSP system implementation? ¤

Because of the smoothness of $H1(\omega)$, Property 6.3, this limit is well defined as an integral. It may be easier to convince yourself of (6.12) as the limiting form of (6.11) if you approximate the integral (6.12) using the "rectangle rule" and get (6.11). The sequence $\{g_n\}$, defined by (6.12), is the **inverse discrete-time Fourier transform (IDTFT)**.

Of course, we would like to have $\{g_n = h_n\}$ uniquely. That is, we want the DTFT followed by the IDTFT to be the identity operation. To show this, we will use (6.4) to substitute for $H1(\omega)$ in (6.12) and interchange the order of the (finite) sum and integral. The argument proceeds just as in the case of the DFT (**Chapter 3**).

$$g_n = \frac{1}{2 \cdot \pi} \cdot \int_0^{2 \cdot \pi} e^{i \cdot \omega \cdot n} \cdot \left[\sum_m \exp(-(i \cdot (\omega \cdot m))) \cdot h_m \right] d\omega$$

Interchanging the order of the integration and finite sum, we get

$$g_n = \sum_m h_m \cdot I_{m,n} \qquad\qquad I_{m,n} = \frac{1}{2 \cdot \pi} \cdot \int_0^{2 \cdot \pi} e^{i \cdot \omega \cdot (n-m)} d\omega$$

The integral $I_{m,n}$ is easily evaluted. It is clearly 1 when m=n; otherwise it is

$$I_{m,n} = \frac{\sin(\pi \cdot (n-m))}{\pi \cdot (n-m)} \qquad\qquad (n \neq m)$$

which is clearly zero. Thus

$$I_{m,n} = \delta(m,n)$$

We now have

$$g_n = \sum_m h_m \cdot \delta(m,n)$$

Evaluating the sum gives $g_n = h_n$, as was to be proved.

We have now established the inverse discrete-time Fourier transform.

inverse discrete-time Fourier transform: $\qquad h_n = \frac{1}{2 \cdot \pi} \cdot \int_0^{2 \cdot \pi} e^{i \cdot n \cdot \omega} \cdot H1(\omega) \, d\omega$

It may be amusing to plot $I_{m,n}$.

$$nn := 0..24 \qquad mm := 0..24 \qquad I_{nn,mm} := \frac{1}{2 \cdot \pi} \cdot \int_0^{2 \cdot \pi} e^{i \cdot \omega \cdot (nn - mm)} \, d\omega$$

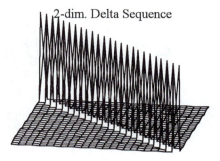

2-dim. Delta Sequence

I

Property 6.6 The DTFT has period 2π and therefore (6.12) can be written

$$h_n = \frac{1}{2 \cdot \pi} \cdot \int_{-\pi}^{\pi} e^{i \cdot \omega \cdot n} \cdot H1(\omega) \, d\omega \qquad\qquad (6.13)$$

Because $H1(\omega)$ and $\exp(i\omega n)$ both have a period of 2π in ω, we may take the limits on the integral as $[-\pi,\pi]$, which we will see is sometimes convenient.

IDTFT Computation

The evaluation of the IDTFT (6.12) or (6.13) can be done by several methods. The most generally useful is the numerical approximation of the IDTFT with the IDFT, implemented by the IFFT. In fact, as we will see, the approximation for finite-length sequences is exact, within numerical error.

Numerical Computation

In the actual implementation of a DSP system, the IDTFT would very likely be computed numerically by approximating it with the IDFT, implemented with the IFFT. This is also probably the quickest way to compute the IDTFT even for modeling and analysis. If the DTFT is that of a finite sequence, then the IDTFT can be computed exactly, within numerical error, by the IDFT. We demonstrate this with an example.

Example 6.6

If we are given a system function, we can get the frequency response. We can then approximate the integral of the IDTFT by the rectangle rule, thereby getting the IDFT, which can be implemented by a fast algorithm, the IFFT. This is a practical method. Suppose we are given the system function

$$a := 0.9 \qquad M := 16 \qquad H_{\exp}(z) := \frac{1 - \left(a \cdot z^{-1}\right)^M}{1 - a \cdot z^{-1}}$$

We set

$$z(\omega) := \exp(i \cdot \omega) \qquad H1_{\exp}(\omega) := H_{\exp}(z(\omega))$$

Now we define the sample points

$$K := 32 \qquad k := 0 .. K - 1 \qquad \omega_k := \frac{2 \cdot \pi}{K} \cdot k$$

and the frequency samples

$$Ha_k := H1_{\exp}\left(\omega_k\right) \qquad idft(v) := \frac{1}{\sqrt{K}} \cdot cfft(v)$$

We invert with the IDFT and plot it. We also compare it with the known, truncated exponential IR, h.

$$ha := idft(Ha) \qquad h_k := if\left(k < M, a^k, 0\right)$$

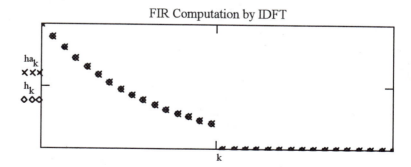

FIR Computation by IDFT

Thus we are able to *precisely* compute the FIR using the IDFT. ‡

PROBLEM 6.3

Vary K in Example 6.6 and explain the results. Plot the frequency response, in particular its phase. What distinguishes it from the previous examples, especially the MA filter's frequency response phase? ‡

The observation of Example 6.6, that the IDTFT can be exactly computed by the IDFT, can be argued more generally as follows. Suppose we are given a sequence - say an FIR of length M, which we can zero pad to a length N>=M. Then we have noted that the DFT - the N-periodic frequency response - is exactly obtained by sampling the DTFT at the frequencies $\{\omega_k=(2\pi/N)k,\ k=0,...,N-1\}$. Then the IDFT gives the M length sequence - the FIR - zero padded to length N, for any N>=M. We state this more concisely in the following property.

Property 6.7 Let H1(ω) be the DTFT of the finite, M-length sequence {h}. Then the IDTFT of H1(ω) is the IDFT of the sequence $\{H_k=H1(\omega_k),\ \omega_k=(2\pi/M)k,\ k=0,...,M-1\}$.

EXERCISE 6.8 Compute the IR of the 5-by-7 FIR of Example 6.3 using the numerical computation of Property 6.7. The required declarations are of this form.

$$H57_k = H1_{5X7}(\omega_k) \qquad h57a = idft(H57)$$

Plot the FIR {h57a} and compare to that found in Example 6.3, {h57}. ¤

The inverse DTFT, as an integral over a finite region, could be evaluated, for each value of n of interest, using standard numerical integration algorithms present in mathematical software such as Mathcad. However, we have already noted that computing the IDTFT by this method takes a long time. Again, the IDFT is much more likely to be implemented in any practical DSP system.

Power Series and Symbolic Computation

For relatively short FIR filters, the simplest method is this. If we are given the system function H(z), we just express it as a power series in z^{-1} and read out the the FIR using the definition (6.6). The symbolic mathematics capability of Mathcad can be useful to get the power series. We give a simple example.

Example 6.7 _____
Suppose we are given the system function of Example 6.1 with M=4.

$$\frac{z^4 - 1}{4 \cdot z^3 \cdot (z - 1)}$$

We enclose an instance of z in the form and choose **Expand to Series...** from the **Symbolic** menu. We get

$$\frac{1}{4} \cdot z^{(-3)} + \frac{1}{4} \cdot z^{(-2)} + \frac{1}{4} \cdot z^{(-1)} + \frac{1}{4}$$

We read out the IR as (1/4,1/4,1/4,1/4), which we know to be correct. ‡

EXERCISE 6.9 Enclose an instance of z in this last form and choose **Polynomial Coefficients** from the **Symbolic** menu. Note that the order will be in increasing powers of z. You can now define a vector h with this form for further use. ¤

One can also use the symbolic mathematics capabilty of Mathcad to compute ZTs and their inverses. (The inverse z transform, IZT, is given a formal definition below.)

Example 6.8 _____

Suppose we are given the system function

$$\frac{z^4 - 1}{4 \cdot z^3 \cdot (z - 1)}$$

After selecting an instance of z, we choose **Transforms** then **Inverse Z Transform** from the **Symbolic** menu, obtaining

$$\frac{1}{4} \cdot \Delta(n - 3) + \frac{1}{4} \cdot \Delta(n - 2) + \frac{1}{4} \cdot \Delta(n - 1) + \frac{1}{4} \cdot \Delta(n)$$

Observing that the symbolic engine denotes the unit impulse sequence with Δ, rather than with δ, we read out the IR (1/4,1/4,1/4,1/4). (This may require a moment's thought: We haven't used such a cumbrous notation to represent an FIR!) ‡

Contour Integration in the Complex Plane

Finally, the IDTFT (6.13) can be evaluated using integration in the complex z-plane. As the integrand is a function of ω only as $\exp(i\omega)$, we substitute $z = \exp(i\omega)$. Note that $dz = i\omega \ \exp(i\omega) \ d\omega$ so that $d\omega = (iz)^{-1}dz$. As ω varies through 2π radians, z travels once around the unit circle C in the complex plane. Thus (6.13) becomes the **contour integral**

$$h_n = \frac{1}{2 \cdot \pi \cdot i} \cdot \oint_C z^{n-1} \cdot H(z) \, dz \qquad (6.14)$$

This alternate form (6.14) gives us a formal definition of the **inverse z transform (IZT)**. A useful analytic technique for rational $H(z)$ is to evaluate (6.14) by the method of residues. We do not pursue this evaluation method here.

Project 6.1

Approximate, with the DFT, the DTFT of each of the simple FIRs of **Project 2.2**. Check by plotting the DTFT computed by hand or symbolically. ‡

References

Jackson (1996), Sec. 6.2
Oppenheim and Schafer (1989), Sec. 2.6 - 2.9
Oppenheim and Willsky (1997), Chap. 5
Proakis and Manolakis (1996), Sec. 4.2

7 Discrete-Time Fourier Transform Properties

We saw in **Chapter 6** that the DTFT is the appropriate frequency response characterization of FIR filters in applications involving indefinitely long input sequences. It is the commonly used frequency response and the object of most design methods. More generally, the DTFT was defined for the aperiodic extension of any finite-length sequence. As indefinitely long sequences are not practically observable, the effect of truncation on the DTFT is one important property we will study. An important property, conceptually, has to do with the IDTFT of a product of two DTFTs: We shall see that it is the aperiodic convolution of the two IDTFTs.

Many of the DTFT properties are analogous to the properties of the DFT. They are modified in form as the IDFT is an integral instead of a finite sum. Their proofs are quite similar to the proofs of the DFT properties. The delta sequence nature of $I_{m,n}$ of (**6.10**) is used in place of the $S_{k,k1}$ of (**3.7**), for example.

We recall the definitions of the DTFT and IDTFT.

DTFT:
$$X1(\omega) = \sum_{n=-\infty}^{\infty} e^{-i\cdot\omega\cdot n}\cdot x_n \qquad (7.1)$$

IDTFT:
$$x_n = \frac{1}{2\cdot\pi}\cdot\int_{0}^{2\cdot\pi} e^{i\cdot n\cdot\omega}\cdot X1(\omega)\, d\omega \qquad (7.2)$$

Example 7.1

We will use the illustration of an FIR of length M; its DTFT is easily computed using the sum of a finite geometric sequence and was given in **Exercise 6.3**.

FIR length: $\qquad M := 16 \qquad m := 0..M - 1$

FIR: $\qquad a := 0.9 \qquad h_m := a^m$

DTFT:

$$H1(\omega) := \frac{1 - \left(a \cdot e^{-i \cdot \omega}\right)^M}{1 - a \cdot e^{-i \cdot \omega}}$$

‡

Properties

Property 7.1 The DTFT has period 2π.

We have already noted this periodicity, a consequence of the periodicity of exp(iω). We illustrate it with **Example 7.1**.

$$\omega := -2\cdot\pi, -2\cdot\pi + 0.05 .. 4\cdot\pi$$

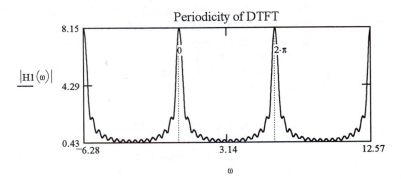

Property 7.2 The DTFT of a real sequence is Hermitian symmetric, H1(-ω)=conj(H1(ω)), which may be expressed as H1(2π-ω)=conj(H1(ω)).

The proof is simple.

$$H1(-\omega) = \sum_{n=-\infty}^{\infty} e^{-i \cdot (-\omega) \cdot n} \cdot h_n = \overline{\left[\sum_{n=-\infty}^{\infty} e^{-i \cdot \omega \cdot n} \cdot h_n \right]} = \overline{H1(\omega)}$$

Now use the 2π periodicity of the DTFT to note that H1(-ω)=H1(2π-ω).

Example 7.2 _____

We illustrate this property with **Example 7.1**.

$$\omega := 0, 0.05 .. 2 \cdot \pi$$

Hermitian Symmetry of DTFT

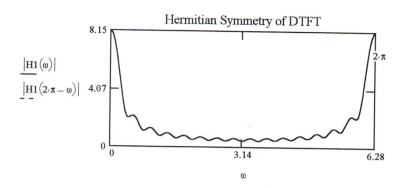

$|H1(\omega)|$

$\overline{|H1(2 \cdot \pi - \omega)|}$

Hermitian Symmetry of DTFT

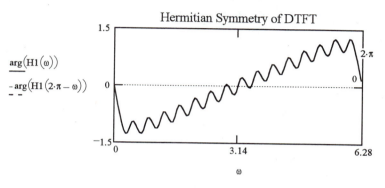

$\arg(H1(\omega))$

$- \overline{\arg(H1(2 \cdot \pi - \omega))}$

Clearly the plots are the same. ‡

PROBLEM 7.1

Let HR(ω) and HI(ω) be, respectively, the real and imaginary parts of H1(ω). Then they are, respectively, even and odd functions expressible as HR(2π-ω)=HR(ω) and HI(2π-ω)=-HI(ω). ‡

Recall that the aperiodic translate of a finite-length sequence {h} is defined as the translate of its aperiodic extension {he} (**Chapter 1**). The next property follows easily from the DTFT definition with a simple change of summing index.

Property 7.3: Aperiodic time translation Given a sequence {h$_n$, n=0,1,...} with DTFT H1(ω), the DTFT of the translated sequence {he$_{n-nd}$, n=0,1,...}, nd>=0 an integer, is exp(-iωnd) H1(ω).

Example 7.3 _____

Continuing with Example 7.1, we can illustrate Property 7.3 for a delay nd by choosing N larger than M+nd and sampling the DTFT by computing the DFT of length N. As we know, we can sample the DTFT as densely as we like by choosing a sufficiently large N.

delay: $\qquad$ $nd := 16$

DFT length: $\qquad$ $N := 128 \qquad n := 0 .. N - 1$

aperiodic
extension $\qquad$ $he_n := (n<M) \cdot h_n \qquad\qquad dft(v) := \sqrt{N} \cdot icfft(v)$
and its DFT:

$\qquad\qquad\qquad\qquad\qquad\qquad\qquad\qquad\qquad He := dft(he)$

aperiodically
delayed sequence $\qquad hed_n := if(n<nd, 0, he_{n-nd}) \qquad Hed := dft(hed)$
and its DFT:

We compare the directly computed DTFT Hed with its asserted
form (call it Ht), sampled at the appropriate frequencies and using
the known DTFT H1.

$$\omega_n := \frac{2 \cdot \pi}{N} \cdot n \qquad\qquad Ht_n := \exp(-i \cdot \omega_n \cdot nd) \cdot H1(\omega_n)$$

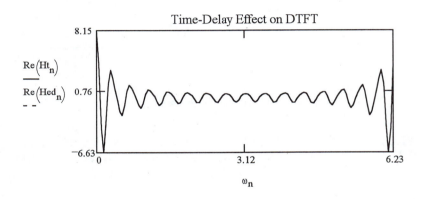

Time-Delay Effect on DTFT

$\mathrm{Re}(Ht_n)$ ———

$\mathrm{Re}(Hed_n)$ $- -$

(y-axis: 8.15, 0.76, −6.63; x-axis: 0, 3.12, 6.23)

ω_n

Clearly the plots are the same. ‡

▓ **EXERCISE 7.1** Plot the imaginary parts in the above plot. ¤

Because any IDTFT H1(ω) has period 2π, H1(ω-ω_d) for any
frequency translation ω_d is welldefined and clearly ω_d enters only as
pod(ω_d,2π). The next property follows easily from the IDTFT
definition with a change of summing index.

Property 7.4: Periodic frequency translation Given a DTFT
H1(ω) with IDTFT {h_n}, the IDTFT of the translated DTFT H1(ω-ω_d) is
{exp(iω_dn) h_n}.

Example 7.4

We illustrate this property by using the IDFT after sampling the known DTFT H1(ω) of Example 7.1. We have, in Example 7.3, already computed its IDTFT {he}.

frequency translation:

$$\omega d := \frac{\pi}{6}$$

sampled known DTFT:

$$H1s_n := H1\left(\omega_n\right)$$

sampled, translated known DTFT:

$$G_n := H1\left(\omega_n - \omega d\right)$$

IDTFT of G:

$$idft(v) := \frac{1}{\sqrt{N}} \cdot cfft(v) \qquad g := idft(G)$$

asserted form:

$$ht_n := \exp(i \cdot \omega d \cdot n) \cdot he_n$$

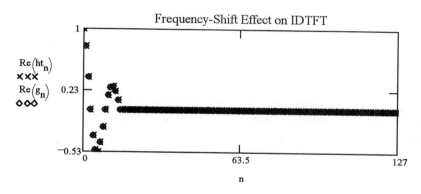

Frequency-Shift Effect on IDTFT

Clearly the plots are the same. ‡

▓ **EXERCISE 7.2** Plot the imaginary parts in the above plot. ¤

The following properties are appropriate restatements of analogous properties of the DFT.

Property 7.5: Plancherel's Identity Given a sequence {x_n} with DTFT X1(ω),

$$\sum_m \left(\left|h_m\right|\right)^2 = \frac{1}{2 \cdot \pi} \cdot \int_0^{2 \cdot \pi} \left(\left|H1(\omega)\right|\right)^2 d\omega$$

Example 7.5

We illustrate this property with our running Example 7.1.

$$c1 := \sum_m \left(|h_m| \right)^2 \qquad\qquad c1 = 5.082$$

$$c2 := \frac{1}{2\cdot\pi} \cdot \int_0^{2\cdot\pi} \left(|H1(\omega)| \right)^2 d\omega \qquad\qquad c2 = 5.082 \qquad ‡$$

Property 7.6: Parseval's Identity Given sequences $\{f_n, n=0,1,...\}$ with DTFT $F1(\omega)$ and $\{g_n, n=0,1,...\}$ with DTFT $G1(\omega)$,

$$\sum_n f_n \cdot \overline{g_n} = \frac{1}{2\cdot\pi} \cdot \int_0^{2\cdot\pi} F1(\omega)\cdot \overline{G1(\omega)} \, d\omega$$

Example 7.6

To illustrate this property, we may take $\{f_n = h_n\}$ and define a new sequence.

finite-length sequence, aperiodically extended:
$$M2 := 24 \qquad b := 0.9$$
$$ge_n := if\left(n < M2, b^n, 0\right)$$

known DTFT:
$$G1(\omega) := \frac{1 - \left(b\cdot e^{-i\cdot\omega}\right)^{M2}}{1 - b\cdot e^{-i\cdot\omega}}$$

Then we compute:

$$c1 := \sum_n he_n \cdot \overline{ge_n} \qquad\qquad c1 = 5.082$$

$$c2 := \frac{1}{2\cdot\pi} \cdot \int_0^{2\cdot\pi} H1(\omega)\cdot \overline{G1(\omega)} \, d\omega \qquad\qquad c2 = 5.082 \qquad ‡$$

EXERCISE 7.3 Choose other sequences for f and g and verify Properties 7.5 and 7.6. ¤

PROBLEM 7.2   Prove that Property 7.5 is a corollary of Property 7.6. ‡

PROBLEM 7.3   Prove Property 7.6, similar to **Property 4.6**, using the delta sequence (**6.10**)in place of (**3.7**). ‡

Just as Plancherel's and Parseval's properties for the DFT had a geometric interpretation, so do they for the DTFT. However, the mathematics are more complicated, as we are now dealing with sequences of indefinite length and with functions. We will not belabor this. Suffice it to say that the Plancherel's property equates two norms, one for sequences and one for functions. And Parseval's property equates two inner products, one for sequences and one for functions.

DTFT and Aperiodic Convolution

Suppose that we change the dummy summing index to m on the left side of Parseval's Identity and take $f_m=h_m$ and $g_m=x_{n-m}$, both real sequences. Then $F1(\omega)=H1(\omega)$ and, by Property 7.3, $G1(\omega)=\exp(-i\omega n)\text{conj}[X1(\omega)]$. So Parseval's Identity now reads

$$\sum_m h_m \cdot x_{n-m} = \frac{1}{2\cdot\pi} \cdot \int_0^{2\cdot\pi} e^{i\,\cdot\omega\cdot n} \cdot (H1(\omega)\cdot X1(\omega))\, d\omega$$

We recognize the left side as the aperiodic convolution of {h} and {x} and the right side as the IDTFT of the product of the DTFTs of {h} and {x}. Thus we have established the following property.

Property 7.7: Frequency domain multiplication The IDTFT of the product of two DTFTs is the aperiodic convolution of the two IDTFTs.

Example 7.7 _____

To illustrate this property, we may take the FIR {h_n} of Example 7.1 and {x_n} to be the sequence {g_n} of Example 7.6.

FIR, aperiodically extended: $M := 16$ $a := 0.9$

$he_n := (n<M)\cdot a^n$ $N = 128$

known DTFT: $H1(\omega) := \dfrac{1 - \left(a\cdot e^{-i\,\cdot\omega}\right)^M}{1 - a\cdot e^{-i\,\cdot\omega}}$

finite-length sequence, aperiodically extended:	$M2 := 24 \qquad b := 0.9$	

$$xe_n := if\left(n < M2, b^n, 0\right)$$

known DTFT:

$$X1(\omega) := \frac{1 - \left(b \cdot e^{-i \cdot \omega}\right)^{M2}}{1 - b \cdot e^{-i \cdot \omega}}$$

We calculate the aperiodic convolution.

aperiodic convolution:

$$y\,LS_n := \sum_{m=0}^{M-1} he_m \cdot (n - m \geq 0) \cdot xe_{n-m}$$

We now calculate the IDTFT form asserted by Property 7.7 to also be the aperiodic convolution. We could use Mathcad's built-in integration algorithm but this is very time consuming. So we use samples at the frequencies $\{\omega_n = n(2\pi/N),\ n=0,...,N-1\}$ as already defined in Example 7.3.

asserted aperiodic convolution, IDTFT approximated by IDFT:

$$H1s_n := H1\left(\omega_n\right) \qquad X1s_n := X1\left(\omega_n\right)$$

$$y\,RS := idft\left(\overrightarrow{(H1s \cdot X1s)}\right)$$

We plot these two sequences.

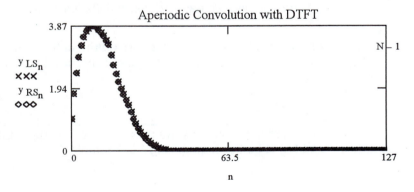

The plots are clearly the same. Thus we have exemplified Property 7.7. ‡

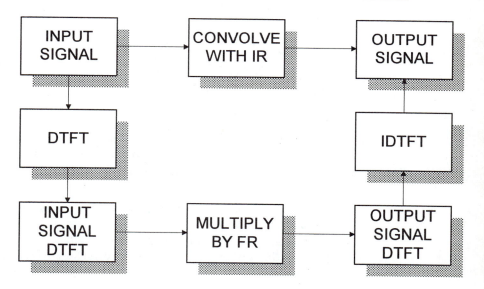

■ **EXERCISE 7.4** Choose other sequences for {h} and {x} and verify Property 7.7. ¤

■ **EXERCISE 7.5** Compute the IDTFT using Mathcad's built-in integration algorithm in place of the IDFT approximation. You may want to decrease N to a little larger than M+M2-1, depending on your computer, to reduce the computation time. ¤

Property 7.7 gives us an important *theoretical*, alternative method of computing the aperiodic convolution. It is summarized in the following sketch. We may term it the **frequency domain, or DTFT, method of filtering**. In this case we are referring to the aperiodic convolution definition of filtering. You may want to contrast this with the DFT method of filtering already discussed (**Chapter 4**).

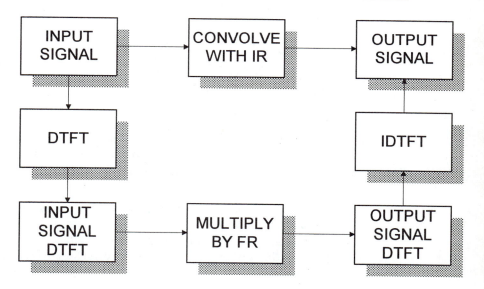

INPUT SIGNAL	CONVOLVE WITH IR	OUTPUT SIGNAL
DTFT		IDTFT
INPUT SIGNAL DTFT	MULTIPLY BY FR	OUTPUT SIGNAL DTFT

Truncation and Spectral Estimation

The next property has interesting theoretical and practical consequences. Whereas Property 7.7 was for multiplication in the frequency domain, Property 7.8 is for multiplication in the time domain.

Property 7.8: Time domain multiplication The DTFT Z1(ω) of a product of sequences, $\{z_n = w_n \, x_n\}$, is the periodic convolution of the DTFTs of $\{w_n\}$ and $\{x_n\}$, that is, W1(ω) and X1(ω), respectively.

$$Z1(\omega) = \frac{1}{2\cdot\pi} \cdot \int_0^{2\cdot\pi} W1(\omega - u) \cdot X1(u) \, du$$

To prove this property, we compute the DTFT Z1(ω) of the product $\{z_n = w_n \, x_n\}$ using the IDTFT representation of $\{x_n\}$.

$$Z1(\omega) = \sum_n e^{-i \cdot \omega n} \cdot w_n \cdot \frac{1}{2\cdot\pi} \cdot \int_0^{2\cdot\pi} e^{i \cdot u \cdot n} \cdot X1(u) \, du$$

Now we interchange the order of integration and sum to obtain

$$Z1(\omega) = \frac{1}{2\cdot\pi} \cdot \int_0^{2\cdot\pi} X1(u) \cdot \sum_n e^{-i \cdot (\omega - u) \cdot n} \cdot w_n \, du$$

We recognize the DTFT of $\{w_n\}$ with argument (ω-u) and so the property is established. Note that the convolution is a periodic convolution as both W1(ω) and X1(ω) have period 2π.

We make an important application of Property 7.8, namely, when Z1(ω) is used as an estimate of the DTFT, or spectrum, X1(ω). Let $\{x_n\}$ represent an arbitrarily long data sequence with DTFT X1(ω). (We discuss in the next section when we may define the DTFT for an infinite-length sequence.) Suppose the latter is unknown and we wish to compute it from an observation of $\{x_n\}$. In practice, we can only observe a finite-length segment of $\{x_n\}$, namely the **truncated** data $\{z_n = w_n x_n\}$. The finite-length sequence $\{w_n\}$ is called a **window** sequence. Given the finite-length sequence $\{z_n\}$, we compute its DFT: With the zero padding technique, we can thereby obtain samples of the DTFT Z1(ω) to whatever detail we desire. However, Z1(ω) is *not* X1(ω); rather, it is the result of the convolution described by Property 7.8. It is appropriate to term X1(ω) an **idealized model** because it is defined by a sequence, $\{x_n\}$, of arbitrarily large length and hence unobservable. In this context, Z1(ω) is called a **spectral estimate** of X1(ω).

This leads us to pose the problem of choosing a window w_n with a good DTFT W1. The window is not necessarily of constant value. In fact, we usually want a nonconstant window, as we will discuss later in connection with this measurement problem (**Chapter 15** and **Chapter 26**) and also FIR filter design (**Chapter 12** and **Chapter 13**). But we already have some insight into this problem as we now point out. Note that the DTFT of an M-length window is a rational function of exp(iω) with exactly M complex zeros. Therefore, it is impossible to confine the DTFT to an interval within $[0,2\pi]$.

Example 7.8

We define a relatively long sequence x_n with a simple DTFT.

"long" data sequence:

$$NN := 512 \qquad nn := 0 .. NN - 1$$

$$\omega1 := \frac{2 \cdot \pi}{NN} \cdot 32 \qquad \omega2 := \frac{2 \cdot \pi}{NN} \cdot 80$$

$$x_{nn} := 0.05 \cdot \cos(\omega1 \cdot nn) + 0.075 \cdot \cos(\omega2 \cdot nn)$$

We truncate this sequence with a simple, uniform window.

window:

$$MM := 16 \qquad w_{nn} := if(nn < MM, 1, 0)$$

truncated data:

$$z_{nn} := w_{nn} \cdot x_{nn}$$

We now compute samples of the three DTFTs, W1, X1 and Z1, using the DFT, and plot them.

DFT:

$$dft(v) := \sqrt{NN} \cdot icfft(v)$$

DFT ~ DTFT:

$$X := dft(x) \qquad W := dft(w) \qquad Z := dft(z)$$

$$\omega_{nn} := \frac{2 \cdot \pi}{NN} \cdot nn$$

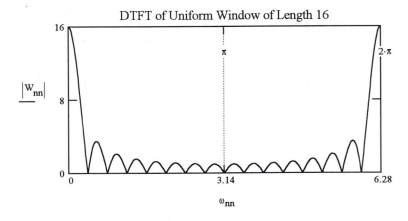

DTFT of Uniform Window of Length 16

ω_{nn}

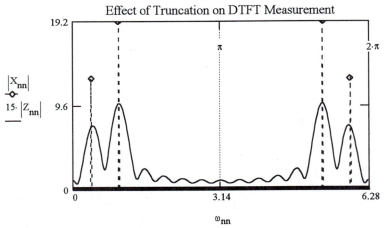

Effect of Truncation on DTFT Measurement

ω_{nn}

We see that the truncation can make inferences about X1 from Z1 quite problematic. ‡

EXERCISE 7.6 Vary the parameters in Example 7.8 and observe Z1. For example, vary M with the other parameters fixed. Then try markedly different amplitudes on the cosine sequences. Notice that the window can be varied only by changing its length, M. This changes its DTFT's **main lobe width**, defined as the distance between zeros enclosing the maximum. But it does not change the relative heights of the subsidiary maxima, or **sidelobe levels**. ¤

■ **EXERCISE 7.7** Experience with Example 7.8 and Exercise 7.6 suggests that it is of interest to consider a nonconstant sequence for a window. Recall that the FIR for the **5-by-7** filter has a tapered shape that results in a DTFT with much lower sidelobe level, albeit at the cost of a broader mainlobe width. Suppose we use a fairly pronounced taper, resulting in a triangular-shaped window, in place of the rectangular-shaped window.

$$\text{MT} := 31 \qquad \text{mT} := 0.. \text{MT} \quad \text{wT}_{mT} := \text{if}\left(\text{mT} < \frac{\text{MT}}{2}, \text{mT}, \text{MT} - \text{mT}\right)$$

Repeat Example 7.8 and Exercise 7.6 using this window. ¤

Infinitely Long Sequences

It can be useful to consider the DTFT of signal sequences of unlimited length. While not observable, they can be useful as idealized models. Their mathematical analysis may be easier than that for finite-length signals - with the significant proviso that we have developed the needed theory and manipulative skills. In fact, numerous theories of Fourier transforms have been established. Such a discussion would draw us far afield so we will be content here to formally develop only what we shall need in our DSP study.

First, note that the DTFT of a sequence $\{x_n\}$ will exist provided that $\{x_n\}$ is absolutely summable. This is established by the simple bound

$$|X1(\omega)| = \left|\sum_n e^{-i \cdot \omega \cdot n} \cdot x_n\right| \le \sum_n |x_n| \quad \text{¤}$$

It may be shown that $X1(\omega)$ for such a sequence is uniformly continuous. This is sufficient to ensure that the IDTFT exists and equals $\{x_n\}$. The proof is the same as we gave for finite-length sequences in **Chapter 6** but the interchange of sum and integral can be justified now using the uniform continuity property. It can be shown that the above properties all hold for this family of sequences.

■ **EXERCISE 7.8** Show that if f is absolutely summable, then

$$\sum_{n=-\infty}^{\infty} (|f_n|)^2 < \infty \qquad \text{and} \qquad \sum_{n=\infty}^{\infty} f_n \cdot \overline{g_n} < \infty$$

Then the left sides of Plancherel's and Parseval's Identities are in fact finite. ¤

This theory is adequate to handle all practical cases of interest to us, including stable infinite impulse responses that we discuss later (**Chapter 18**). However, it does not encompass the conceptually important complex exponential sequence and certain idealized frequency responses commonly referred to in DSP. We discuss these below.

Sinusoidal Sequences

Recall how we introduced the DFT in **Chapter 3**. We observed that the complex exponential family {{exp{i(2π/N)kn, n=0,...,N}, k=0,...,N-1} was invariant under the periodic convolution of period N. We were naturally led to identify the N-periodic frequency response, or DFT. Suppose we try to introduce the DTFT in a similar way. We can easily observe the invariance of the complex exponential family {{exp(iωn), n=...,-1,0,1,...}, ω in [0,2π]} under the aperiodic convolution and the natural appearance of the DTFT.

$$y_n = \sum_{m=-\infty}^{\infty} h_m e^{i \cdot \omega \cdot (n-m)} = e^{i \cdot \omega \cdot n} \sum_{m=-\infty}^{\infty} e^{-i \cdot \omega \cdot m} \cdot h_m = e^{i \cdot \omega \cdot n} \cdot H1(\omega)$$

As long as {h} is absolutely summable - for example, the aperiodic extension of a finite sequence - there will be no mathematical problems.

But suppose we wanted to, in theory, apply the DTFT method of computing the aperiodic convolution in this case. The members of this complex exponential family are not absolutely summable and so do not have a DTFT under the theory mentioned. If we wish to persist in this effort, we need a more encompassing theory for the DTFT. We will only formally indicate how this might be done, sufficient for our purposes.

We define an entity called the δ-**function** with the sole property we will use - the **sifting property**. For a broad class of functions f,

$$\int_{-\infty}^{\infty} f(u) \cdot \delta(\omega - u) \, du = f(\omega)$$

With this construct we can formally derive the DTFT of a complex exponential.

Example 7.9

The DTFT of $\exp(i\omega_1 n)$, $0<\omega_1<2\pi$, is $2\pi\delta(\omega-\omega_1)$. We use the sifting property of the δ-function to compute the IDTFT:

$$\frac{1}{2\cdot\pi}\cdot\int_0^{2\cdot\pi} e^{i\cdot n\cdot\omega}\cdot 2\cdot\pi\cdot\delta(\omega-\omega_1)\,d\omega = e^{i\cdot\omega_1\cdot n} \qquad \ddagger$$

EXERCISE 7.9 Show that, for ω_1 in $[0,2\pi]$,

$\text{DTFT}\{\cos(\omega_1 n)\}=\pi[\delta(\omega+\omega_1)+\delta(\omega-\omega_1)]$ and

$\text{DTFT}\{\sin(\omega_1 n)\}=(-i)\pi[\delta(\omega+\omega_1)-\delta(\omega-\omega_1)]$. ¤

To retrace the above discussion of truncation, particularly Example 7.8, the ideal, infinitely long sequence $\{x_n\}$ would be composed of two cosine waves whose DTFT is given in terms of δ-functions. As these DTFTs are not functions, they do not have graphs. It is conventional to draw a vertical arrow at the frequencies where the δ-functions sift. We can imply this information in the DFT for N-length sequences by choosing the very long sequence to have an integer number of cycles for the cosine components. This is a suggested practice we follow when possible.

Ideal, Naive Frequency Responses

There are several types of frequency responses commonly referred to in DSP that do not fall within the above theory. The most common one is the so-called **ideal low-pass filter** FR, which is a constant over a low-pass frequency band and zero elsewhere. As such a DTFT is discontinuous, the IDTFT is not absolutely summable. Such an IR is not likely to be of practical interest: Because its values are finite (you can easily show this), it is of infinite length and it must decay quite slowly as n goes to infinity. A consequence is that the present value of the output may significantly depend on values of the input far from the present. In fact, we will later call them *unstable* impulse responses, and they are avoided in filter design. Clearly such an FR is only naively regarded as "ideal"!

Example 7.10

Consider the following ideal low-pass FR

$$H1(\omega)=1, \; |\omega|<\omega c \qquad H1(\omega)=0, \omega c\leq|\omega|\leq\pi \qquad (-\pi<\omega<\pi)$$

Its FR is the IDFT

$$h_n = \frac{1}{2\cdot\pi}\cdot\int_{-\omega c}^{\omega c} e^{i\cdot n\cdot\omega}\cdot 1\ d\omega$$

We evaluate this integral using Mathcad's symbolic engine. We enclose the right side and choose **Evaluate** then **Evaluate Symbolically** from the **Symbolic** menu. We find the IR

$$h_n = \frac{1}{\pi}\cdot\frac{\sin(n\cdot\omega c)}{n}$$

This IR is of infinite length and falls off very slowly; in fact, it is not absolutely summable. ‡

▨ **EXERCISE 7.10** Is the IR of Example 7.10 causal? ¤

PROBLEM 7.4   Derive the IR of Example 7.10 using the known integral of an exponential. ‡

Example 7.11 _____
An example of another kind of ideal FR is

$$\text{sgn}(\omega) := \text{if}(\omega<0,-1,\text{if}(\omega=0,0,1))\qquad\qquad (-\pi<\omega<\pi)$$

This function is called the **signum** function whose value is $\omega/|\omega|$ except at $\omega=0$ where it is taken as 0. Since this function is discontinuous, it cannot be the DTFT of an absolutely summable sequence. While the computation of the IDTFT is easily formally done (we know the integral of an exponential!), we use Mathcad's symbolic mathematics capability. We type in the form we wish to compute.

Symbolic IDTFT:
$$\frac{1}{2\cdot\pi}\cdot\int_{-\pi}^{0} e^{i\cdot n\cdot\omega}\cdot(-1)\ d\omega + \frac{1}{2\cdot\pi}\cdot\int_{0}^{\pi} e^{i\cdot n\cdot\omega}\cdot(1)\ d\omega$$

Then we enclose the entire expression and choose **Evaluate Symbolically** from the **Symbolic** menu, obtaining

$$\frac{1}{(2\cdot\pi)}\cdot\left(\frac{i}{n}-\frac{i}{n}\cdot\exp(-i\cdot n\cdot\pi)\right) + \frac{1}{(2\cdot\pi)}\cdot\left(\frac{-i}{n}\cdot\exp(i\cdot n\cdot\pi)+\frac{i}{n}\right)$$

Finally, we choose **Simplify** from the **Symbolic** menu, obtaining the form

$$-i \cdot \frac{(\cos(n \cdot \pi) - 1)}{(\pi \cdot n)}$$

Note that the sequence is imaginary, as is predictable from the oddness of the DTFT. Also, as predicted, the sequence is not absolutely summable. We will use this DTFT as an unattainable "ideal" in designing a Hilbert transform FIR filter (**Chapter 11**). ‡

EXERCISE 7.11 Notice that the IDTFT of Example 7.11 appears to be indeterminant at n=0. Complete Example 7.11 by computing the IDTFT at n=0 using its definition. ¤

EXERCISE 7.12 We will soon encounter the DTFT $i\omega$, $-\pi<\omega<\pi$, as the FR of an unattainable ideal discrete-time differentiator to be approximated by an FIR filter. Use Mathcad's symbolic mathematics capability to show that the IDTFT is the non-absolutely summable sequence

$$h_n = -i \cdot \left(\frac{\pi}{n} \cdot \cos(n \cdot \pi)\right)$$

Clarify the situation at n=0. ¤

EXERCISE 7.13 Compute the DTFT of the one-sided, infinite, exponential sequence $a^n \Phi(n)$, $|a|<1$, where $\Phi(n)$ is the built-in unit step sequence. Do this using the known sum of an infinite geometric series and check the computation using the symbolic mathematics capability of Mathcad. (Here there is no anomaly: The sequence is absolutely summable.) ¤

DFT Approximation to DTFT

When the sequence $[x_n]$ is of infinite length, the DFT is no longer guaranteed to be samples of the DTFT. It is of interest to get a measure of the degree of approximation. The following problem gives some results in that direction.

PROBLEM 7.5

Consider an infinite sequence $\{x_n, n=0,1,...\}$ with DTFT $X1(\omega)$. Suppose the sequence is truncated to a length N, forming the sequence $\{x_n, n=0,1,...,N-1\}$ with DFT $\{X_k, k=0,...,N-1\}$. At the sample points $\{\omega_k=(2\pi/N)k, k=0,...,N-1\}$ we wish to compare X_k and $X1(\omega_k)$. Define the mean-square error

$$\text{MSE} = \frac{1}{N} \cdot \sum_{k=0}^{N-1} \left(X_k - X1(\omega_k) \right)^2$$

Show that

$$\text{MSE} = \sum_{n=N}^{\infty} \sum_{m=N}^{\infty} x_n \cdot x_m \cdot \delta(\text{pod}(m-n,N),0)$$

Furthermore, show that the MSE can be written in the form

$$\text{MSE} = \sum_{n=N}^{\infty} \sum_{\kappa = 1 - \text{floor}\left(\frac{n}{N}\right)}^{\infty} x_n \cdot x_{n+\kappa \cdot N}$$

Finally, show that the MSE has an upper bound:

$$\text{MSE} \le \left(\sum_{n=N}^{\infty} |x_n| \right)^2 \qquad \ddagger$$

▓ **EXERCISE 7.14** Compute the two forms of the MSE and the bound of Problem 7.5 for the exponential sequence {$x_n = a^n \Phi(n)$, $|a| < 1$}. We know the DTFT from Exercise 7.13. ¤

▓ **EXERCISE 7.15** Compute the two forms of the MSE and the bound of Problem 7.5 for the simple MA sequence of length M. When M<=N the MSE must be zero. Observe this. We know the DTFT from **Example 6.2**. ¤

Project 7.1

In this project we anticipate the discussion of the next two chapters. Consider an FIR $\{h_m, m=0,...,M\}$ of length M+1 with M even. Temporarily define the sequence $\{g_m=h_{m-M/2}, m=-M/2,...,M/2\}$. For $\{g_m\}$ (i) even, (ii) odd and (iii) neither even nor odd, compute the FR of the corresponding FIRs $\{h_m\}$ using the DFT to sample the DTFT and plot the magnitude and phase. Comment especially on the nature of the phase. (You should use the phase unwrapping algorithm (**Chapter 3**) for clarity.) For each of the FIRs you considered, write down the ZT and plot its poles and zeros. Comment especially on the nature of the zeros. ‡

References

Jackson (1996), Sec. 6.2
Oppenheim and Schafer (1989), Secs. 2.6 - 2.9
Oppenheim and Willsky (1997), Chap. 5
Proakis and Manolakis (1996), Sec. 4.3

8 FIR Filters with Linear Phase

We have noticed in the examples that the phase of FIR filters can be piecewise linear. Recall that this phase property held for the simple MA filter (**Example 6.1**). And it also held for the 5-by-7 filter (**Example 6.2**), predictably as it is the cascade of simple MAs. But it did not hold for the truncated exponential FIR of **Problem 6.1**. What distinguished the two cases was a symmetry present in the IRs for the first two examples that was absent in the third. This piecewise linear phase is important because filters with such a property do not disperse signals passing through them; all frequency components are given the same delay. This is important in digital communication systems. We noticed that the delay associated with an (M+1)-length simple MA filter is (M/2) and is attributable to the linear phase (M/2), which explicitly appears in the phase of its frequency response. We shall now show that a certain symmetry - and also a certain asymmetry - in the IR implies a piecewise linear phase.

Types

To conform to widely used notation for FIR filters, we shall here assume that the FIR length is (M+1). The IR will be denoted by the sequence $\{h_n, n=0,...,M\}$. We also assume that h_0 and h_M are not zero so that the filter is actually of length (M+1). The **midpoint** of the FIR is M/2 (whether M is odd or even). An FIR is **even about its midpoint** if $h_m=h_{M-m}$. An FIR is **odd about its midpoint** if $h_m=-h_{M-m}$. There are four possibilities: an FIR may have M even or odd and be even or odd about its midpoint. These possibilities are called Types I - IV and are defined in the following examples.

Example 8.1 _____
We consider the case of an FIR even about its midpoint with M even. This defines **Type I**. As $h_{M/2}=h_{M-M/2}$ is an identity, there is no restraint imposed on $h_{M/2}$ by the evenness condition. ‡

$$M := 8 \quad N := M + 1 \quad n := 0..N-1 \quad h1_n := \text{if}\left(n \leq \frac{M}{2}, n+1, M-n+1\right)$$

Type I: M Even, FIR Even...

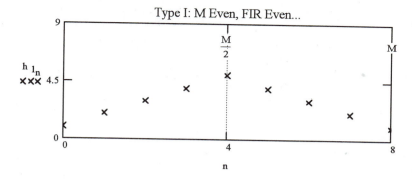

EXERCISE 8.1 Give another example of a Type I FIR. ¤

Example 8.2

We consider the case of an FIR even about its midpoint with M odd. This defines **Type II**. ‡

$$M := 7 \quad N := M + 1 \quad n := 0..N - 1 \quad h2_n := \text{if}\left(n < \frac{M}{2}, n + 1, M - n + 1\right)$$

Type II: M Odd, FIR Even...

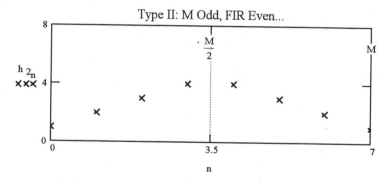

EXERCISE 8.2 Give another example of a Type II FIR. ¤

Example 8.3

We consider the case of an FIR odd about its midpoint with M even. This defines **Type III**. As $h_{M/2} = -h_{M-M/2}$, necessarily $h_{M/2} = 0$. ‡

$$M := 8 \quad N := M + 1 \quad n := 0..N - 1$$

$$h3_n := \text{if}\left[n < \frac{M}{2}, n + 1, \text{if}\left[n = \frac{M}{2}, 0, -(M - n + 1)\right]\right]$$

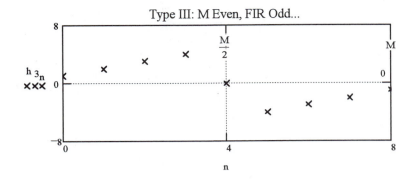

Type III: M Even, FIR Odd...

■ **EXERCISE 8.3** Give another example of a Type III FIR. ¤

Example 8.4

We consider the case of an FIR odd about its midpoint with M odd.
This defines **Type IV**. ‡

$$M := 7 \quad N := M + 1 \quad n := 0 .. N - 1 \quad h4_n := \text{if}\left[n < \frac{M}{2}, n + 1, -(M - n + 1)\right]$$

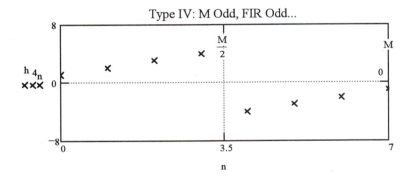

Type IV: M Odd, FIR Odd...

■ **EXERCISE 8.4** Give another example of a Type IV FIR. ¤

FIR Even about Its Midpoint

We establish the piecewise linearity of the phase of the FR in the
case of an FIR even about its midpoint. We detail the M-odd case
and more briefly discuss the M-even case.

Type II

Property 8.1 If an FIR is even about its midpoint and M is odd, then
its frequency response has a piecewise linear phase.

We write out the system function definition and break the finite sum into two parts to enable use of the evenness of the IR.

$$M := 7 \qquad N := M + 1 \qquad n := 0 .. N - 1 \qquad h := h_2$$

$$H(z) := \sum_{n=0}^{\frac{M-1}{2}} h_n \cdot z^{-n} + \sum_{n=\frac{M+1}{2}}^{M} h_n \cdot z^{-n}$$

In the second sum, we set m=M-n and then use the symmetry assumption $h_{M-m}=h_m$. As both sums are then over the same set of indices, we can combine them.

$$H(z) := z^{-\frac{M}{2}} \cdot \sum_{n=0}^{\frac{M-1}{2}} h_n \cdot \left[z^{-\left(n - \frac{M}{2}\right)} + z^{\left(n - \frac{M}{2}\right)} \right] \qquad (8.1)$$

The frequency response is obtained by setting z=exp(iω). We recognize the cosine that then appears. As usual, we set H1(ω)=H(exp(iω)).

$$H1(\omega) := e^{-i \cdot \frac{M}{2} \cdot \omega} \cdot \sum_{n=0}^{\frac{M-1}{2}} h_n \cdot 2 \cdot \cos\left[\left(n - \frac{M}{2} \right) \cdot \omega \right] \qquad (8.2)$$

The linear phase (-ωM/2) is explicitly evident in the frequency response (8.2). But note that this may not be the entire phase, because the summation defines a function, say R(ω), which, while clearly real, is not necessarily nonnegative and hence cannot generally be the magnitude of the frequency response. The magnitude is in fact |R(ω)| and any changes in sign of R(ω) must be accounted for in the complete phase - by π jumps at the isolated points where R(ω) may change sign. Thus we can only obtain piecewise linearity in the phase. This is quite evident when we plot R(ω) and the frequency response magnitude and phase in this specific example.

$$K := 128 \qquad k := 0 .. K - 1 \qquad \varepsilon := 10^{-6} \qquad \omega_k := \frac{2 \cdot \pi}{K} \cdot k + \varepsilon$$

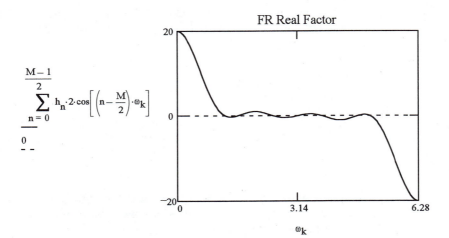

$$\frac{\displaystyle\sum_{n\,=\,0}^{\frac{M-1}{2}} h_n \cdot 2 \cdot \cos\left[\left(n - \frac{M}{2}\right) \cdot \omega_k\right]}{0}$$
- -

FR Real Factor

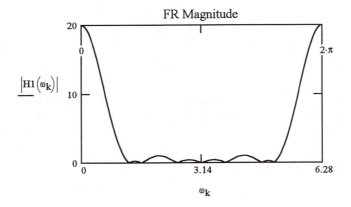

FR Magnitude

$\left|\overline{H1\left(\omega_k\right)}\right|$ 10

We compute the phase with the unwrapping algorithm to avoid π jump artifacts due to the arg function itself.

$$\theta_0 := \arg\left(H1\left(\omega_0\right)\right) \qquad \theta_k := \mathrm{if}\left(k=0, \theta_0, \theta_{k-1} + \arg\left(H1\left(\omega_k\right) \cdot \overline{H1\left(\omega_{k-1}\right)}\right)\right)$$

FR Phase

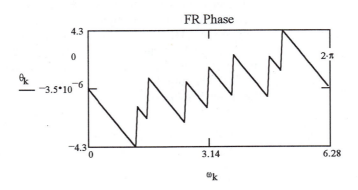

$\dfrac{\theta_k}{}$ $-3.5 \cdot 10^{-6}$

The phase indeed appears to be piecewise linear. Notice that between the first zeros on either side of the maximum of the FR magnitude, the phase is strictly linear.

Returning to eq. (8.1), suppose that z_0 is a zero of H(z). As z_0 cannot be zero, we have

$$0 = \sum_{n=0}^{\frac{M-1}{2}} h_n \cdot \left[\left(\frac{1}{z_0} \right)^{\left(n - \frac{M}{2} \right)} + (z_0)^{\left(n - \frac{M}{2} \right)} \right]$$

(8.3)

But (8.3) is invariant to inverting z_0. Thus, if z_0 is a zero of H(z) then $1/z_0$ must be as well. This implies an interesting pattern for the zeros that we discuss in general later. For now we plot the M zeros for this example.

$$hr_n := h_{N-n-1} \quad zeros := polyroots(hr) \quad m := 0 .. M-1 \quad \omega := 0, \frac{2 \cdot \pi}{64} .. 2 \cdot \pi$$

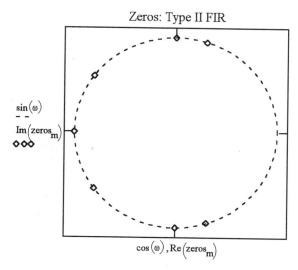

Zeros: Type II FIR

$$zeros = \begin{bmatrix} -1 \\ -0.809 - 0.588i \\ -0.809 + 0.588i \\ -1.156 \cdot 10^{-8} - 1i \\ 1i \\ 0.309 + 0.951i \\ 0.309 - 0.951i \end{bmatrix}$$

FIR Filters with Linear Phase

EXERCISE 8.5 Satisfy yourself that, in this plot, if z_0 is a zero, then $1/z_0$ is also a zero. ¤

EXERCISE 8.6 Repeat the above considerations for a Type II FIR with the example you chose for Exercise 8.2. ¤

Type I

Property 8.2 If an FIR is even about its midpoint and M is even, then its frequency response has a piecewise linear phase.

When M is even, we have (analogously to (8.1))

$$H(z) := z^{-\frac{M}{2}} \cdot \left[\sum_{n=0}^{\frac{M}{2}-1} h_n \cdot \left[z^{-\left(n-\frac{M}{2}\right)} + z^{\left(n-\frac{M}{2}\right)} \right] + h_{\frac{M}{2}} \right]$$

So the frequency response is, setting z=exp(iω),

$$H1(\omega) := e^{-i \cdot \frac{M}{2} \cdot \omega} \cdot \left[\sum_{n=0}^{\frac{M}{2}-1} h_n \cdot 2 \cdot \cos\left[\left(n-\frac{M}{2}\right) \cdot \omega \right] + h_{\frac{M}{2}} \right]$$

The linear phase again appears in an exponential multiplying a real but not necessarily nonnegative quantity. Thus, again, the FR phase will be piecewise linear in general.

PROBLEM 8.1 Plot the FR magnitude and phase and the zeros for the Type I FIR h_1. ‡

FIR Odd about Its Midpoint

We establish the piecewise linearity of the phase of the FR in the case of an FIR odd about its midpoint. We detail the M-odd case and more briefly discuss the M-even case.

Type IV

Property 8.3 If an FIR is odd about its midpoint and M is odd, then its frequency response has a piecewise linear phase.

We write out the transfer function definition and break the finite sum into two parts to enable use of the oddness of the IR.

$$M := 7 \qquad N := M + 1 \qquad n := 0 .. N - 1 \qquad h := h_4$$

$$H(z) := \sum_{n=0}^{\frac{M-1}{2}} h_n \cdot z^{-n} + \sum_{n=\frac{M+1}{2}}^{M} h_n \cdot z^{-n}$$

In the second sum, we set m=M-n and then use the asymmetry assumption $h_{M-m} = - h_m$. As both sums are then over the same set of indices, we can combine them.

$$H(z) := z^{-\frac{M}{2}} \cdot \sum_{n=0}^{\frac{M-1}{2}} h_n \cdot \left[z^{-\left(n - \frac{M}{2}\right)} - z^{\left(n - \frac{M}{2}\right)} \right] \qquad (8.4)$$

The frequency response is obtained by setting z=exp(iω). We recognize the sine that then appears. We need to multiply by i/i, leaving i=exp(iπ/2) explicit. As usual, we set H1(ω)=H(exp(iω)).

$$H1(\omega) := e^{-i \cdot \frac{M}{2} \cdot \omega + i \cdot \frac{\pi}{2}} \cdot \sum_{n=0}^{\frac{M-1}{2}} h_n \cdot 2 \cdot \sin\left[\left(n - \frac{M}{2}\right) \cdot \omega \right] \qquad (8.5)$$

The linear phase (-ωM/2) is explicitly evident in the frequency response (8.5). But note that this may not be the entire phase because the summation defines a function, say Q(ω), that, while clearly real, is not necessarily nonnegative and hence cannot generally be the magnitude of the frequency response. Rather, the magnitude is |Q(ω)| and any changes in sign of Q(ω) must be accounted for in the complete phase - by π jumps at the isolated points where Q(ω) may change sign. Thus we can only obtain piecewise linearity in the phase. In this specific example, Q(ω) is entirely of one sign: negative!

$$K := 128 \qquad k := 0 .. K - 1 \qquad \varepsilon := 10^{-6} \qquad \omega_k := \frac{2 \cdot \pi}{K} \cdot k + \varepsilon$$

FR Real Factor

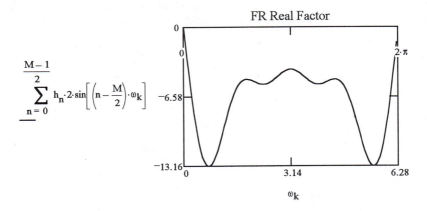

$$\dfrac{\displaystyle\sum_{n=0}^{\frac{M-1}{2}} h_n \cdot 2 \cdot \sin\left[\left(n - \dfrac{M}{2}\right) \cdot \omega_k\right]}{}$$

FR Magnitude

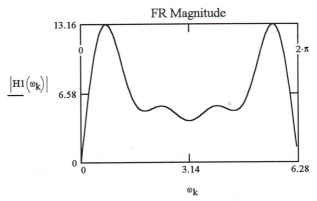

$$\dfrac{\left|H1\left(\omega_k\right)\right|}{}$$

We compute the phase with the unwrapping algorithm to avoid π jump artifacts due to the arg function itself.

$$\theta_0 := \arg\left(H1\left(\omega_0\right)\right) \qquad \theta_k := \text{if}\left(k = 0, \theta_0, \theta_{k-1} + \arg\left(H1\left(\omega_k\right) \cdot \overline{H1\left(\omega_{k-1}\right)}\right)\right)$$

FR Phase

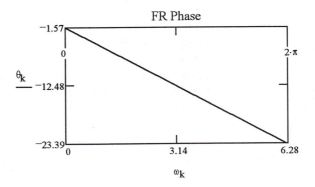

$$\dfrac{\theta_k}{}$$

Returning to eq. (8.4), suppose that z_0 is a zero of H(z). As z_0 cannot be zero, we have

$$0= \sum_{n=0}^{\frac{M-1}{2}} h_n \cdot \left[\left(\frac{1}{z_0}\right)^{n-\frac{M}{2}} - (z_0)^{\left(n-\frac{M}{2}\right)} \right] \qquad (8.6)$$

But (8.6) is invariant to inverting z_0. This implies that if z_0 is a zero of H(z) then $1/z_0$ must be as well. This is the same phenomenon that occurred for FIRs even about their midpoint. For the present we make a plot of the zeros of this example.

$$hr_n := h_{N-n-1} \qquad zeros := polyroots(hr) \qquad m := 0..M-1 \qquad \omega := 0, \frac{2\cdot\pi}{64}..2\cdot\pi$$

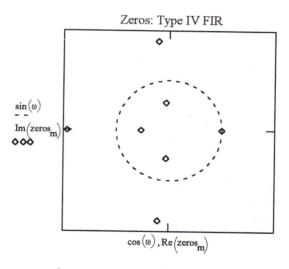

Zeros: Type IV FIR

$$zeros = \begin{bmatrix} -1.922 \\ -0.52 \\ -0.214 - 1.798i \\ -0.214 + 1.798i \\ -0.065 + 0.549i \\ -0.065 - 0.549i \\ 1 \end{bmatrix}$$

EXERCISE 8.7 Observe, in this plot, the pattern of zeros. Can you partition them into a singlet, a doublet and a quadruplet? ¤

EXERCISE 8.8 Repeat the above considerations for a Type IV FIR with the example you chose for Exercise 8.4. ¤

Type III

Property 8.4 If an FIR is odd about its midpoint and M is even, then its frequency response has a piecewise linear phase.

When M is even, we have, analogously to (8.1),

$$H(z) := z^{-\frac{M}{2}} \cdot \left[\sum_{n=0}^{\frac{M}{2}-1} h_n \cdot \left[z^{-\left(n-\frac{M}{2}\right)} - z^{\left(n-\frac{M}{2}\right)} \right] + h_{\frac{M}{2}} \right]$$

So the frequency response is, setting z=exp(iω) and remembering that $h_{M/2}=0$,

$$H1(\omega) := e^{-i \cdot \frac{M}{2} \cdot \omega + i \cdot \frac{\pi}{2}} \cdot \left[\sum_{n=0}^{\frac{M}{2}-1} h_n \cdot 2 \cdot \sin\left[\left(n-\frac{M}{2}\right) \cdot \omega \right] \right]$$

The linear phase again appears, in an exponential multiplying a real but not necessarily nonnegative quantity. Thus, again, the FR phase will be piecewise linear in general. And, there is the π/2 phase shift.

PROBLEM 8.2 Plot the FR magnitude and phase and the zeros for the Type III FIR h_3. ‡

Patterns of Zeros

We observed above that for all four types of FIR filters that we are discussing, if z_0 is a zero then so is $1/z_0$. Of course, for a real IR, if z_0 is a zero then so is its complex conjugate $\text{conj}(z_0)$. Implied, then, are the following observations.

Property 8.5 For an FIR that is even or odd about its midpoint, we have the following zero patterns.

1. If z_0 is a complex zero, with $|z_0|$ not 1 and $\text{Im}(z_0)$ not 0, then z_0 occurs as a member of the **complex quadruplet** $(z_0, \text{conj}(z_0), 1/z_0, 1/\text{conj}(z_0))$.

2. If z_0 is a complex zero on the unit circle, with $|z_0|=1$ and $\text{Im}(z_0)$ not 0, then $1/z_0=\text{conj}(z_0)$ and so z_0 appears as a member of the **complex doublet** $(z_0, \text{conj}(z_0))$.

3. If z_0 is a real zero, with $|z_0|$ not 1, then $\text{conj}(z_0)=z_0$ and so z_0 appears as a member of the **real doublet** $(z_0, 1/z_0)$.

4. If z_0 is +1 or -1, then $z_0=1/z_0=\text{conj}(z_0)$ and so z_0 appears as a **singlet**.

Concerning the zeros at +1 and -1, there is more to be said.

PROBLEM 8.3

(a) For an FIR that is even about its midpoint, show that

$$H(z) := z^{-M} \cdot H\left(z^{-1}\right) \tag{8.7}$$

(b) For an FIR that is odd about its midpoint, show that

$$H(z) := -\left(z^{-M} \cdot H\left(z^{-1}\right)\right) \qquad \ddagger \tag{8.8}$$

EXERCISE 8.9 Show, now with (8.7) and (8.8), that if z_0 is a zero then so is $1/z_0$ for all four types of FIRs. Confirm this by plotting the zeros in the four examples introduced here. ¤

EXERCISE 8.10 Evaluate (8.7) at z=-1 and conclude that, for M odd, z=-1 necessarily is a zero. ¤

EXERCISE 8.11 Evaluate (8.8) at z=+1 and conclude that z=+1 necessarily is a zero. ¤

■ **EXERCISE 8.12** Evaluate (8.8) at z=-1 and conclude that for M even z=-1 necessarily is a zero. ¤

We summarize these results.

Property 8.6 A Type II FIR must have a zero at z=-1. A Type III FIR must have zeros at z=-1 and z=+1. A Type IV FIR must have a zero at z=+1.

With regard to FIR design, remembering that z=+1 corresponds to $\omega=0$ and z=-1 corresponds to $\omega=\pi$, some observations can be made at this point.

1. Types II and III FIRs should not be used for a high-pass design.
2. Types III and IV FIRs should not be considered for a low-pass design.
3. If a $\pi/2$ phase shift is required, as in a differentiator or a Hilbert transform, a Type III or Type IV FIR should be used.

PROBLEM 8.4

In some design problems, even though a linear phase may be desired, practical restraints may result in only an approximately linear phase. In a design study for a portable, video-on-demand, wireless communication system, the minimization of power consumption dominated design considerations (Meng, et al.). To be at all feasible, the system had to use data compression and a method called subband decomposition was chosen. This scheme employed two FIR filters to decompose the signal frequencies into low and high passbands. As a result of much design compromise and simulation, the FIRs were chosen to be

$$h_{LO}=(3,6,2,-1) \qquad h_{HI}=(1,2,-6,3)$$

Plot the magnitude and phase of the FR of each filter. How linear are the phases? Also plot the magnitude and phase of the overall FR of their parallel combination. How near the FR of an ideal delay is it? Plot the zero pattern of each filter. Do they occur in the special patterns discussed here? ‡

Project 8.1

For each of the four types of FIR filters exemplified above, define at least one new example. For each example, (i) plot the FR, magnitude and phase, and note the piecewise linear phase, and (ii) make a pole-zero plot and note the zero pattern. ‡

Project 8.2

Consider the **backward difference** FIR defined by M=1 and $h_0=1$, $h_1=-1$. What type FIR is it? Find the zeros of the transfer function and make a pole-zero plot. Compute and plot the frequency response and determine the frequency range over which this filter acts approximately as a first-order differentiator. Illustrate its action by sampling an analog signal, adjusting the sampling rate to control the accuracy. ‡

Project 8.3

Consider the **second backward difference** FIR defined by M=2 and $h_0=h_2=1$, $h_1=-2$. What type FIR is it? Find the zeros of the transfer function and make a pole-zero plot. Compute and plot the frequency response and determine the frequency range over which this filter acts approximately as a second-order differentiator. Illustrate its action by sampling an analog signal, adjusting the sampling rate to control the accuracy. ‡

Project 8.4

For each of the simple FIRs of **Project 2.2**, identify the even or odd FIRs and predict whether or not the FR phase will be piecewise linear. Plot the FR magnitude and phase and verify your predictions. Find the zeros, make a pole-zero plot and verify that they are consistent with your predictions and with Properties 8.5 and 8.6. ‡

References

Jackson (1996), Sec. 5.3
Meng, et al. (1995)
Oppenheim and Schafer (1989), Sec. 5.7.3
Proakis and Manolakis (1996), Sec. 8.2.1

9 FIR Filters: Geometric View

We have seen that the frequency response of an FIR filter is a rational function of z=exp(iω) and that the roots of the numerator can be complex. More precisely, for an FIR of length M+1, the only possible pole is z=0, of order M, and the M zeros must, if complex, occur in complex conjugate pairs. And we have noted that, if the FIR is odd or even about its midpoint, then the FIR filter will have a piecewise linear phase and the zeros will appear in special quadruplets, doublets and singlets.

System Function Factored Form

The design of an FIR filter can be said to be the placement of zeros in the complex plane. We do not directly place zeros in more sophisticated design procedures - although we certainly do so implicitly. But we can at least perform a "rough" design by this technique. The general form of the transfer function is, for an FIR of length M+1,

$$H(z) = \frac{\left[\prod_{m=0}^{M-1} (z - z_m) \right]}{z^M}$$

We note that the magnitude of the corresponding frequency response, H1(ω)=H(exp(iω)), cannot be effected by the pole: |exp(iMω)|=1. The phase of the frequency response does have a contribution, exp(-iMω), from the pole. As ω increases from 0 to 2π, this phase contribution decreases linearly from 0 to -2πM.

Suppose we write each factor of the numerator of the frequency response H1(ω) in magnitude and phase form:

$$a(\omega, m) = \left| e^{i \cdot \omega} - z_m \right| \qquad\qquad \alpha(\omega, m) = \arg\left(e^{i \cdot \omega} - z_m \right)$$

Then

$$H1(\omega, M) = e^{-i \cdot M \cdot \omega} \prod_{m=0}^{M-1} a(m,\omega) \cdot e^{i \cdot \alpha(m,\omega)}$$

and so the frequency response magnitude is

$$H1m(\omega, m) = \prod_{m=0}^{M-1} a(\omega, m)$$

and

$$\arg(H1(\omega, m)) = \sum_{m=0}^{M-1} \alpha(m,\omega) \ - M \cdot 2 \cdot \pi$$

Consider just one of the factors in isolation as ω increases from 0 to 2π. We shall draw its pole-zero diagram and plot its frequency response magnitude and phase.

$$z_0 := 0.9 \cdot e^{i \cdot \frac{\pi}{3}} \qquad F1(\omega) := e^{i \cdot \omega} - z_0 \qquad K := 64 \qquad k := 0 .. K \qquad v_k := \frac{2 \cdot \pi}{K} \cdot k$$

Pole-Zero Plot

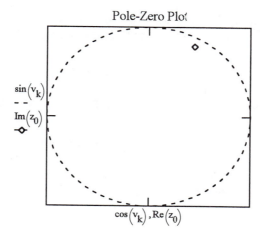

We imagine the vector (z-z₀) drawn from z_0 to an arbitrary
z=exp(iω): As ω increases from 0 to 2π, z moves from z=1
counterclockwise around the unit circle, past z_0, and back to z=1.
The magnitude of this vector, |z-z₀|, clearly has a local minimum
when arg(z)=arg(z_0). Furthermore, there is a relatively rapid change
of phase near z such that arg(z)=arg(z_0). For example, when z_0 is
near the unit circle, this change is very rapid and nearly +π. The
total phase change is +2π. These simple geometric ideas allow us
to predict the general nature of the frequency response of this
factor, which we now plot.

$$\theta_0 := \arg\left(F1\left(v_k\right)\right) \qquad \theta_k := \mathrm{if}\left(k=0, \theta_0, \theta_{k-1} + \arg\left(F1\left(v_k\right) \cdot \overline{F1\left(v_{k-1}\right)}\right)\right)$$

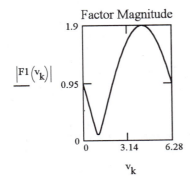

Factor Magnitude

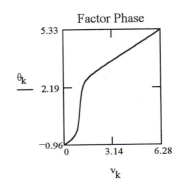

Factor Phase

▦ **EXERCISE 9.1** (a) Discuss the magnitude and phase behavior of
F1(ω) when |z₀|>1. What is the net phase contribution as ω
increases from 0 to 2π?
(b) Vary the magnitude and angle of the zero and observe the
variety of behavior of the magnitude and phase of this factor. ¤

▦ **EXERCISE 9.2** Show that an FIR filter of length (M+1) with M1
(M1<=M, of course) zeros outside the unit circle will have a net
phase change (as ω increases from 0 to 2π) of (-2π M1) rad. ¤

We can now use our understanding of the behavior of each factor of
H1(ω) to often qualitatively predict the behavior of its amplitude and
phase - and to design, at least crudely, FIR filters. This analysis is
called the **geometric view**.

Examples of FIR Filters with Linear Phase

We now give some examples of FIR design using the geometric point of view. We assume that we want a real impulse response and a piecewise linear phase. We will attempt the design of low-pass, bandpass, and high-pass filters. We also want to illustrate the use of a variety of the special zeros patterns.

▨ **EXERCISE 9.3 (Review)** Can a Type III or IV FIR be a low-pass filter? Can a Type II FIR be a high-pass filter? If we want an FIR with a $\pi/2$ phase shift, corresponding to a multiplier i in the FR, which types of FIRs would we use? ¤

Type I

Example 9.1 _____

We design a high-pass FIR with a cutoff frequency about $\pi/2$. So we should reduce the FR magnitude for $|\omega|<\pi/2$ by placing zeros on or near the arc of the unit circle for $0<=\omega<=\pi/2$. We consider a Type I FIR; we do not want a Type II FIR with its zero at $\omega=\pi$. So we choose an even M of manageable size, say, M=8.

We can use a complex doublet with one of its zeros at an angle $\omega=\pi/2$ to give a definite cutoff. We can use a complex quadruplet with one of its zeros at an angle $\omega=\pi/4$ and a real doublet with positive zeros to pull down the FR magnitude in the stopband. We can adjust the radii to get a desired response.

$$M := 8 \qquad m := 0 .. M-1 \qquad ze_0 := 0.99999 \cdot e^{i \cdot \frac{\pi}{2}} \qquad ze_1 := \overline{ze_0}$$

$$ze_2 := 0.75 \cdot e^{i \cdot \frac{\pi}{4}} \qquad ze_3 := \overline{ze_2} \qquad ze_4 := \frac{1}{ze_2} \qquad ze_5 := \frac{1}{\overline{ze_2}}$$

$$ze_6 := 0.5 \qquad ze_7 := \frac{1}{ze_6}$$

We form the transfer function using these zeros and an Mth-order pole at z=0.

$$H_I(z) := \frac{1}{z^M} \cdot \prod_m \left(z - ze_m \right)$$

We make a pole-zero plot for this system function.

Type I Pole-Zero Plot

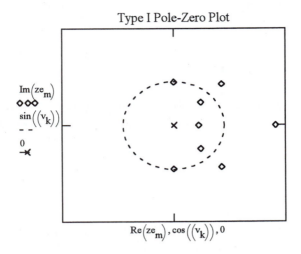

$$\text{Im}\big(ze_m\big)$$
$$\sin\big((v_k)\big)$$
$$0$$

$$\text{Re}\big(ze_m\big), \cos\big((v_k)\big), 0$$

We now plot the frequency response.

$$K := 64 \quad k := 0..K-1 \quad \omega_k := k \cdot \frac{2 \cdot \pi}{K} \quad H_{I_k} := H_I\big(e^{i \cdot \omega_k}\big) \quad Hm_k := \Big|H_{I_k}\Big|$$

Type I FIR FR Magnitude

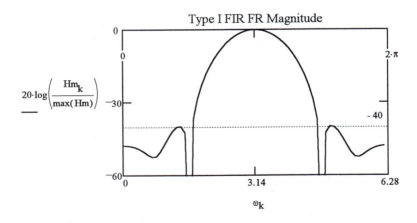

$$20 \cdot \log\left(\frac{Hm_k}{\max(Hm)}\right)$$

$$\omega_k$$

We note that the FIR is a high-pass filter. It has a -40db sidelobe level that could find application, but a rather nonuniform gain over the passband. We compute the phase of the FR.

$$\theta_0 := \arg\big(H_{I_0}\big) \qquad \theta_k := \text{if}\bigg(k=0, \theta_0, \theta_{k-1} + \arg\Big(H_{I_k} \cdot \overline{H_{I_{k-1}}}\Big)\bigg)$$

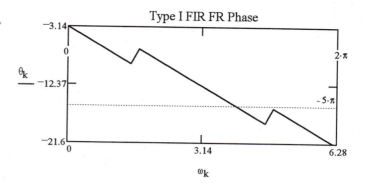

Type I FIR FR Phase

The phase is clearly piecewise linear. Since M1=3 zeros are outside the unit circle, the total phase shift should be, and is, 2π M1=-6π.

We now compute the impulse response by the IDFT, using the frequency samples.

$$h_I := \frac{1}{\sqrt{K}} \cdot \text{cfft}\left(H_I\right)$$

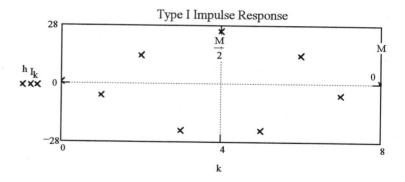

Type I Impulse Response

As expected, the impulse response is even about its midpoint (n=M/2=4). ‡

EXERCISE 9.4 Verify that the IR is real. ¤

EXERCISE 9.5 Vary the choice of zeros in Example 9.1 and observe the effects on the FR and IR. You may wish to vary M. You may also wish to violate the special zero patterns we discovered in Chapter 8. ¤

Type II

Example 9.2

We design a low-pass FIR with a cutoff frequency about $\pi/2$. So we should reduce the FR magnitude for $|\omega|>\pi/2$ by placing zeros on or near the arc of the unit circle for $\pi/2<=\omega<=\pi$. We consider a Type II FIR with its zero at $\omega=\pi$ and we choose an odd M of manageable size, say, M=7.

We can use a complex doublet with one of its zeros at an angle $\omega=\pi/2$ to give a definite cutoff. We can use a complex quadruplet with one of its zeros at an angle $\omega=3\pi/4$ and the required real singlet at z=-1 to pull down the FR magnitude in the stop band. We adjust the radii to achieve a desirable response.

$$M := 7 \qquad m := 0 .. M - 1 \qquad ze_0 := 0.99999 \cdot e^{i \cdot \frac{\pi}{2}} \qquad ze_1 := \overline{ze_0}$$

$$ze_2 := 0.75 \cdot e^{i \cdot \frac{3 \cdot \pi}{4}} \qquad ze_3 := \overline{ze_2} \qquad ze_4 := \frac{1}{ze_2} \qquad ze_5 := \frac{1}{\overline{ze_2}}$$

$$ze_6 := -0.9999$$

We form the transfer function using these zeros and an Mth-order pole at z=0.

$$H_{II}(z) := \frac{1}{z^M} \cdot \prod_m \left(z - ze_m \right)$$

We make a pole-zero plot for this system function.

Type II Pole-Zero Plot

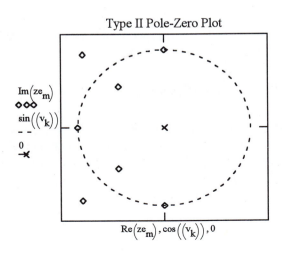

$$\text{Re}\left(ze_m\right), \cos\left(\left(v_k\right)\right), 0$$

We now plot the frequency response.

$$H_{II_k} := H_{II}\left(e^{i \cdot \omega_k}\right) \qquad Hm_k := \left|H_{II_k}\right|$$

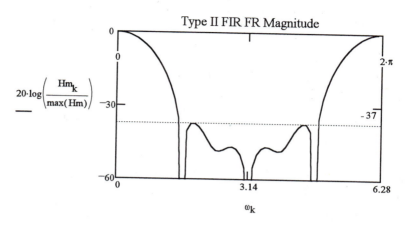

Type II FIR FR Magnitude

We note that the FIR is a low-pass filter. It has a -37 db sidelobe level, but a rather nonuniform gain over the passband. We now compute the phase of the FR.

$$\theta_0 := \arg\left(H_{I_0}\right) \qquad \theta_k := \text{if}\left(k{=}0, \theta_0, \theta_{k-1} + \arg\left(H_{II_k} \cdot \overline{H_{II_{k-1}}}\right)\right)$$

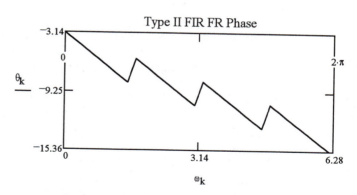

Type II FIR FR Phase

The phase is clearly piecewise linear. Since M1=2 zeros are outside the unit circle, the total phase shift should be, and is, 2π M1=-4π.

We now compute the impulse response by the IDFT, using the frequency samples.

$$h_{II} := \frac{1}{\sqrt{K}} \cdot \text{cfft}\left(H_{II}\right)$$

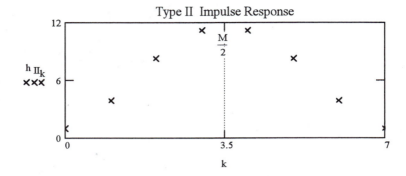

Type II Impulse Response

As expected, the impulse response is even about its midpoint (n=M/2=3.5). ‡

EXERCISE 9.6 Verify that the IR is real. ¤

EXERCISE 9.7 Vary the choice of zeros in Example 9.2 and observe the effects on the FR and IR. You may wish to vary M. You may also wish to violate the special zero patterns we discovered in Chapter 8. ¤

Type III

Example 9.3

We design an FIR that, first, will reject frequencies below $\pi/4$ and from $3\pi/4$ to π. (Of course, the FR in the band $\pi<\omega<2\pi$ is then fixed by Hermitian symmetry.) So we should reduce the FR magnitude for ω in these rejection bands by placing zeros on or near the arcs of the unit circle for $0<=\omega<\pi/4$ and $3\pi/4<=\omega<=\pi$. Second, we want a $\pi/2$ phase shift over the passband. For example, we may want to perform a Hilbert transform on the signals in that band. (We discuss the use of such a filter in generating a single-sideband, amplitude-modulated sequence in **Chapter 11**.) A Type III FIR with its zeros at $\omega=0$ and $\omega=\pi$ and its $\pi/2$ phase shift is an obvious candidate. So we choose an even M of manageable size, say, M=14.

We note that there are required singlets at z=1 and z=-1. We can try a complex doublet at angle $\omega=\pi/4$ and another at angle $\omega=3\pi/4$. To reduce the response between these zeros, we add a doublet at angle $\omega=\pi/8$ and another at angle $\omega=7\pi/8$ forming, together, a complex quadruplet.

$$M := 14 \qquad m := 0 \,..\, M - 1 \qquad ze_0 := 0.99999 \qquad ze_1 := -0.99999$$

$$ze_2 := 0.99999 \cdot e^{i \cdot \frac{3 \cdot \pi}{4}} \qquad ze_3 := \overline{ze_2} \qquad ze_4 := 0.99999 \cdot e^{i \cdot \frac{\pi}{4}} \qquad ze_5 := \overline{ze_4}$$

$$ze_6 := 0.9 \cdot e^{i \cdot \frac{\pi}{8}} \qquad ze_7 := \overline{ze_6} \qquad ze_8 := \frac{1}{ze_6} \qquad ze_9 := \overline{ze_8}$$

$$ze_{10} := 0.9 \cdot e^{i \cdot \frac{7 \cdot \pi}{8}} \qquad ze_{11} := \overline{ze_{10}} \qquad ze_{12} := \frac{1}{ze_{10}} \qquad ze_{13} := \overline{ze_{12}}$$

We form the transfer function using these zeros and an Mth-order pole at z=0.

$$H_{III}(z) := \frac{1}{z^M} \cdot \prod_m \left(z - ze_m \right)$$

We make a pole-zero plot for this system function.

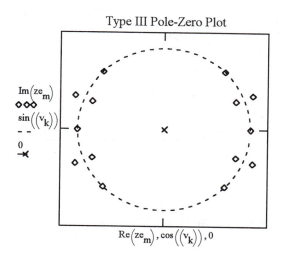

Type III Pole-Zero Plot

$\mathrm{Re}(ze_m), \cos\left(\left(v_k\right)\right), 0$

We now plot the frequency response.

$$H_{III_k} := H_{III}\left(e^{i \cdot \omega_k} \right) \qquad Hm_k := \left| H_{III_k} \right|$$

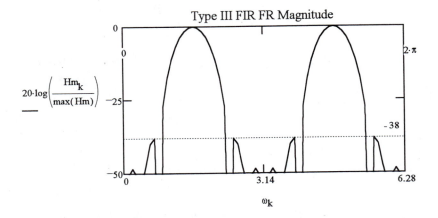

Type III FIR FR Magnitude

We note that the FIR is a bandpass filter. It has a -38 db sidelobe level, but a rather nonuniform gain over the passband. We now compute the phase of the FR.

$$\theta_0 := \arg\left(H_{I_0}\right) \qquad \theta_k := \text{if}\left(k{=}0, \theta_0, \theta_{k-1} + \arg\left(H_{III_k} \cdot \overline{H_{III_{k-1}}}\right)\right)$$

Type III FIR FR Phase

The phase is clearly piecewise linear. Since M1=4 zeros are outside the unit circle, the total phase shift should be, and is, $2\pi M1 = -8\pi$.

We now compute the impulse response by the IDFT, using the frequency samples.

$$h_{III} := \frac{1}{\sqrt{K}} \cdot \text{cfft}\left(H_{III}\right)$$

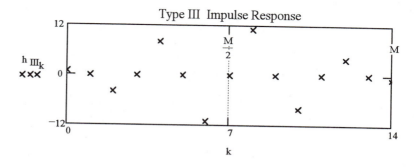

Type III Impulse Response

As expected, the impulse response is odd about its midpoint (M/2=7). ‡

▨ **EXERCISE 9.8** Verify that the IR is real. ¤

▨ **EXERCISE 9.9** Vary the choice of zeros in Example 9.3 and observe the effects of the FR and IR. You may wish to vary M. You may also wish to violate the special zero patterns we discovered in Chapter 8. ¤

Type IV

PROBLEM 9.1

As in Examples 9.1 through 9.3, state a problem specification that would lead the designer to choose a Type IV FIR filter. Make a pole-zero plot, plot the FR magnitude and phase, and compute and plot the IR, verifying that it is real and odd. ‡

PROBLEM 9.2

The FIRs were found by sampling the FR and using the IDFT, a numerical procedure that is efficient. One can also find the FIR by expanding the factored form of H(z) - e.g., H_i(z) above - into a power series in z^{-1} from which the FIR is simply read out, in principle a symbolic procedure. Find the FIRs of Examples 9.1, 9.2 and 9.3 using the symbolic mathematics capability of Mathcad. Which procedure do you prefer? ‡

Project 9.1

Recall that in **Project 8.2**, a very simple Type IV FIR performed approximately as a differentiator. We wish to improve the approximation over a specified band - say $0<=\omega<=\pi/4$. By placing zeros in the complex plane, design an FIR that will perform as a differentiator over this frequency band. Illustrate your design by differentiating a long signal by the method of fast convolution. ‡

Project 9.2

Recall that in **Project 8.3**, a very simple Type IV FIR performed approximately as a second-order differentiator. We wish to improve the approximation over a specified band - say $0 <= \omega <= \pi/4$. By placing zeros in the complex plane, design an FIR that will perform as a second-order differentiator over this frequency band. Illustrate your design by differentiating a long signal by the method of fast convolution. ‡

References

Jackson (1996), Sec. 5.3
Oppenheim and Schafer (1989), Sec. 5.7.3
Proakis and Manolakis (1996), Sec. 8.2.1

10 FIR Design by Frequency Sampling

We now consider an important design method for FIR filters. It gives us an opportunity to further our understanding of FIR filters while providing a useful design procedure that, as we will see, is part science and part art. That is, there will still be a trial-and-error fitting process based on our experience gained using the method. The use of mathematical software such as Mathcad is demonstrated forcefully.

FIR Characterization by Frequency Samples

Suppose an FIR $\{h_n, n=0,...,N-1\}$ has length $N=M+1$. Then its system function, or ZT, is of the form

$$H(z)= \sum_{n=0}^{M} h_n \cdot z^{-n}$$

(10.1)

Its frequency response, or DTFT, is

$$H1(\omega)=H\left(e^{i \cdot \omega}\right)$$

(10.2)

Given a frequency response, we may sample it at the **sampling frequencies** $\{\omega_k, k=0,...,M\}$ and obtain the **frequency samples** $\{H_k, k=0,...,M\}$:

sampling
frequencies: $k := 0 .. M$ $\omega_k = \frac{2 \cdot \pi}{N} \cdot k$

frequency
samples: $H_k = H1\left(\omega_k\right)$

Eq. (10.2) now reads

$$H_k= \sum_{n=0}^{M} e^{-i \cdot \left(\frac{2 \cdot \pi}{N}\right) \cdot k \cdot n} \cdot h_n$$

(10.3)

which we recognize as the DFT of the sequence $\{h_n, n=0,...,M\}$. We know that the latter sequence can be recovered from the $\{H_k, k=0,...,M\}$ sequence by the IDFT.

$$h_n = \frac{1}{N} \cdot \sum_k e^{\,i \cdot \left(\frac{2 \cdot \pi}{N}\right) \cdot n \cdot k} \cdot H_k$$

We have made these observations before. But here we emphasize that the frequency samples $\{H_k, k=0,...,M\}$ determine the FIR $\{h_n, n=0,...,M\}$ which, in turn, determines the frequency response (DTFT) via (10.2) for all frequencies as well as the transfer function (ZT) via (10.1) for all z (not 0). The computation of the FIR $\{h_n, n=0,...,M\}$ from the frequency samples $\{H_k, k=0,...,M\}$ is efficiently done by the IFFT; the computation of the frequency response is computed to arbitrarily fine detail by zero padding the FIR to a sufficient length NP and computing the DFT/FFT of length NP.

Reviewing this discussion, we realize that we have a means of designing FIR filters. For a filter of length N=M+1, we choose the set of frequency samples $\{H1(\omega_k), k=0,...,M\}$ that represent a sampling of a **posed frequency response desideratum**. We can then find the FIR using the IDFT and hence find the frequency response to any practically required detail.

The procedure is not as simple as it may appear! If the FIR is to be real, the symmetry conditions noted earlier for the DFT must be satisfied. If the FIR is to be causal, the phase must be properly chosen. And the implicit frequency interpolation may yield, when examined, an unattractive approximation to the posed frequency response. Nevertheless, this **method of design by frequency sampling**, with a little experience and art, is very useful and can result in computationally efficient filters. It is true that we can find an explicit analytic form for the implicit interpolation of the DTFT for all ω. However, this form is not of direct interest to us here because its direct computation is generally much slower than the FFT/IFFT method described above.

PROBLEM 10.1

The frequency interpolation implicitly performed by the frequency sampling method can be written as

$$H1(\omega) = \sum_{k=0}^{M} H_k \cdot f(\omega, k)$$

where $f(\omega,k)$ is the interpolation function. Find $f(\omega,k)$. ‡

Design Restraints

Symmetry

The 2π period and Hermitian symmetry of the FR H1(ω) (**Property 7.2**) imply that the sequence of frequency samples has the property

$$H_k = \overline{H_{N-k}}$$

To show this, we note the string of equalities conj(H_k)=H(exp(i(-ω_k)))= H(exp(i(2π-ω_k)))=H(exp(iω_{N-k}))=H_{N-k} . It directly follows that the frequency sample magnitudes Hm_k obey

$$Hm_k = Hm_{N-k}$$

and that the frequency sample phases obey

$$\arg\left(H_k\right) = - \arg\left(H_{N-k}\right)$$

Note that, when N is even, the frequency sample $H_{N/2}$ must be real.

Causality

To ensure a causal filter we must impose the linear phase -(M/2)ω which, when sampled at ω_k, gives -((N-1)/N)πk . Note that when N is even the zero phase required by the reality of $H_{N/2}$ must be explicitly imposed.

Linear Phase

To ensure a piecewise linear phase, there may be additional restraints (as summarized in **Chapter 8**) which can carry over to restraints on the frequency samples. A Type II FR must have $H_{N/2}$=0. A Type III FR must have H_0=0. A Type IV FR must have H_0=0. Note that a Type III FIR filter has a zero at ω=π but, as N is odd, ω=π is not a sample.

We have already noted that certain types are not amenable to some designs. Types II and III should not be considered for a high-pass design. Types III and IV should not be considered for a low-pass design. Types III and IV should be considered when a π/2 phase shift, or i, FR factor is needed, as in differentiation and Hilbert transform filters.

Low-Pass Filter Design

To illustrate the basic ideas of design by frequency sampling, we consider the design of a low-pass, piecewise linear phase, real, causal FIR filter. We shall pose an **ideal low-pass frequency response** desideratum that we will discover is naive, and we will, by trial and error, modify it. All necessary calculations are rapidly made with the FFT/IFFT.

We first pose a desired frequency response magnitude that is a constant over $(-2\pi/8, 2\pi/8)$, and 0 otherwise. Since we are going to make all required calculations with the DFT/IDFT, we actually want the frequency samples in DFT order, corresponding to sampling the desired frequency response over $(0, 2\pi)$.

We define the frequency samples which, for a real filter, must have an even magnitude and an odd phase. We choose a filter length of N=32. Then M=N-1=31 is odd and $2\pi/8 = \omega_k$ with k=N/8. Since we want a low-pass filter, we choose a Type II FIR filter, which is defined by an even FIR and M odd. The zero at z=-1, or $\omega = +/-\pi$, implies the restraint $H_{N/2} = 0$. We define the frequency samples for k=0,...,N/2 and then use the restraint $H_{N-k} = conj(H_k)$ to complete the definition.

$$N := 32 \qquad\qquad k := 0..\,N-1 \qquad kk := 0..\frac{N}{2}$$

magnitude design:
$$Hm_{kk} := if\!\left(kk \leq \frac{N}{8}, 1, 0\right)$$

The phase will be the minimal, linear phase for a causal filter and must be chosen to be odd. Also, when N is even, the phase of the N/2 sample is always zero.

phase design:
$$ph_{kk} := if\!\left[kk < \frac{N}{2}, -\frac{(N-1)}{N} \cdot kk \cdot \pi, 0\right]$$

We form the FR for k in [0,N/2] and complete its definition.

FR design:
$$H_{kk} := Hm_{kk} \cdot \exp\!\left(i \cdot ph_{kk}\right)$$

symmetry imposed:
$$H_k := if\!\left(k \leq \frac{N}{2}, H_k, \overline{H_{N-k}}\right)$$

We compute the FIR and plot it, verifying that it is real and even about its midpoint. We also find the interpolated frequency response by first zero padding the sequence to a longer length and then computing the DFT.

$$\text{idft}(v) := \left(\frac{1}{\sqrt{N}}\right) \cdot \text{cfft}(v) \qquad h := \text{idft}(H) \qquad n := 0 .. N - 1$$

$$NN := 16 \cdot N \qquad nn := 0 .. NN - 1 \qquad \text{dft}(v) := \sqrt{NN} \cdot \text{icfft}(v)$$

$$he_{nn} := \text{if}(nn < N, h_{nn}, 0) \qquad He := \text{dft}(he) \qquad He_{nn} := |He_{nn}|$$

$$Hel_{nn} := 20 \cdot \log(He_{nn} + 0.0001) \qquad Hml_k := 20 \cdot \log(|H_k| + 0.001)$$

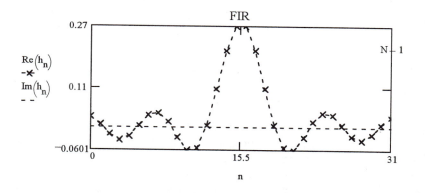

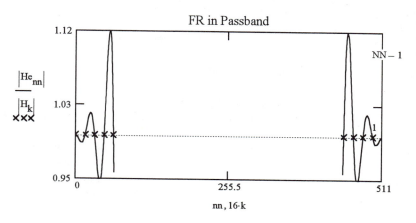

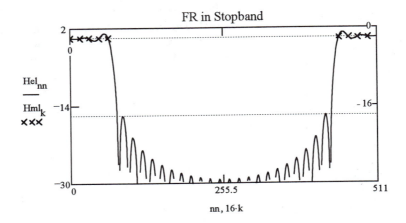

FR in Stopband

$$\frac{\text{Hel}_{nn}}{\text{Hml}_k}$$
$$\times\times\times$$

nn, 16·k

This filter design is not particularly desirable. The first sidelobe is about -16 db and there is a passband ripple of maximum value about 12%. We can improve on the sidelobe level and passband ripple, as we will discover, by admitting a **transition band** where |H1(ω)| may be allowed to decrease less rapidly. In an application of the filter, this band may be made available by choosing an appropriate sampling frequency. After discussing sampling in **Chapter 15**, we will see how such a transition band can be made available in our discussion of interpolation in **Chapter 16** .

We will later discuss the design of FIR filters that are considered best according to a selected criterion. Such optimum filters are found by solving an optimization problem. These solutions are generally relatively complicated. But for now, we are interested in good design, by which we mean that the frequency response magnitude shall have the following properties.

1. The passband fluctuations, or ripple, shall be of small magnitude.
2. The stopband should be less than some specified level.
3. The transition band should be of a practical width.
4. For some applications, the FR magnitude shall have maxima that are about equal, a so-called equiripple characteristic.

Various best and good solutions are all valuable in design, especially because it is not usually feasible to incorporate all desired features into an optimality criterion and all practical restraints a priori into a design algorithm.

With these informal criteria for good design in mind, we can choose, by trial and error, the frequency samples in a transition band. The numerical and plotting features of Mathcad render this procedure practical.

Transition Bands

One Transition Sample

We introduce a nonzero frequency sample just outside the passband and adjust this sample value until the approximation is "close" to the desired ideal frequency response outside the transition band. We are able to get the passband ripple to less than about 3% and the stopband ripple to about -29 db.

$$Hm_{\frac{N}{8}+1} := 0.5 \qquad H_{kk} := Hm_{kk} \cdot \exp\left(i \cdot ph_{kk}\right)$$

$$H_k := if\left(k \le \frac{N}{2}, H_k, \overline{H_{N-k}}\right)$$

We compute the FIR and plot it, verifying that it is real and even about its midpoint. We also find the interpolated frequency response by first zero padding the sequence to a longer length and then computing the DFT.

$$idft(v) := \left(\frac{1}{\sqrt{N}}\right) \cdot cfft(v) \qquad h := idft(H) \qquad n := 0 .. N-1$$

$$NN := 16 \cdot N \qquad nn := 0 .. NN-1 \qquad dft(v) := \sqrt{NN} \cdot icfft(v)$$

$$he_{nn} := if\left(nn < N, h_{nn}, 0\right) \qquad He := dft(he) \qquad He_{nn} := \left|He_{nn}\right|$$

$$Hel_{nn} := 20 \cdot log\left(He_{nn} + 0.0001\right) \qquad Hml_k := 20 \cdot log\left(\left|H_k\right| + 0.001\right)$$

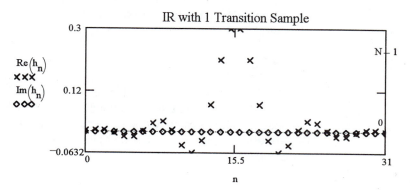

IR with 1 Transition Sample

n

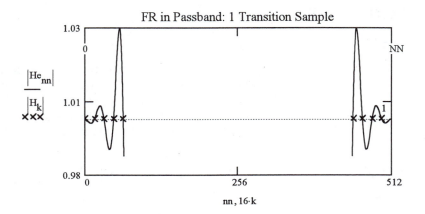

FR in Passband: 1 Transition Sample

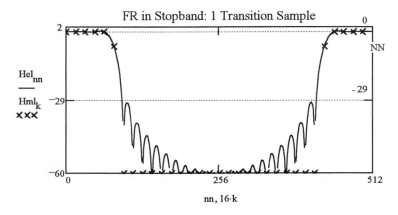

FR in Stopband: 1 Transition Sample

⬚ **EXERCISE 10.1** Vary the single transition sample and observe the FR. Verify that the phase is piecewise linear. What value gives the least passband ripple? (You should be able to achieve 0.35%.) With what sidelobe level? What value gives the least, nearly equiripple? (You should be able to achieve -42 db.) With what passband ripple? ¤

Two Transition Samples

We now introduce a second frequency sample in a transition band and adjust these sample values until the approximation is close to the desired ideal frequency response outside the transition band. We are able to get the passband ripple to about 1.5% and the stopband ripple to about -43 db.

$$Hm_{\frac{N}{8}+1} := 0.7 \qquad Hm_{\frac{N}{8}+2} := 0.2 \qquad H_{kk} := Hm_{kk} \cdot \exp\left(i \cdot ph_{kk}\right)$$

$$H_k := if\left(k \le \frac{N}{2}, H_k, \overline{H_{N-k}}\right)$$

We compute the FIR and plot it, verifying that it is real and even about its midpoint. We also find the interpolated frequency response by first zero padding the sequence to a longer length and then computing the DFT.

$$\text{idft}(v) := \left(\frac{1}{\sqrt{N}}\right) \cdot \text{cfft}(v) \qquad h := \text{idft}(H) \qquad n := 0 .. N - 1$$

$$NN := 16 \cdot N \qquad nn := 0 .. NN - 1 \qquad \text{dft}(v) := \sqrt{NN} \cdot \text{icfft}(v)$$

$$he_{nn} := \text{if}\left(nn < N, h_{nn}, 0\right) \qquad He := \text{dft}(he) \qquad He_{nn} := \left| He_{nn} \right|$$

$$Hel_{nn} := 20 \cdot \log\left(He_{nn} + 0.0001\right) \qquad Hml_{k} := 20 \cdot \log\left(\left|H_{k}\right| + 0.001\right)$$

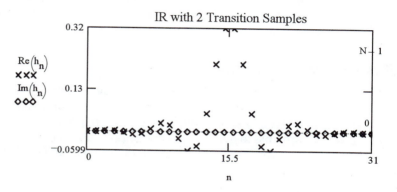

IR with 2 Transition Samples

n

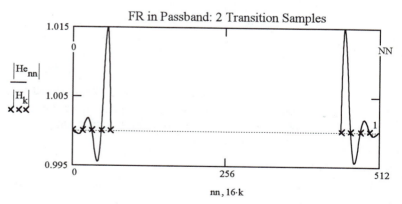

FR in Passband: 2 Transition Samples

nn, 16·k

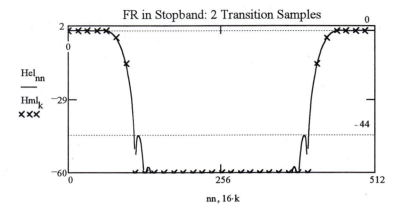

FR in Stopband: 2 Transition Samples

$\dfrac{\text{Hel}_{nn}}{\text{Hml}_k}$
×××

nn, 16·k

▨ **EXERCISE 10.2** Repeat Exercise 10.1, now varying the two transition samples. You should be able to achieve passband ripple as low as 0.25% and a fairly equiripple stopband ripple as low as -55 db - but not simultaneously! ¤

Three Transition Samples

We now introduce a third frequency sample in a transition band and adjust these sample values until the approximation is close to the desired ideal frequency response outside the transition band. We are able to get the passband ripple to less than 0.1% and the stopband ripple to about -50 db with a nearly equiripple character.

$$\text{Hm}_{\frac{N}{8}+1} := 0.97 \qquad \text{Hm}_{\frac{N}{8}+2} := 0.7 \qquad \text{Hm}_{\frac{N}{8}+3} := 0.2$$

$$H_{kk} := \text{Hm}_{kk} \cdot \exp\left(i \cdot ph_{kk}\right) \qquad H_k := \text{if}\left(k \le \frac{N}{2}, H_k, \overline{H_{N-k}}\right)$$

We compute the FIR and plot it, verifying that it is real and even about its midpoint. We also find the interpolated frequency response by first zero padding the sequence to a longer length and then computing the DFT.

$$\text{idft}(v) := \left(\frac{1}{\sqrt{N}}\right) \cdot \text{cfft}(v) \qquad h := \text{idft}(H) \qquad n := 0.. N-1$$

$$NN := 16 \cdot N \qquad nn := 0.. NN - 1 \qquad \text{dft}(v) := \sqrt{NN} \cdot \text{icfft}(v)$$

$$he_{nn} := \text{if}\left(nn < N, h_{nn}, 0\right) \qquad He := \text{dft}(he) \qquad He_{nn} := \left|He_{nn}\right|$$

$$\text{Hel}_{nn} := 20 \cdot \log\left(He_{nn} + 0.0001\right) \qquad \text{Hml}_k := 20 \cdot \log\left(\left|H_k\right| + 0.001\right)$$

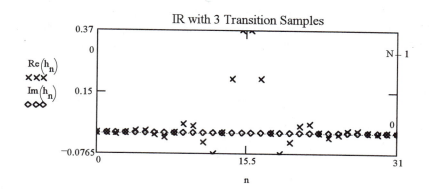

IR with 3 Transition Samples

n

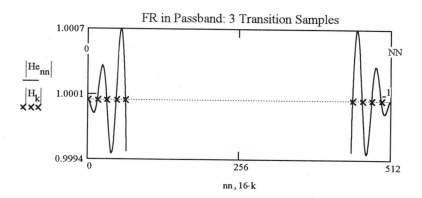

FR in Passband: 3 Transition Samples

$nn, 16 \cdot k$

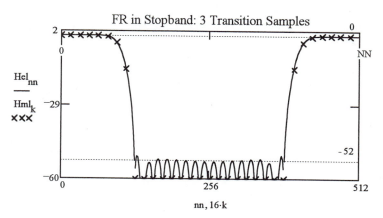

FR in Stopband: 3 Transition Samples

$nn, 16 \cdot k$

We regard the solution achieved with three transition samples as a "good" design. In fact, we will later use it to illustrate a practical smoothing filter in an interpolation scheme.

EXERCISE 10.3 Repeat Exercise 10.1, now varying the three frequency samples. You should be able to achieve a passband ripple as low as 0.1% and a nearly equiripple stopband ripple of -60 db - but not simultaneously! ¤

EXERCISE 10.4 With the above-cited criteria for good design in mind, compare the frequency response magnitudes of (i) this design by frequency sampling, (ii) the 5x7 filter and (iii) the simple MA FIR. ¤

EXERCISE 10.5 Make a pole-zero plot for the FIR filter with three transition samples and plot the phase of the FR. ¤

EXERCISE 10.6 Change the FIR length. How do these results change? ¤

A Related High-Pass Filter

Bandpass and high-pass filters can be designed directly by the frequency sampling method. Interesting examples are considered in the Projects. However, it is worth noting that there is a simple way to get a high-pass filter design from a low-pass filter design. Imagine a low-pass FR $H1_{lo}(\omega)$ that is translated by π: We may guess that this would define the FR of a high-pass filter $H_{hi}(\omega)=H1_{lo}(\omega-\pi)$.

Example 10.1 _____

We apply this idea to the low-pass filter we have designed above. Note that because N was even, shifting $H1(\omega)$ by π is equivalent to shifting the frequency samples by N/2. This can readily be done using the periodicity of both.

$$\text{pod}(nn, NN) := \text{mod}(NN + \text{mod}(nn, NN), NN)$$

$$H_{hi_{nn}} := He_{\text{pod}\left(nn - \frac{NN}{2}, NN\right)} \qquad Hm_{hi_{nn}} := \left| H_{hi_{nn}} \right|$$

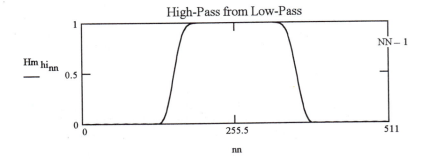

High-Pass from Low-Pass

$$h_{hi} := \frac{1}{\sqrt{NN}} \cdot \text{cfft}\left(H_{hi} \right)$$

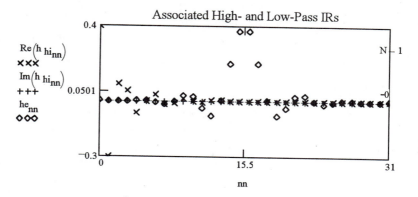

Associated High- and Low-Pass IRs

We see that the IR of the high-pass filter is in fact real and has a simple relation to the IR of the low-pass filter. We state it in the following problem. ‡

PROBLEM 10.2

Given the FR H1(ω) of a real IR, prove that H1a(ω)=H1($\omega-\pi$) is Hermitian symmetric and that the real IR ha_n is equal to $(-1)^n h_n$. ‡

Project 10.1

Using the frequency sampling method for FIR design, design a low-pass filter that differentiates in the band $(-\pi/4,\pi/4)$. The designed filter should conform closely to the criteria for good design discussed above. You will discover that a transition region is needed. Illustrate your design by differentiating an interesting signal. Also illustrate your design by differentiating an interesting long signal, using fast convolution - either the overlap-add or overlap-save method. ‡

Project 10.2

A **bank of filters** is used as part of a **real-time spectral estimator**, which estimates the energy in a set of frequency bands defined as follows.

Band # 1   800 - 1200 Hz
Band # 2   1200 - 1600 Hz
Band # 3   1600 - 2000 Hz

The analog waveform, whose spectrum is to be so analyzed, has negligible frequency content above 3200 Hz. A set of three FIR filters is to be designed, one for each band, by the method of frequency sampling.

Complete the design specifications. Design the set of filters and identify all critical parameters. State clearly your reasons for all choices. Simulate your design with an interesting signal. ‡

Project 10.3

 Two FIR filters are to be used, in parallel, as a **crossover network** in an audio system. One, a low-pass filter, is connected to a **woofer**; the other, a high-pass filter, is connected to a **tweeter**. Each filter must protect the other's speaker from out-of-band energy. The overall network frequency response should be as smooth as possible. Assume the following parameters:

sampling frequency	32 KHz
crossover frequency	2 KHz
high-pass FIR FR	-30 db @ 1 KHz
low-pass FIR FR	-30 db @ 4 KHz

Design the FIR filters by the method of frequency sampling, clearly explaining all critical parameters and design choices. Simulate your design with an interesting signal. ‡

References

Jackson (1996), Sec. 9.2
Proakis and Manolakis (1996), Sec. 8.2.3

11 FIR Design for SSB-AM Communications

Communication systems are one of the most important areas of application of DSP. The application of digital communication techniques is expanding rapidly and this area's needs are a driving force in the application and development of DSP. Digital processing systems are now replacing traditional analog processing systems, sometimes in system components such as receivers. We apply skills learned to this point to a significant filter design problem that arises in a specific analog communication system design.

Single-Sideband Waveform

A common analog communication method is amplitude modulation (AM). Conventional AM broadcast radio requires a bandwidth twice that of the modulation waveform m(t). However, there is a special type of AM modulation, called single-sideband amplitude modulation (SSB-AM) that requires only half the bandwidth of conventional AM, albeit needing a more complicated receiver. In principle, an SSB-AM waveform is derived from a double-sideband amplitude modulated waveform with a filter that removes one of the sidebands. In practice, it is easier to construct an economical filter when the modulation does not have very low frequencies - as in voice or telephone transmission.

The SSB-AM transmitter can use a phase-shift method to generate the single-sideband waveform, given the modulation m(t). The following scheme is called a Hartley modulator.

1. A local oscillator has an output, $\cos(v_c t)$, called the **in-phase carrier**. The local oscillator output is passed through a $\pi/2$ **phase shifter**, producing the **quadrature carrier** $\sin(v_c t)$.

2. The **modulation** m(t) is also passed through a $\pi/2$ phase shifter. Its output is called the **Hilbert transform, HT**, $m_H(t)$, of m(t).

3. The modulation is **mixed** with (multiplied by) the in-phase carrier to form $m(t)\cos(v_c t)$. The Hilbert transform $m_H(t)$ is mixed with the quadrature carrier to form $m_H(t)\sin(v_c t)$.

4. The last two waveforms are summed to form the **single-sideband amplitude modulated (SSB-AM)** waveform.

The π/2 phase shifter is called a **Hilbert transform** filter.

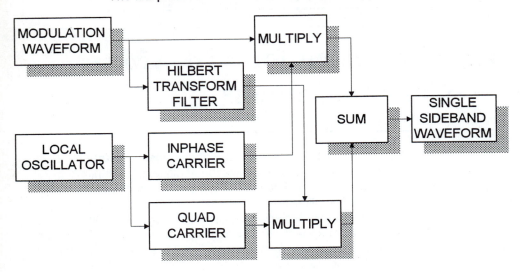

We will perform the Hartley modulator operations with a digital signal processor. The processor's input is the sampled modulation and its output, a single-sideband sequence, is converted to an analog waveform for transmission.

We now see how the π/2 phase shift operation on the sampled sequence can be interpreted as a digital filtering. Consider first a sampled modulation that is the cosine sequence

$$m_n = \frac{1}{2} \cdot \left(e^{i \cdot \omega 1 \cdot n} + e^{-i \cdot \omega 1 \cdot n} \right)$$

It has a DTFT that is the sum of the δ-functions located at ω=ω1 and ω=-ω1:

$$M1(\omega) = \pi \cdot (\delta(\omega - \omega 1) + \delta(\omega + \omega 1))$$

The π/2 phase-shifted sequence is the sine sequence

$$m_H(t) = \frac{1}{2} \cdot \left[e^{i \cdot \left(\omega 1 \cdot n - \frac{\pi}{2} \right)} + e^{-i \cdot \left(\omega 1 \cdot n - \frac{\pi}{2} \right)} \right]$$

Because exp(-iπ/2)=-i and exp(iπ/2)=1,

$$m_H(t) = \frac{-i}{2} \cdot \left(e^{i \cdot \omega 1 \cdot n} - e^{-i \cdot \omega 1 \cdot n} \right)$$

which has DTFT

$$M1_H(t) = -i \cdot \pi \cdot (\delta(\omega - \omega 1) - \delta(\omega + \omega 1))$$

We observe that $M1_H(\omega)$ is obtained from $M1(\omega)$ by multiplying by $-i$ and by **sgn(ω)**, which is the sign of ω and called the **signum** function. We interpret this factor, $-i$ sgn(ω), as the FR of a linear filter. Then we may write

$$M1_H(\omega) = (-i \cdot sgn(\omega)) \cdot M1(\omega)$$

This relation holds in general: Since a sampled, real modulation can be represented by a weighted sum of cosine sequences and since the $\pi/2$ phase shifter is realized by a linear filter, we have a general description of the latter's operation on the former.

FIR Hilbert Transform Filter Design

Thus we wish to design a digital Hilbert transform filter. Its frequency response (DTFT) has a period 2π and ideally is to be

$$H1(\omega) = -i \cdot sgn(\omega) \qquad , -\pi < \omega < \pi \qquad (11.1)$$

We already have enough experience to know that the discontinuity at $\omega = 0$ can only be approximated with a practical filter. To allow a transition region, we assume that very low frequencies are not present in the modulation.

EXERCISE 11.1 Show that $H1(\omega)$ defined by (11.1) is Hermitian symmetric. ¤

We seek an FIR design whose linear phase can be chosen to make the filter causal. If we choose a Type III or Type IV filter, we get the $\pi/2$ phase shift that we need. Both types have a zero necessarily at $\omega = 0$; also, the Type III has a zero at $\omega = \pi$. We assume that the expected signal sequence frequencies are in the band (ω_1, ω_2), where $0 < \omega_1 < \omega_2 < \pi$. We assume we may use otherwise unspecified bands for transition bands.

So, the problem we pose is the design of an FIR filter by the frequency sampling method. The filter is to compute the Hilbert transform over a specified band of frequencies $0 < \omega_1 < \omega_2 < \pi$. A Type III with zeros necessarily at $\omega = 0$ and $\omega = \pi$ is chosen. The desired frequency response is, imposing Hermitian symmetry,

$$H1(\omega) = -i \quad , \; 0 < \omega_1 < \omega < \omega_2 < \pi \,, \quad H1(\omega) = \overline{H1(2 \cdot \pi - \omega)}$$

First we define the magnitude Hm(ω) of the frequency response H1(ω). The magnitude must be even. We assume a filter length N=(M+1) and assume, for simplicity, that ω_1 and ω_2 are expressible as (2π/N)k, where k is an integer. We shall use the art of the design method that we learned in designing a low-pass filter to make a good initial choice of transition samples. Our choice can later be modified by trial and error as needed.

frequency sample index:
$$M := 32 \qquad N := M + 1 \qquad k := 0 .. N - 1$$

band frequencies:
$$\omega_1 := \frac{2 \cdot \pi}{N} \cdot 4 \qquad \omega_2 := \frac{2 \cdot \pi}{N} \left(\frac{N - 1}{2} - 4 \right)$$

half-range frequency index:
$$kk := 0 .. \frac{N - 1}{2}$$

frequency samples:
$$Hm_{kk} := if\left[(kk \geq 4) \cdot \left(kk \leq \frac{N - 1}{2} - 4 \right), 1, 0 \right]$$

transition region frequency samples:
$$Hm_3 := 0.97 \qquad Hm_2 := 0.7 \qquad Hm_1 := 0.2$$

$$Hm_{\frac{N-1}{2} - 3} := 0.98 \qquad Hm_{\frac{N-1}{2} - 2} := 0.707 \qquad Hm_{\frac{N-1}{2} - 1} := 0.2$$

This magnitude is multiplied by $-i \, sgn(\omega)$. Of course, $sgn(\omega)=1$ for ω in [0,π].

signum factor:
$$H_{kk} := -i \cdot Hm_{kk}$$

Now we include the phase necessary for causality and complete the definition of the frequency samples over the range of ω from 0 to π.

causal phase:
$$ph_{kk} := \frac{-(N - 1)}{N} \cdot kk \cdot \pi \qquad H_{kk} := H_{kk} \cdot exp\left(i \cdot ph_{kk} \right)$$

We complete the definition of the frequency samples by imposing Hermitian symmetry.

Hermitian symmetry:
$$H_k := if\left(k \leq \frac{N - 1}{2}, H_k, \overline{H_{N - k}} \right)$$

We compute the impulse response h.

$$idft(v) := \left(\frac{1}{\sqrt{N}}\right) \cdot cfft(v) \qquad\qquad h := idft(H)$$

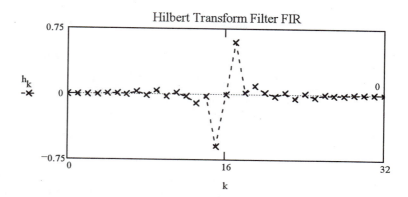

Hilbert Transform Filter FIR

EXERCISE 11.2 Verify that the IR h is real and odd about its midpoint. ¤

PROBLEM 11.1

Compute the IR of the ideal Hilbert transform FR (11.1). Plot it with a suitable translation and compare with the IR h of our design. ‡

We now find the interpolated frequency response by first zero padding the sequence to a longer length and then computing the DFT.

$$NN := 8 \cdot N \qquad\qquad nn := 0 .. NN - 1 \qquad\qquad dft(v) := \sqrt{NN} \cdot icfft(v)$$

$$he_{nn} := if\left(nn < N, h_{nn}, 0\right) \qquad\qquad He := dft(he) \qquad\qquad \delta := 10^{-4}$$

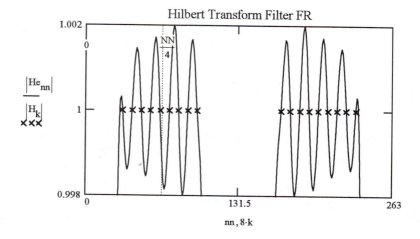

Hilbert Transform Filter FR

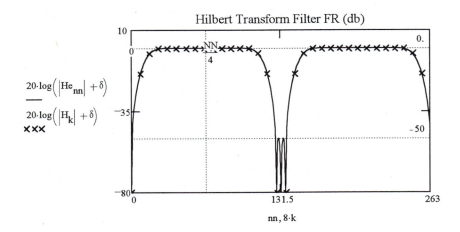

Hilbert Transform Filter FR (db)

$$\frac{20 \cdot \log\left(\left|He_{nn}\right| + \delta\right)}{20 \cdot \log\left(\left|H_k\right| + \delta\right)}$$
$\times\times\times$

nn, 8·k

Thus, using three transition samples in each transition region results in an apparently good frequency response. There is about a 0.2% ripple in the passband and a maximum response of -50 db near ω=0 and ω=π. We shall see whether the filter design is adequate by simulating its use in an SSB-AM modulator.

▨   **EXERCISE 11.3** Plot the phase of the FR and verify that it is piecewise linear. ¤

PROBLEM 11.2 Make a pole-zero plot for this design and verify that the zeros occur in the allowed quadruplets, doublets and singlets of a Type III FIR. ‡

Hilbert Transform Filter Test

We can check the operation of our filter design by using it to compute the Hilbert transform of a sequence for which we know the exact Hilbert transform.

First we synthesize a simple signal and compute its Hilbert transform, using our filter.

$$N := 256 \quad n := 0..N-1 \qquad mod_n := \cos\left(\frac{2 \cdot \pi}{N} \cdot 32 \cdot n\right) + 2 \cdot \cos\left(\frac{2 \cdot \pi}{N} \cdot 40 \cdot n\right)$$

Note Choosing the frequencies of the modulation sequence in the form $(2\pi/N)k$, k integer, renders verisimilitude to the DFT of the finite sequence in suggesting the DTFT of the infinite sequence. That is, the locations of the nonzero values of the DFT occur at the scaled locations of the impulse functions of the DTFT.

EXERCISE 11.4 Show that the Hilbert transform of $\cos(\omega_o n)$ is $\sin(\omega_o n)$ using a simple trigonometric identity. ¤

Thus, the known Hilbert transform of the modulation is

$$\text{mod}_{\text{Hex}_n} := \sin\left(\frac{2\cdot\pi}{N}\cdot 32\cdot n\right) + 2\cdot\sin\left(\frac{2\cdot\pi}{N}\cdot 40\cdot n\right)$$

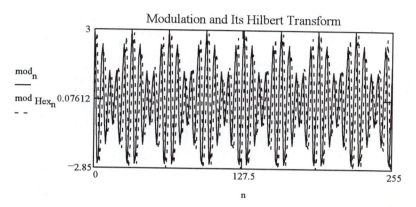

Modulation and Its Hilbert Transform

mod_n

$\text{mod}_{\text{Hex}_n}$ 0.07612

We now examine the spectral content of the modulation and its known Hilbert transform.

$$\text{dft}(v) := \sqrt{N}\cdot\text{icfft}(v) \quad \text{MOD} := \text{dft}(\text{mod}) \qquad \text{MOD}_{\text{Hex}} := \text{dft}\left(\text{mod}_{\text{Hex}}\right)$$

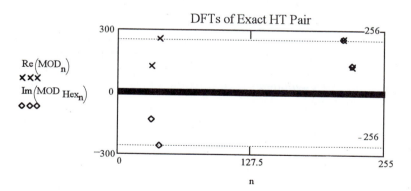

DFTs of Exact HT Pair

$\text{Re}\left(\text{MOD}_n\right)$
×××
$\text{Im}\left(\text{MOD}_{\text{Hex}_n}\right)$
◇◇◇

EXERCISE 11.5 Compute the DTFTs of $\cos(\omega_o n)$ and its Hilbert transform $\sin(\omega_o n)$. Show that the first is purely real and the second purely imaginary. ¤

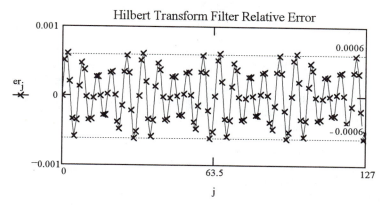

Hilbert Transform Filter Relative Error

The FIR filter is thus approximating the Hilbert transform to within about 0.06% error on this particular modulation. We plot their DFTs below.

$$\text{SMOD}_H := \text{dft}\left(\text{smod}_H\right) \qquad \text{SMOD}_{Hexd} := \text{dft}\left(\text{smod}_{Hexd}\right)$$

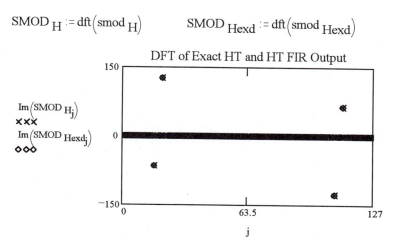

DFT of Exact HT and HT FIR Output

▦ **EXERCISE 11.6** Try other modulation forms and examine the resulting error. ¤

SSB-AM Modulator Simulation

We can arrange a simulation of our filter in the Hartley modulator and see if we do get a sampled SSB-AM waveform to good accuracy. We use a convenient carrier frequency. Also, because the HT FIR has a delay of M/2, we delay the modulation itself by M/2.

SSB-AM carrier:

$$k_{AM} := 25 \qquad \omega_{AM} := \frac{2 \cdot \pi}{J} \cdot k_{AM}$$

modulation segment with filter delay:	$$\text{smod}_j := \text{mod}_{(j+J)} - \frac{M}{2}$$	
DSB-AM (in-phase):	$$\text{sinph}_j := \text{smod}_j \cdot \cos\left(\omega_{AM} \cdot j\right)$$	$$\text{SINPH} := \text{dft}(\text{sinph})$$
DSB-AM (quadrature phase):	$$\text{squad}_j := \text{smod}_{H_j} \cdot \sin\left(\omega_{AM} \cdot j\right)$$	$$\text{SQUAD} := \text{dft}(\text{squad})$$
SSB-AM (sampled) waveform:	$$\text{ssb}_j := \text{sinph}_j + \text{squad}_j$$	$$\text{SSB} := \text{dft}(\text{ssb})$$

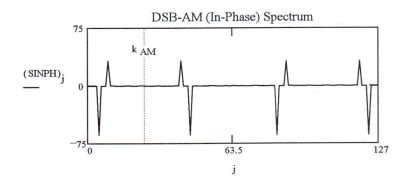

DSB-AM (In-Phase) Spectrum

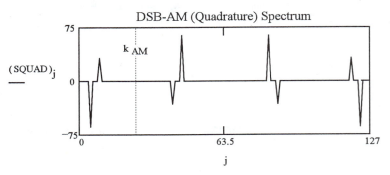

DSB-AM (Quadrature) Spectrum

We see the DSB-AM spectra in the in-phase and quadrature waveforms, centered on the carrier ωc.

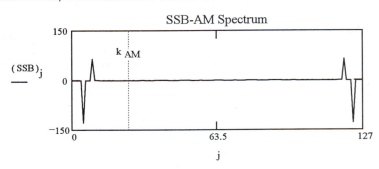

SSB-AM Spectrum

Thus we have an SSB-AM sequence on the carrier ωc. We replot the spectrum on a log scale to examine the fine detail.

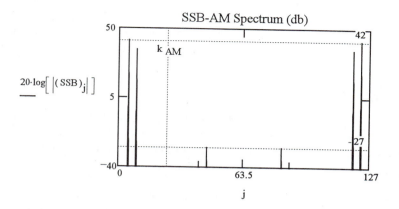

SSB-AM Spectrum (db)

The quality of the filter's generation of an SSB-AM sequence by the filter appears to be very good. The undesired upper sideband is about -70 db relative to the desired lower sideband.

EXERCISE 11.7 Show that the difference of the in-phase and quadrature waveforms results in an SSB-AM waveform with the upper sideband of the DSB-AM waveform. ¤

PROBLEM 11.3 Make up a small table of Hilbert transforms, starting with these. You might also like to establish some properties. Is it linear? Is it causal? Is it invariant? ‡

h_n	$HT\{h_n\}$
$\delta(n)$	$(n\neq 0)\cdot\dfrac{\cos(\pi\cdot n)-1}{2\cdot\pi n}$
$\exp\left(i\cdot\omega_0\cdot n\right)$	$\exp\left(i\cdot\omega_0\cdot n\right)\cdot\left(-i\cdot\operatorname{sgn}\left(\omega_0\right)\right)$
$\cos\left(\omega_0\cdot n\right)$	$\sin\left(\omega_0\cdot n\right)$
$\sin\left(\omega_0\cdot n\right)$	$-\cos\left(\omega_0\cdot n\right)$

Project 11.1

Design a Hilbert transform FIR filter of length 31 and compare to the designs in the second reference at the end of the chapter. ‡

Project 11.2

 Model and simulate a coherent receiver for SSB-AM. Explain why it works. What is the effect when the local oscillator has a frequency and/or phase error? Use the method of design by frequency sampling to design the required low-pass filter. ‡

Project 11.3

The bandwidth efficiency of SSB-AM has led to its use in analog telephone coaxial transmission systems. In applications such as television the bandwidth efficiency is a desirable property, but video waveforms have very low frequencies. To make a practical filter possible, the technique of vestigial-sideband modulation, VSB-AM, is employed. It is also proposed for use in the HDTV system. It imposes a certain restraint on the filter (Gibson, Sec. 5.4). Repeat the considerations of this chapter, including filter design by the method of frequency sampling, for a VSB-AM system. ‡

References

Gibson (1993), Sec 5.4, Figure P.5.19
Proakis and Manolakis (1996), Sec 8.2.6

12 FIR Design by Windows

As we have seen at several points, particularly in the design of a low-pass filter by the frequency sampling method (**Chapter 10**), low sidelobe levels in the frequency response magnitude of an FIR filter have occurred in conjunction with a taper in the IR. We could view this taper as being achieved by multiplying the sin(n)/n-type response - associated with the ideal low-pass frequency response - by a window sequence that produces the taper. Thus we are led to the idea of attempting to directly choose such a taper, or **window**, sequence that will result in some desirable attributes of the frequency response magnitude of the FIR filter.

Convolution in Frequency: Animation

Multiplication of the window sequence by the ideal low-pass filter's FIR is profitably viewed alternatively in the frequency domain. As we know (**Property 7.8**), multiplication of these two sequences in the time domain results in the (periodic) convolution of the DTFT of the window with the ideal filter's frequency response, FR. After a bit of thought, we see that such an operation could perform a smoothing of the ideal filter's FR. Certainly it will remove the discontinuity present in the ideal filter's FR. In fact, if the window's DTFT is narrow relative to the bandwidth of ideal frequency response, we can anticipate that the transition region width will be about that of the window's DTFT mainlobe. And we can expect that the resultant ripple of the filter will be roughly equal in the passband and the stopband. Further, we expect that there will be sign changes in the window's DTFT: It is a rational function of $\exp(i\omega)$. This should result in the filter's ripple being somewhat less than the ripple of the window's DTFT: We expect some averaging in the convolution summation.

Example 12.1 _____

We recall the periodic convolution in the frequency domain that results when we multiply two sequences together in the time domain. Here we let the window sequence $\{w_n\}$ have DTFT $W1(\omega)$ and let the ideal low-pass filter's frequency response be $H1_i(\omega)$. Then the FR of the resulting filter is

periodic convolution (frequency domain):	$H1(\omega) = \dfrac{1}{2 \cdot \pi} \cdot \displaystyle\int_0^{2 \cdot \pi} W1(\omega - u) \cdot H1_I(u) \, du$

We assume that the window sequence is the constant 1 and of length M. Then its DTFT is found by modifying **Example 6.1**. However, we will set the phase, due to causality, to zero: then we will have purely real functions of ω to plot, which will be easier to understand.

window length: $\qquad M := 21$

noncausal window DTFT:
$$W1(\omega) := \text{if}\left[\omega=0, M, \frac{\sin\left(\dfrac{M}{2} \cdot \omega\right)}{\sin\left(\dfrac{1}{2} \cdot \omega\right)}\right]$$

The DTFT of the ideal low-pass filter is taken to be

ideal filter FR/DTFT:
$$H1_I(\omega) := \text{if}\left[\left(\omega \leq \frac{\pi}{2}\right) + \left(\omega \geq \frac{3 \cdot \pi}{2}\right), 1, 0\right] \qquad (0<=\omega<=2\pi)$$

We sample these sequences densely so that we will be able to make a plot of them and their periodic convolution.

frequency sample points: $\qquad N := 64 \qquad n := 0 .. N - 1 \qquad \omega_n := \dfrac{2 \cdot \pi}{N} \cdot n$

DTFT sample sequences: $\qquad W_n := W1(\omega_n) \qquad\qquad H_{I_n} := H1_I(\omega_n)$

$$pod(n, N) := \text{mod}(N + \text{mod}(n, N), N)$$

sampled periodic convolution (freq. domain):
$$H_n := \frac{1}{N} \cdot \sum_{m=0}^{N-1} W_{pod(n-m,N)} \cdot H_{I_m}$$

animation/movie frame variable: $\qquad F := \text{FRAME} \qquad F := 26$

animated, plotted output: $\qquad \text{Hplot}_n := \text{if}(n \leq F, H_n, -10)$

$m := 0 .. N - 1$

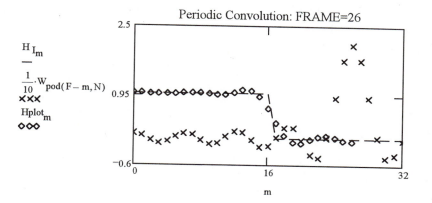

Periodic Convolution: FRAME=26

H_{I_m}
___

$\dfrac{1}{10} \cdot W_{pod}(F-m,N)$
✗✗✗

$Hplot_m$
◇◇◇

Note that we have plotted the DTFTs only to N/2 vice N-1. Also, values of the convolution for indices greater than FRAME have been set arbitrarily low so as to not appear on the plot. And we have scaled down the window's DTFT for better plot visibility. ‡

EXERCISE 12.1 Enter a special value of F in the range 0 to 32 to the right of its declaration as FRAME and push F9 to recompute the plot. Carefully note whether our predictions about the filter's FR were accurate. After you thoroughly understand this exercise, *remove all special declarations of F other than as FRAME.* ¤

We can now create an animation of Exercise 12.1. Be sure that F is declared only as FRAME above. Remember that the **Math** mode must be **Automatic Mode**. Select **Window**, then **Animation**, then **Create...** from the menu above, obtaining the Create Animation dialogue box to set up the animation parameters. Enclose the above plot by dragging the mouse across it. Then, in the dialogue box, set up the desired range of the FRAME variable. Choose FRAME to run from 0 to 32 for the animation. Then select **Animate**; the creation of the animation will take several seconds, depending on your computer. A **Playback** window will appear on the screen and you can play the animation and also step it through the frames. If desired, use **Save as...** to save the animation file for later playback. The resulting file size is 438 Kbytes.

EXERCISE 12.2 Playback the animation step-by-step and repeat the analysis of Exercise12.1. ¤

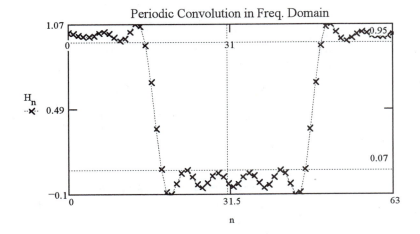

We conclude that our predictions of the effect of convolving the window's DTFT with the ideal low-pass filter's frequency response are borne out generally.

We will define and study properties of some of the common windows that have been proposed and used in DSP filter design practice. Then we will discuss how they can be employed in FIR filter design. These windows are also useful in another context, that of spectral estimation. (Recall the discussion in **Chapter 7**.) Windows are also discussed in conjunction with spectral density estimation (**Chapter 26**).

Windows

We will discuss some simple windows that are common in DSP. They each have a fixed shape and a single parameter M that determines their length. We can observe that their DTFTs' mainlobe width is inversely proportional to M, but their relative sidelobe level is independent of M. This discussion will lead us naturally to the problem of designing an optimal window (**Chapter 13**).

Rectangular Window

Of course, merely truncating a sequence is equivalent to multiplying the sequence by a finite sequence of uniform values. We call such a sequence, in this context, a **rectangular** window. We take its length as M+1.

$$M := 32 \qquad m := 0..M \qquad wR_m := \frac{1}{M+1}$$

As usual, we see the DTFT to sufficient detail by zero padding the sequence to sufficient length.

$$N := 32 \cdot (M+1) \quad n := 0..N-1 \qquad weR_n := \text{if}\left(n \leq M, wR_n, 0\right)$$

$$dft(v) := \sqrt{N} \cdot \text{icfft}(v) \qquad WR := dft\left(weR\right) \qquad Wm_n := \left| WR_n \right|$$

$$\delta := 10^{-6} \qquad WdbR_n := 20 \cdot \log\left(\frac{Wm_n}{\max(Wm)} + \delta\right)$$

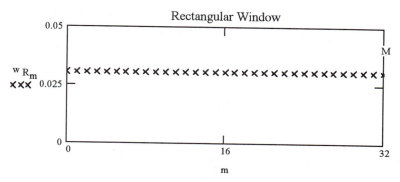

Rectangular Window

Location of first zero:

$$\omega R := \frac{2 \cdot \pi}{M+1} \qquad \omega_n := n \cdot \frac{2 \cdot \pi}{N}$$

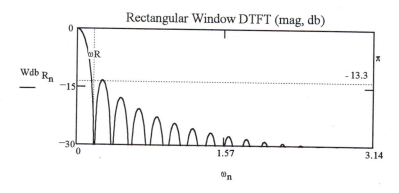

Rectangular Window DTFT (mag, db)

Note that we have plotted the frequency response only to π.

We see that the first null, a measure of the width of the window's DTFT, is $2\pi/(M+1)$. We will use this as a reference as it is the narrowest of the window types we will discuss. Also, we note that the first and highest sidelobe level is -13.3 db. This will be seen to be the highest level of the window types we will discuss.

 ▦ **EXERCISE 12.3** Compute the relative energy between the **first zeros** - the positive zero nearest ω=zero and the negative zero nearest ω=zero - when W_R is plotted for ω over ($-\pi,\pi$). ¤

PROBLEM 12.1 Recall that the DFT of a finite length (M) uniform sequence was computed in Problem 3.3 and used in Example 6.1 to get the DTFT, eq. (6.7a). Plot (6.7a) and compare it to the DTFT computed numerically here. ‡

Triangular Window

One obvious way to lower the relative sidelobes of a frequency response magnitude is by simply squaring it. In the time domain, this corresponds to convolving the rectangular window with itself, resulting in a **triangular** window.

$$w_{T_m} := if\left(m < \frac{M}{2}, m, M - m\right)$$

Note that the length of this sequence is actually M-1. The DTFT is found to sufficient detail by zero padding the sequence to sufficient length.

$$we_{T_n} := if\left(n \le M, w_{T_n}, 0\right)$$

$$W_T := dft\left(we_T\right) \qquad Wm_n := \left|W_{T_n}\right| \qquad Wdb_{T_n} := 20 \cdot log\left(\frac{Wm_n}{max(Wm)} + \delta\right)$$

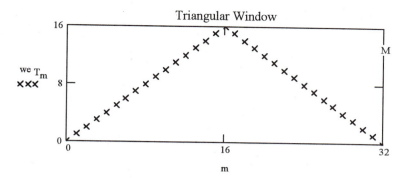

Triangular Window

Location of first zero:
$$\omega T := 2 \cdot \frac{2 \cdot \pi}{M}$$

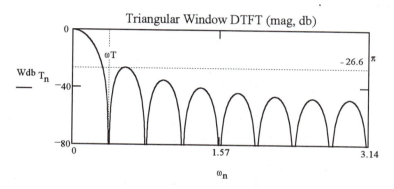

Triangular Window DTFT (mag, db)

Note that we have plotted the frequency response only to π.

We see that the first null, a measure of the width of the window's DTFT, is twice $2\pi/M$, close to our expectation. Also, we note that the first and highest sidelobe level is -26.6 db, exactly as we expect.

EXERCISE 12.4 Compute the relative energy between the first zeros when W_T is plotted for ω over $(-\pi,\pi)$. ¤

PROBLEM 12.2 Compute the DTFT of the triangular window, plot it and compare it to the numerical computation here. ‡

Hanning Window

Another common window is the **Hanning**, or **raised cosine**, window. Note that its length is actually M-1.

$$\text{w}\,\text{C}_m := \frac{1}{2} \cdot \left(1 - \cos\left(\frac{2 \cdot \pi}{M} \cdot m\right) \right)$$

We compute the DTFT of this window.

$$\text{we}\,\text{C}_n := \text{if}\left(n \leq M, \text{w}\,\text{C}_n, 0 \right)$$

$$\text{W}\,\text{C} := \text{dft}\left(\text{we}\,\text{C}\right) \qquad \text{Wm}_n := \left| \text{W}\,\text{C}_n \right| \qquad \text{Wdb}\,\text{C}_n := 20 \cdot \log\left(\frac{\text{Wm}_n}{\max(\text{Wm})} + \delta \right)$$

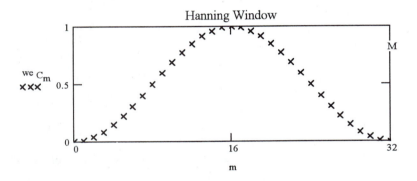

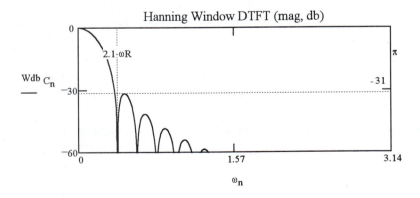

Note that we have plotted the frequency response only to π.

We see, by trial and error using the plot markers, that the first null, a measure of the width of the window's DTFT, is a little more than twice $2\pi/(M+1)$ - nearly the same as the triangular window. Relative to the triangular window, one could say that the Hanning window has less taper near its center but more severe taper near its edges. Also, we note that the first and highest sidelobe level is -31 db, lower than that of the triangular window.

EXERCISE 12.5 Compute the relative energy between the first zeros when W_C is plotted for ω over $(-\pi,\pi)$. ¤

PROBLEM 12.3 Compute the DTFT of the Hanning window, plot it and compare it to the numerical computation here. Which method do you prefer? ‡

Hamming Window

The **Hamming** window is a modification of the Hanning window and is of length M+1.

$$w M_m := 0.54 - 0.46 \cdot \cos\left(\frac{2 \cdot \pi}{M} \cdot m\right)$$

We compute the DTFT of this window.

$$we M_n := if\left(n \leq M, w M_n, 0\right)$$

$$W M := dft\left(we M\right) \quad Wm_n := \left|W M_n\right| \quad Wdb M_n := 20 \cdot \log\left(\frac{Wm_n}{max(Wm)} + \delta\right)$$

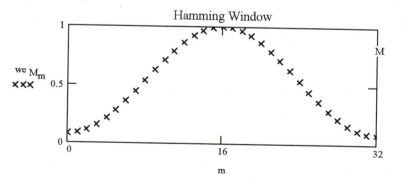

Hamming Window

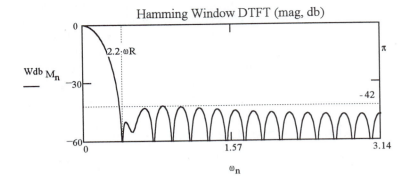

Hamming Window DTFT (mag, db)

Note that we have plotted the frequency response only to π.

We see that the first null, a measure of the width of the window's DTFT, is about 2.2 times $2\pi/(M+1)$. Also, we note that the highest sidelobe level is -42 db. Note that the highest sidelobe peak is not the first sidelobe; the stopband is roughly equiripple.

EXERCISE 12.6 Compute the relative energy between the first zeros when W_M is plotted for ω over $(-\pi,\pi)$. ¤

PROBLEM 12.4 Compute the DTFT of the Hamming window, plot it and compare it to the numerical computation here. Which method do you prefer? ‡

Blackman Window

The **Blackman** window is a modification of the Hanning or Hamming window and is of length M-1.

$$w_{B_m} := 0.42 - 0.5 \cdot \cos\left(\frac{2\cdot\pi}{M}\cdot m\right) + 0.08\cdot\cos\left(\frac{4\cdot\pi}{M}\cdot m\right)$$

We compute the DTFT of this window.

$$we_{B_n} := if\left(n \le M, w_{B_n}, 0\right)$$

$$W_B := dft\left(we_B\right) \quad Wm_n := \left|W_{B_n}\right| \quad Wdb_{B_n} := 20\cdot\log\left(\frac{Wm_n}{\max(Wm)} + \delta\right)$$

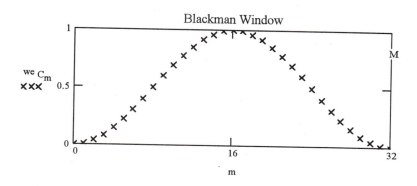
Blackman Window

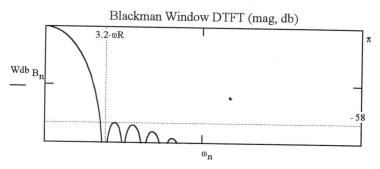
Blackman Window DTFT (mag, db)

Note that we have plotted the frequency response only to π.

We see that the first null, a measure of the width of the window's DTFT, is about 3.2 times $2\pi/(M+1)$. Also, we note that the first and highest sidelobe level is -58 db. This window, or FIR, has a frequency response magnitude with a very low sidelobe level, but a large cost in transition region width is evident.

EXERCISE 12.7 Compute the relative energy between the first zeros when W_B is plotted for ω over $(-\pi,\pi)$. ¤

PROBLEM 12.5 Compute the DTFT of the Blackman window, plot it and compare it to the numerical computation here. Which method do you prefer? ‡

EXERCISE 12.8 Verify the following tabular entries for window attributes, using the above results. Vary M and note the results, especially the cases of M odd or even. ¤

TABLE I

attribute	window type				
	rect	triang	Han	Ham	Black
max sidelobe of window	-13.3	-26.6	-31	-42	-58
first null (relative) of window	1	2	2.1	2.2	3.2

PROBLEM 12.6 Try your own hand at designing a window. Note its attributes and compare them to those in Table I. ‡

FIR Design Procedure

We can now summarize the basic ideas of windows use in FIR design. A practical FIR filter design incorporates a transition region. The width of this region is matched to the mainlobe width of the window's DTFT: this determines the window's - and hence the FIR filter's - length. The ideal filter's cutoff frequency is centered in the transition region. The sidelobe specification determines the allowable window types, and generally the shortest FIR is chosen.

This design method results in the following tabulation of (i) filter sidelobe level achieved and (ii) the width of the transition region, relative to that of the rectangular window. Notice that the latter is generally larger than estimated in Table I.

TABLE II

attribute	window type				
	rect	triang	Han	Ham	Black
max sidelobe of filter	-21	-27	-44	-53	-74
first null (relative) of filter, f	0.9	1.8	3.1	3.3	5.5

Thus, based on this experience, the window (and FIR) length is given by

$$M = f \cdot \frac{2 \cdot \pi}{\Delta}$$

(12.1)

where, if ωc is the edge of the passband and ωr is the start of the stopband, the width Δ of the transition region is

$$\Delta = \omega r - \omega c$$

Example 12.2

We design a low-pass filter with specifications that lead us to select a window with a Hamming weighting.

passband cutoff frequency:	$\omega c := \dfrac{2 \cdot \pi}{10}$
stopband frequency:	$\omega r := \dfrac{3}{2} \cdot \omega c$
transition region bandwidth:	$\Delta := \omega r - \omega c$
passband cutoff (ideal filter):	$\omega tr := \dfrac{\omega r + \omega c}{2}$
stopband relative attenuation (db):	$A := 50$

From Table II we see that either a Hamming or a Blackman window would result in an FIR filter meeting the sidelobe specification, but we choose a Hamming window as it will be shorter. Then we use (12.1) to get the window and FIR length.

$$f := 3.3 \qquad M := f \cdot \frac{2 \cdot \pi}{\Delta} \qquad M = 66 \qquad M := ceil(M) \qquad M = 66$$

The Hamming window may now be defined.

$$n := 0 .. M \qquad w M_n := 0.54 - 0.46 \cdot \cos\left(\frac{2 \cdot \pi}{M} \cdot n\right)$$

The FIR filter designed to approximate the Hilbert transform computes

$$M := 32 \quad m := 0 .. M \qquad\qquad \mathrm{mod}\,H_n := \sum_m h_m \cdot \mathrm{if}\left(n - m < 0, 0, \mathrm{mod}_{n-m}\right)$$

The delayed (by M/2) version of the analytically computed Hilbert transform can be used for comparison.

$$\mathrm{mod}\,Hexd_n := \mathrm{if}\left(n - \frac{M}{2} < 0, 0, \mathrm{mod}\,Hex_{n - \frac{M}{2}}\right)$$

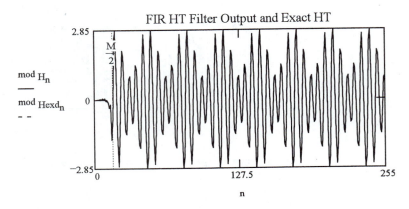

mod H_n

mod $Hexd_n$

- -

FIR HT Filter Output and Exact HT

We see that after an initial transient the FIR filter computes a very good approximation to the Hilbert transform.

It is of interest to take a segment of the transform and its approximation after the initial filter transient and examine the error. In practice, the filter would be operating on a very long data sequence.

subsequence index: $\qquad J := 128 \qquad j := 0 .. J - 1 \qquad \mathrm{dft}(v) := \sqrt{J} \cdot \mathrm{icfft}(v)$

subsequences: $\qquad \mathrm{smod}\,H_j := \mathrm{mod}\,H_{j+J} \qquad \mathrm{smod}\,Hexd_j := \mathrm{mod}\,Hexd_{j+J}$

normalized error: $\qquad er_j := \mathrm{smod}\,Hexd_j - \mathrm{smod}\,H_j \qquad er_j := \dfrac{er_j}{\max\left(\mathrm{smod}\,H\right)}$

We now truncate and weight the IR of the "ideal" low-pass filter hid.

IR of ideal low-pass filter:

$$hid_n := if\left[n = \frac{M}{2}, \frac{\omega tr}{\pi}, \frac{\sin\left[\omega tr \cdot \left(n - \frac{M}{2}\right)\right]}{\pi \cdot \left(n - \frac{M}{2}\right)}\right]$$

truncation with window:

$$h_n := hid_n \cdot w M_n$$

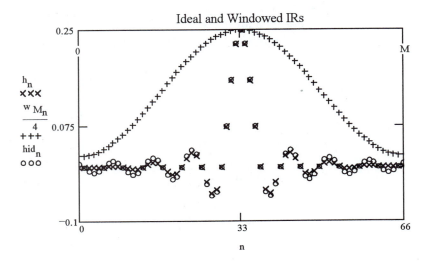

Ideal and Windowed IRs

To see greater detail in the frequency response, we zero pad h to a length 16*M. We first plot both the passband ripple and the stopband ripple on a linear scale.

$$K := 16 \cdot M \quad k := 0 .. K - 1 \quad he_k := if(k < M + 1, h_k, 0) \quad w_k := k \cdot \frac{2 \cdot \pi}{K}$$

$$dft(v) := \sqrt{K} \cdot icfft(v) \quad H := dft(he) \quad \varepsilon := 10^{-10} \quad H_k := if\left(\left|H_k\right| = 0, \varepsilon, H_k\right)$$

$$\omega c = 0.628 \qquad \omega r = 0.942$$

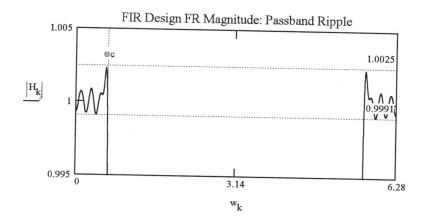

FIR Design FR Magnitude: Passband Ripple

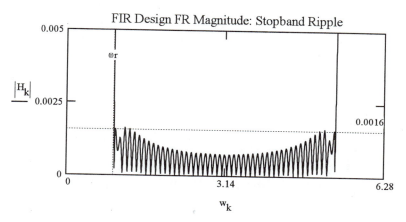

FIR Design FR Magnitude: Stopband Ripple

We see that the passband ripple is about 0.34% and the stopband ripple is about 0.32%: they are nearly equal, conforming to our prediction at the outset.

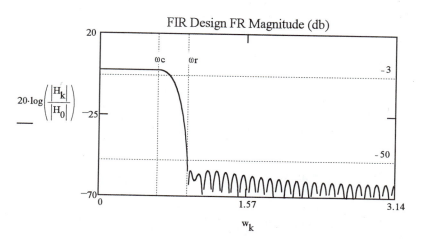

FIR Design FR Magnitude (db)

We see that the design meets the specification. However, it is not a tight design, in that the maximum sidelobe level is about -5 db below the stopband specification and the 3 db bandwidth of the passband is larger than required.

We plot the phase of the FIR filter.

$$\theta_0 := \arg\left(H_0\right) \qquad \theta_k := \text{if}\left(k{=}0, \theta_0, \theta_{k-1} + \arg\left(H_k \cdot \overline{H_{k-1}}\right)\right)$$

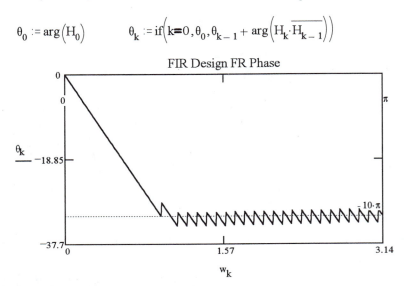

FIR Design FR Phase

As we expect, the FIR filter has a piecewise linear phase and is linear over the passband of the filter. ‡

Project 12.1

Using the windows method, design an FIR filter with piecewise linear phase that meets the following specifications:

passband cutoff frequency:	$\omega c := \dfrac{2 \cdot \pi}{10}$
stopband frequency:	$\omega r := 2 \cdot \omega c$
transition region bandwidth:	$\Delta := \omega r - \omega c$
passband cutoff of ideal filter:	$\omega tr := \dfrac{\omega r + \omega c}{2}$
stopband relative attenuation (db):	$A := 70$ ‡

Project 12.2

As in Project 12.1 except A = 50. ‡

Project 12.3

As in Project 12.1 except A = 40. ‡

Project 12.4

As in Project 12.1 except A = 25. ‡

Project 12.5

As in **Project 10.1** except use the method of windows. ‡

Project 12.6

As in **Project 10.2** except use the method of windows. ‡

Project 12.7

As in **Project 10.3** except use the method of windows. ‡

Project 12.8

As in **Project 11.1** except use the method of windows. ‡

Project 12.9

As in Example 12.1, create animations for the periodic convolution of the ideal low-pass FR with the DTFTs of the other windows discussed in this chapter. ‡

References

Jackson (1996), Sec. 9.1
Oppenheim and Schafer (1989), Secs. 7.4, 7.5
Proakis and Manolakis (1996), Sec. 8.2.2

13 FIR Design with an Optimal Window

We have now discussed several windows parametrized by their length (**Chapter 12**). Their use in FIR filter design resulted in a frequency response magnitude with low sidelobes, which came at the cost of a wider mainlobe and a greater length than the ideal filter. We now directly address the following problem: what window, for a given length, maximizes its DTFT content in a specified frequency band?

This specified band corresponds approximately to a specified transition region width in the FIR filter. If we could manage to contain all of the content of the DTFT in the specified band, there would be no sidelobes. But a window of finite length has a rational DTFT and therefore cannot be zero except at isolated points - so we cannot do that well. We choose to measure content of the DTFT by **energy**, the integral of the squared modulus. Such a choice is mathematically convenient and reasonable for our purpose. Thus, assuming that we can find these windows, they will be parametrized by (i) their length and (ii) the width of the low-pass band where we wish to contain as much of their energy as possible.

Optimal Window Criterion

Suppose the window is defined by the sequence $\{w_n, n=0,...,N-1\}$, which has DTFT $W1(\omega)$. The ratio of the energy of $W1(\omega)$ in a specified low-pass band $(-\Omega/2, \Omega/2)$ to the total energy of $W1(\omega)$ is

$$r = \frac{\dfrac{1}{2\cdot\pi}\cdot\displaystyle\int_{-\frac{\Omega}{2}}^{\frac{\Omega}{2}} \left(\left|W1(\omega)\right|\right)^2 d\omega}{\dfrac{1}{2\cdot\pi}\cdot\displaystyle\int_{-\pi}^{\pi} \left(\left|W1(\omega)\right|\right)^2 d\omega} \qquad (13.1)$$

where

$$W1(\omega)= \sum_{n=0}^{N-1} e^{-i\cdot\omega\cdot n}\cdot w_n \tag{13.2}$$

We want to maximize r by choice of the window sequence $\{w_n, n=0,...,N-1\}$, so we need to express (13.1) directly in terms of $\{w_n, n=0,...,N-1\}$. We use Parseval's relation to do this for the denominator.

$$\frac{1}{2\cdot\pi}\cdot\int_{-\pi}^{\pi} \left(\left|W1(\omega)\right|\right)^2 d\omega = \sum_{n=0}^{N-1} \left(\left|w_n\right|\right)^2 \tag{13.3}$$

In the numerator of (13.1), we substitute (13.2) and interchange the order of the finite sums with the integral. We then see that we need to evaluate the integral

$$\gamma_{n-m} = \frac{1}{2\cdot\pi}\cdot\int_{-\frac{\Omega}{2}}^{\frac{\Omega}{2}} e^{i\cdot\omega\cdot(n-m)}\,d\omega$$

We find analytically that when n=m, $\gamma_0 = \Omega/2\pi$ and, otherwise,

$$\gamma_{n-m} = \frac{\Omega}{2\cdot\pi}\cdot\frac{\sin\left[\frac{\Omega}{2}\cdot(n-m)\right]}{\frac{\Omega}{2}\cdot(n-m)} \tag{13.4}$$

Thus the numerator has the form

$$\sum_{n=0}^{N-1}\sum_{m=0}^{N-1} w_n\cdot w_m\cdot\gamma_{n-m}$$

and so

$$r = \frac{\displaystyle\sum_{n=0}^{N-1} \sum_{m=0}^{N-1} w_n \cdot w_m \cdot \gamma_{n-m}}{\displaystyle\sum_{n=0}^{N-1} (|w_n|)^2} \qquad (13.5)$$

Geometric View

Suppose we rewrite (13.5) in vector notation. Then the numerator is an inner product and the denominator is a squared norm:

$$r = \frac{w \cdot (\Gamma \cdot w)}{(|w|)^2} \qquad (13.6)$$

where the N-by-N matrix Γ has elements $\Gamma_{m,n} = \gamma_{m-n}$ that depend on (m,n) only as |m-n|. Thus Γ is symmetric and of a "stripe form" called a **Toeplitz** matrix, a matrix form that arises often in DSP.

As our first attempt to understand this **optimization problem**, consider the form (13.6) when w is replaced by u=w/|w|, a unit norm vector. Then

$$r = u \cdot (\Gamma \cdot u) \qquad (13.7)$$

If Γu were unit norm - it nearly will be, as we will see, when we have most of the relative energy in the desired band - then we should choose u, if possible, to make u and Γu colinear. After all, the inner product of two unit vectors is the cosine of the angle between them, which is maximized at angle zero. Thus we guess that we should choose u such that, for λ a constant,

$$\lambda \cdot u = \Gamma \cdot u \qquad \text{or} \qquad \lambda \cdot w = \Gamma \cdot w \qquad (13.8)$$

For an alternate argument for (13.8), recall the Cauchy-Schwarz Inequality, which states that for two vectors f and g,

$$\left(|f \cdot g| \right)^2 \le (|f|)^2 \cdot (|g|)^2 \qquad (13.9)$$

with equality if and only if

$$\lambda \cdot f = g \qquad (13.10)$$

where λ is a constant. Setting f=w and g=Γw in (13.9), taking the square root and dividing by the squared norm of w, we get

$$r \le |\lambda|_0 \tag{13.11}$$

where, by (13.10),

$$\lambda \cdot w = \Gamma \cdot w \tag{13.12}$$

The matrix equation (13.12) says that our desired solution has an **invariant direction** when multiplied by Γ: it is called a **characteristic**, or **eigen-**, **vector** of the matrix Γ. We recall some facts from linear algebra about symmetric matrices that are positive definite - note that r is a ratio of nonnegative numbers.

1. There are N solution pairs {(λ_n, w_n), n=0,...,N-1}, where the {λ_n, n=0,...,N-1} are called **characteristic**, or **eigen-**, **values**.
2. The characteristic values are real and may be ordered $0 < \lambda_N <= .... <= \lambda_0 <= 1$, the last inequality because r<=1.
3. The characteristic vectors {w_n, n=0,...,N-1} are real and orthogonal.

In view of (13.11), the solution to our problem is the sequence {w_0, n=0,...,N-1} and the attained value of r is λ_0.

Finding the solution is in fact generally a problem of numerical analysis. That is the case here. This is a much-studied problem, and good solution algorithms appear in many application software packages, including Mathcad. Indeed, this demonstrates one of the strengths of an interactive book written in a high-level mathematical programming language.

Optimal Window Computation

We illustrate the computation of a **maximum energy window**. We first define the matrix Γ.

$$N := 32 \qquad n := 0 .. N - 1 \qquad m := 0 .. N - 1 \qquad \Omega := \frac{2 \cdot \pi}{8}$$

$$\gamma(y) := \text{if}\left[y = 0, \frac{\Omega}{2 \cdot \pi}, \frac{\Omega}{2 \cdot \pi} \cdot \frac{\sin\left(\frac{\Omega}{2} \cdot y\right)}{\frac{\Omega}{2} \cdot y} \right] \qquad \Gamma_{m,n} := \gamma(m - n)$$

We now find the characteristic values and order them in decreasing size.

$\lambda := \text{eigenvals}(\Gamma)$

$L := \text{reverse}(\text{sort}(\lambda))$

$L =$

	0
0	0.999946
1	0.997657
2	0.960125
3	0.722844
4	0.273763
5	0.042175
6	$3.312594 \cdot 10^{-3}$
7	$1.707293 \cdot 10^{-4}$
8	$6.431638 \cdot 10^{-6}$
9	$1.856095 \cdot 10^{-7}$
10	$4.221797 \cdot 10^{-9}$
11	$7.72347 \cdot 10^{-11}$
12	$1.153914 \cdot 10^{-12}$

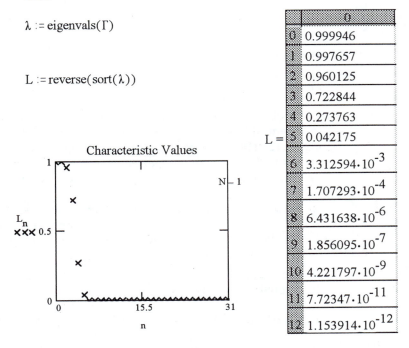

Characteristic Values

Clearly the first element of the sorted vector of characteristic values and its associated characteristic vector are the solution to our problem.

$\text{wopt} := \text{eigenvec}\left(\Gamma, L_0\right)$

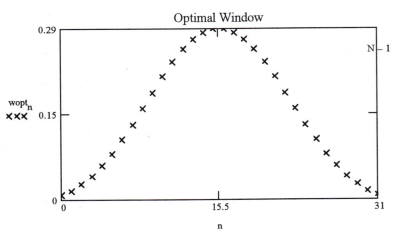

Optimal Window

As we may have expected, there is a pronounced taper to the window. The fraction of energy that is contained in the desired frequency interval seems quite large: 0.999 946!

The DTFT corresponding to the optimal window is computed to sufficient detail in the usual way by zero padding.

$$NN := 16 \cdot N \qquad nn := 0 .. NN - 1 \qquad we_{nn} := if\left(nn < N, wopt_{nn}, 0\right)$$

$$\omega_{nn} := \frac{2 \cdot \pi}{NN} \cdot nn \qquad dft(v) := \sqrt{NN} \cdot icfft(v)$$

$$Wel := dft(we) \qquad Wm_{nn} := \left| Wel_{nn} \right| \qquad Wm_{nn} := \frac{Wm_{nn}}{max(Wm)} + 10^{-8}$$

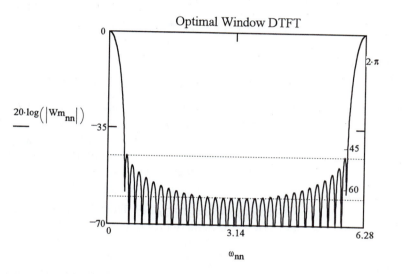

Optimal Window DTFT

EXERCISE 13.1 Choose various values of Ω and N and note the shape of the optimal window, the fraction of energy in the specified bandwidth and the sidelobe level of the window's DTFT. ¤

EXERCISE 13.2 For the same window length, and several Ω, make a comparison with the windows discussed in Chapter 12. Make clear your basis of comparison. ¤

It turns out that the maximum relative energy r depends on N and Ω approximately only as their **time-bandwidth product**, TBP=NΩ/2π. We delay a discussion of this until later. However, this is an important clue that leads us to a simplified FIR design procedure, as we now discuss.

FIR Filter Design

To apply these optimal windows to FIR filter design by the method of windows, we need to gain some experience that will help us formulate some practical guides. We will discuss the design of a low-pass filter. One can obtain other types of filters by transformation, as we discuss at various points.

Conventionally, a low-pass filter FR is specified by a passband cutoff frequency ωc, a stopband initial frequency ωr and a maximum allowable sidelobe level, SLL, in db. Also, the conventional design by the windows technique sets the ideal filter's cutoff frequency to be $\omega tr=(\omega c+\omega r)/2$, centered between ωc and ωr. The transition bandwidth of the filter is of course $\omega r-\omega c$. Thus, the specified parameters are $(\omega c,\omega r,SLL)$.

We need to see how to use these specifications to fix a length N and a bandwidth Ω to define the optimal window. Based on our discussions in Chapter 12, we take $\Omega=\omega r-\omega c$. That is, we want the DTFT of the optimal window to be confined as well as possible to a bandwidth equal to the transition bandwidth of the filter we are designing. It remains to specify the optimal window's length N. We find out how to do this as follows.

We directly design many FIR filters for various specifications. We learn by this empirical procedure that the time-bandwidth product TBP=$N\Omega/2\pi$ is the critical design parameter. That is, we find that the specified SLL mainly determines the required TBP, with only a weak dependence on Ω otherwise and on ωtr. We find N using the definition of the TBP and Ω and so the optimal window is specified. We complete the filter design by the method of windows.

The critical empirical relation giving the required TBP in terms of the specified SLL is

$$ f := \begin{pmatrix} -9.059 \\ -12.802 \\ -0.28 \end{pmatrix} \quad TBPfn(SLL) := \frac{-f_1 - \sqrt{(f_1)^2 - 4 \cdot f_2 \cdot (f_0 - SLL)}}{2 \cdot f_2} \tag{13.13} $$

The formula will lead to good filter designs for SLL<-35 db and $\Omega<\omega tr/2$. The resulting TBP is greater than 2. Then the FR magnitude will fall to less than the SLL for $\omega<\omega r$.

EXERCISE 13.3 For SLL values of (-20,-30,...,-90), find the required TBP using (13.13). ¤

As we said, the required window length N is determined by the definition of TBP. We can write it in the form

$$\text{Nfn}(\text{SLL}, \Omega) := \text{ceil}\left(\frac{2 \cdot \pi}{\Omega} \cdot \text{TBPfn}(\text{SLL})\right)$$

(13.14)

EXERCISE 13.4 For SLL values of (-20,-30,...,-90) and some values of Ω, find the required window length using (13.14). ¤

Example 13.1

Suppose the critical frequencies and the SLL are specified.

passband cutoff frequency:	$\omega c := 1 - \dfrac{2 \cdot \pi}{32}$	**stopband frequency:**	$\omega r := 1 + \dfrac{2 \cdot \pi}{32}$
	$\omega c = 0.80365$		$\omega r = 1.19635$

filter sidelobe level (db): $\text{SLL} := -72$

These determine the optimal window parameters N and Ω and ideal filter cutoff frequency ωtr, as we discussed.

optimal window bandwidth parameter:	$\Omega := \omega r - \omega c$	**passband cutoff of ideal filter:**	$\omega \text{tr} := \dfrac{\omega r + \omega c}{2}$
	$\Omega = 0.392699$		$\omega \text{tr} = 1$

optimal window length: $N := \text{Nfn}(\text{SLL}, \Omega)$ $N = 72$

It is of interest to note the required TBP.

required time-bandwidth product: $\text{TBP} := \dfrac{N \cdot \Omega}{2 \cdot \pi}$ $\text{TBP} = 4.5$

We can now find the optimal window, as we have shown above.

$n := 0 .. N - 1$ $m := 0 .. N - 1$ $M := N - 1$

$$\gamma(y) := \text{if}\left[y=0, \frac{\Omega}{2 \cdot \pi}, \frac{\Omega}{2 \cdot \pi} \cdot \frac{\sin\left(\frac{\Omega}{2} \cdot y\right)}{\frac{\Omega}{2} \cdot y}\right]$$ $\Gamma_{m,n} := \gamma(m - n)$

$\lambda := \text{eigenvals}(\Gamma)$ $L := \text{reverse}(\text{sort}(\lambda))$ $w_{OE} := \text{eigenvec}(\Gamma, L_0)$

We truncate the ideal filter's IR with the optimal window.

$$hid_n := if\left[n = \frac{M}{2}, \frac{\omega tr}{\pi}, \frac{\sin\left[\omega tr \cdot \left(n - \frac{M}{2}\right)\right]}{\pi \cdot \left(n - \frac{M}{2}\right)}\right] \qquad h_n := hid_n \cdot w\,OE_n$$

We plot the optimal window and FIR normalized to emphasize their shapes.

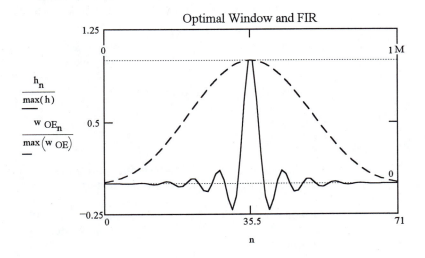

$$\frac{h_n}{max(h)}$$

$$\frac{w\,OE_n}{max\left(w\,OE\right)}$$

Optimal Window and FIR

We now compute the FR to examine its SLL. To see greater detail in the frequency response, we zero pad h sufficiently.

$$K := 32 \cdot N \qquad k := 0..K - 1 \qquad he_k := if\left(k < N, h_k, 0\right)$$

$$\omega_k := k \cdot \frac{2 \cdot \pi}{K} \qquad dft(v) := \sqrt{K} \cdot icfft(v) \qquad H := dft(he)$$

$$Hm_k := if\left(\left|H_k\right| = 0, 10^{-10}, \left|H_k\right|\right)$$

$$Hmax := max(Hm) \qquad Hmdb_k := 20 \cdot \log\left(\frac{Hm_k}{Hmax}\right)$$

We can plot the FR and see whether the specifications were met.

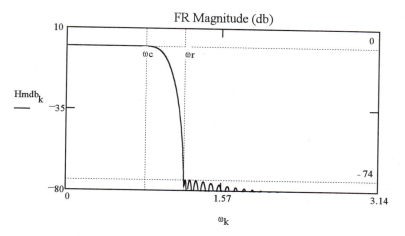

FR Magnitude (db)

We examine the sidelobe level more carefully. We see that it is -74 db, exceeding the specification of -72 db. If we shorten the FIR to length 71, we see that it is -71.6 db, close to the specified -72 db and possibly satisfactory.

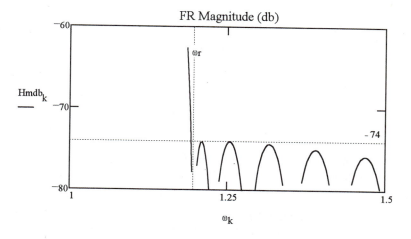

FR Magnitude (db)

It is of interest to see the passband ripple: its total excursion is about 0.05%. This was not specified, of course.

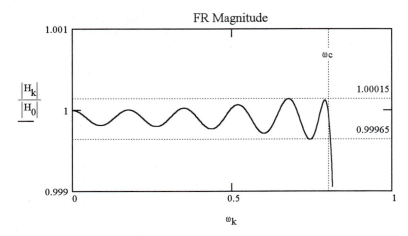

FR Magnitude

$$\theta_0 := \arg\left(H_0\right) \qquad \theta_k := \mathrm{if}\left(k{=}0, \theta_0, \theta_{k-1} + \arg\left(H_k \cdot \overline{H_{k-1}}\right)\right)$$

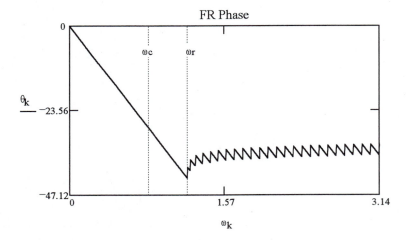

FR Phase

As we expected, the FIR filter has a piecewise linear phase that is linear over the passband of the filter. ‡

■ **EXERCISE 13.5** Choose some other values of SLL and inspect the resulting filter designs. You can also choose other values of (ωc,ωr). ¤

Kaiser Approximation

Kaiser has proposed a design procedure that uses an approximation to the optimal window (Kuo and Kaiser). The two parameters of his design are the window length M and a parameter β that plays a role similar to the TBP. Given the specification of a passband cutoff frequency ωc, a stopband frequency ωr and the attenuation in the stopband, he gives empirically derived formulas for M and β.

Example 13.2

We illustrate the design of an FIR filter by the windows method using a Kaiser window of length M+1 to approximate the optimal window. We also compare the design with that of Example 13.1 where the optimal window was used.

passband cutoff (-3db) frequency:	$\omega c := 1 - \dfrac{2 \cdot \pi}{32}$	stopband frequency:	$\omega r := 1 + \dfrac{2 \cdot \pi}{32}$

transition region bandwidth:	$\Delta := \omega r - \omega c$	passband cutoff of ideal filter:	$\omega tr := \dfrac{\omega r + \omega c}{2}$

stopband relative attenuation (-db):	$A := 72$	(note A>21)

We use the following formulas to get the window length M+1 and shape parameter β.

$$M := \text{ceil}\left(\frac{A - 7.95}{14.36 \cdot \Delta} \cdot 2 \cdot \pi\right) \qquad M = 72 \qquad N_K := M + 1$$

$$\beta 1 := 0.1102 \cdot (A - 8.7) \qquad \beta 2 := 0.5482 \cdot (A - 21)^{0.4} + 0.07886 \cdot (A - 21)$$

$$\beta := \text{if}(A < 50, \beta 2, \beta 1) \qquad \beta = 6.97566$$

Notice that the Kaiser window is of length $N_K = 73$, whereas the optimal window's length is 72.

The optimal window is now approximated as a ratio of modified Bessel functions $I_0(\ )$. (Kaiser used a power series approximation to the Bessel functions; we avoid this as the Bessel functions are built-in functions in Mathcad.)

$$nn := 0 .. N_K - 1$$

$$\beta arg_{nn} := \beta \cdot \sqrt{1 - \left(1 - 2 \cdot \frac{nn}{M}\right)^2} \qquad w_{K_{nn}} := \frac{I0\left(\beta arg_{nn}\right)}{I0(\beta)} \qquad (13.15)$$

We compare the Kaiser window with the optimal window and see that they are very similar in shape.

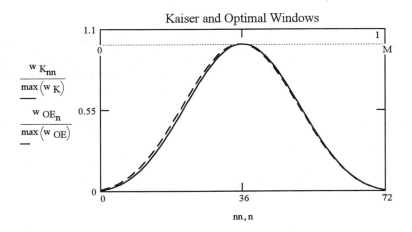

We now apply the window to the IR of the ideal low-pass filter.

$$hid_{nn} := if\left[nn = \frac{M}{2}, \frac{\omega tr}{\pi}, \frac{\sin\left[\omega tr \cdot \left(nn - \frac{M}{2}\right)\right]}{\pi \cdot \left(nn - \frac{M}{2}\right)}\right] \qquad h_{K_{nn}} := hid_{nn} \cdot w_{K_{nn}}$$

To see greater detail in the frequency response, we zero pad h sufficiently.

$$KK := 32 \cdot N_K \qquad kk := 0 .. KK - 1 \qquad he_{K_{kk}} := if\left(kk < N_K, h_{K_{kk}}, 0\right)$$

$$\omega\omega_{kk} := kk \cdot \frac{2 \cdot \pi}{KK} \qquad dft(v) := \sqrt{KK} \cdot icfft(v) \qquad H_K := dft\left(he_K\right)$$

$$Hm_{K_{kk}} := if\left(\left|H_{K_{kk}}\right| = 0, 10^{-10}, \left|H_{K_{kk}}\right|\right)$$

$$Hmax_K := max\left(Hm_K\right) \qquad Hmdb_{K_{kk}} := 20 \cdot log\left(\frac{Hm_{K_{kk}}}{Hmax_K}\right)$$

We plot the FR magnitudes of the FIRs designed with the Kaiser approximation to the optimal window and with the optimal window.

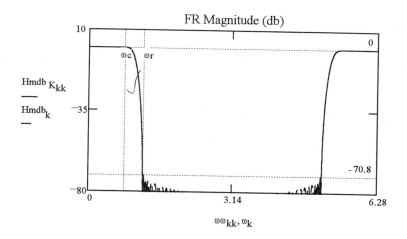

We examine the sidelobe level more carefully. We see that it is -70.8 db, close to the specified -72 db and presumably satisfactory. An optimal window is better while of length 71. Note that the optimal filter has a more equiripple character.

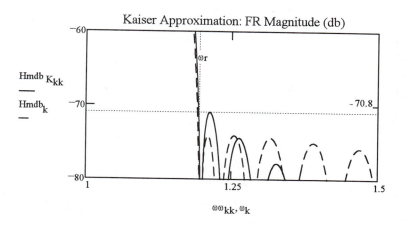

It is of interest to see the passband ripple: its total excursion is about 0.052%, almost the same as the optimal FR. But, again, note that the optimal filter has a more equiripple character.

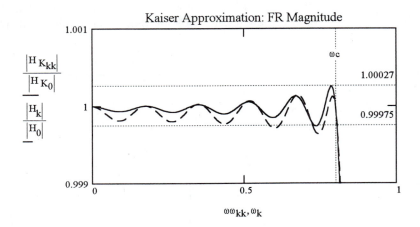

Kaiser Approximation: FR Magnitude

$$\theta_{K_0} := \arg\left(H_{K_0}\right) \qquad \theta_{K_{kk}} := \mathrm{if}\left(kk\!=\!0,\theta_{K_0},\theta_{K_{kk-1}} + \arg\left(H_{K_{kk}} \cdot \overline{H_{K_{kk-1}}}\right)\right)$$

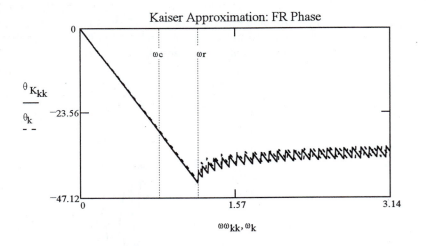

Kaiser Approximation: FR Phase

The Kaiser FIR filter also has a piecewise linear phase that is linear over the passband of the filter. ‡

▦   **EXERCISE 13.6** Choose some other values of SLL and inspect the resulting filter designs. You can also choose other values of ($\omega c,\omega r$). You should coordinate this exercise with Exercise 13.5 for meaningful comparisons. ¤

Time-Bandwidth Product Parameter

We have asserted that the time-bandwidth parameter, TBP=$N\Omega/2\pi$, is a critical, simplifying parameter in understanding and applying the optimal (maximum energy) window. We now study this.

Maximum Energy

We want to study the dependence of r_{max} on N and Ω. In particular, we wish to see whether r_{max} depends, at least approximately, on N and Ω only as their product. So what we would like to do is make many computations of r_{max} for an interesting set of TBPs, each of which is achieved by various pairs (N,Ω). We can then plot all these values of r_{max} versus TBP and see if they lie on, or near, a common curve.

We could, of course, repeat the above computations many times, once for each of the (N,Ω) pairs. This would be rather tedious: we would have to make up a table for the results and then define and enter, element by element, vectors for the plot. If we could somehow place our above computations inside a programming loop that selected Ns and Ωs, then we could store each r_{max} in an array, making all of them available for plotting. We can do precisely that in Mathcad, which has a simple, elegant programming capability for functions. (A sufficient introduction to this function programming capability is given in the chapter **A Mathcad Tutorial**.)

We need the N-by-N kernel matrix G and we would like it to depend on the specific N and W selected by the for loops. We can do this by defining it with a function program.

$$\Gamma(N,\Omega) := \begin{array}{|l} \text{for } m \in 0..N-1 \\ \quad \text{for } n \in 0..N-1 \\ \qquad \Gamma_{m,n} \leftarrow \text{if}\left[m-n{=}0, \dfrac{\Omega}{2\cdot\pi}, \dfrac{\Omega}{2\cdot\pi}\cdot\dfrac{\sin\left[\dfrac{\Omega}{2}\cdot(m-n)\right]}{\left[\dfrac{\Omega}{2}\cdot(m-n)\right]}\right] \\ \Gamma \end{array}$$

We can now call this function inside another program that has two loops that set up values for N and Ω. In effect, we have managed to create a four-dimensional array. Of course, explicit matrices are restricted to two dimensions in Mathcad, expressed in terms of two range variables.

EXERCISE 13.7 Construct the above program yourself. (If necessary, refer to the Mathcad User's Guide.) Display Γ for some small values of N to confirm that it is an N-by-N matrix array. ¤

For each choice of N and Ω we want to find the largest characteristic value. We gather the statements above that find the largest characteristic value into a function program.

$$\text{lambda}(N,\Omega) := \begin{vmatrix} \lambda \leftarrow \text{eigenvals}(\Gamma(N,\Omega)) \\ L \leftarrow \text{reverse}(\text{sort}(\lambda)) \\ \text{lambda} \leftarrow L_0 \end{vmatrix}$$

$$\text{lambda}\left(8, \frac{2 \cdot \pi}{5}\right) = 0.948453$$

EXERCISE 13.8 Compute lambda(N,Ω) for other choices of N and Ω. ¤

We can now embed this computation inside two loops. It is convenient to have the outside loop select a set of useful TBPs. The inside loop can then select a set of desired Ωs. N will be computed inside the inner loop using the definition of TBP. We store all the largest characteristic values in a matrix R, from which we can generate the desired plot.

$$R := \begin{vmatrix} \text{for } j \in 0..4 \\ \quad \begin{vmatrix} \text{tbp} \leftarrow 1 + j \\ \text{for } k \in 0..4 \\ \quad \begin{vmatrix} \Omega \leftarrow \frac{2 \cdot \pi}{2^{2+k}} \\ N \leftarrow \text{tbp} \cdot \frac{2 \cdot \pi}{\Omega} \\ \lambda \leftarrow \text{lambda}(N,\Omega) \\ R_{j,k} \leftarrow \lambda \end{vmatrix} \end{vmatrix} \\ R \end{vmatrix}$$

Computation time is about 20 sec on a 300 MH Pentium II

EXERCISE 13.9 Display R as a matrix and confirm that it is a 5-by-5 matrix. Construct the above function program yourself. ¤

Thus, for each value of TBP, we are computing r_{max} for five (N, Ω) pairs. The TBP, Ω and N values used in the program are

$$j := 0..4 \qquad tbp_j := 1 + j \qquad k := 0..4 \qquad \Omega_k := \frac{2 \cdot \pi}{2^{2+k}}$$

$$N_{j,k} := (1 + j) \cdot \left(2^{2+k}\right)$$

▦ **EXERCISE 13.10** Display the values of tbp, W and N employed. ¤

We now want to plot r_{max} as stored in R. Note that each row of R is r_{max} for a set of (N, Ω) that gives the same TBP. If we plot each column of R versus TBP we should see a close clumping of points for each TBP - if our hypothesis is correct, namely that r_{max} should depend, at least approximately, on N and Ω only as their TBP.

▦ **EXERCISE 13.11** Make the indicated plot of r_{max}. Note its exponential appearance. ¤

We see, in view of Exercise 13.11, that it is more interesting to plot $\ln(1 - r_{max})$ versus TBP. Then a plot of $\ln(1 - r_{max})$ versus TBP will be nearly linear and amenable to a low-order polynomial fit.

$$y := \overrightarrow{\ln(1 - R)}$$

Examining the plot following Problem 13.1, we see that the points fall close to a curve, which is nearly a straight line. This confirms our conjecture: r_{max} depends on N and Ω nearly only as their TBP and 1-r falls off approximately exponentially with increasing TBP. We would like to find this curve.

PROBLEM 13.1 Mathcad has built-in regression functions that can allow us to devise a least squares polynomial curve through the data points in the plot of ln(1-R) vs TBP. We have multiple points at each value of TBP: Mathcad's built-in regression functions assume just one. Show that we can form the average of the data at each value of TBP and then use Mathcad's built-in regression functions without a cost in least-square error. ‡

In view of Problem 13.1, we preprocess the data y to give one data point, the average, for each TBP value.

$$y_{ave_j} := \frac{1}{5} \cdot \sum_{i=0}^{4} y_{j,i}$$

We now use Mathcad's built-in regression algorithm to find a second-order polynomial curve fitting the data points with the least-square error, LSE.

$vs := regress(tbp, y_{ave}, 2)$ $f := submatrix(vs, 3, 5, 0, 0)$

$fit_2(t) := f_0 + f_1 \cdot t + f_2 \cdot t^2$ $tbpx := 0.5, 0.6 .. 5.5$

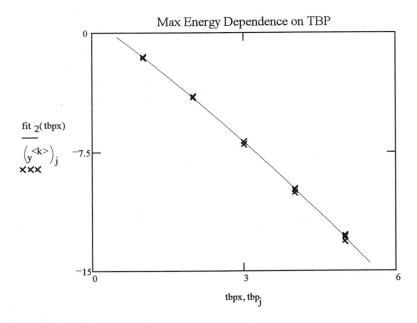

Max Energy Dependence on TBP

$\overline{fit_2(tbpx)}$

$\left(y^{<k>}\right)_j$
$\times\times\times$

tbpx, tbp$_j$

■ **EXERCISE 13.12** Display y_{ave}, vs, and f. ¤

The inverse of this LSE fit gives us the required TBP for a specified maximum relative energy r.

PROBLEM 13.2

Show that the inverse of the LSE fit is

$$TBPfn(r) := \frac{-f_1 - \sqrt{(f_1)^2 - 4 \cdot f_2 \cdot (f_0 - \ln(1 - r))}}{2 \cdot f_2} \qquad ‡ \qquad (13.16)$$

■ **EXERCISE 13.13** Compute the required TBP for r in the set (0.9, 0.99, 0.999, 0.9999, 0.99999). ¤

Design Procedure

Suppose that we want to find an optimal window, confined to a bandwidth Ω with relative energy r. We use the function TBPfn to find the required TBP for the specified r. We use the definition of TBP to find the required N. We can then find the window optimal for the parameters (N,Ω) with a function that uses the programmed functions we devised above.

Example 13.3

Suppose the bandwidth Ω and required maximum energy r are specified. We want to find the optimal window.

$$\Omega := \frac{2 \cdot \pi}{10} \qquad r := 0.9999 \qquad TBP := TBPfn(r) \qquad TBP = 3.81062$$

$$N := \text{ceil}\left[TBP \cdot \left(\frac{2 \cdot \pi}{\Omega} \right) \right] \qquad N = 39$$

$$w(N, \Omega) := \text{eigenvec}(\Gamma(N, \Omega), \text{lambda}(N, \Omega))$$

To plot w, defined as a function, we need to define an equivalent vector, say ww, and a range variable, say nn.

$$ww := w(N, \Omega) \qquad\qquad nn := 0 .. N - 1$$

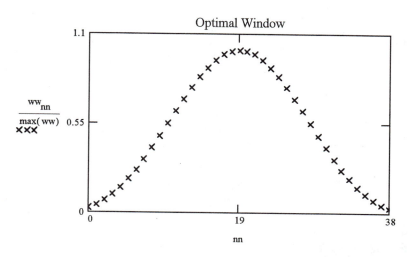

This exemplifies a rather efficient procedure. ‡

EXERCISE 13.14 Repeat Example 13.3 for other values of (r,Ω). ¤

FIR Design

To render efficient the design of an FIR filter by the method of windows using an optimal window, we want a procedure very similar to the one just discussed. Now the desired sidelobe level, SLL, is specified instead of the desired relative energy r. We hope to show that the specified SLL determines the required TBP, approximately independently of the other specified parameters, $(\omega c, \omega r)$. We leave this work to Project 13.1. We have already given the resulting functional dependence of TBP on SLL above.

Example 13.4

Suppose the design parameters are specified as in Example 13.1.

passband cutoff frequency: $\omega c := 1 - \dfrac{2 \cdot \pi}{32}$ **stopband frequency:** $\omega r := 1 + \dfrac{2 \cdot \pi}{32}$

filter sidelobe level (db): $SLL := -72$ $\Omega := \omega r - \omega c$

We can now find the optimal window's length N.

$$f := \begin{pmatrix} -15.28 \\ -9.586 \\ -0.73 \end{pmatrix} \qquad TBPfn(SLL) := \frac{-f_1 - \sqrt{(f_1)^2 - 4 \cdot f_2 \cdot (f_0 - SLL)}}{2 \cdot f_2}$$

$$Nfn(SLL, \Omega) := ceil\left(\frac{2 \cdot \pi}{\Omega} \cdot TBPfn(SLL)\right) \qquad N := ceil(Nfn(SLL, \Omega))$$

$$w(N, \Omega) := eigenvec(\Gamma(N, \Omega), lambda(N, \Omega))$$

The design of the FIR filter and examination of its FR is completed as in Example 13.1. This exemplifies a rather efficient procedure. ‡

EXERCISE 13.15 Repeat Example 13.4 for other values of SLL and $(\omega c, \omega r)$. ¤

Project 13.1

Derive the functional relation TBPfn(SLL) (13.13). One approach you can use is that illustrated to find the functional relation TBPfn(r) (13.16). You must study its independence of other parameters, as discussed in the chapter. ‡

Project 13.2

By direct computation, one can show that the FIR designed with the Kaiser window has a smaller transition region width, for comparable sidelobe level, than the single parameter window types we discussed in **Chapter 12**. Verify the entries in the following tabulation (Oppenheim and Schafer (1989), p. 231). ‡

β	relative width	sidelobe level	comparison type
2	1.5	-29	Bartlett (1.8,-27)
4	2.6	-45	Hanning (3.1,-44)
5	3.2	-54	Hamming (3.3,-53)
7	4.5	-72	Blackman (5.5,-74)
8	5.1	-81	

Project 13.3

As in **Project 12.5** except use the optimal window. ‡

Project 13.4

As in **Project 12.6** except use the optimal window. ‡

Project 13.5

As in **Project 12.7** except use the optimal window. ‡

Project 13.6

As in **Project 12.8** except use the optimal window. ‡

Project 13.7

In a digital communication system using **pulse amplitude modulation, PAM**, the pulse p(t) must be carefully designed to have (i) a specified bandwidth 2Ω, (ii) zeros at the sampling times $\{nT, n=+/-1,+/-2,...\}$ and (iii) rapidly decreasing sidelobes, the last for low **intersymbol interference, ISI**. We can choose the form

$$p(t) = q(t) \cdot \frac{\sin\left(\pi \cdot \dfrac{t}{T}\right)}{\left(\pi \cdot \dfrac{t}{T}\right)} \qquad\qquad q(0) = 0$$

The second factor ensures that (i) and (ii) are met, and q is to be chosen to meet (iii). We choose to maximize the relative energy ρ of q in $[-T_q/2, T_q/2]$. If we were able to get all the energy so contained, there could be no sidelobes. But the finite bandwidth restraint precludes that possibility. With ρ defined by the first form, show that it may be written in the second form.

$$\rho = \frac{\displaystyle\int_{-T_q}^{T_q} (|q(t)|)^2 \, dt}{\displaystyle\int_{-\infty}^{\infty} (|q(t)|)^2 \, dt} \qquad \rho = \frac{\displaystyle\int_{-1}^{1} \int_{-1}^{1} f(\omega) \cdot f(u) \cdot \frac{\sin(c \cdot (\omega - u))}{\pi \cdot (\omega - u)} \, d\omega \, du}{\displaystyle\int_{-1}^{1} (|f(\omega)|)^2 \, d\omega}$$

where $f(\omega) = Q(\Omega\omega)$, Q is the Fourier transform of q and the time-bandwidth product $c = \Omega T_q/2$ is the only way the parameters Ω and T_q enter. With an argument analogous to that used in this chapter, show that f must solve the **integral equation**

$$\lambda \cdot f(\omega) = \int_{-1}^{1} \frac{\sin(c \cdot (\omega - u))}{\pi \cdot (\omega - u)} \cdot f(u) \, du \qquad , \ -1 <= \omega <= 1$$

 This equation is famous! Its solutions are called **prolate speroidal wave functions** and can be found only numerically. Find them and discuss how to finish solving this optimal pulse design problem. In practice, including the latest HDTV design, a so-called raised cosine spectrum (Gibson) is chosen for F. Compare this choice. ‡

References

Gibson (1993), Sec. 8.2
Jackson (1966), pp. 230 - 233
Kuo and Kaiser (1966), Chap. 7
Oppenheim and Schafer (1989), Sec. 7.5

14 FIR Design for Equiripple

We have noticed that the frequency response magnitude of some of our studied FIR filters have had nearly equal local maxima in their stopband. Examples are the 5-by-7 FIR filter and the lowpass filter we designed with the frequency sampling method (**Chapter 10**). This can be a desirable property, as when interference is fairly uniformly distributed over the stopband and its presence in any subband is equally injurious to performance. In such a situation, we can be led to formulate a design problem minimizing the maxima in a specified band of frequencies. This is a well-known **minimax** optimization problem with a long history in numerical analysis and approximation theory. Solution algorithms appropriate to DSP applications are now standard in DSP software.

To gain insight into this approximation problem and because the more advanced algorithms are somewhat complicated, we offer an introductory discussion that will nonetheless lead to useful approximate solutions. Our discussion adopts an approximation to the minimax solution discussed in Press, et al. (1986).

Approximation with Chebyshev Polynomials

We consider the problem of approximating the frequency response magnitude of an FIR filter with an equiripple, or **Chebyshev**, approximation. We will assume the IR is even about its midpoint and of length (2M+1). Then the filter will have a piecewise linear phase, and a delay of M will result in a causal filter. We know how to do this with a linear phase on the frequency response.

We may then write the frequency response

$$H1(\omega) = \sum_{m=-M}^{M} e^{-i \cdot \omega \cdot n} \cdot h_m$$

in the form

$$H1(\omega) = h_0 + 2 \cdot \sum_{m=1}^{M} h_m \cdot \cos(m \cdot \omega) \qquad (-\pi <= \omega <= \pi) \qquad (14.1a)$$

Since H1(ω) is an even function of ω, we can restrict the approximation problem to ω such that $-\pi <= \omega <= 0$, and we do so.

We introduce the **Chebyshev polynomial of order m (m=0,1,...)**:

$$T(\cos(\omega), m) = \cos(m \cdot \omega) \qquad (-\pi <= \omega <= \pi)$$

or, setting x=cos(ω),

$$T(x, m) = \cos(m \cdot \mathrm{acos}(x)) \qquad (-1 <= x <= 1) \qquad (14.2)$$

Thus, as ω ranges over $[-\pi, 0]$, x=cos(ω) ranges uniquely over $[-1,1]$. Now, setting H1(acos(x))=f(x), we have

$$f(x) = h_0 + 2 \cdot \sum_{m=1}^{M} h_m \cdot T(x, m) \qquad (-1 <= x <= 1) \qquad (14.1b)$$

For a given FIR h, (14.1b) gives f as a series expansion using Chebyshev polynomials. The design problem is rather the inverse: given an f, we would like to find the FIR h. Of course, generally we are not astute enough to choose an f that has exactly the representation (14.1b). Thus we want to choose h so that the right side aproximates f with the property that the maximum errors are about equal. To gain some insight into how to do this, we first need to learn about the properties of Chebyshev polynomials and series such as (14.1b).

We compute a few Chebyshev polynomials to see what they look like. It is convenient in Mathcad to sample x and define T(x_n,m) as an array, $TC_{n,m}$.

$$N := 64 \qquad n := 0..N \qquad x_n := -1 + n \cdot \frac{2}{N}$$

$$M := 16 \qquad m := 0,1..M \qquad TC_{n,m} := \cos\left(m \cdot \mathrm{acos}\left(x_n\right)\right) \qquad (14.3)$$

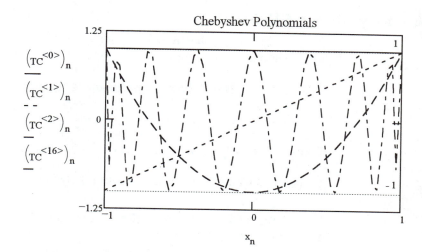

Chebyshev Polynomials

$\left(TC^{<0>}\right)_n$

$\left(TC^{<1>}\right)_n$

$\left(TC^{<2>}\right)_n$

$\left(TC^{<16>}\right)_n$

x_n

EXERCISE 14.1 Plot the Chebyshev polynomials for other orders. Note that the zero order is constant, the first order is linear, the second order is quadratic and then higher orders are oscillatory between -1 and 1. ¤

A surface plot summarizes this family of curves.

Chebyshev Polynomials to Order 16

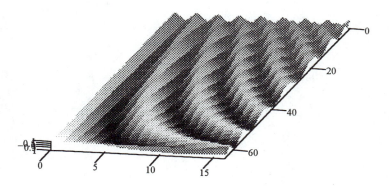

TC

Chebyshev Polynomial Properties

We discuss some salient properties of the Chebyshev polynomials, with illustrations but without proofs.

Property 14.1 The Chebyshev polynomials solve the recursion

$$T(x,0)=1 \qquad T(x,1)=x$$

$$T(x,m+1)=2 \cdot x \cdot T(x,m) - T(x,m-1) \qquad (m>=2) \qquad (14.4)$$

It is clear now that $T(x,m)$ is an mth-order polynomial in x.

▨ **EXERCISE 14.2** Use the recursion to compute a few Chebyshev polynomials. ¤

In view of (14.2), we have the following two properties.

Property 14.2 $|T(x,m)|<=1$.

Property 14.3 $T(x,m)$ has m zeros $\{xo_{k,m}\}$ in [-1,1] at, for m>0,

$$xo_{k,m} = \cos\left(\frac{k+\frac{1}{2}}{m} \cdot \pi\right) \qquad (k=0,\dots,m-1) \qquad (14.5)$$

For example,

$$\mu := 8 \qquad k := 0 .. \mu - 1 \qquad xo_{k,\mu} := \cos\left(\pi \cdot \frac{k+\frac{1}{2}}{\mu}\right) \qquad xo^{<\mu>} = \begin{bmatrix} 0.981 \\ 0.831 \\ 0.556 \\ 0.195 \\ -0.195 \\ -0.556 \\ -0.831 \\ -0.981 \end{bmatrix}$$

Notice that these zeros are distributed over [-1,1].

Property 14.4 $T(x,m)$ has m+1 extrema in [-1,1] at, for m>0,

$$xe_{k,m} := \cos\left(\frac{k}{m} \cdot \pi\right) \qquad (k=0,\dots,m) \qquad (14.6)$$

For example,

$$k := 0 .. \mu \qquad xe_{k, \mu} := \cos\left(\pi \cdot \frac{k}{\mu}\right) \qquad xe^{\langle\mu\rangle} = \begin{bmatrix} 1 \\ 0.924 \\ 0.707 \\ 0.383 \\ 0 \\ -0.383 \\ -0.707 \\ -0.924 \\ -1 \end{bmatrix}$$

Notice that these extrema are distributed over [-1,1].

Property 14.5 The Chebyshev polynomials are mutually orthogonal over [-1,1] with respect to the weight function 1/sqrt(1-x^2). This condition may be written

$$I_{m,n} = \int_{-1}^{1} \frac{T(x,m) \cdot T(x,n)}{\sqrt{1 - x^2}} \, dx \qquad \begin{aligned} I_{m,n} &= 0 & (m \neq n) \\[2mm] I_{m,m} &= \frac{\pi}{2} & (m = n \neq 0) \\[2mm] I_{0,0} &= \pi & (m = n = 0) \end{aligned} \qquad (14.7)$$

PROBLEM 14.1

Compute some orthogonality conditions (14.7). ‡

Property 14.6 The **Nth-order approximation** to f,

$$f_N(x) = \sum_{k=1}^{N} c_k \cdot T(x, k-1) \; - \frac{1}{2} \cdot c_1 \qquad (14.8)$$

where

$$c_j := \frac{2}{N} \cdot \sum_{k=1}^{N} f\left(\cos\left(\frac{\left(k - \frac{1}{2}\right)}{N} \cdot \pi\right)\right) \cdot \cos\left[(j-1) \cdot \frac{k - \frac{1}{2}}{N} \cdot \pi\right] \qquad (14.9)$$

is *exact* at the N zeros of T(x,N).

PROBLEM 14.2

Choose a specific f, e.g., f(x) = cos[(4π)x], which will vary by four periods over [-1,1]. Implement (14.8) and (14.9) and check Property 14.6. Begin with a small N and increase it slowly, checking to see if the assertion is met. You will see that the quality of the approximation improves suddenly. ‡

An Approximation

Suppose that, in (14.8), N is chosen to be very large. Now suppose we approximate f with only the first M terms of (14.9), the {c_j} still computed with (14.8). If the {c_j} are decreasing rapidly for j near M, then the error is dominated by $c_{M+1}T(x,M)$, where T(x,M) is an oscillatory function over [-1,1] with (M+1) extrema of unity value smoothly distributed over [-1,1]. Then we will hopefully have a good approximation to the minimax approximation to f(x). *This is the idea that we hope to exploit.*

So we will consider the **truncated approximation**

$$c_j := \frac{2}{N} \cdot \sum_{k=1}^{N} f\left(\cos\left(\frac{\left(k-\frac{1}{2}\right)}{N}\cdot\pi\right)\right) \cdot \cos\left[(j-1)\cdot\frac{k-\frac{1}{2}}{N}\cdot\pi\right] \quad \square$$

$$f_{a_n} := \sum_{j=1}^{M} c_j \cdot T_{n,k} - \frac{1}{2}\cdot c_1 \square \qquad (14.10)$$

With a certain amount of trial and error, we hope to find a satisfactory approximation (14.10). In contrast, the minimax approximation requires a considerably more sophisticated algorithm.

A trial-and-error design procedure can go as follows.

1. Choose the desired frequency response magnitude f(x) for x in [-1,1], corresponding to H1(ω) for ω in [-π,0].
2. Choose a sufficiently large N and compute the {c_j} using (14.8) and compute the approximation f_N using (14.9). Compare f and f_N and adjust N to get the error very small.
3. Examining the c_j, choose M and compute the truncated approximation f_a using (14.10). Observe the error; note in particular how nearly equiripple it is, and compare it to the first ignored term.
4. Iterate 3 as necessary.
5. Iterate 2 as necessary.

Example Filter Design

Example 14.1

We define a frequency response to be approximated. We define it as 1 over a passband and -40 db over a stopband. We want a small, nearly equiripple error in the passband and the stopband. We allow a transition region where we do not require a close approximation. A bit of experience shows that it is helpful to smoothly connect the specified levels in the transition region. We do this by fitting an exponential by trial and error, inside the transition region.

design passband cutoff: $xcd := 0.6$ **fitting point:** $xc := 0.5$

design stopband cutoff: $xsd := -0.1$ **fitting point:** $xs := 0.0$

desideratum: $f(x) := \text{if}\left[x < xs, 10^{-2}, \text{if}\left[x < xc, \exp\left[-\frac{1}{2} \cdot \left(\frac{x - xc}{0.167} \right)^2 \right], 1 \right] \right]$

$\delta := 0.01$ $NN := \dfrac{2}{\delta}$ $n := 0 .. NN$ $x_n := -1 + n \cdot \delta$ $fs_n := f(x_n)$

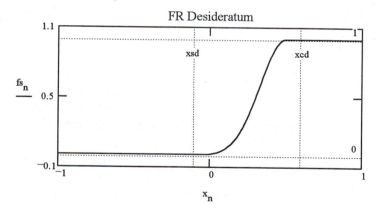

FR Desideratum

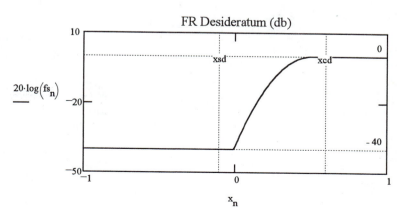

FR Desideratum (db)

We compute the coefficients (14.8) for the approximation (14.9) of the function f.

$$N := 128 \qquad k := 1..N \qquad j := 1..N$$

$$c_j := \frac{2}{N} \cdot \sum_k \left[f \left[\cos \left[\pi \cdot \frac{\left(k - \frac{1}{2}\right)}{N} \right] \right] \cdot \cos \left[\frac{\pi \cdot (j - 1) \cdot \left(k - \frac{1}{2}\right)}{N} \right] \right]$$

$$T(x,m) := \cos(m \cdot \mathrm{acos}(x)) \qquad f_N(x) := \sum_k c_k \cdot T(x, k - 1) - \frac{c_1}{2}$$

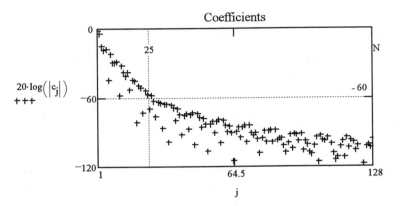

Coefficients

Notice that the c_j fall off less rapidly after j about 25. So we hazard that choosing a truncation length less than 25 enhances the possibility of a nearly equiripple approximation.

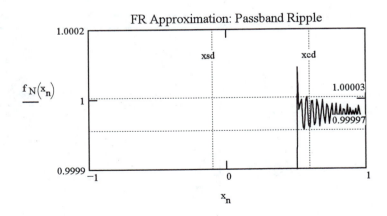

FR Approximation: Passband Ripple

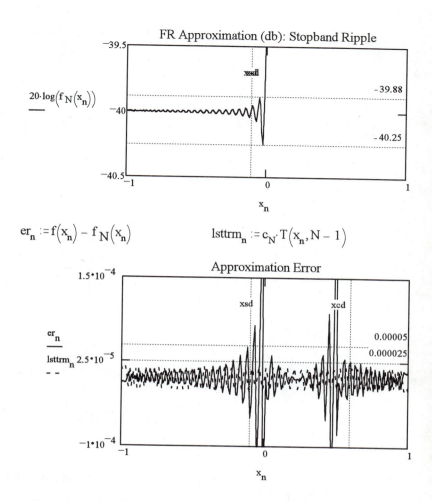

FR Approximation (db): Stopband Ripple

$$20 \cdot \log(f_N(x_n))$$

$$er_n := f(x_n) - f_N(x_n) \qquad\qquad lsttrm_n := c_N \cdot T(x_n, N - 1)$$

Approximation Error

$$\frac{er_n}{lsttrm_n}$$

The approximation error is very small - less than 0.0025% in the passband and less than 0.005% in the stopband. So we now consider the truncated approximation, denoted fa. Examining the values of c_j above, we select a value of M in the region where the c_j are rapidly decreasing.

$$M := 25 \qquad m := 1 .. M \qquad T(x, m) := \cos(m \cdot a\cos(x))$$

$$fa(x) := \sum_{m} c_m \cdot T(x, m - 1) - \frac{c_1}{2}$$

Desideratum & Approximation

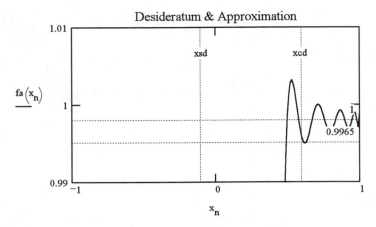

Desideratum & Approximation (db)

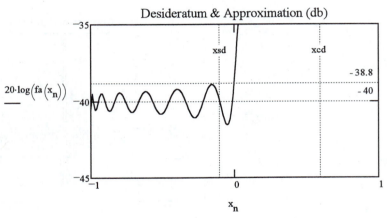

We examine the error and compare it with the first ignored term in the series for fa.

$$er_n := f(x_n) - fa(x_n) \qquad\qquad nextterm_n := c_{(M+1)} \cdot T(x_n, M)$$

Approximation Error and the Next Term

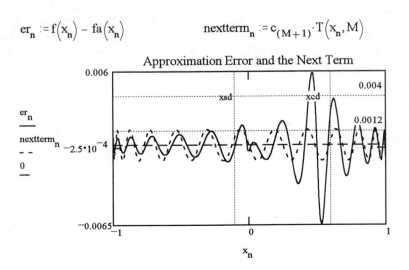

We see that the error is fairly well approximated by the first ignored term in the series for fa over the stopband. As a consequence, the error is approximately equiripple in the stopband. In the stopband, the ripple magnitude is about -58 db. The error in the passband is about 0.4%. It is nearly equiripple except near xcd. This indicates that we should move the fitting point xc a little farther into the transition region. We leave this as an exercise. The FIR has a length of 51.

We now plot the impulse response - recall eqs. (14.1a) and (14.1b).

$$MM := 2 \cdot M + 1 \qquad mm := 0..\, MM - 1 \qquad MM = 51$$

$$h_{mm} := \text{if}\left[mm > M, \frac{c_{(mm-M)+1}}{2}, \text{if}\left[mm < M, \frac{c_{(M-mm)+1}}{2}, 0.5 \cdot c_1 \right] \right]$$

We now verify our design by computing and displaying the frequency response computed from the impulse response.

$$K := 32 \cdot MM \qquad k := 0..\, K \qquad h_k := \text{if}\left(k < MM, h_k, 0\right) \qquad hdft := \sqrt{K} \cdot \text{icfft}(h)$$

$$\omega cd := a\cos(xcd) \qquad \omega sd := a\cos(xsd) \qquad \omega_k := k \cdot \frac{2 \cdot \pi}{K}$$

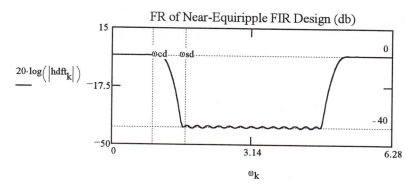

FIR Design: FR in Passband

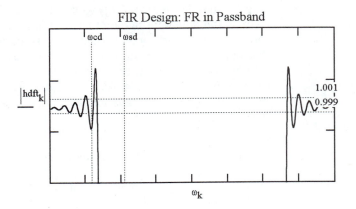

FIR Design: FR in Stopband (mag, db)

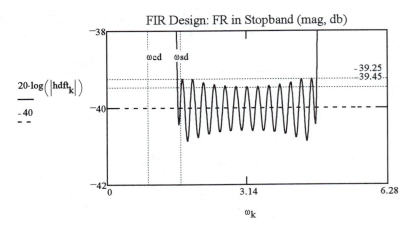

We see that the response in the stopband is a nearly equiripple within 0.2 db The passband has a ripple maximum of about 0.1%. The FIR filter IR is of length 51. ‡

PROBLEM 14.3

In Example 14.1, change the nature of the approximation in the transition region and note the resultant design. You can vary the connection points within the transition region. Also, you can try different functional connections, such as a straight line. ‡

PROBLEM 14.4

Try a design with a shorter FIR length. In some applications, a relatively short length may be required to minimize the computations. ‡

Note The computation of the entire document requires about 40 seconds on a 66 MHz 486.

Project 14.1

Design a bandpass filter using an approximately equiripple design.‡

Project 14.2

Design a high-pass filter using an approximately equiripple design.‡

Project 14.3

As in **Project 10.1**, but use an approximately equiripple design. ‡

Project 14.4

As in **Project 10.2**, but use an approximately equiripple design. ‡

Project 14.5

As in **Project 10.3**, but use an approximately equiripple design. ‡

Project 14.6

As in **Project 11.1**, but use an approximately equiripple design. ‡

References

Press, et al. (1986), pp. 147 - 151
Oppenheim and Schafer (1989), Secs. 7.6, 7.7
Proakis and Manolakis (1996), Sec. 8.2.4

15 Sampling Analog Signals

At the outset we noted that digital signals are commonly derived by sampling an analog waveform. Even when this is not done, it can be convenient to consider a fictitious analog waveform to better understand certain operations upon the digital signal. We now turn to a study of the sampling operation.

Aliasing and Adequate Sampling

The analysis of analog filters and their actions on analog waveforms, just as in the discrete-time case we have discussed throughout, is greatly clarified by mapping the signals and filters to the frequency domain using, in this case, the Fourier transform. The operation of sampling is also greatly clarified by examining it in the frequency domain. We consider an analog waveform xa(t) with an FT Xa(v); we shall denote the frequency variable associated with the FT by v to distinguish it from the frequency variable ω associated with the DTFT. Recall that the **Fourier transform (FT)** is

$$Xa(v) = \int_{-\infty}^{\infty} e^{-i \cdot v \cdot t} \cdot xa(t)\, dt \qquad (15.1)$$

and the **inverse Fourier transform (IFT)** is

$$xa(t) = \frac{1}{2 \cdot \pi} \cdot \int_{-\infty}^{\infty} e^{i \cdot t \cdot v} \cdot Xa(v)\, dv \qquad (15.2)$$

We now sample the analog waveform at the instants $\{t_n = n\, T_s, n=0,+/-1,...\}$, obtaining the sequence of samples $\{x_n = xa(t_n), n=0,+/-1,...\}$. This sequence will have a representation as an IDTFT (**Chapter 6**):

$$x_n = \frac{1}{2 \cdot \pi} \cdot \int_{-\pi}^{\pi} e^{i \cdot n \cdot \omega} \cdot X1(\omega)\, d\omega \qquad (15.3)$$

But it also has the representation

$$x_n = \frac{1}{2 \cdot \pi} \cdot \int_{-\infty}^{\infty} e^{i \cdot n \cdot Ts \cdot v} \cdot Xa(v) \, dv \tag{15.4}$$

obtained by sampling the representation (15.2).

We would like to relate the two representations (15.3) and (15.4), and thereby relate $X1(\omega)$ and $Xa(v)$. Since (15.3) involves an integral over $(-\pi, \pi)$, it seems a good idea to break the integral of (15.4) into a sum of integrals, each expressible as an integral over an interval of width 2π. Then, with changes of the dummy variables of integration, we will be able to write each as an integral over $(-\pi, \pi)$. Finally, interchanging order of summing and integration, we will have a form to compare with (15.3).

After a try or two, we see that we should break the infinite integral of (15.4) into an infinite sum of integrals, the mth such integral over the interval $[(m-1/2)vs, (m+1/2)vs]$, where the sampling frequency $vs = 2\pi/Ts$.

$$x_n = \frac{1}{2 \cdot \pi} \cdot \sum_{m=-\infty}^{\infty} \int_{\left(m - \frac{1}{2}\right) \cdot vs}^{\left(m + \frac{1}{2}\right) \cdot vs} e^{i \cdot n \cdot Ts \cdot v} \cdot Xa(v) \, dv$$

In the mth integral, we change the dummy variable of integration by the substitution $Tsv = \omega + m2\pi$ and recognize that $\exp(inm2\pi) = 1$ to get the form

$$\frac{1}{Ts} \cdot \left[\frac{1}{2 \cdot \pi} \cdot \int_{-\pi}^{\pi} e^{i \cdot n \cdot \omega} \cdot Xa\left(\frac{\omega - m \cdot 2 \cdot \pi}{Ts} \right) d\omega \right] \tag{15.5}$$

We now have

$$x_n = \int_{-\pi}^{\pi} e^{i \cdot n \cdot \omega} \cdot \frac{1}{Ts} \cdot \sum_{m=-\infty}^{\infty} Xa\left(\frac{\omega - m \cdot 2 \cdot \pi}{Ts} \right) d\omega$$

Comparing to (15.3), we have the relation

$$X1(\omega) = \frac{1}{Ts} \cdot \sum_{m=-\infty}^{\infty} Xa\left(\frac{\omega - m \cdot 2 \cdot \pi}{Ts}\right) \tag{15.6}$$

This relation shows the well-known **aliasing** artifact caused by sampling an analog waveform. The DTFT X1 is the sum of an infinite number of translated and scaled replicas of Xa called **aliases**. We will call (15.6) the **aliased FT**.

EXERCISE 15.1 The DTFT X1(ω) has period 2π. Show that the right side of (15.6) has period 2π. ¤

PROBLEM 15.1

Let f(t) = exp(-|t|). Compute its FT F(v). ‡

Example 15.1 _____

We illustrate (15.6). We choose a double-sided exponential analog waveform h(t) = exp(-|t|) for which we have computed the FT H(v) in Problem 15.1. Note that both h and H are of infinite extent. We examine H1(ω) over (-π,π) and add enough terms so that the change in the plot is imperceptible if we add more terms; we find this out by trial and error. We also plot the scaled version of Xa(v) itself for comparison.

$$ha(t) := e^{-|t|} \qquad Ha(v) := \frac{1}{1+v^2} \qquad \omega c := 1$$

$$Ts := 1 \qquad M := 10 \qquad H1(\omega) := \frac{1}{Ts} \cdot \sum_{m=-M}^{M} Ha\left(\frac{\omega - m \cdot 2 \cdot \pi}{Ts}\right)$$

$$\omega := -\pi, -\pi + 0.1 .. \pi$$

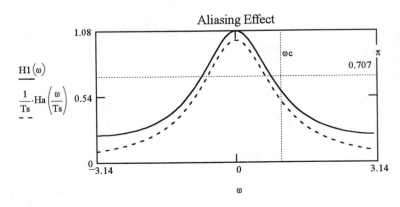

We see that H1(ω) differs considerably from the rescaled Ha(ν) due to aliasing effects. ‡

 EXERCISE 15.2 Vary Ts in Example 15.1 and observe the aliasing effects. ¤

EXERCISE 15.3 Suppose a critical frequency ωc is specified as 1. Adjust Ts until the -3 db relative value of H1(ω) occurs there. ¤

PROBLEM 15.2

An obvious method of obtaining a digital filter, given an analog filter, is to simply sample the analog filter's IR to obtain the digital filter's IR. If the -3 db cutoff frequency of the digital filter is specified, then Ts is thereby specified. Choose an h(t) other than the one of Example 15.1 and repeat the analysis. ‡

Given an analog filter, one may wish to perform the filtering with a digital filter. One first uses an ADC to sample the analog waveform, which has usually been prefiltered with an analog filter to help reduce aliasing effects. Second, one does digital filtering. Third, one uses a DAC to recover the filtered analog waveform. Choosing the digital filter's IR to be the samples of the analog filter's IR is a design method called the **impulse invariant** method. As the above discussion points out, the sole design parameter is the sample period Ts. If it is chosen to satisfy a cutoff specification, as illustrated in Exercise 15.3 and Problem 15.2, then Ts cannot be independently chosen to control aliasing. Therefore this design method, though conceptually simple, is not highly regarded and will not be further considered here.

The effects of aliasing depend on the application. A dramatic example is the creation of false images in image processing systems. (An example is discussed in **Chapter 31**.) The system design problem is often to control the effects of aliasing, avoidance being impractical.

We have plotted X1, which has period 2π, over the period (-π,π), which is probably most natural when relating the DTFT to the FT. However, if we are relating the DTFT to the DFT (as we often do for the latter's computational attractiveness when implemented as an FFT), it is more natural to select the period (0,2π).

$\omega := 0, 0.1 .. 2 \cdot \pi$

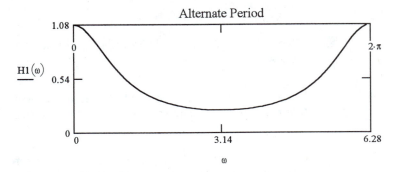

Alternate Period

$\dfrac{H1(\omega)}{}$

We note that if the analog waveform is bandlimited to $(-\Delta/2, \Delta/2)$, then by choosing Ts sufficiently small, we can avoid any overlap of the aliases. In this case, we have the simple relation

$$X1(\omega) = \frac{1}{Ts} \cdot Xa\left(\frac{\omega}{Ts}\right) \qquad (-\pi < \omega < \pi) \qquad (15.7)$$

The **Nyquist condition**, or **adequate sampling condition**, for no overlap of the aliases is

$$vs > \Delta \qquad (15.8)$$

and then the relation between v and ω is simply

$$\omega = Ts \cdot v \qquad (15.9)$$

so that, as v ranges from $-\Delta/2$ to $\Delta/2$, ω ranges from a frequency greater than $-\pi$ to a frequency less than π. In other words, the analog frequency range $(-\Delta/2, \Delta/2)$ is mapped by a simple scaling $(1/Ts)$ into the digital frequency range $(-\pi, \pi)$. Of course, if the analog waveform's bandwidth is infinite, a simple, linear scaling mapping is impossible.

Shannon Interpolation

Under the condition (15.8) of adequate sampling, we can recover the analog waveform from the sample sequence, as we now show. This is not unexpected since then $X1(\omega)$ is a scaled replica of $Xa(v)$. We begin with the representation (15.2) of xa(t), explicitly modifying it to show its bandlimit.

$$xa(t) = \frac{1}{2 \cdot \pi} \cdot \int_{-\frac{vs}{2}}^{\frac{vs}{2}} e^{i \cdot t \cdot v} \cdot Xa(v) \, dv$$

We now substitute for $Xa(v)$ using (15.7).

$$xa(t) = \frac{1}{2 \cdot \pi} \cdot \int_{-\frac{vs}{2}}^{\frac{vs}{2}} e^{i \cdot t \cdot v} \cdot (Ts \cdot X1(Ts \cdot v)) \, dv$$

In turn, we use the DTFT definition of $X1(\omega)$ in terms of the sample sequence $\{x_n = xa(nTs), n = 0, +/-1, ...\}$ to get

$$xa(t) = \frac{1}{2 \cdot \pi} \cdot \int_{-\frac{vs}{2}}^{\frac{vs}{2}} e^{i \cdot t \cdot v} \cdot \left[Ts \cdot \sum_{n=-\infty}^{\infty} e^{-i \cdot Ts \cdot n \cdot v} \cdot xa(n \cdot Ts) \right] dv$$

▣ **EXERCISE 15.4** Interchange the order of summation and integration in this last form and evaluate the integral of $\exp(i(t-nTs)v$. ¤

Thus we have derived the **Shannon interpolation formula.**

$$xa(t) = \sum_{n=-\infty}^{\infty} xa(n \cdot Ts) \cdot \frac{\sin\left[(t - n \cdot Ts) \cdot \frac{\pi}{Ts} \right]}{\left[(t - n \cdot Ts) \cdot \frac{\pi}{Ts} \right]}$$

(15.10)

We plot the **interpolation function.**

$$ifn(t) := if\left[t = 0, 1, \frac{\sin\left(t \cdot \frac{\pi}{Ts} \right)}{\left(t \cdot \frac{\pi}{Ts} \right)} \right]$$

$$t := -7 \cdot Ts, -7 \cdot Ts + \frac{Ts}{10} \, .. \, 7 \cdot Ts$$

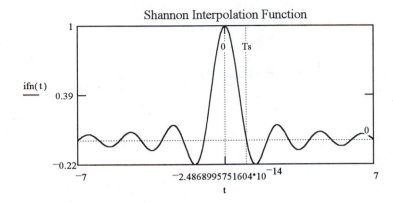

Shannon Interpolation Function

EXERCISE 15.5 An interpolation function used in (15.10) must have two essential properties. What are these? What is an undesirable attribute of this interpolation function? ¤

Suppose we are given a sequence and we wish to see more of its detail by somehow increasing the sample density. We have in mind an underlying, smooth analog waveform that has been adequately sampled and we now want to see it more densely sampled. Shannon's interpolation formula gives us a method to find such an interpolation. Given a sequence, we can, by means of (15.10), reconstruct to any desired detail - in other words, for an arbitrarily dense set of samples $\{t_n\}$ - a real or virtual bandlimited analog waveform.

Example 15.2 _____

We illustrate Shannon's interpolation function by using it to more densely sample an analog waveform.

$v1 := 2 \cdot \pi \cdot 211$ $v2 := 2 \cdot \pi \cdot 667$

analog waveform: $sa(t) := 2 \cdot \cos(v1 \cdot t) + \cos(v2 \cdot t)$

Nyquist frequency: $v_N := 2 \cdot v2$

sampling factor: $f := 2$

sampling frequency: $v_s := f \cdot v_N$ $v_s = 1.676 \cdot 10^4$

sample period: $T_s := \dfrac{2 \cdot \pi}{v_s}$ $T_s = 3.748 \cdot 10^{-4}$

Shannon interpolation function:

$$\text{ifn}(t) := \text{if}\left[t \neq 0, \frac{\sin\left(\pi \cdot \dfrac{t}{T_s}\right)}{\pi \cdot \dfrac{t}{T_s}}, 1\right]$$

We form the sampled sequence, trying to keep the length of the waveform sampled constant.

sample index: $\qquad N := 10 \cdot f \qquad n := 0 .. N - 1$

sample sequence: $\qquad s_n := sa\left(n \cdot T_s\right)$

Form the interpolated sequence using (15.10) and interpolate by a density factor of 8.

interpolation: a slow calculation! $\quad M := 8 \cdot N \quad m := 0 .. M \quad r_m := \displaystyle\sum_n s_n \cdot \text{ifn}\left(m \cdot \dfrac{T_s}{8} - n \cdot T_s\right)$

$$t := 0, \frac{0.1}{660} .. \frac{5}{660}$$

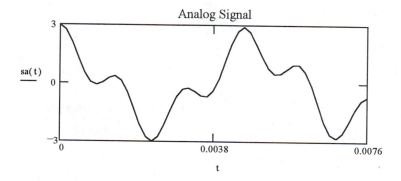

Analog Signal

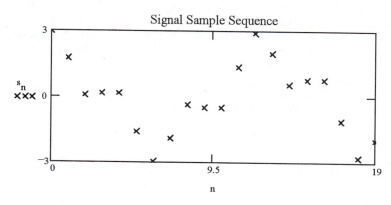

Signal Sample Sequence

Interpolated Sequence

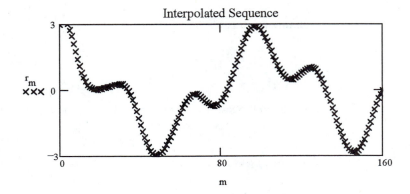

It is also of interest to plot the spectrum of the sampled waveform, computed by the DFT/FFT. We make an extension, by zero padding, of the sequence to see more detail in the spectrum.

$$se_m := if\left(m<N, s_m, 0\right) \qquad dft(v) := \sqrt{M} \cdot icfft(v) \qquad sdft := dft(se)$$

$$v_m := m \cdot \frac{2 \cdot \pi}{M} \cdot \frac{1}{T_s} \qquad\qquad f = 2$$

Sample Sequence DTFT

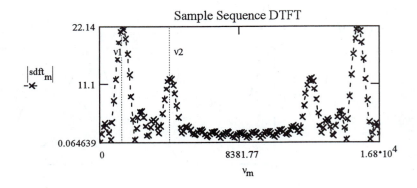

The FT of the analog waveform is composed of "delta functions" located at the frequencies $v1$ and $v2$. There are artifacts in the plot indicating this. This is the general effect of truncation characterized by a convolution; see (15.13) below. We discuss this next. ‡

EXERCISE 15.6 In Example 15.2, vary f and carefully observe the behavior in all plots. ¤

Example 15.3

We will use the animation capability of Mathcad to create a movie of the aliasing due to sampling. We associate the frame variable FRAME with the sampling frequency and plot the resulting DTFT of the sampled sequence. (You may need to review how to create an animation: see **Chapter 2**. Remember to make sure **Math** is in **Automatic Mode**.)

We directly specify the analog signal's FT, or spectrum, and plot it. It must be symmetric about v = 0 for a real function.

FT:
$$Sa(v) := (|v| > 100) \cdot (|v| < 200) \cdot \left(\frac{100 + |v|}{300} \right)$$

FT frequency:
$$v := -300, -295 .. 300$$

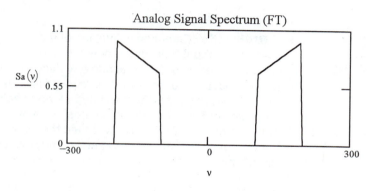

Analog Signal Spectrum (FT)

We now implement the effect of sampling the analog signal in the frequency domain of the sample sequence, that is, the DTFT domain, as described by (15.6). We shall restrict the aliasing phenomenon so that we need only consider the n=0 and n=1 terms of (15.6) for ω in [0,2π], one period of the DTFT.

maximum frequency: $v_{max} := 200$

Nyquist frequency: $v_N := 2 \cdot v_{max}$

sampling factor: $f := 2 - \dfrac{FRAME}{10}$

(**FRAME is restricted, say to 0 to 14)**

sampling frequency: $v_s := f \cdot v_N$

$v_s = 800$

sampling period: $T_s := \dfrac{2 \cdot \pi}{v_s}$

$T_s = 7.854 \cdot 10^{-3}$

DTFT:
$$S(\omega) := \frac{1}{T_s} \cdot Sa\left(\frac{\omega}{T_s}\right) + \frac{1}{T_s} \cdot Sa\left(\frac{\omega - 2\cdot\pi}{T_s}\right)$$
(approximating (15.6))

DTFT frequency:
$$\omega := 0, 0.1 .. 2\cdot\pi$$

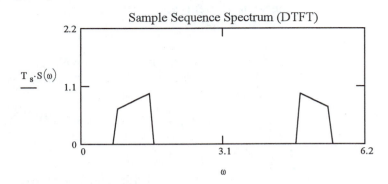

EXERCISE 15.7 Enter special values of the sampling factor f ranging from about 2 down to about 0.6. Over this range, do the n=0 and n=1 terms of (15.6) accurately describe $S(\omega)$? For each value of f, push F9 to recompute and carefully observe the plot. For what set of values of f is there overlap of the spectral parts? For what values of f can the original analog waveform be recovered? Which part of the DTFT could be called the alias? For what f? After you thoroughly understand this exercise, remove all special declarations of f other than that involving FRAME. ¤

EXERCISE 15.8 Create an animation of Exercise 15.4 with FRAME running from 0 to 14. Playback the animation. Repeat the analysis asked for in that exercise. Define another analog spectrum, or FT, and repeat the analysis. You might like to consider one or a few sinusoids. (Be careful to approximate (15.6) accurately.) ¤

This example and its included exercises show that the FT domain and DTFT domain descriptions give us considerable insight into the sampling operation. ‡

PROBLEM 15.3 Using (15.6) and the FT given above, sketch by hand the DTFT for ω over the period $[0, 2\pi]$ for several of the suggested sampling factors. Do you prefer to let Mathcad do the sketches/plots? ‡

Truncation

Models of analog systems that employ waveforms of infinite extent are common. Useful models of DSP systems can employ sequences of infinite length. However, in practical DSP, only a finite-length sample sequence of an analog waveform is processed, and it is often important to explicitly model this limitation.

For example, when sampling an analog waveform modeled as infinite in extent, the sample sequence model is of infinite length. We can then imagine the latter to be truncated to a finite length. In practice, we would do this with a window. We have already discussed this in **Chapter 7**. Our intent here is often to make the DTFT as accurate a replica of the FT as possible.

Finally, as our actual computations are often done with the DFT/FFT, we note that the DFT is simply the appropriate set of samples of the DTFT of the truncated sequence.

Thus, the relation between the DFT and the FT may be summarized as a sampling of the DTFT that results from the convolution of the aliased FT (15.6) with the DTFT, W1(ω), of a selected window.

$$X1(\omega) = \frac{1}{2 \cdot \pi} \cdot \int_{-\pi}^{\pi} W1(\omega - \mu) \cdot \frac{1}{Ts} \cdot \sum_{m = -\infty}^{\infty} Xa\left(\frac{\mu - m \cdot 2 \cdot \pi}{Ts}\right) d\mu \qquad (15.11)$$

DFT X_k: $\quad k = (0 .. N - 1) \qquad \omega_k = \frac{2 \cdot \pi}{N} \cdot k \qquad X_k = X1(\omega_k) \qquad (15.12)$

Obviously, the relation between the DFT X_k and the FT $Xa(v)$ is not a simple one!

However, if xa(t) is bandlimited and adequately sampled, then (15.11) simplifies to

$$X1(\omega) = \frac{1}{2 \cdot \pi} \cdot \int_{-\pi}^{\pi} W1(\omega - \mu) \cdot \frac{1}{Ts} \cdot Xa\left(\frac{\mu}{Ts}\right) d\mu \qquad (15.13)$$

Still, X_k is not a sample of Xa: rather, it is a sample of the periodic convolution of the window's DTFT with Xa (suitably scaled) smearing detail in the latter. An important problem is spectral estimation - in this case the estimation of Xa with X1, or, practically, with the DFT $\{X_k\}$. Window choice plays a role in spectral estimation. We have already discussed windows in conjunction with designing FIR filters and we apply this experience to this problem of spectral estimation.

Spectral Estimation

As mentioned above, the relation (15.13),

$$X1(\omega) = \frac{1}{2 \cdot \pi} \cdot \int_{-\pi}^{\pi} W1(\omega - \mu) \cdot \frac{1}{Ts} \cdot Xa\left(\frac{\omega}{Ts}\right) d\mu$$

leads naturally to the question of choosing a window function for the truncation of the analog waveform or, equivalently, choosing a window sequence for the truncation of the sequence of samples of the (adequately) sampled analog waveform.

We know from our experience with FIR filters that a finite sequence will have a rational DTFT so that it can be zero on at most a finite set of ω's in $[0, 2\pi]$. The best that we can hope to do, generally speaking, is to confine the window as much as possible to a specified, relatively small ω-set, which we call the **resolution** of the spectral estimate. We have already offered, in __Chapter 13__, a definition of "best confinement" in our discussion of an optimal window for FIR design by the windows method and furthermore found the solution to be easily computed by Mathcad. There is no need to resort to Kaiser's approximation of these optimal windows.

While special situations may dictate otherwise, these optimal energy windows offer a good general solution to the problem of choosing a window for spectral (FT) estimation. Optimal energy windows are particularly useful because they do not depend on the spectrum (FT), which is unknown. We do presumably know the resolution required in the spectrum estimate.

Example 15.4

We shall illustrate how the optimal window may be used in spectral estimation. We shall assume an analog waveform with a known spectrum, or FT, in order to show how the accuracy is related to the choice of optimal window parameters (Ω, N), the resolution and the window length. Recall (**Problem 13.1**) that, to a good approximation, the fraction of the energy confined to Ω depends on Ω and N only as the time-bandwidth product TBP=$\Omega N/2\pi$.

analog frequencies: $\qquad K := 4 \qquad k := 1 .. K \qquad va_k := k \cdot 2 \cdot \pi \cdot 10^3$

analog signal: $\qquad s_a(t) := \sum_k \left(1 + \frac{k}{2}\right) \cdot \cos\left(va_k \cdot t\right)$

analog signal spectrum/FT: $\qquad S_a(v) = \sum_k \left(1 + \frac{k}{2}\right) \cdot \frac{1}{2} \cdot \left(\delta\left(v + va_k\right) + \delta\left(v - va_k\right)\right)$

We imagine a long sample sequence that will be truncated by the optimal window.

$$v_s := 3 \cdot va_K \qquad\qquad T_s := \frac{2 \cdot \pi}{v_s} \qquad NN := 512 \qquad\qquad nn := 0 .. NN - 1$$

$$s_{nn} := s_a\left(nn \cdot T_s\right) \qquad\qquad \frac{v_s}{2 \cdot \pi} = 1.2 \cdot 10^4 \qquad\qquad T_s = 8.333 \cdot 10^{-5}$$

sample sequence frequencies: $\qquad \left(T_s \cdot va\right)^T = (\; 0 \quad 0.524 \quad 1.047 \quad 1.571 \quad 2.094 \;)$

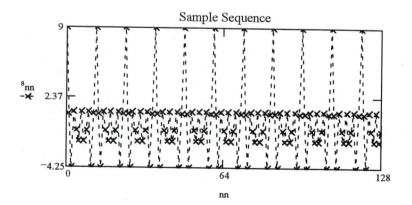

Sample Sequence

We now specify the resolution and and window length and find the optimal window sequence. We can use the plot given in **Chapter 13** to find the TBP required for a given percent energy to fall in the resolution interval. Given the window length N, the resolution Ω is determined.

$$\Omega := 2 \cdot \pi \cdot 250 \cdot T_s \quad N := 128 \quad n := 0 .. N - 1 \quad m := 0 .. N - 1 \quad \Omega = 0.131$$

We copy and paste the required Mathcad statements from **Chapter 13**.

$$\gamma(y) := if\left[y=0, \frac{\Omega}{2 \cdot \pi}, \frac{\Omega}{2 \cdot \pi} \cdot \frac{\sin\left(\frac{\Omega}{2} \cdot y\right)}{\frac{\Omega}{2} \cdot y}\right] \qquad \Gamma_{m,n} := \gamma(m - n)$$

$$\lambda := eigenvals(\Gamma) \quad L := reverse(sort(\lambda)) \qquad wopt := eigenvec\left(\Gamma, L_0\right)$$

$$TBP := \frac{\Omega \cdot N}{2 \cdot \pi} \qquad\qquad TBP = 2.667$$

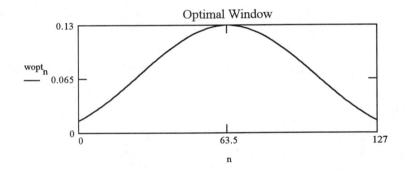

We now truncate the sample sequence with the optimal window and then compute the DFT/FFT: this is our estimate of the FT.

$$str_n := wopt_n \cdot s_n \qquad\qquad Str := \sqrt{N} \cdot icfft(str)$$

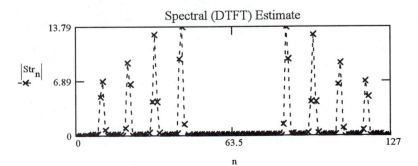

The artifacts of the four frequencies in the spectral estimate are evidence of the pure sinusoidal structure of the analog waveform. ‡

EXERCISE 15.9 Change the resolution Ω for a fixed window length N, and note the effect on the spectral (FT) estimate. Change the window length, for a fixed resolution, and note the effect on the spectral (FT) estimate. ¤

PROBLEM 15.4 Use a rectangular window for Example 15.4 and compare the spectral estimate with that of the optimal window. ‡

Project 15.1

Illustrate the use of a window in spectral (FT) estimation. Explain your choice of window and window length. Can you think of a signal model and restraint that could lead to rectangular window choice? ‡

References

Jackson (1996), Sec. 6.1
Oppenheim and Schafer (1975), Sec. 1.7
Oppenheim and Schafer (1989), Secs. 3.1 - 3.3
Proakis and Manolakis (1996), Secs. 1.4.1 - 1.4.2

16 Interpolation

Given a signal sequence corresponding to an adequately sampled real or virtual analog waveform, we may wish to see more detail in the waveform. To do this, we increase the sample density or sample rate by a process called **interpolation**. We shall discuss two methods of interpolation: the choice of method depends on the computational facility available.

We have already discussed the Shannon interpolation formula, **15.10**, and adapted it to provide more dense sampling of a sequence. But it was not very practical in that it required considerable computation.

Zero Injection Method

In this method we ask for an increase L in sample density and seek, not perfect, but accurate interpolation. We can then design a practical FIR to give sample interpolation with this scheme, which involves injecting L-1 zeros between each pair of samples of the sequence to be interpolated. As often before, the frequency domain point of view greatly clarifies the operation.

Let $\{x_n, n=0,1,...,N\}$ be a finite sequence with DTFT $X1(\omega)$. For illustration, we define a specific sequence and compute the DTFT to any accuracy desired with the DFT/FFT.

$$N := 64 \quad n := 0..N - 1$$

sequence:
$$x_n := \cos\left(\frac{2\cdot\pi}{N}\cdot 3\cdot n\right) + \cos\left(\frac{2\cdot\pi}{N}\cdot 6\cdot n\right)$$

sequence DFT:
$$X := \sqrt{N}\cdot\text{icfft}(x) \qquad \omega_n := n\cdot\left(2\cdot\frac{\pi}{N}\right)$$

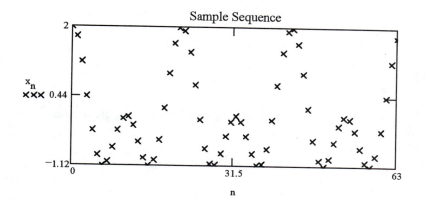

Sample Sequence

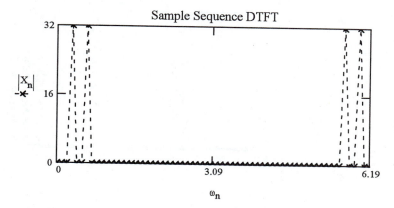

Sample Sequence DTFT

We form the sequence $\{y_n, n=0,1,...\}$ by injecting zeros into the sequence $\{x_n, n=0,1,...\}$.

interpolation factor:

$$L := 4 \qquad\qquad nn := 0..L \cdot N - 1$$

injected sequence:

$$y_{nn} := if\left(mod(nn, L) = 0, \frac{x_{nn}}{L}, 0\right)$$

injected sequence DFT:

$$Y := \sqrt{L \cdot N} \cdot icfft(y) \qquad\qquad \omega_{nn} := nn \cdot \left(2 \cdot \frac{\pi}{L \cdot N}\right)$$

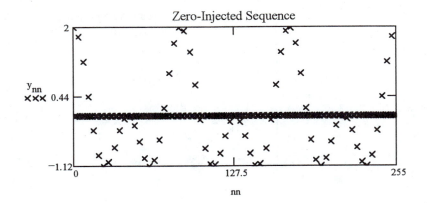

Zero-Injected Sequence

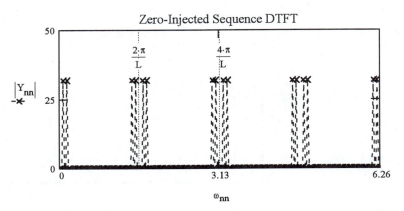

Zero-Injected Sequence DTFT

We see that the DTFT X1 has been rescaled in frequency by the factor L to form the DTFT Y1. (It is important to remember that any DTFT has period 2π.)

EXERCISE 16.1 Show analytically that $Y1(\omega)=X1(L\omega)$. ¤

Note that $Y1(\omega)$ will have period $2\pi/L$. The L-1 replications of the spectrum are called **images**. We distinguish them from aliases because no overlapping effect is present here.

Suppose, out of curiosity, that we low-pass filter $\{y_n\}$ so as to retain just the rescaled DTFT of $\{x_n\}$ centered at 0. We can do this with an ideal filter as follows.

ideal low-pass filter:
$$Yf_{nn} := if\left[\left(nn>\frac{N}{2}\right)\cdot\left(nn<N\cdot L-\frac{N}{2}\right), 0, Y_{nn}\right] \qquad (16.1)$$

filtered injected sequence:

$$yf := \frac{1}{\sqrt{N \cdot L}} \cdot cfft(Yf)$$

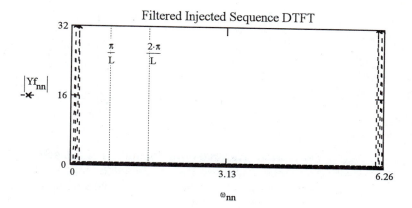

Filtered Injected Sequence DTFT

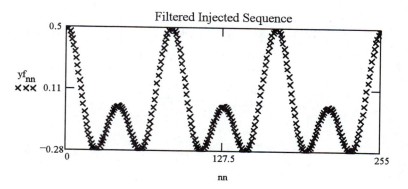

Filtered Injected Sequence

We interpret the sequence $\{yf_n\}$ as a more dense sampling of an analog waveform that was adequately sampled to form the sequence $\{x_n\}$. In our illustration we know, of course, that the analog waveform can be taken as

$$T_s := 10^{-4} \qquad x(t) := \cos\left(\frac{2 \cdot \pi}{N} \cdot 4 \cdot \frac{t}{T_s}\right) + 2 \cdot \cos\left(\frac{2 \cdot \pi}{N} \cdot 8 \cdot \frac{t}{T_s}\right)$$

where T_s is a sampling period. We plot it.

$$t := 0, \frac{T_s}{10} \ .. \ N \cdot L \cdot \frac{T_s}{10}$$

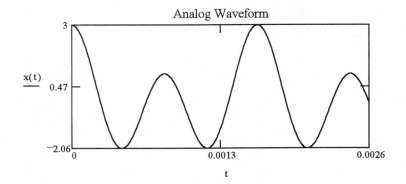

Analog Waveform

$\frac{x(t)}{}$ 0.47

3

−2.06

0   0.0013   0.0026

t

Derivation We write down the details of this scheme for a general sequence $\{x_n, n=0,+/-1,...\}$. We want to find a relation for yf in terms of the real or virtual analog signal xa. We begin with yf's representation as an IDTFT.

$$yf_n=\frac{1}{2\cdot\pi}\cdot\int_{-\pi}^{\pi} e^{i\cdot n\cdot\omega}\cdot Y1(\omega)\,d\omega \qquad Y1(\omega)=H1(\omega)\cdot X1(L\cdot\omega)$$

The filter passes just one image of Y1, that centered on $\omega=0$. If the filter is ideal, then it has FR

$$H1(\omega)=if\left(|\omega|<\frac{\pi}{L},1,0\right)$$

So

$$yf_n=\frac{1}{2\cdot\pi}\cdot\int_{-\frac{\pi}{L}}^{\frac{\pi}{L}} e^{i\cdot n\cdot\omega}\cdot X1(\omega)\,d\omega$$

We change the dummy variable of integration to u = Lω. Now

$$yf_n=\frac{1}{L}\cdot\left[\frac{1}{2\cdot\pi}\cdot\int_{-\pi}^{\pi} e^{i\cdot\frac{n}{L}\cdot u}\cdot X1(u)\,du\right]$$

Under the assumption of adequate sampling there exists a real or vitual analog waveform with FT Xa related to X1 by (**15.7**):

$$X1(u) = \frac{1}{Ts} \cdot Xa\left(\frac{u}{Ts}\right)$$

Using this in the last expression for yf and making the change of dummy variable of integration $v = u/Ts$, we have

$$yf_n = \frac{1}{L} \cdot \left[\frac{1}{2 \cdot \pi} \cdot \int_{-\pi}^{\pi} e^{i \cdot \left(n \cdot \frac{Ts}{L}\right) \cdot v} \cdot Xa(v)\, dv \right]$$

But we recognize the right side as the IFT representation of xa, evaluated at the time instant n(Ts/L). So

Interpolation property: $$yf_n = \frac{1}{L} \cdot xa\left(n \cdot \frac{Ts}{L}\right)$$

Thus we have established that yf is an L times more dense sampling of the real or virtual analog waveform associated with the sequence x_n.

Our discussion assumed the use of an idealized **smoothing filter**. It is of practical interest to design an FIR filter for this purpose when the sequence to be interpolated is long. We discuss this next. If in fact the data can be brought entirely into a computer capable of computing its DFT, then we could use the ideal filter. However, in this case there is an alternate method that we will discuss later.

FIR Interpolation Filter

For a realizable digital filter we choose a causal, piecewise linear phase FIR filter for the following reasons.

1. The filter is of finite length and so stable.
2. The linear phase assures no dispersive distortion of the signal sequence.
3. A fraction (L-1)/L samples of the injected sequence are zero and do not require actual multiplication.
4. The even symmetry of the FIR can be exploited to reduce the required computation by one-half.

Because we want a low-pass filter, we clearly want a Type I or Type II FIR filter. It is also quite clear that we want a frequency response that passes the frequencies with uniform gain near zero while rejecting all the images with equal attenuation: this leads to an equiripple design criterion. Note that the required transition band can be controlled by the sampling frequency, given that the sequence was actually derived by sampling an analog waveform. The availability of a transition band is also affected by the choice of the **interpolation factor** L.

Interpolation with the 5-by-7 Filter

Example 16.1 _____

We illustrate this interpolation scheme with the **5-by-7** filter discussed earlier. Its frequency response has a desirable, closely equiripple stopband character of a fairly low (-30 db) level. It is does not have an especially uniform gain over its passband, but it is a simple filter to implement; it is just two accumulators.

We must now fit the parameters of the interpolation scheme to the selected filter. The 5-by-7 filter's frequency response has a first zero at $2\pi/7$. We choose L so that π/L is about this frequency: the value L=4 is suitable. Then the lowest scaled replica of $X1(\omega)$ falls in the mainlobe, or passband, of the filter, and the (L-1)=3 other replicas, or images, fall in the stopband. The sampling frequency can be chosen to facilitate this fit. If we decide we do not want the first image to fall in the mainlobe, then we need to use a sampling frequency just (7/6) times the Nyquist frequency: this is a modest increase in the number of samples and hence the computation.

PROBLEM 16.1   Show that if we decide we do not want the first image to fall in the mainlobe, then we need to use a sampling frequency just (7/6) times the Nyquist frequency. ‡

We compute the output by the DFT method, although this method may not be the most efficient for such a short FIR.

$$h_{5_{nn}} := \mathrm{if}\left(nn<5,\frac{1}{5},0\right) \qquad H_5 := \sqrt{N \cdot L} \cdot \mathrm{icfft}(h_5)$$

$$h_{7_{nn}} := \mathrm{if}\left(nn<7,\frac{1}{7},0\right) \qquad H_7 := \sqrt{N \cdot L} \cdot \mathrm{icfft}(h_7) \qquad H := \overrightarrow{(H_5 \cdot H_7)}$$

$$Y := \sqrt{N \cdot L} \cdot \mathrm{icfft}(y) \qquad Yf := \overrightarrow{(H \cdot Y)} \qquad yff := \frac{1}{\sqrt{N \cdot L}} \cdot \mathrm{cfft}(Yf)$$

We would like to compare this interpolation with the L-times more densely sampled waveform. For this comparison we note that the filter output has a delay of 5.

$$xd_{nn} := \cos\left(\frac{2\cdot\pi}{N}\cdot 3\cdot\frac{nn-5}{L}\right) + \cos\left(\frac{2\cdot\pi}{N}\cdot 6\cdot\frac{nn-5}{L}\right) \qquad Xd := \sqrt{N\cdot L}\cdot\text{icfft}(xd)$$

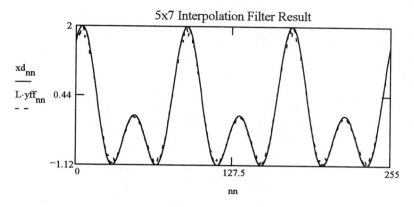

5x7 Interpolation Filter Result

As we see, the interpolation is reasonably accurate except at its extrema. It is of considerable interest to plot the various spectra.

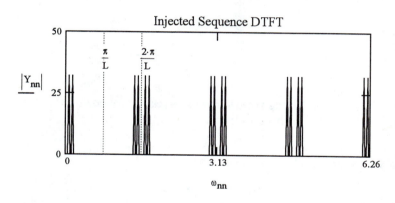

Injected Sequence DTFT

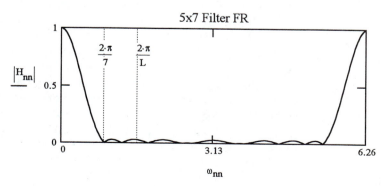

5x7 Filter FR

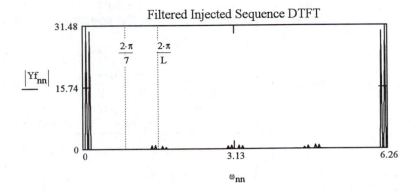

Filtered Injected Sequence DTFT

Note that the image spectra have not been entirely suppressed. Also note that the spectral lines are not quite equal, due to the nonuniform gain of the 5-by-7 FIR.

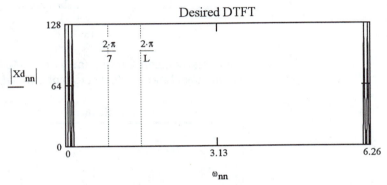

Desired DTFT

These plots show the explanatory power of mathematical software such as Mathcad. ‡

Zero Padding the DFT

In this method we ask for an increase in sample density by L and, taking advantage of the finiteness of the sequence, achieve a perfect interpolation.

We are by now routinely zero padding a finite sequence to compute the DFT to sample the DTFT to a desired accuracy. A little thought shows that we should be able to sample the IDTFT to a desired accuracy by zero padding the DTFT. We do need to take care in the zero padding, however. The DFT is indexed asymmetrically over $[0, N-1]$ corresponding to ω in $[0, 2\pi]$ in the DTFT. Thus the zeros must be added in the center of the DFT sequence, which corresponds to adding zeros on both ends of the symmetrically indexed and sampled DTFT sequence. We must zero pad in this manner to preserve the Hermitian symmetry of the real DFT.

Example 16.2

Suppose we interpolate the sequence {x_n, n=0,...,N-1} by this method.

$$Xzp_{nn} := 0 \qquad Xzp_{nn} := if\left(nn \leq \frac{N}{2}, X_{nn}, if\left(nn \leq \frac{L \cdot N}{2}, 0, \overline{Xzp_{L \cdot N - nn}}\right)\right)$$

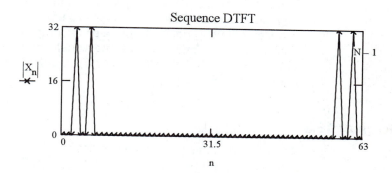

Sequence DTFT

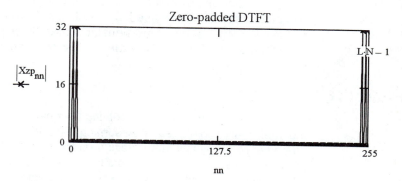

Zero-padded DTFT

The zero padding is clear. We now compute the IDFT and compare the result with the L-times more densely sampled analog waveform.

$$xint := \frac{1}{\sqrt{L \cdot N}} \cdot cfft(Xzp) \qquad xdd_{nn} := cos\left(\frac{2 \cdot \pi}{N} \cdot 3 \cdot \frac{nn}{L}\right) + cos\left[\frac{2 \cdot \pi}{N} \cdot 6 \cdot \left(\frac{nn}{L}\right)\right]$$

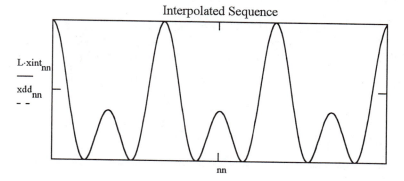

Interpolated Sequence

We see that this method can be highly accurate, subject only to numerical error. ‡

Project 16.1

We have noted that the FIR interpolation filter should have an equiripple character. We learned how to design such a filter by trial and error, using the frequency sampling method (**Chapter 10**). For L=4, so design the filter and simulate its use. (The design problem is not completely specified: you need to complete it.) What do you think of this criterion? For the same signal, compare its performance with that of the 5-by-7 filter. Did you make a fair comparison? Explain. ‡

Project 16.2

The FIR interpolation filter may be designed for an equiripple frequency response magnitude (**Chapter 14**). For L=4, find the equiripple filter and simulate its use. (The design problem is not completely specified: you need to complete it.) What do you think of this criterion? For the same signal, compare its performance with that of the 5-by-7 filter. Did you make a fair comparison? Explain. ‡

Project 16.3

The design problem for the smoothing filter can be eased by doing the interpolation in stages. (i) Assuming L=4, design the FIR smoothing filter by any of our design methods. (The frequency sampling method may be simplest here.) (ii) Now do the interpolation in two stages, each with L=2. Design the smoothing filters. (iii) Compare the number of complex operations used in the two schemes. (iv) Simulate your designs with an interesting signal. The digital sequences to be interpolated are limited to a bandwidth of $2\pi/16$. ‡

References

Jackson (1996), Secs. 5.3, 13.1
Oppenheim and Schafer (1989), Secs. 3.6.1 - 3.6.2
Proakis and Manolakis (1996), Sec. 10.3

17 Sampling Digital Signals

At the outset we noted that digital signals are commonly derived by sampling an analog waveform. Likewise, one can derive new digital signals by sampling, or **decimating**, digital signals. The operation of sampling a digital sequence is greatly clarified by examining the operation in the frequency domain. We consider a digital signal $\{x_n\}$ with a DTFT $X1(\omega)$:

$$x_n = \frac{1}{2 \cdot \pi} \cdot \int_0^{2 \cdot \pi} e^{i \cdot n \cdot \omega} \cdot X1(\omega) \, d\omega \tag{17.1}$$

We form the sampled, or decimated, sequence $\{y_n\}$ by taking every Kth sample of the sequence $\{x_n\}$:

$$y_n = x_{K \cdot n} \tag{17.2}$$

The sequence $\{y_n\}$ has a DTFT $Y1(\omega)$ and so has the representation

$$y_n = \frac{1}{2 \cdot \pi} \cdot \int_0^{2 \cdot \pi} e^{i \cdot n \cdot \omega} \cdot Y1(\omega) \, d\omega \tag{17.3}$$

But, in view of (17.1) and (17.2), it also has the representation

$$y_n = \frac{1}{2 \cdot \pi} \cdot \int_0^{2 \cdot \pi} e^{i \cdot K \cdot n \cdot \omega} \cdot X1(\omega) \, d\omega \tag{17.4}$$

We would like to relate the two representations (17.3) and (17.4), and thereby relate $Y1(\omega)$ to $X1(\omega)$. We proceed in a manner quite similar to our discussion of sampling analog waveforms in **Chapter 15**.

Aliasing and Adequate Sampling

We try to rewrite (17.4) with the exponential appearing with argument $n\omega$, as in (17.3). So, in the right side of (17.4), we set $u = K\omega$, getting the form

$$y_n = \frac{1}{K} \cdot \left[\frac{1}{2 \cdot \pi} \cdot \int_0^{2 \cdot \pi \cdot K} e^{i \cdot n \cdot u} \cdot X1\left(\frac{u}{K}\right) du \right] \qquad (17.5)$$

We break the finite integral of (17.5) into the sum of K integrals, each over an interval of width 2π. We get

$$y_n = \sum_{k=0}^{K-1} \frac{1}{K} \cdot \left[\frac{1}{2 \cdot \pi} \cdot \int_{k \cdot 2 \cdot \pi}^{(k+1) \cdot (2 \cdot \pi)} e^{i \cdot n \cdot u} \cdot X1\left(\frac{u}{K}\right) du \right]$$

In each integral separately, we set $v = u - k2\pi$. Then,

$$y_n = \sum_{k=0}^{K-1} \frac{1}{K} \cdot \left[\frac{1}{2 \cdot \pi} \cdot \int_0^{2 \cdot \pi} e^{i \cdot n \cdot (v + k \cdot 2 \cdot \pi)} \cdot X1\left(\frac{v + k \cdot 2 \cdot \pi}{K}\right) dv \right]$$

We recognize that $\exp(ink2\pi) = 1$ and hence

$$y_n = \frac{1}{K} \cdot \sum_{k=0}^{K-1} \frac{1}{2 \cdot \pi} \cdot \int_0^{2 \cdot \pi} e^{i \cdot n \cdot v} \cdot X1\left(\frac{v + k \cdot 2 \cdot \pi}{K}\right) dv \qquad (17.6)$$

or

$$y_n = \frac{1}{2 \cdot \pi} \cdot \int_0^{2 \cdot \pi} e^{i \cdot n \cdot v} \cdot \frac{1}{K} \cdot \sum_{k=0}^{K-1} X1\left(\frac{v + k \cdot 2 \cdot \pi}{K}\right) dv \qquad (17.7)$$

Comparing (17.7) and (17.3), we have

$$Y1(\omega) = \frac{1}{K} \cdot \sum_{k=0}^{K-1} X1\left(\frac{\omega + k \cdot 2 \cdot \pi}{K}\right) \qquad (17.8)$$

This relation shows the **aliasing** caused by sampling. The DTFT Y1 is the sum of a finite number, K, of translated and scaled replicas of X1 called **aliases**.

EXERCISE 17.1 Choose an X1(ω), then sketch Y1(ω) as given by (17.8). ¤

PROBLEM 17.1

Compare, step by step, this derivation of the form of the DTFT of a sampled sequence with the derivation of the form of the DTFT of a sampled analog waveform given in <u>**Chapter 15**</u>. ‡

We may interpret this sampling result as follows. By decimating, or sampling, a sequence, the variations in the sequence are more rapid and we can expect that the spectrum will be broader. This renders agreeable the frequency scaling given by Y1(ω)=X1(ω/K)/K. But this cannot be the correct relation because then Y1(ω) would have period K2π. But we can force the 2π periodicity by adding in (K–1) translates {X1((ω+k2π)/K), k=1,...,K–1}. This is exactly (17.8)!

Example 17.1

We illustrate (17.8). We construct a simple DTFT in [0,2π], in DFT order, and choose K=4.

$$X1(\omega) := \text{if}\left[\omega \le \pi, \exp\left[-\frac{\omega^2}{2\cdot\left(\frac{\pi}{32}\right)}\right], \exp\left[-\frac{(2\cdot\pi-\omega)^2}{2\cdot\left(\frac{\pi}{32}\right)}\right]\right]\cdot(\omega \ge 0)\cdot(\omega \le 2\cdot\pi)$$

$$\omega := 0, 0.1 .. 2\cdot\pi$$

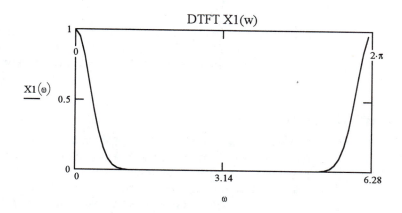

DTFT X1(w)

$$K := 4 \qquad Y1(\omega) := \frac{1}{K}\cdot\sum_{k=0}^{K-1} X1\left(\frac{\omega + k\cdot 2\cdot\pi}{K}\right)$$

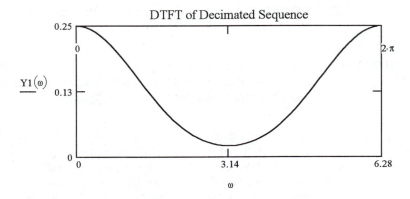

The effect of aliasing is evident: the spectrum X1 is stretched and the aliases overlap. ‡

Adequate Sampling

We note that if the $\{x_n\}$ is bandlimited to $(-\Omega/2, \Omega/2)$, then we can avoid any overlap of the aliases if $K\Omega/2 < \pi$. That is, for **adequate sampling**,

$$\frac{2 \cdot \pi}{K} > \Omega \tag{17.9}$$

In this case, we have the simple relation

$$Y1(\omega) = \frac{1}{K} \cdot X1\left(\frac{\omega}{K}\right) \qquad (-\pi < \omega < \pi) \tag{17.10}$$

Comparing these results to those for sampling an analog signal, we see that K plays the role of Ts and $2\pi/K$ plays the role of the sampling frequency vs. We call K the **sampling period**.

Interpolation

In the absence of side information, if we are given the sequence $\{y_n\}$, there is no way to recover the decimated sequence $\{x_n\}$. We could fill in the missing samples in an arbitrary manner. But if $\{y_n\}$ adequately samples a real or virtual sequence $\{x_n\}$ then we should be able to recover $\{x_n\}$ from the sample sequence $\{y_n\}$. We now prove this. Our argument closely parallels that for the Shannon interpolation formula of <u>**Chapter 15**</u>.

We begin with the IDTFT representation of $\{x_n\}$ and strive to involve the sample sequence $\{y_n\}$ explicitly.

$$x_n = \frac{1}{2 \cdot \pi} \cdot \int_{-\frac{\pi}{K}}^{\frac{\pi}{K}} e^{i \cdot n \cdot \omega} \cdot X1(\omega) \, d\omega$$

We use the assumption that $\{x_n\}$ is adequately sampled at the period K, which further allows us to use (17.10) relating X1 and Y1.

$$x_n = \frac{1}{2 \cdot \pi} \cdot \int_{-\frac{\pi}{K}}^{\frac{\pi}{K}} e^{i \cdot n \cdot \omega} \cdot K \cdot Y1(K \cdot \omega) \, d\omega$$

We explicitly bring in the samples by using the definition of the DTFT Y1:

$$x_n = \frac{1}{2 \cdot \pi} \cdot \int_{-\frac{\pi}{K}}^{\frac{\pi}{K}} e^{i \cdot n \cdot \omega} \cdot K \cdot \sum_{m = -\infty}^{\infty} e^{-i \cdot m \cdot K \cdot \omega} \cdot y_m \, d\omega$$

Now we interchange the order of integration and summation.

$$x_n = \sum_{m = -\infty}^{\infty} y_m \cdot \frac{K}{2 \cdot \pi} \cdot \int_{-\frac{\pi}{K}}^{\frac{\pi}{K}} e^{i \cdot (n - m \cdot K) \cdot \omega} \, d\omega$$

▓ **EXERCISE 17.2** Evaluate the integral in this last form for $\{x_n\}$. ¤

So we find the desired interpolation formula to reconstruct the sequence $\{x_n\}$.

Interpolation formula: $\quad x_n = \displaystyle\sum_{m=-\infty}^{\infty} y_m \cdot \dfrac{\sin\left[(n - m \cdot K) \cdot \dfrac{\pi}{K}\right]}{\left[(n - m \cdot K) \cdot \dfrac{\pi}{K}\right]}$ $\qquad$ (17.11)

Note that the interpolation sequence $\{\sin[n\pi/K]/[n\pi/K]\}$ has the desired property of being one at time n=0 and zero for n otherwise. It also has the undesirable property of falling off slowly, requiring many computations for an accurate reconstruction for each x_n. Thus the result is mainly of theoretical interest. We have already discussed efficient interpolation methods in **Chapter 16**.

PROBLEM 17.2

Compare, step by step, this derivation of the interpolation formula of a sampled sequence with the derivation of the interpolation formula of an analog waveform given in **Chapter 15**. ‡

We now consider an example of interpolation with this interpolation formula.

Example 17.2 _____
Consider the following sequence.

$$N := 128 \qquad\qquad n := 0 .. N - 1 \qquad\qquad \omega_n := n \cdot \frac{2 \cdot \pi}{N}$$

$$x_n := \cos\left(\frac{2 \cdot \pi}{N} \cdot 10 \cdot n\right) + 2 \cdot \cos\left(\frac{2 \cdot \pi}{N} \cdot 20 \cdot n + \frac{\pi}{3}\right) \qquad X := \sqrt{N} \cdot \text{icfft}(x)$$

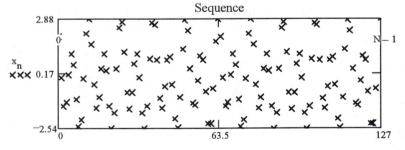
Sequence

DFT (Magnitude)

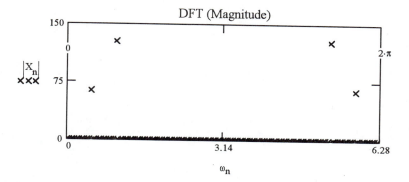

$$\omega_n$$

We form the sequence $\{y_n\}$ by sampling at period K, with N/K integer here, from the sequence $\{x_n\}$.

$$K := 2 \quad nn := 0 .. \frac{N}{K} - 1 \quad y_{nn} := x_{K \cdot nn} \qquad Y := \sqrt{\frac{N}{K}} \cdot icfft(y) \qquad u_{nn} := nn \cdot \frac{2 \cdot \pi}{\left(\frac{N}{K}\right)}$$

Sampled Sequence

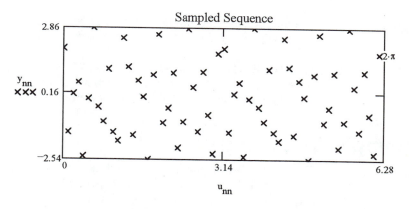

$$u_{nn}$$

DFT (Magnitude)

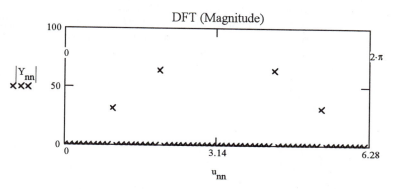

$$u_{nn}$$

$$\text{xint}_n := \sum_{m=0}^{\frac{N}{K}-1} y_m \cdot if\left[n-m\cdot K=0,1, \frac{\sin\left[(n-m\cdot K)\cdot \frac{\pi}{K}\right]}{\left[(n-m\cdot K)\cdot \frac{\pi}{K}\right]}\right]$$

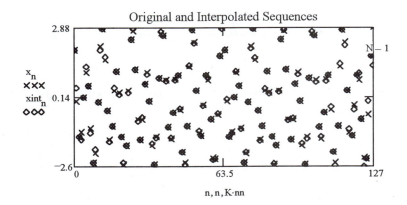

Original and Interpolated Sequences

We see that the interpolation is fairly accurate, except near the endpoints where the interpolation is based on fewer samples. ‡

EXERCISE 17.3 Increase K (note that N/K must be an integer) and note the DTFT of {y_n} to see when aliasing begins. Note carefully the corresponding interpolations. At what K does aliasing begin? ¤

Sample Averaging

The data rate is commonly reduced by averaging adjacent samples. This seems to be a reasonable procedure with noisy data that may be rare or expensive data. Our intuition would be that it is advantageous, relative to discarding samples, to average data to reduce the effect of noise. Suppose we are given a sequence {x_n, n=0,1,...}. We form a new sequence {y_n, n=0,1,...} according to the following prescription.

$$K := 4 \quad nn := 0 .. \frac{N}{K} - 1$$

$$\text{yave}_{nn} := \frac{1}{K} \cdot \sum_{k=0}^{K-1} (K \cdot nn - k \geq 0) \cdot x_{K \cdot nn - k} \qquad (17.12)$$

$$Y := \sqrt{\frac{N}{K}} \cdot icfft(\text{yave}) \qquad u_{nn} := nn \cdot \frac{2 \cdot \pi}{\left(\frac{N}{K}\right)}$$

We can better understand the processing (17.12) if we consider it as the result of two concatenated operations: filtering and decimation. We now understand both of these operations. We introduce the auxiliary sequence $\{z_n\}$ and observe the following.

$$z_n := \frac{1}{K} \cdot \sum_{k=0}^{K-1} \text{if}(n-k<0, 0, x_{n-k})$$ (17.13)

1. The sequence $\{z_n, n=0,1,...\}$ is a filtering of the sequence $\{x_n, n=0,1,...\}$ by a simple MA of length K and weights 1/K.
2. The sequence $\{y_n, n=0,1,...\}$ is a K-fold decimation of the sequence $\{z_n, n=0,1,...\}$.

The MA multiplies its well-known frequency response by the DTFT of the data sequence. Thus the MA should be wellmatched to the bandwidth of the sequence to be smoothed. It will give a distortion of the sequence - and a delay of K/2 - which will have to be balanced against noise averaging. Of course, a more sophisticated filter should be used. We leave this to a project.

Example 17.3

We illustrate the idea of sample rate reduction by sample averaging and compare it with sample decimation in a noisy situation.

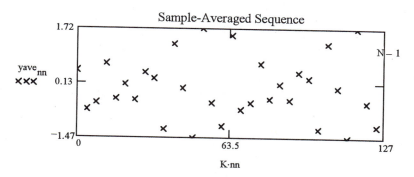

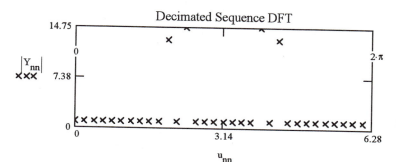

Of course, the simple MA filter has poor sidelobe behavior. If the data sequence has additive noise, then we might use a nonrectangular window to remove more of the noise. The amount of noise suppression depends on the noise spectrum.

$$\text{var} := 10.0 \qquad\qquad \text{no} := \text{rnorm}(N, 0, \text{var}) \qquad\qquad xc := x + \text{no}$$

$$\text{yave}_{nn} := \frac{1}{K} \cdot \sum_{k=0}^{K-1} (K \cdot nn - k \geq 0) \cdot xc_{K \cdot nn - k}$$

$$\text{ydec}_{nn} := xc_{nn \cdot K}$$

We compare these sequences.

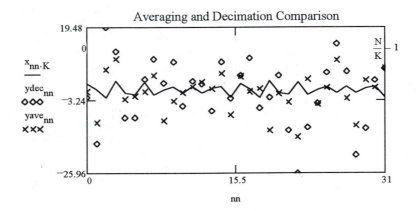

$x_{nn \cdot K}$
___

ydec_{nn}
◇◇◇

yave_{nn}
✕✕✕

Averaging and Decimation Comparison

A measure for comparison of yave and ydec is the mean-square error with x. (yave is not perfectly aligned with ydec, as the MA gives a delay of K/2, which is decimated to a delay of 1/2.)

$$\text{MSE}_{\text{ave}} := \sum_{nn=0}^{\frac{N}{K}-1} \left(x_{K \cdot nn} - \text{yave}_{nn} \right)^2 \qquad\qquad \text{MSE}_{\text{ave}} = 1.353 \cdot 10^3$$

$$\text{MSE}_{\text{dec}} := \sum_{nn=0}^{\frac{N}{K}-1} \left(x_{K \cdot nn} - \text{ydec}_{nn} \right)^2 \qquad\qquad \text{MSE}_{\text{dec}} = 3.393 \cdot 10^3$$

Thus the indication of the plot, that yave is a closer approximation to x than ydec, is borne out by the MSE computation. ‡

EXERCISE 17.4 Arrange the parameters of the illustration so that a larger K can be used without aliasing. Then comment on the improved noise reduction, if any. ¤

Interpolation-Decimation by a Rational Factor

We have been studying methods to vary the sample spacing by interpolation and decimation for integer factors. By concatenating interpolation with a factor L and decimation with a factor K, we can change the sample spacing by the factor K/L.

The need for changing the sample period may be required to transfer data between DSP systems with different sample periods. This is common in entertainment systems and may have been made difficult intentionally. Also, for efficiency in computation a single DSP system may use two or more sample periods. Such systems are called **multirate DSP systems**.

Example 17.4

We exemplify changing the sample period by a rational factor K/L using the methods we have implemented.

$$N := 128 \qquad n := 0 .. N - 1 \qquad x_n := \cos\left(\frac{2 \cdot \pi}{N} \cdot 4 \cdot n\right) + 2 \cdot \cos\left(\frac{2 \cdot \pi}{N} \cdot 7 \cdot n + \frac{\pi}{3}\right)$$

$$X := \sqrt{N} \cdot \mathrm{icfft}(x) \qquad u_n := \frac{2 \cdot \pi}{N} \cdot n$$

Sequence

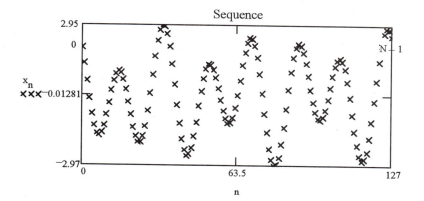

Sequence DFT

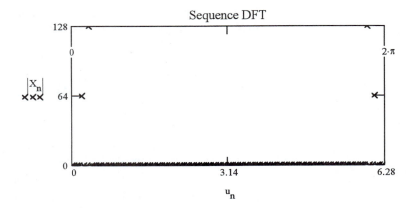

We form the sequence $\{y_n, n=0,1,...\}$ by injecting zeros into the sequence $\{x_n, n=0,1,...\}$.

$$L := 5 \qquad NN := L \cdot N \qquad nn := 0 .. NN - 1 \qquad v_{nn} := \frac{2 \cdot \pi}{NN} \cdot nn$$

$$y_{nn} := if\left(mod(nn, L) = 0, x_{\frac{nn}{L}}, 0\right) \qquad\qquad Y := \sqrt{L \cdot N} \cdot icfft(y)$$

Zero-Injected Sequence

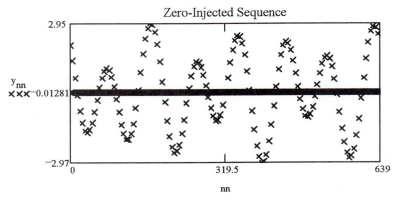

Injected Sequence DFT

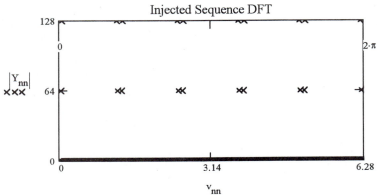

We low-pass filter $\{y_n\}$ to retain only the rescaled DTFT of $\{x_n\}$ centered at 0. We do this here with an ideal filter.

$$Yf_{nn} := if\left[\left(nn > \frac{N}{2}\right) \cdot \left(nn < NN - \frac{N}{2}\right), 0, Y_{nn}\right] \qquad yf := \frac{1}{\sqrt{NN}} \cdot cfft(Yf) \quad \textbf{(17.14)}$$

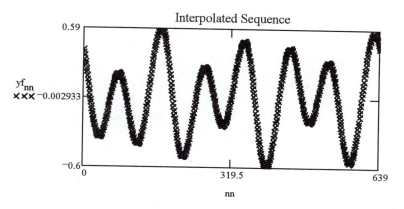

We form the decimated sequence $\{z_n, n=0,1,...\}$ by deleting samples from the sequence $\{yf_n, n=0,1,...\}$.

$$K := 3 \qquad MM := \frac{NN}{K} \qquad j := 0 .. MM - 1 \qquad w_j := j \cdot \frac{2 \cdot \pi}{MM}$$

$$z_j := yf_{K \cdot j} \qquad Z := \sqrt{MM} \cdot icfft(z)$$

Decimated Sequence

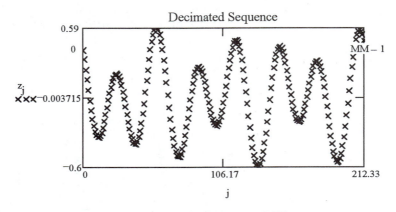

z_j
×××−0.003715

Decimated Sequence DFT

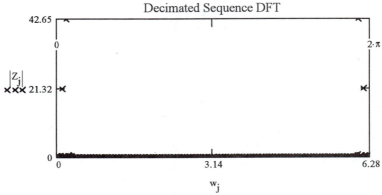

$|Z_j|$
××× 21.32

$$zdd_j := \cos\left(\frac{2\cdot\pi}{N}\cdot 4\cdot\frac{K}{L}\cdot j\right) + 2\cdot\cos\left(\frac{2\cdot\pi}{N}\cdot 7\cdot\frac{K}{L}\cdot j + \frac{\pi}{3}\right)$$

Interpolated and Decimated Sequences

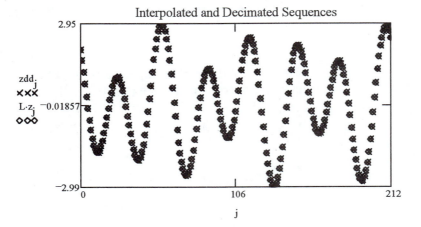

zdd_j
×××
$L\cdot z_j$ −0.01857
◇◇◇

We verify that this scheme changes the sample period by the factor K/L. ‡

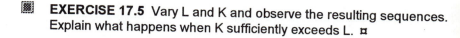 **EXERCISE 17.5** Vary L and K and observe the resulting sequences. Explain what happens when K sufficiently exceeds L. ¤

Project 17.1

In the above discussion of decimation by sample averaging, a simple MA was used. It has high sidelobes, allowing a relatively large amount of noise to pass. Also, it has a decidedly nonuniform mainlobe, thereby nonuniformly weighting the signal sequence DTFT and resulting in a distorted signal. So we wish to apply our knowledge of FIR design to better reject out-of-band noise and pass the signal without distortion. Suppose the signals to be expected are all well confined to $(-\pi/8, \pi/8)$ and the additive noise is white over $(-\pi, \pi)$. Using any of the FIR design methods we have studied, design a filter for this application. Compare its MSE with the MSE of simple decimation. ‡

References

Jackson (1996), Sec. 13.1
Oppenheim and Schafer (1989), Sec. 3.6
Proakis and Manolakis (1996), Secs. 10.1 - 10.4

18 Linear Difference Equations

We have at this point almost exclusively discussed digital filters with a finite-length impulse response and we have emphasized processing finite-length sequences. This restriction allowed us to discuss many important DSP topics that did not require mathematical models of infinite-length sequences and their attendant, more difficult theory. We recall that the starting point (**Chapter 2**) for the discussion of FIR filters was the input-output relation

$$y_n = \sum_{m=0}^{M} b_m \cdot x_{n-m} \tag{18.1}$$

Of course, **differences** of the indices of the input sequence $\{x_n\}$ appear. Curiosity could lead us to consider a form that also involved differences of the input:

$$\sum_{k=0}^{N} a_k \cdot y_{n-k} = \sum_{m=0}^{M} b_m \cdot x_{n-m} \tag{18.2}$$

The relation (18.2) is called a **linear difference equation (LDE)**. The form (18.2) has appeal because it is a natural form for digital computation. Note that the number of real multiplies-adds, for each y_n, is about M+N+2, assuming $a_0 = 1$.

Difference Equations

Assuming that $a_0 = 1$ without loss of generality - as we can just divide through by a_0 and redefine the a_k and b_m - we rearrange (18.2) into the form

$$y_n = -\sum_{k=1}^{N} a_k \cdot y_{n-k} + \sum_{m=0}^{M} b_m \cdot x_{n-m} \tag{18.3}$$

As was the case with (18.1), (18.3) is not completely defined until the set of sequences upon which it is to be subjected are defined. We take these to be sequences defined on the set of indices [0,1,...). Then, in (18.3), any sequence member referenced with a negative index is understood to be defined as zero. This eliminates a solution, called the **homogeneous solution**, that does not depend on the input. In DSP we are normally interested in the solution, called the **particular solution**, determined by the input sequence. *We understand that any further reference in this and others chapters to (18.3) assumes this completed definition.*

Causality

The LDE (18.3) defines a causal operation, or filter. As now y_n has no solution part independent of x_n and only the present and finite past indices appear in (18.3), it is causal by definition.

Linearity

It is also a linear operation. That is, if y1 solves (18.3) for input x1 and y2 solves (18.3) for input x2, then form $y=\alpha y1+\beta y2$. Using the corresponding right sides of (18.3) and the linearity of the finite sums, we find

$$y_n = -\sum_{k=1}^{N} a_k \cdot y_{n-k} + \sum_{m=0}^{M} b_m \cdot \left(\alpha \cdot x1_{n-m} + \beta \cdot x2_{n-m}\right)$$

Invariance

The operation (18.3) is also an invariant operation. That is, if $\{y_n\}$ is the solution to (18.3) for input $\{x_n\}$ then $\{y_{n-nd}\}$, nd >= 0, is the solution to (18.3) for the input $\{x_{n-nd}\}$.

$$y_{n-nd} = -\sum_{k=1}^{N} a_k \cdot y_{n-nd-k} + \sum_{m=0}^{M} b_m \cdot x_{n-nd-m}$$

We see that we can simply translate the input and output sequences together and still satisfy (18.3). This property accrues because the coefficients $\{a_k\}$ and $\{b_m\}$ in (18.3) do not depend on n.

There is some common nomenclature used with an LDE. If all the $a_k=0$ in (18.3), then (18.3) is called a **moving average (MA)** computation, as we know. If M=0 in (18.3), then (18.3) is called an **autoregressive (AR)** computation. If N>0 and M>0, (18.3) is called an **autoregressive-moving average (ARMA)** computation. We see that (18.3) generally computes the present value, y_n, of the output sequence as a sum of two sums. One is a weighted sum of present and a finite number of past inputs; it is called the **nonrecursive part**. The other sum is a weighted sum of a finite number of past outputs; it is called the **recursive part**. The **order** of the LDE is the maximum of N and M.

The presence of the AR part of (18.3) admits a new class of filters that can have interesting frequency responses while remaining computationally very attractive. However, two fundamentally new phenomena can now arise. First, because the output is computed recursively, even though the input may be a finite-length sequence, the output sequence may be of infinite length. Such systems are said to have an **infinite impulse response (IIR)**. Second, the recursive calculation can be unstable. That is, the output sequence $\{y_n\}$ can grow without bound, with increasing n, even for an input sequence $\{x_n\}$ composed of bounded numbers. Naturally, we are interested in conditions sufficient to prevent instability. But first we consider an example.

Example 18.1 _____
Consider the following first-order AR system, with a single, real parameter a.

$$n=0 \qquad y_0 = x_0$$

(18.4)

$$n>0 \qquad y_n = -a \cdot y_{n-1} + x_n$$

We implement this recursion in Mathcad, computing the system's output for a unit impulse input sequence, the system's IR, to a length N.

$$N := 64 \qquad n := 0 .. N-1 \qquad x_n := \delta(n,0)$$

$$a := -0.9 \qquad y_0 := x_0 \qquad y_n := \text{if}\left(n=0, x_0, -a \cdot y_{n-1} + x_n\right) \quad \ddagger$$

PROBLEM 18.5

Show that, if {h_n, n=0,1,...} is a real sequence, then H(z)*=H(z*). Then show that if z_m is such that H(z_m)=0, then necessarily H(z_m*)=0. And, if p_k is such that 1/H(p_k)=0, then necessarily 1/H(p_k*)=0. ‡

PROBLEM 18.6

Using (18.8), show that the IR is causal. ‡

Example 18.3 _____

A simple digital filter with an IIR is the **quadratic resonator**, defined by the following coefficient vectors. We have already found its IIR in Example 18.2.

$$r := 0.85 \quad \theta := \frac{\pi}{4} \quad \beta := 0.99 \quad a := \begin{bmatrix} 1 \\ -2 \cdot r \cdot \cos(\theta) \\ r^2 \end{bmatrix} \quad b := \begin{bmatrix} 1 \\ 0 \\ -\beta^2 \end{bmatrix}$$

The numerator of the transfer function (18.8) is the polynomial

$$n(z) := z^2 - \beta^2$$

so the zeros of the transfer function are $z_0=\beta$ and $z_1=-\beta$. The denominator polynomial of (18.8) is

$$d(z) := z^2 - 2 \cdot r \cdot \cos(\theta) \cdot z + r^2$$

so the poles of the transfer function are $p_0=r \exp(i\theta)$ and $p_1=r \exp(-i\theta)$. The pole-zero plot is

z0re := -β	z1re := β	p0re := r·cos(θ)	p1re := p0re
z0im := 0	z1im := 0	p0im := r·sin(θ)	p1im := -p0im

$$\omega := 0, 2 \cdot \frac{\pi}{128} .. 2 \cdot \pi$$

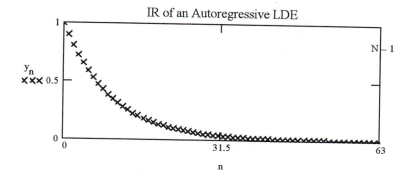

IR of an Autoregressive LDE

▦ **EXERCISE 18.1** Vary parameter a and note that the behavior appears to be exponential. Describe the plot when |a|<1 and when |a|>1. ¤

PROBLEM 18.1

Calculating the recursion for a few iterations and making an induction, show that the IIR is an exponential sequence. ‡

▦ **EXERCISE 18.2** Change the input to the system (18.4) to a sinusoid and repeat Exercise 18.1. ¤

This simple example of an AR system exhibits behavior generally encountered in an IIR corresponding to a linear difference equation: the growth or decay is exponentially fast. We now generalize these observations.

We can, in principle, find the IR of the system defined by (18.3) by recursive evaluation. We may be able to find a useful expression for h_n for any n. We may also find that the sequence $\{h_n\}$ does not converge. In Example 18.1, $h_n=a^n$ so that, for |a|>1, $|h_n|$ increases without limit as n increases without limit.

Knowing the IR h_m for m=0,...,n, the output y_n may be computed using the linearity and invariance of (18.3). For any input $\{x_n\}$, y_n will depend on x_n as $h_0 x_n$, upon x_{n-1} as $h_1 x_{n-1}$ and so on, because of the invariance property of (18.3). By the linearity of (18.3), y_n will be the sum of all of these contributions:

$$y_n = \sum_{m=0}^{n} h_m \cdot x_{n-m} \qquad (18.5)$$

That is, the output sequence $\{y_n\}$ is given by the **convolution** of the IR $\{h_n\}$ and the input sequence $\{x_n\}$.

Note that, as n increases without limit, the sum consists of a possibly unlimited number of terms and so y_n will be defined only if the convolution sum converges. Suppose that $\{x_n\}$ is a **bounded sequence**: that is, there is a B<∞ such that x_n<B for all n=0,1,.... Then we would like y_n to be bounded for all n=0,1,.... We note the string of inequalities

$$|y_n| := \left| \sum_{m=0}^{n} h_m \cdot x_{n-m} \right| \leq \sum_{m=0}^{n} |h_m| \cdot |x_{n-m}| \leq B \cdot \sum_{m=0}^{n} |h_m|$$

Then, as n increases without limit, y_n will be bounded if the IR $\{h_n\}$ is absolutely summable; that is, if

$$\sum_{m=0}^{\infty} |h_m| < \infty \qquad (18.6)$$

PROBLEM 18.2

Show that if a specific IIR is not absolutely summable, then there is a bounded input sequence such that y_n is unbounded. ‡

Stability Definition Thus we make the following definition: the system (18.3) is **stable** if and only if its IR $\{h_n\}$ is absolutely summable.

EXERCISE 18.3 Show that the IIR of Example 18.1 is absolutely summable. ¤

We would like to have an alternative way to characterize a stable system. This is in part because the convolution (18.5) is not a practical direct implementation for an IIR. Rather, (18.3) is the computationally attractive form. It is completely specified by the $\{a_k\}$ and $\{b_m\}$. In fact, we can note that only the $\{a_k\}$ can be involved in the question of stability.

 EXERCISE 18.4 Show that the IR of (18.3) depends on all the $\{b_m\}$. ¤

Stability Criterion The system (18.3) is stable if and only if the roots $\{p_0,...,p_{N-1}\}$ of the Nth-order **characteristic polynomial** of coefficients $(a_0,a_1,...,a_N)$ have magnitude less than 1: $|p_n| < 1$. Geometrically, the roots of the characteristic polynomial must lie within the unit circle in the complex (z) plane.

We do not prove this assertion. We also note without proof that the IR itself can be expressed in terms of the $\{p_0,...,p_{N-1}\}$. We cite the case when the roots are all distinct. Then, for appropriate constants $\{c_j\}$ determined by $\{y_{-j}=0, j=1,...,N\}$,

$$h_n := \sum_{j=1}^{N} c_j \cdot \left(p_j\right)^n \quad \square$$

It is clear with this representation that $\{h_n\}$ is absolutely summable if and only if $|p_j|<1$, $j=1,...,N$.

EXERCISE 18.5 Find the characteristic root of the system of Example 18.1. ¤

Example 18.2

We consider a second-order ARMA system, defined by a specific set of parameters.

$$r := 0.9 \qquad \theta := \frac{\pi}{4} \qquad \beta := 0.99 \qquad a := \begin{bmatrix} 1 \\ -2 \cdot r \cdot \cos(\theta) \\ r^2 \end{bmatrix} \qquad b := \begin{bmatrix} 1 \\ 0 \\ -\beta^2 \end{bmatrix}$$

We implement the recursion (18.3) in Mathcad, computing the system's output for a unit impulse input sequence, the system's IR, to a length N. ‡

$$N := 64 \qquad n := 0 .. N - 1 \qquad x_n := \delta(n, 0)$$

$$y_0 := b_0 \cdot x_0 \qquad y_1 := -a_1 \cdot y_0 + \left(b_0 \cdot x_1 + b_1 \cdot x_0\right)$$

$$y_n := \text{if}\left[n \geq 2, \left(-a_1 \cdot y_{n-1} - a_2 \cdot y_{n-2}\right) + \left(b_0 \cdot x_n + b_1 \cdot x_{n-1} + b_2 \cdot x_{n-2}\right), y_n\right]$$

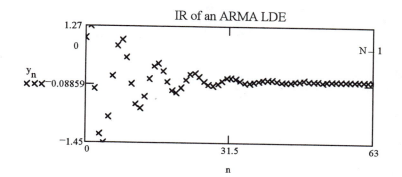

IR of an ARMA LDE

EXERCISE 18.6 Vary the parameter r in Example 18.2. Describe the plot when r<1 and when r>1. Also vary θ and β and describe the effects. ¤

PROBLEM 18.3 Write out the characteristic polynomial and find the characteristic roots of the system of Example 18.2 and hence a condition for stability. ‡

EXERCISE 18.7 Change the input to the system (18.4) to a sinusoid and repeat the analysis requested in Exercise 18.6. ¤

PROBLEM 18.4 Show that the simple MA, which we have hitherto written in nonrecursive form, may be written in recursive form. ‡

Frequency Response

As with FIR filters, it is again true that the nature of IIR filters can be greatly clarified by examining the filtering operation in the frequency domain of the DTFT. We must consider the DTFT of infinite length sequences in order to generally define the frequency response of an IIR filter. Fortunately, for a stable filter - the only kind of interest to us here - the IIR is absolutely summable and the DTFT is well defined (**Chapter 7**).

Taking the DTFT of (18.3) and using its **Property 7.3** concerning time delay, we find

$$\sum_{k=0}^{N} a_k e^{-i \cdot \omega \cdot k} \cdot Y1(\omega) = \sum_{m=0}^{M} b_m e^{-i \cdot \omega \cdot m} \cdot X1(\omega)$$

from which we find that the frequency response $H1(\omega)=Y1(\omega)/X1(\omega)$ is

$$H1(\omega) = \frac{\displaystyle\sum_{m=0}^{M} b_m e^{-i \cdot \omega \cdot m}}{\displaystyle\sum_{k=0}^{N} a_k e^{-i \cdot \omega \cdot k}} \tag{18.7}$$

The right side of (18.7), H[exp(iω)], is a rational function of exp(iω). Clearly we can reverse the steps that led from (18.2) to (18.7). Therefore, for every linear difference equation (18.3), there is a related rational frequency response (18.7) and vice versa. Thus the **coefficient vectors** a=(a_0,...,a_N) and b=(b_0,...,b_M) determine the LDE, the frequency response and the poles and zeros of the system function.

■ **EXERCISE 18.8** Find the FR of Example 18.1. Then reverse the steps and find the LDE from the FR. ¤

■ **EXERCISE 18.9** Find the FR of Example 18.2. Then reverse the steps and find the LDE from the FR. ¤

The system function H(z) is H1(ω)=H(exp(iω)) with exp(iω) replaced by z. From (18.7),

$$H(z) = \frac{\sum_{m=0}^{M} b_m \cdot z^{-m}}{\sum_{k=0}^{N} a_k \cdot z^{-k}} \tag{18.8a}$$

In factored form the transfer function is

$$H(z) = z^{N-M} \cdot \frac{\left[b_0 \cdot \prod_{m=0}^{M-1} (z - z_m) \right]}{\left[a_0 \cdot \prod_{n=0}^{N-1} (z - p_n) \right]} \tag{18.8b}$$

Note that the roots of the characteristic polynomial of the LDE are the poles {p_n} of the system function H(z). For a stable system, these poles lie inside the unit circle. The zeros of the transfer function are the roots {z_m} of the polynomial of coefficients (b_0,...,b_M). For a real IR, any complex roots must occur in complex conjugate pairs.

Pole-Zero Plot

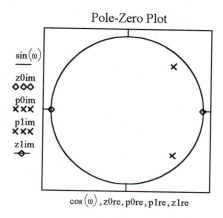

$\dfrac{\sin(\omega)}{}$

z0im
◇◇◇

p0im
✗✗✗

p1im
✗✗✗

z1im
◆

$\cos(\omega), z0re, p0re, p1re, z1re$

The frequency response is

$$H1(\omega) := \frac{n(\exp(i \cdot \omega))}{d(\exp(i \cdot \omega))}$$

Resonator FR Magnitude

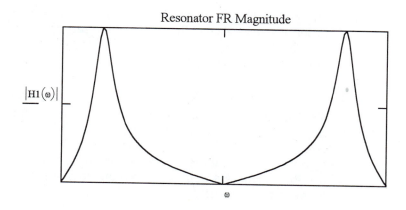

$\overline{|H1(\omega)|}$

ω

Resonator FR Phase

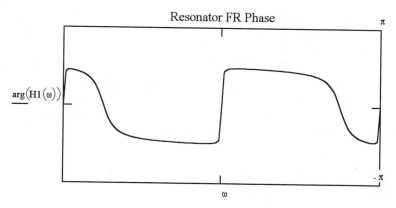

π

$\overline{\arg(H1(\omega))}$

$-\pi$

ω

We note that the phase of the frequency response is nonlinear, as is generally true of IIR filters. Note that the total phase shift, as ω increases from 0 to 2π, is zero. We can predict this based on the geometric view, which was discussed in Chapter 9 for FIR filters and which we will discuss in Chapter 19 for IIR filters. ‡

 EXERCISE 18.10 Vary the parameters (r,θ,β) and observe the variation of the FR. In particular, note the behavior for $\beta=0$. ¤

Computation

If the digital filter is specified in terms of its poles, zeros and a **gain** $k=b_o/a_0$, then the factored form (18.8b) of H(z) may be formed. Setting $z=\exp(i\omega)$ gives the FR, which may be plotted to arbitrary accuracy. By expanding the numerator and denominator polynomials of H(z), one gets the power series form (18.8a) from which the coefficients $\{a_k\}$ and $\{b_m\}$ may be read out. The symbolic capability of Mathcad can be helpful in doing this. Then the LDE (18.3) can implement the actual computation of the output, given an input. As the design methods we will discuss all lead to such an initial specification of the filter's poles, zeros and gain, and as the LDE is an efficient computational algorithm, this will be our **standard procedure**.

Note that in this standard procedure we do not have to compute the IIR. The direct implementation of the convolution (18.5) would require a truncation of the IIR to achieve a finite number of computations. Such a truncation alters the FR, as discussed in **Chapter 15**. For sufficient accuracy, the truncation is likely so long that the convolution would require more computation than the LDE for each output value y_n.

Example 18.4 _____

We show the effect of truncation of the IIR on the FR in the first-order LDE of Example 18.1.

$$a := 0.9 \qquad\qquad x_n := a^n{}_0$$

For an infinite-length sequence, the condition $|a|<1$ ensures that $\{x_n, n=0,1,...\}$ is absolutely summable and hence the DTFT exists. ‡

 EXERCISE 18.11 Show that the DTFT of this exponential sequence is

$$X1(\omega) := \frac{1}{1 - a \cdot e^{-i \cdot \omega}}$$ ¤

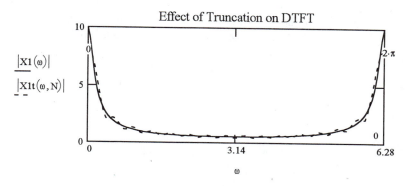

EXERCISE 18.12 Show that the DTFT of this exponential sequence truncated to length N is

$$N := 16 \qquad X1t(\omega, N) := \frac{1 - \left(a \cdot e^{-i \cdot \omega}\right)^N}{1 - a \cdot e^{-i \cdot \omega}}$$

¤

We plot these two forms for comparison.

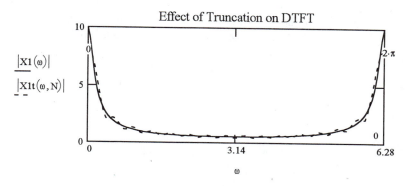

EXERCISE 18.13 Vary N in Example 18.4 and observe the quality of the approximation. ¤

Of course, the DTFT of the truncated IIR is accurately sampled by the DFT.

$$n := 0 .. N - 1 \qquad a := 0.9 \qquad xx_n := a^n \qquad \omega\omega_n := \frac{2 \cdot \pi}{N} \cdot n$$

$$dft(v) := \sqrt{N} \cdot icfft(v) \qquad XX := dft(xx)$$

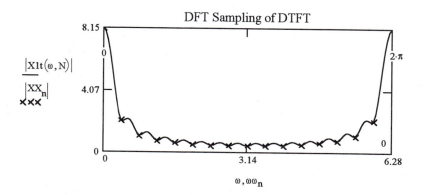

Example 18.5 _____

Suppose that we are given the N=2 poles, the M=N=2 zeros and the gain k=b₀/a₀=1 of a filter. Then its system function H(z) is of the form (18.8b).

numerator: $\quad (z - z_0) \cdot (z - z_1)$

denominator: $\quad (z - p_0) \cdot (z - p_1)$

We want to find the LDE coefficient vectors a and b, which are the coefficients of polynomials in negative powers of z and ordered in *decreasing* powers of z. If we divide the numerator and denominator polynomials by z^2, we get such polynomials.

numerator: $\quad \left(1 - z_0 \cdot \dfrac{1}{z}\right) \cdot \left(1 - z_1 \cdot \dfrac{1}{z}\right)$

denominator: $\quad \left(1 - p_0 \cdot \dfrac{1}{z}\right) \cdot \left(1 - p_1 \cdot \dfrac{1}{z}\right)$

$\dfrac{1}{w}$

The symbolic engine of Mathcad can find the polynomial coefficients, ordered in *increasing* powers of the dummy variable. We can use the variable substitution capability of the symbolic engine to get what we want. We type 1/w on the worksheet - as at the left, enclose it and choose **Copy** from the **Edit** menu. Then we enclose an instance of z in either form and choose **Substitute for Variable** from the **Symbolic** menu. We get, in turn,

numerator: $\quad (1 - z_0 \cdot w) \cdot (1 - z_1 \cdot w)$

denominator: $\quad (1 - p_0 \cdot w) \cdot (1 - p_1 \cdot w)$

Now we enclose an instance of w in either expression and choose **Polynomial Coefficients** from the **Symbolic** menu. We get, in turn,

$$\mathbf{b} \quad \begin{bmatrix} 1 \\ -z_1 - z_0 \\ z_0 \cdot z_1 \end{bmatrix} \qquad\qquad \mathbf{a} \quad \begin{bmatrix} 1 \\ -p_1 - p_0 \\ p_0 \cdot p_1 \end{bmatrix}$$

Note that the polynomial coefficients are in order of *increasing* powers of w, which is decreasing powers of z, just what we want! Given specific numerical values, we can implement the filter (18.3).

‡

Note For a detailed discussion of linear difference equations, see Roberts and Mullis (1987).

Project 18.1

Choose three zeros and three poles appropriate to a low-pass ARMA IIR filter. While we will develop some insight into choosing the poles and zeros in the next section, we should be able to do this here with a little thought. Carry out the standard procedure discussed in this section, using the techniques displayed. In particular, plot the FR showing that the filter is indeed low-pass, implement the LDE and compute the output sequence for an interesting input sequence. ‡

Project 18.2

An autoregressive IIR filter has the coefficient vector b simply the scalar 1 and one of

$$
a_1 := \begin{bmatrix} 1 \\ 0 \\ 1.183 \\ 0 \\ 0.41 \end{bmatrix}
\qquad
a_2 := \begin{bmatrix} 1 \\ -1.895 \\ 1.502 \\ -0.575 \\ 0.09 \end{bmatrix}
\qquad
a_3 := \begin{bmatrix} 1 \\ 1.895 \\ 1.502 \\ 0.575 \\ 0.09 \end{bmatrix}
$$

Determine in each case whether the filter is low-pass, bandpass or high-pass. While doing so, for each case exhibit the rational and factored forms of H(z), (18.8a) and (18.8b), repectively, and plot the FRs. ‡

References

Jackson (1996), Sec. 4.2
Oppenheim and Schafer (1989), Secs. 2.5, 5.2
Proakis and Manolakis (1996), Sec. 2.4
Roberts and Mullis (1987), Sec. 2.6

19 IIR Filters: Geometric View

The system function H(z) of an IIR filter described by a linear difference equation is, as we have seen, a rational function of z. It may be characterized by its poles and zeros and a gain constant. We can glean considerable insight into IIR filters (and discover simple designs) by considering the various factors contributing to the factored form (18.8) of the system function. We have already done this for FIR filters. For IIR filters, though, the poles do not have to be at the origin of the z-plane: for a stable filter they must be within the unit circle and for a real IR they must, if complex, occur in conjugate pairs. A little experience with the placement of poles and zeros leads us to realize that because we can place the poles away from z=0, we can, for the same order LDE, get greater selectivity of, for example, a low-pass band. We pay for this greater selectivity with a nonlinear phase that results from moving the poles away from the origin, and we are not able to pair them with their reciprocals (as we can with zeros) because the latter are outside the unit circle.

Pole-Zero Patterns

We discuss a series of illustrations to build up an understanding of IIR filters.

Example 19.1 _____

We consider again the simple IIR filter of **Example 18.1**, described by the first-order LDE

$$y_n := a \cdot y_{n-1} + x_n$$ (19.1)

Taking the DTFT of this equation and setting z=exp(iω) yields the system function

$$H(z) := \frac{z}{z-a}$$ (19.2)

This IIR filter has a zero at z=0 and a pole at z=a. If this filter is to be stable, we must have |a|<1. For this filter to have a real IR, a must be real. So we assume that -1<a<1. Let us separately consider the factor due to the pole.

pole factor: $a := 0.97$ $f(z) := \dfrac{1}{z - a}$ $z(x,y) := x + i \cdot y$

We use a surface plot (over the z-plane) to show this factor. We set the surface 0 outside the unit circle to see the frequency response.

plotting mesh: $N := 33$ $m := 0 .. N - 1$ $x_m := -1.2 + \dfrac{2.4}{N} \cdot m$

$n := 0 .. N - 1$ $y_n := -1.2 + \dfrac{2.4}{N} \cdot n$

pole factor surface: $fs_{m,n} := \mathrm{if}\!\left[\left(x_m\right)^2 + \left(y_n\right)^2 \le 1, \left| f\!\left(z\!\left(x_m, y_n\right)\right) \right|, 0 \right]$

Real Pole Factor

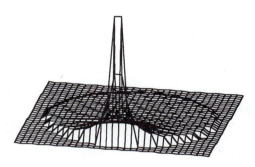

fs

The real axis is directed downward and the imaginary axis toward the right. The elevation around the unit circle gives the frequency response, with low frequencies nearest and high frequencies farthest. Note that the most dramatic influence of a pole is over a rather small area in the z-plane but it is perceptible at all frequencies. The filter is clearly a low-pass filter.

Imagining the complex phasor from the pole to the complex number exp($i\omega$), this phasor has least magnitude when ω is zero, so the system function magnitude will have a maximum there. As ω travels around the unit circle once, said phasor will rotate through a total phase of 2π, resulting in a total phase shift of -2π for the factor. Also, the phase change is most rapid as the pole is passed as ω goes through zero. If the pole is quite near the unit circle, the phase change will be nearly π.

The other factor of the system function H(z) is the numerator polynomial z. The zero at the origin of the z-plane clearly has no effect on the magnitude of the system function: the phasor from z=0 to exp(iω) is exp(iω) and it has magnitude unity . But, as ω increases from 0 to 2π the phase of said phasor increases linearly from 0 to +2π.

Therefore, the magnitude of H(z) is determined by the pole and the total phase shift is zero, with a rapid change of nearly -π near ω=0 if the pole is near the unit circle. ‡

$$H(z) := \frac{z}{z-a}$$

$$\omega := 0, \frac{2 \cdot \pi}{64} .. 2 \cdot \pi$$

$$Hs_{m,n} := if\left[\left(x_m\right)^2 + \left(y_n\right)^2 \le 1, H\left(z\left(x_m, y_n\right)\right), 0 \right]$$

$$Hsm := \overrightarrow{|Hs|}$$

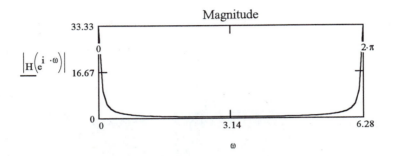

Magnitude

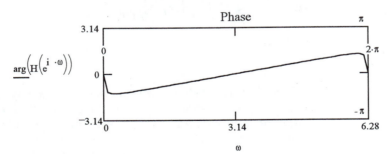

Phase

System Function H(z)

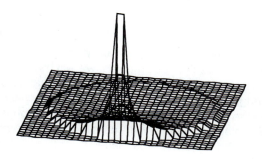

Hsm

Pole-Zero Plot

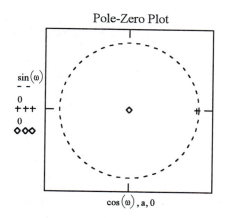

EXERCISE 19.1 Vary a in Example 19.1 and observe the variety of possible frequency responses. What range of a results (i) in a low-pass filter or (ii) in a high-pass filter? What controls the sharpness of the passband? ¤

PROBLEM 19.1

Design a low-pass filter with a -3 db cutoff of $\pi/8$. Make a pole-zero plot, a surface plot of the magnitude of the system function and a plot of the FR. ‡

PROBLEM 19.2

Design a high-pass filter with a -3 db cutoff of $7\pi/8$. Make a pole-zero plot, a surface plot of the magnitude of the system function and a plot of the FR. ‡

EXERCISE 19.2 In Example 19.1, remove the zero and note the effect on the magnitude and phase of the frequency response. Can you predict the phase? What is the corresponding LDE? What are possible benefits of having the zero? ¤

It should be clear now that we can only have either a low-pass or a high-pass filter with one pole, with or without a zero at the origin. To get a bandpass filter using poles, we will have to introduce a complex conjugate pair of poles. We expect that the maximum of the FR magnitude will be at or near the frequencies equaling the angles of the poles. If we use no zeros, the total phase shift of the system function will be -4π, with most rapid change near the pole angles. We can use two zeros placed near z=+/-1, which should increase the sharpness of the filter and also result in a total phase shift of zero in the system function. We now see if our predictions, based on this geometric view, are correct.

Example 19.2 _____

We consider a second-order ARMA defined as follows.

system
poles:
$$r := 0.85 \quad \theta := \frac{\pi}{4} \quad p1 := r \cdot e^{i \cdot \theta} \quad p2 := \overline{p1}$$

system
zeros:
$$z1 := 0.99 \qquad z2 := -0.99$$

system
function:
$$H(z) := \frac{(z - z1) \cdot (z - z2)}{(z - p1) \cdot (z - p2)}$$

We use a surface plot (over the z-plane) to show this factor. We set the surface 0 outside the unit circle to see the frequency response as an **elevation**. ‡

$$Hs_{m,n} := if\left[\left(x_m\right)^2 + \left(y_n\right)^2 \le 1, H\left(z\left(x_m, y_n\right)\right), 0 \right] \qquad Hsm := \overrightarrow{|Hs|}$$

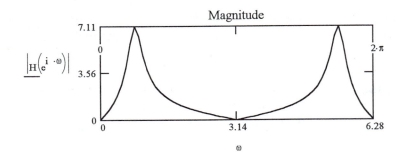

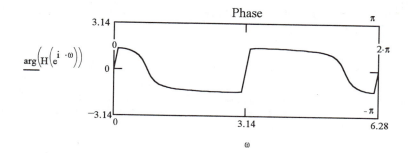

Phase

$$\underline{\arg\left(H\left(e^{i\cdot\omega}\right)\right)}$$

System Function H(z)

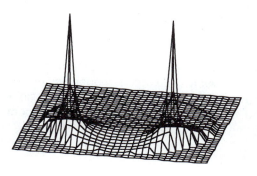

Hsm

Pole-Zero Plot

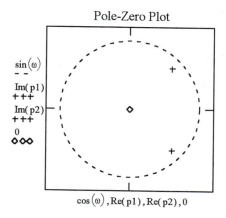

$\underline{\sin(\omega)}$

$\underset{+++}{\mathrm{Im}(p1)}$

$\underset{+++}{\mathrm{Im}(p2)}$

$\underset{\Diamond\infty}{0}$

$\cos(\omega), \mathrm{Re}(p1), \mathrm{Re}(p2), 0$

EXERCISE 19.3 Vary r and θ in Example 19.1 and observe the variety of possible frequency responses. What controls the sharpness of the passband? What controls the frequencies in the passband? ¤

Write down the LDE corresponding to this system function. ¤

In Example 19.2, remove the zeros and note the effect on the magnitude and phase of the frequency response. Can you predict these effects on the magnitude and phase? What is the corresponding LDE? What are possible benefits of having the zeros? ¤

PROBLEM 19.3

Design a bandpass filter, corresponding to a second-order LDE, with a center frequency of $\pi/4$ and bandwidth between -3 db cutoff frequencies of $\pi/8$. The system function magnitude should be as small as possible outside the passband. Make a pole-zero plot, a surface plot of the magnitude of the system function and a plot of the FR. ‡

PROBLEM 19.4

Design a bandpass filter with a center frequency of $\pi/2$ and bandwidth between -3 db cutoff frequencies of $\pi/4$. The system function magnitude should be as small as possible outside the passband. Make a pole-zero plot, a surface plot of the magnitude of the system function and a plot of the FR. ‡

Design of a Unity Gain Resonator

We wish to design a narrowband filter to recover a sinusoidal sequence of frequency $\omega c=1.0$. The filter should reject frequencies from 0 to 0.75 and from 1.25 to π with an attenuation of at least 25 db. We assume that the filter has a unity maximum gain. For speed of computation in application, we assume that the filter will be implemented by a second-order LDE. We place the two allowed zeros at z=+1 and z=-1. Such a filter is called a **unity gain resonator**. We will implement the IIR filter and simulate it.

The **design procedure** has two steps. First, we determine the pole locations as accurately as possible using trial and error with graphical assist. Second, we use a built-in optimization algorithm of Mathcad to refine the solution.

We will complete the standard procedure outlined in **Chapter 18** by implementing the filter with the LDE. We can then simulate it for an interesting input.

stop band frequencies: $\qquad \omega 1 := 0.75 \qquad \omega 2 := 1.25$

We try a design with a conjugate pair of poles near the unit circle at the frequency $\omega c = 1$. The radial placement of the poles is adjusted by trial and error.

system poles: $\qquad \omega c := 1.0 \qquad \rho := 0.987 \quad p1 := \rho \cdot \exp(i \cdot \omega c) \qquad p1c := \overline{(p1)}$

system zeros: $\qquad z1 := 1 \qquad z2 := -1$

We can now plot the frequency response, see how we did, and, adjusting the filter parameters (k, ρ) by trial and error, move close to the specifications. Since the bandwidth is narrow, we shall have to plot many frequency points to capture the maximum accurately.

frequency response: $\qquad k := 0.0129 \qquad H1(\omega) := k \cdot \dfrac{\left(e^{i \cdot \omega} - z1\right) \cdot \left(e^{i \cdot \omega} - z2\right)}{\left(e^{i \cdot \omega} - p1\right) \cdot \left(e^{i \cdot \omega} - p1c\right)}$

check specifications: $\qquad 20 \cdot \log\left(\left|\dfrac{H1(\omega 1)}{H1(\omega c)}\right|\right) = -26.643$

$\left|H1(\omega c)\right| = 0.999 \qquad\qquad 20 \cdot \log\left(\left|\dfrac{H1(\omega 2)}{H1(\omega c)}\right|\right) = -25.174$

$\omega := 0, \dfrac{2 \cdot \pi}{1024} .. 2 \cdot \pi \qquad \varepsilon := 0.0001$

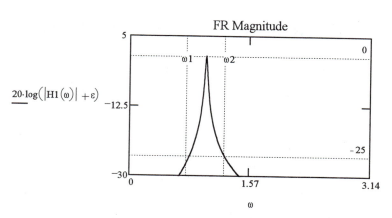

FR Magnitude

We notice that, when the specification is met at $\omega 2$, the specification is even better met at $\omega 1$. This is due to the asymmetry about ωc of the FR magnitude. Note that the FR magnitude has been plotted only for ω in $[0, \pi]$.

Optimization Algorithm

We may use Mathcad's **Find** algorithm to further refine our design specified by the parameters k,ρ,θ. This is an algorithm that attempts to solve numerically a problem posed in terms of equality and inequality restraints on a function f. This is exactly the problem we have here. It is also very much worth our time to learn to use such an algorithm. As the specifications are in terms of the magnitude to the FR, we make explicit the parameter dependencies of the magnitude-squared of the FR. Mathcad's FIND function seems to require a fairly explicit display of f, without use of user-defined functions. This algorithm is itself a search algorithm and may or may not converge; if it converges it may or may not converge to the desired solution. *Thus any found solution must always be checked.* Also, the convergence is strongly affected by the initial estimates of the parameters: the graphical trial-and-error procedure enabled by Mathcad is a powerful assist in getting good initial estimates for the algorithm.

$$f(\omega, k, \rho, \theta) := \left(\left| k \cdot \frac{1 - \exp(-i \cdot 2 \cdot \omega)}{1 - 2 \cdot \rho \cdot \cos(\theta) \cdot \exp(-i \cdot \omega) + \rho^2 \cdot \exp(-i \cdot 2 \cdot \omega)} \right| \right)^2$$

We need to define an initial value for θ. We choose it to be ωc=1.

$\theta := \omega c$

We enter a **solve block**, in Mathcad's terminology.

Given

equality constraint: $f(\omega c, k, \rho, \theta) = 1$

$f(\omega 1, k, \rho, \theta) \leq 10^{-2.5}$

inequality constraints:

$f(\omega 2, k, \rho, \theta) \leq 10^{-2.5}$

$$\begin{bmatrix} ko \\ \rho o \\ \theta o \end{bmatrix} := Find(k, \rho, \theta)$$
   $ERR = 0$
$$\begin{bmatrix} ko \\ \rho o \\ \theta o \end{bmatrix} = \begin{pmatrix} 0.013 \\ 0.987 \\ 1 \end{pmatrix}$$

We check the solution.

$$f(\omega c, ko, po, \theta o) = 1$$

$$10 \cdot \log(f(\omega 1, ko, po, \theta o)) = -26.643445$$

$$10 \cdot \log(f(\omega 2, ko, po, \theta o)) = -25.173907$$

So the solution does satisfy the specifications.

  EXERCISE 19.6 Is the maximum gain actually unity in the design?
¤

PROBLEM 19.5 (a) Suppose the inequality constraint at $\omega 2$ is changed to an equality constraint. What is the result? (b) Suppose the inequality constraint at $\omega 1$ is changed to an equality constraint. What is the result? (c) Suppose all three constraints are equality constraints. What is the result? ‡

Simulation

We simulate the filter's operation using a sequence composed, in addition to the desired sinusoidal sequence, of sequences with frequencies in the bands to be rejected.

$$j := 0..4 \qquad \omega t_0 := 0.5 \qquad \omega t_1 := \omega 1 \qquad \omega t_2 := \omega c \qquad \omega t_3 := \omega 2 \qquad \omega t_5 := 2.0$$

$$N := 256 \qquad\qquad n := 0..N-1 \qquad\qquad x_n := \sum_j \cos(\omega t_j \cdot n)$$

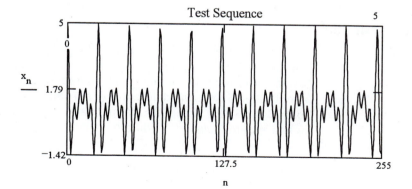

Test Sequence

We implement the filter by its associated LDE:

LDE:
$$y_{n+2} := 2 \cdot \rho \cdot \cos(\omega c) \cdot y_{n+1} - \rho^2 \cdot y_n + k \cdot \left(x_{n+2} - x_n\right) \qquad$$

$$a_1 := 2 \cdot \rho \cdot \cos(\omega c) \qquad\qquad a_2 := \rho^2$$

initial conditions: $\qquad y_0 := k \cdot x_0 \qquad\qquad y_1 := 2 \cdot a_1 \cdot y_0 + k \cdot x_1$

recursion: $\quad m := 0 .. N - 3 \quad y_{m+2} := a_1 \cdot y_{m+1} - a_2 \cdot y_m + k \cdot \left(x_{m+2} - x_m\right)$

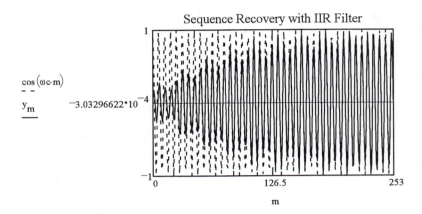

Sequence Recovery with IIR Filter

$\dfrac{\cos\left(\omega c \cdot m\right)}{y_m}$

$-3.03296622 \cdot 10^{-4}$

m

We see that the sinusoid is recovered quite accurately in this example. Note that, as the filter is of quite narrow band, there is a noticeably extended, initial transient. This would, however, be of little consequence in a long sequence.

Project 19.1

An FM stereo waveform consists of (i) two signals, the sum and difference of the left and right audio channels, and (ii) a sinusoid of frequency 19 KHz. The sum signal has frequency content from (about) 0 to 15 KHz; the difference signal has frequency content from 23 to 53 KHz. The FM receiver filters out the 19 KHz sinusoid for use in demodulating the difference signal.

Thus a digital FM receiver requires a digital filter to pass the 19 KHz sinusoid and to reject the two signals. Design a unity gain resonator with at most -25 db gain over the needed rejection bands. Assume a sampling frequency of 120 KHz.

(a) Make an initial trial-and-error solution using Mathcad's graphics.
(b) Refine (and check) the solution with Mathcad's FIND algorithm.
(c) Simulate the action of your design, using its LDE implementation. ‡

Project 19.2

In digital communication it is important for the receiver to synchronize timing with the transmitter. In pulse code modulation, PCM, a sequence of transmitted pulses has the pulse amplitudes determined by the binary symbols sequence to be transmitted. The receiver is assumed to know the pulse period but it must estimate the start, or phase, of the pulse period to make reliable decisions about the transmitted symbols. The basic idea is to use a unity gain resonator that will be excited by the received pulse sequence and whose output's sign will be found, in effect, by a limiter. The times of sign change then give the precise synchronization information needed. For more remarks on an actual implementation, see Ifeachor and Jervis (1993).

Assume that the pulses are transmitted at the rate of 4,800 pulses per second. Then the resonant frequency of an analog resonator would be 4,800 Hz. The received pulse sequence is sampled at the rate of 153,600=32*4,800 samples per second. So the resonant frequency of the digital filter is $2\pi/32$. (Why?)

Design a unity gain resonator for this application, explaining all design choices. In particular, the bandwidth of the filter must be specified. Simulate the resonator with a realistic input, using its LDE implementation. ‡

References

Ifeachor and Jervis (1993), Sec. 7.10.6
Jackson (1996), pp. 50-53
Oppenheim and Schafer (1989), Sec. 5.3
Proakis and Manolakis (1996), Secs. 4.5.2, 4.5.3

20 IIR Filters: Examples

We have defined the general class of digital filters with which we are concerned in this study with the LDE (**18.3**), which is called the ARMA algorithm. When the autoregressive, AR, part is present, the LDE is also an effective computational algorithm for implementing the filter.

The standard procedure we have laid out starts by specifying the filter by its poles, zeros and gain. We have discussed the geometric view (in **Chapter 19**), which gives us insight into how to choose the poles and zeros. For simple filters corresponding to low-order LDEs, this is sufficient to design useful filters. The standard procedure concludes with specifying the LDE with which the filter is implemented.

In particular, we have seen how to design and implement first- and second-order IIR filters. This is more important than it may appear, because the system function of higher-order IIR filters can always be factored into a product of second-order system functions with at most one first-order system. In turn, this means that the filter may be implemented as a sequential, or **cascade**, arrangement of second-order LDEs. We will eventually show how to do this in complete detail in the context of a specific class of IIR filters (**Chapter 22**). We now consider various types of IIR filters, including allpass, notch and comb filters.

Allpass Filters

We have noted that IIR filters have a nonlinear phase, which can be a disadvantage in some applications. But it is possible for an IIR filter to have a constant frequency response magnitude. Such a filter's phase could be used, in principle, to approximately compensate for the phase of an IIR filter that had a desirable frequency response magnitude. That is, the phase of the cascade of the two filters could have a phase that is approximately linear.

It turns out that an allpass-type rational function is also very useful in transforming FRs from one type to another - e.g., from a low-pass FR to a bandpass FR. We discuss this below.

We build up to a general characterization of such a filter with a series of examples.

Example 20.1

First, we consider the frequency response of the following pole-zero pair, which defines a real IIR filter.

real pole: $r := 0.75$ $\omega := 0, \dfrac{2 \cdot \pi}{128} .. 2 \cdot \pi$

system function: $H(z) := |r| \cdot \dfrac{z - \dfrac{1}{r}}{z - r}$

frequency response: $H1(\omega) := H(\exp(i \cdot \omega))$

Pole-Zero Plot

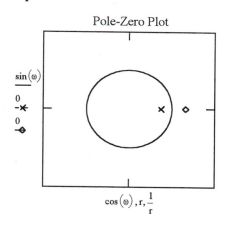

$$\cos(\omega), r, \dfrac{1}{r}$$

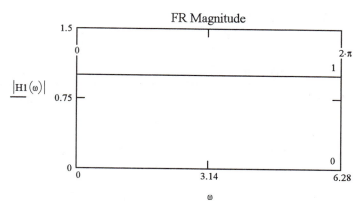

FR Magnitude

ω

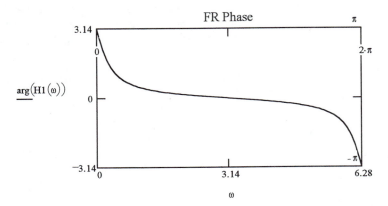

FR Phase

$\arg\left(H1\left(\omega\right)\right)$

We see that such a frequency response has a uniform frequency response magnitude. The phase is that expected from the geometric view. The pole will give a total phase contribution of -2π, whereas the zero outside the unit circle gives a total phase shift contribution of 0. The initial phase of π is due to the zero. ‡

 EXERCISE 20.1 Vary r and observe the resulting FR magnitude and phase. ¤

PROBLEM 20.1 Devise an analytic argument showing that the FR magnitude is a constant. ‡

PROBLEM 20.2 Write down the LDE that implements this IIR filter. ‡

EXERCISE 20.2 Modify the above illustration to a complex pole-zero pair and show that, again, the magnitude of H(exp(iω)) is a constant. (Such a factor is not a system function of a real IIR, but it is a building block for one.) ¤

PROBLEM 20.3 Devise an analytic argument for the constant FR magnitude for the factor of Exercise 20.2. ‡

Example 20.2 _____

We try next the obvious extension to a quadruplet composed of a complex pole and its conjugate, with zeros at the location of their reciprocals.

complex pole: $\rho := 0.75$ $\phi := \dfrac{\pi}{4}$ $p := \rho \cdot e^{i \cdot \phi}$

system function:

$$H(z) := \rho^2 \cdot \frac{\left(z - \dfrac{1}{p}\right) \cdot \left(z - \dfrac{1}{\overline{p}}\right)}{(z - p) \cdot (z - \overline{p})}$$

frequency response:

$$H1(\omega) := H(\exp(i \cdot \omega))$$

Pole-Zero Plot

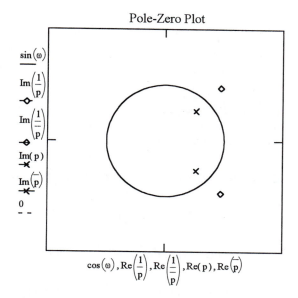

$$\sin(\omega)$$
$$\mathrm{Im}\left(\frac{1}{p}\right)$$
$$\mathrm{Im}\left(\frac{1}{\overline{p}}\right)$$
$$\mathrm{Im}(p)$$
$$\mathrm{Im}(\overline{p})$$
$$0$$

$$\cos(\omega), \mathrm{Re}\left(\frac{1}{p}\right), \mathrm{Re}\left(\frac{1}{\overline{p}}\right), \mathrm{Re}(p), \mathrm{Re}(\overline{p})$$

Because the total phase shift now exceeds 2π, we use the phase unwrapping algorithm as it avoids the confusion of the modularity of the arg( ) function.

$$N := 128 \qquad n := 0 .. N \qquad \omega_n := \frac{2 \cdot \pi}{N} \cdot n$$

$$\theta_0 := \arg\left(H1\left(\omega_0\right)\right) \qquad \theta_n := \mathrm{if}\left(n{=}0, \theta_0, \theta_{n-1} + \arg\left(H1\left(\omega_n\right) \cdot \overline{H1\left(\omega_{n-1}\right)}\right)\right)$$

FR Magnitude

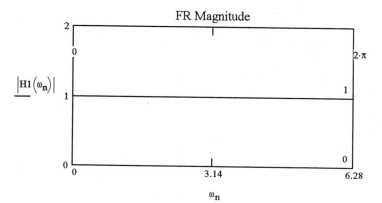

$$\left|H1\left(\omega_n\right)\right|$$

$$\omega_n$$

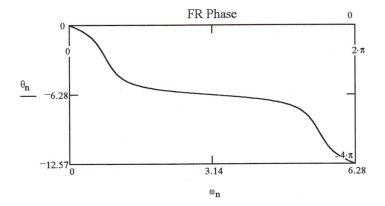

FR Phase

As we expect, the total phase shift is -4π. Each pole contributes -2π total phase shift, while the zeros outside the unit circle make 0 total phase contribution. ‡

EXERCISE 20.3 Vary ρ and θ and note the effect. ¤

PROBLEM 20.4 Modify your analytic argument of Problem 20.3 for this case. ‡

PROBLEM 20.5 Write down the LDE that implements this second-order LDE. ‡

The general situation is now constructed with factors corresponding to the above two cases, a real doublet and a complex quadruplet. Such filters are called **allpass** filters as they pass all frequency components with equal magnitude gain.

Example 20.3

For example, we may combine the two basic building blocks as follows.

system function:
$$H(z) := |r| \cdot \frac{z - \dfrac{1}{r}}{z - r} \cdot \left[(|p|)^2 \cdot \frac{\left(z - \dfrac{1}{p}\right) \cdot \left(z - \dfrac{1}{\overline{p}}\right)}{(z - p) \cdot (z - \overline{p})} \right]$$

frequency response:
$$H1(\omega) := H(\exp(i \cdot \omega))$$

Pole-Zero Plot

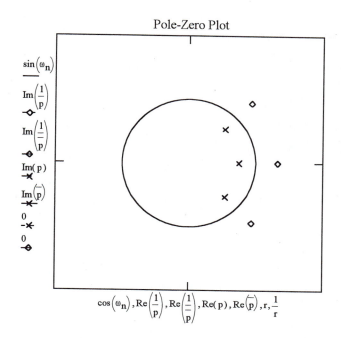

$$\dfrac{\sin(\omega_n)}{}$$

$$\text{Im}\!\left(\dfrac{1}{p}\right)$$

$$\text{Im}\!\left(\dfrac{1}{\overline{p}}\right)$$

$$\text{Im}(p)$$

$$\text{Im}(\overline{p})$$

$$0$$

$$0$$

$$\cos(\omega_n),\ \text{Re}\!\left(\dfrac{1}{p}\right),\ \text{Re}\!\left(\dfrac{1}{\overline{p}}\right),\ \text{Re}(p),\ \text{Re}(\overline{p}),\ r,\ \dfrac{1}{r}$$

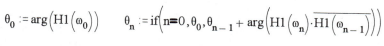

$$\theta_0 := \arg\!\left(H1(\omega_0)\right) \qquad \theta_n := \text{if}\!\left(n=0,\ \theta_0,\ \theta_{n-1} + \arg\!\left(H1(\omega_n)\cdot\overline{H1(\omega_{n-1})}\right)\right)$$

FR Magnitude

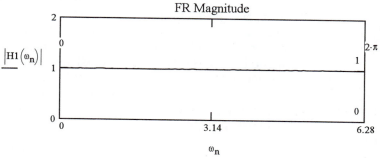

$$\dfrac{|H1(\omega_n)|}{}$$

$$\omega_n$$

FR Phase

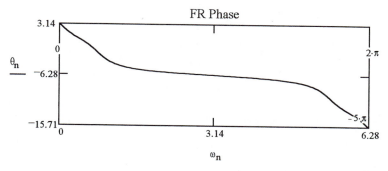

$$\dfrac{\theta_n}{}$$

$$\omega_n$$

‡

EXERCISE 20.4 Vary r, ρ and θ and note the effect. ¤

PROBLEM 20.6   Modify your analytic argument of Problem 20.3 for this case. ‡

PROBLEM 20.7   Write down the LDE that implements the system function made up of a doublet pair and a quadruplet pair. ‡

Notch Filters

Sometimes the purpose of the filter is to eliminate, or reduce, a narrow band of frequencies.

Example 20.4 _____

Suppose we wanted a filter that rejected frequencies very close to zero, but passed other frequencies with approximately uniform gain. Such a filter is called a **DC notch** filter. To do this, we will find the geometric view helpful. First, to get the 0 at ω=0, we place a zero at z=1. To get fairly uniform gain for ω elsewhere, we can place a pole on the real axis, inside the unit circle and very near the zero. Then, for ω well away from 0, the pole and zero phasors are approximately equal, implying that the magnitude will be nearly constant and the phase nearly zero for the system function. For the phase to be defined for all ω, we move the zero just inside the unit circle; in practice this would be allowed by a specification on the rejection level.

pole: $p := 0.8$ **gain:** $k := \left[\left| \dfrac{e^{\,i \cdot \frac{\pi}{2}} - 1}{e^{\,i \cdot \frac{\pi}{2}} - p} \right| \right]^{-1}$

system function: $H(z) := k \cdot \dfrac{z - 0.99999}{z - p}$

frequency response: $H1(\omega) := H\!\left(e^{\,i \cdot \omega}\right)$

Pole-Zero Plot

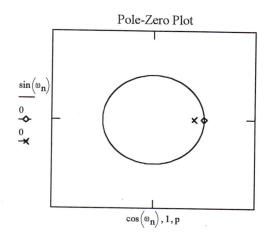

$$\cos\left(\omega_n\right), 1, p$$

$$\theta_0 := \arg\left(\text{H1}\left(\omega_0\right)\right) \qquad \theta_n := \text{if}\left(n=0, \theta_0, \theta_{n-1} + \arg\left(\text{H1}\left(\omega_n\right) \cdot \overline{\text{H1}\left(\omega_{n-1}\right)}\right)\right)$$

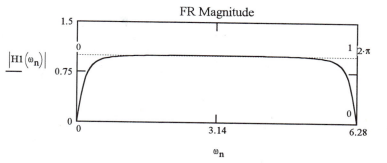

FR Magnitude

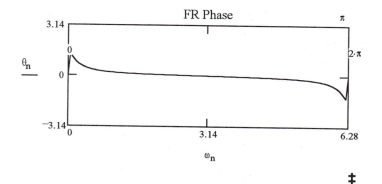

FR Phase

EXERCISE 20.5 Adjust the parameter p and note the resulting effect on the frequency response magnitude and phase. ¤

Example 20.5 _____

We may place notches at a frequency other than ω=0. We can easily construct such a filter generalizing the idea of the DC notch filter.

zeros: $\qquad \phi := \dfrac{\pi}{4} \qquad \rho := 0.99999 \qquad z_1 := \rho \cdot e^{i \cdot \phi} \qquad z_2 := \rho \cdot \overline{z_1}$

poles: $\qquad p := 0.9 \qquad p_1 := p \cdot z_1 \qquad p_2 := \overline{p_1}$

system function: $\qquad H(z) := \dfrac{(z - z_1) \cdot (z - z_2)}{(z - p_1) \cdot (z - p_2)}$

frequency response: $\qquad H1(\omega) := H\left(e^{i \cdot \omega}\right)$

Pole-Zero Plot

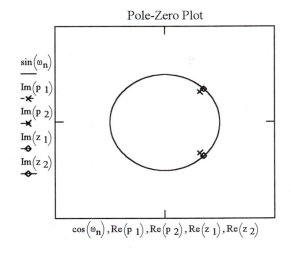

$\overline{\sin(\omega_n)}$
$\mathrm{Im}(p_1)$
$\mathrm{Im}(p_2)$
$\mathrm{Im}(z_1)$
$\mathrm{Im}(z_2)$

$\cos(\omega_n), \mathrm{Re}(p_1), \mathrm{Re}(p_2), \mathrm{Re}(z_1), \mathrm{Re}(z_2)$

$$\theta_0 := \arg\left(H1\left(\omega_0\right)\right) \qquad \theta_n := \mathrm{if}\left(n=0, \theta_0, \theta_{n-1} + \arg\left(H1\left(\omega_n\right) \cdot \overline{H1\left(\omega_{n-1}\right)}\right)\right)$$

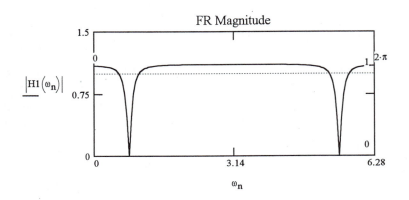

FR Magnitude

$\overline{|H1(\omega_n)|}$

ω_n

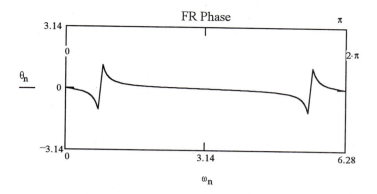

FR Phase

$\frac{\theta_n}{}$

ω_n

▯

EXERCISE 20.6 Adjust parameters p and φ and note the resulting effect on the frequency response magnitude and phase. ¤

Comb Filters

If H(z) is a system function, its frequency response H1(ω) has, of course, a period 2π. Then, for K>0 and integer, $H_K(z)=H(z^K)$ will have a frequency response H1(Kω) with period 2π/K and is called a **comb** filter. (Presumably an imaginative engineer visualized the FR magnitude as a comb!)

Example 20.6

Consider using the DC notch filter as a generator for the comb filter.

$$p := 0.8 \qquad H(z) := k \cdot \frac{z - 0.99999}{z - p} \qquad H1(\omega) := H\left(e^{i \cdot \omega}\right)$$

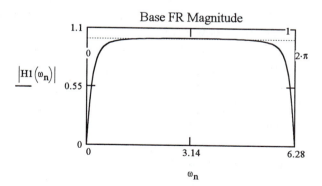

Base FR Magnitude

$\left|H1\left(\omega_n\right)\right|$

ω_n

$$K := 4 \qquad H_K(z) := H\left(z^K\right) \qquad H1_K(\omega) := H1(K \cdot \omega)$$

$$\theta_0 := \arg\left(H1\left(\omega_0\right)\right) \quad \theta_n := if\left(n=0, \theta_0, \theta_{n-1} + \arg\left(H1_K\left(\omega_n\right) \cdot \overline{H1_K\left(\omega_{n-1}\right)}\right)\right)$$

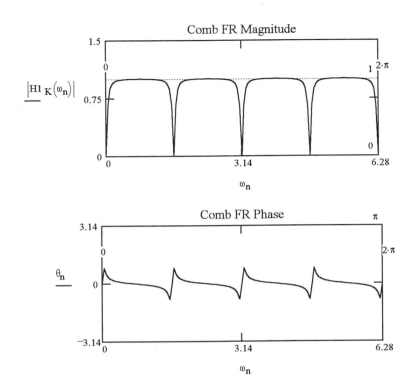

Such a filter could find application in removing interference of a special structure, such as a sinusoid and its harmonics. ‡

Noncausal, Zero Phase Filtering

In many applications, the data sequence to be filtered is recorded or stored in some fashion, and may be brought into the DSP device memory. In these cases, the causality restraint is generally not needed. The following technique effectively filters the data sequence $\{x_n\}$ with a real frequency response.

Step 1 Form the reversed sequence $\{x_{-n}\}$ and filter with frequency response $H1(\omega)$, getting the sequence $\{y_n\}$.

Step 2 Form the reversed sequence $\{y_{-n}\}$ and filter with frequency response $H1(\omega)$, getting the sequence $\{u_n\}$.

It is not difficult to see that the effective frequency response is $|H1(\omega)|^2$, which of course is real.

PROBLEM 20.8 Show that reversing a sequence is equivalent to conjugating its DTFT. Then show that the above scheme does have the asserted frequency response. ‡

Example 20.7

We illustrate this scheme. We define the sequence lengths and the DFT and IDFT.

$$N := 128 \quad n := 0 .. N - 1 \quad \mathrm{dft}(v) := \sqrt{N} \cdot \mathrm{icfft}(v) \quad \mathrm{idft}(v) := \frac{1}{\sqrt{N}} \cdot \mathrm{cfft}(v)$$

We define an input signal that has a full DFT in order to determine the effective frequency response at all frequencies.

$$x_n := \sum_{k=0}^{\frac{N}{2}} \cos\left(\frac{2 \cdot \pi}{N} \cdot k \cdot n\right) \qquad \mathrm{xdft} := \mathrm{dft}(x)$$

We define a simple IIR filter, which will have a phase.

$$a := 0.65 \qquad h_n := a^n \qquad H := \mathrm{dft}(h)$$

The first stage filters the reversed input sequence.

$$xr_n := x_{N-1-n} \qquad \mathrm{xrdft} := \mathrm{dft}(xr)$$

The output is then

$$Y := \overrightarrow{(H \cdot \mathrm{xrdft})} \qquad y := \mathrm{idft}(Y)$$

The second stage filters the reversal of the sequence resulting from the first stage.

$$yr_n := y_{N-1-n} \qquad \mathrm{Yrdft} := \mathrm{dft}(yr)$$

The output is then

$$Z := \overrightarrow{(H \cdot \mathrm{Yrdft})} \qquad z := \mathrm{idft}(Z)$$

The frequency response of the overall operation is then

$$H_{eff} := \overrightarrow{\left(\frac{Z}{\mathrm{xdft}}\right)}$$

We want to compare it to the squared-magnitude of the frequency response of h.

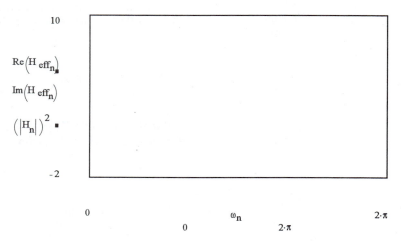

$Re\left(H\,eff_n\right)$

$Im\left(H\,eff_n\right)$

$\left(\left|H_n\right|\right)^2$ ■

We note that $H_{eff}(w)$ is real and that it equals $|H1(w)|^2$, as claimed. ‡

FR Type Transformations

Common types of filters include low-, band- and high- pass and stop filters. These have, in so far as permitted by the rational nature of the FR dictated by their LDE form, FR magnitudes that are either zero or a constant. Thus one could have efficient design procedures for a low-pass digital filter and then transform the design into another type. We will give routine procedures for designing low-pass filters for widely used classes of IIR filters (Chapters 21-23). A filter of another type can then be found by an appropriate transformation. We first recall and adapt a simple low-pass to high-pass transformation.

Low-Pass to High-Pass Transformations

Recall from **Chapter 10** that modifying the FIR $\{h_n,\ n=0,...,M\}$ of a low-pass filter to $\{(-1)^n h_n,\ n=0,...,N-1\}$ resulted in a high-pass filter. The idea was that a low-pass FR is simply translated by π, moving the region of appreciable response from low to high frequencies. Remember that, for the DTFT, these are near π. The exact same argument holds for IIR filters.

For IIR filters, it is more convenient to express the transformation in terms of the $\{a_k\}$ and $\{b_m\}$ vectors that define the FR (18.7):

$$H_{LO}\left(e^{i\cdot\omega}\right) = \frac{\displaystyle\sum_{m=0}^{M} b_m \cdot e^{-i\cdot\omega\cdot m}}{\displaystyle\sum_{k=0}^{N} a_k \cdot e^{-i\cdot\omega\cdot k}}$$

Now suppose we replace ω by $\omega+\pi$. Then, since $\exp(i\pi)=-1$, we have

$$H_{HI}\left(e^{i\cdot\omega}\right) = \frac{\displaystyle\sum_{m=0}^{M} (-1)^m \cdot b_m \cdot e^{-i\cdot\omega\cdot m}}{\displaystyle\sum_{k=0}^{N} (-1)^k \cdot a_k \cdot e^{-i\cdot\omega\cdot k}}$$

So we have a simple procedure to transform a low-pass IIR filter into a high-pass IIR filter. We modify the defining $\{a_k\}$ and $\{b_m\}$ vectors to $\{(-1)^k a_k\}$ and $\{(-1)^m b_m\}$ vectors. Of course, this procedure includes the special case of FIR filters, where $h_m = b_m$.

Low-Pass to Other Type Transformations

Given a system function $H_{LO}(z)$ defining a low-pass digital filter, we define a new system function $H(z)=H_{LO}[g(z)]$, which is intended to be a filter of another type {[low, band, high],[pass, stop]}. For both filters to be implemented by an LDE, they must be rational functions of z. This implies that g(z) must be a rational function of z. To map between pass and stop types with their roughly two-valued FRs, we would like the unit circle - where the FR is found - to be mapped into itself by g(z). This implies that

$$\left|g\left(e^{i\cdot\omega}\right)\right| = 1$$

That is, $g(e^{i\omega})$ has the form of an allpass FR. From Example 20.3 we see that g(z) must be made up of factors of the form

$$|r| \cdot \frac{z - \dfrac{1}{r}}{z - r} \qquad\qquad (|p|)^2 \cdot \frac{\left(z - \dfrac{1}{p}\right)\cdot\left(z - \dfrac{1}{\overline{p}}\right)}{(z - p)\cdot\left(z - \overline{p}\right)}$$

Additionally, we want stable filters to be transformed into stable filters. That is, g(z) should map the unit circle into itself. One can show that this will be true if and only if g(z) is itself the system function of a stable filter. Thus it is required that the poles of g(z) lie within the unit circle.

We leave further discussion to the references, where tables of the common transformations may be found.

Project 20.1

For efficiency and reduced weight, AC generators for vehicles of various types have been designed to generate power with a 440 Hz sinusoid. Suppose that the generator powers a sensor whose output has frequencies from 0 to 2.2 KHz. This sensor output is corrupted by the power generator's harmonics n*440 Hz (n=1,2,...). Design a comb filter to eliminate them. (You will need to complete the design specifications and give a rationale.) Simulate the design, implementing it as a LDE. ‡

Project 20.2

Referring to **Project 19.1**, design a simple notch filter that rejects the 19 KHz subcarrier while minimally affecting the stereo signals. Explain your design. In practice, what limits the bandwidth selection? ‡

References

Jackson (1996), Secs. 4.3, 5.4, 8.4
Oppenheim and Schafer (1989), Secs. 5.4, 7.2
Proakis and Manolakis (1996), Secs. 4.5, 8.4.2

21 IIR Design for Given Magnitude

In some applications, such as most telephony and music reproduction, precise control of phase may not be necessary. Design criteria in such applications may be primarily concerned with the magnitude of the frequency response or, conveniently, the squared-magnitude. We immediately encounter the problem of specifying a real, nonnegative function of ω that, in fact, is either the squared-magnitude of some digital filter or is well-approximated by a member of a family of such functions.

These specification and approximation problems were intensively studied for analog filters more than half a century ago and it is sensible to attempt to take advantage of this knowledge. We need to find a way to relate analog and digital filter designs. There are a number of relations that are used. Sometimes the relation is implicit, as when we replace a differential equation with a related difference equation.

This relation, or mapping, should have some desirable attributes. We would like the frequency response magnitudes to be relatively simply related so that we can anticipate how that of the analog filter design will map to that of the digital filter design. Also, we would like stable analog filters to be mapped into stable digital filters. Finally, we are interested in a rational mapping because our design and implementation techniques for both analog and digital filters assume rational frequency responses corresponding to, respectively, linear differential equations and linear difference equations that allow implementation on, respectively, analog computers and digital computers.

The bilinear map has all of these attributes and is therefore our focus here. We introduce it in an indirect way and then formally recognize, study and apply it.

Given a bona fide squared-magnitude $M1(\omega)=|H1(\omega)|^2$ of a digital filter, there is still the problem of factoring M1 to find H1. The frequency response of a digital filter that is a rational function of $z=\exp(i\omega)$ always has a squared-magnitude that is a ratio of trigonometric functions of ω. We can use trigonometric identities to express the trigonometric functions in terms of $\exp(i\omega)$. Then we can make the substitution $z=\exp(i\omega)$ and find the (generally complex) poles and zeros of the squared-magnitude of the transfer function $M(z)=|H(z)|^2$. Factoring of M to find H is guided by noting that, for a real IR,

$$M\left(e^{i \cdot \omega}\right) = H\left(e^{i \cdot \omega}\right) \cdot H\left(\frac{1}{e^{i \cdot \omega}}\right) \qquad (21.1)$$

and hence that

$$M(z) = H(z) \cdot H\left(\frac{1}{z}\right) \qquad (21.2)$$

Since, for stability, H(z) must have its poles inside the unit circle, H(1/z) must have its poles outside the unit circle: this tells us how to factor the poles of M(z). The zeros are not so restrained, but a desirable way to factor them will be apparent in the two cases we discuss.

PROBLEM 21.1   Prove (21.1). ‡

A Squared-Magnitude Function

Consider the (providently chosen!) proposed squared-magnitude function

$$N := 4 \qquad \omega c := 1 \qquad M1(\omega) := \cfrac{1}{1 + \left[\cfrac{\tan\left(\cfrac{\omega}{2}\right)}{\tan\left(\cfrac{\omega c}{2}\right)}\right]^{2 \cdot N}} \qquad (21.3)$$

▨ **EXERCISE 21.1** Show that ωc is the -3 db cutoff frequency of a low-pass filter. ¤

Noting that

$$\tan\left(\frac{\omega}{2}\right) = (-i) \cdot \frac{e^{i \cdot \omega} - 1}{e^{i \cdot \omega} + 1}$$

we have the continuation of this function from the unit circle to the entire z-plane as

$$(-i) \cdot \frac{z - 1}{z + 1} \tag{21.4}$$

Thus

$$M(z) = \frac{1}{1 + \left[\dfrac{i \cdot \left(\dfrac{z - 1}{z + 1}\right)}{\tan\left(\dfrac{\omega c}{2}\right)}\right]^{2 \cdot N}} \tag{21.5}$$

To find the singularities of this rational function of z, we can simplify M by introducing the invertible change of variable

$$s = \frac{z - 1}{z + 1} \qquad\qquad z = \frac{1 + s}{1 - s} \tag{21.6}$$

The mapping (21.6) is called the **bilinear transformation**. Denoting M, when z is replaced using (21.6), by Mb, we have

$$Mb(s) = \frac{1}{1 + \left(\dfrac{i \cdot s}{\tan\left(\dfrac{\omega c}{2}\right)}\right)^{2 \cdot N}} \tag{21.7}$$

Finally, it is convenient to normalize s by

$$sn = \frac{s}{\tan\left(\dfrac{\omega c}{2}\right)} \tag{21.8}$$

Denoting Mb, when s is replaced by sn, by Mn, we have

$$Mn(sn) = \frac{1}{1 + (-1)^N \cdot sn^{2 \cdot N}} \tag{21.9}$$

We can now note the singularities of Mn. There is no zero in the finite sn-plane but there is a zero of order 2N at sn=∞. The poles are seen to be as follows.

(i) If N is odd, the poles sn_k are the 2N roots of unity.
(ii) If N is even, the poles sn_k are the 2N roots of (-1).

$$k := 0 .. 2 \cdot N - 1 \quad sn_k := if\left(\mod(N,2)=1, e^{i \cdot k \cdot \frac{2 \cdot \pi}{2 \cdot N}}, e^{i \cdot \frac{\pi}{2 \cdot N}} \cdot e^{i \cdot k \cdot \frac{2 \cdot \pi}{2 \cdot N}}\right) \quad (21.10)$$

$$N = 4 \qquad sn = \begin{bmatrix} 0.924 + 0.383i \\ 0.383 + 0.924i \\ -0.383 + 0.924i \\ -0.924 + 0.383i \\ -0.924 - 0.383i \\ -0.383 - 0.924i \\ 0.383 - 0.924i \\ 0.924 - 0.383i \end{bmatrix}$$

s-Plane Pole Plot

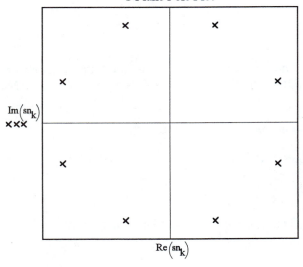

EXERCISE 21.2 Try various values of N and observe the following.
1. There are no purely imaginary poles.
2. (a) When N is odd, there is a real pole at z=+1 for k=0, and a real pole at z=-1 for k=N. (b) When N is even, there are no real poles. ¤

Prove the assertions of Exercise 21.2. ‡

By inverting the maps (21.8) and (21.6), we find that the corresponding z-plane pole locations are

$$t := \tan\left(\frac{\omega c}{2}\right) \quad P_k := \text{if}\left[\text{mod}(N,2)\!=\!1, \dfrac{1+t\cdot e^{i\cdot k \cdot \frac{2\cdot\pi}{2\cdot N}}}{1-t\cdot e^{i\cdot k \cdot \frac{2\cdot\pi}{2\cdot N}}}, \dfrac{1+t\cdot e^{i\cdot(2\cdot k+1)\cdot\frac{\pi}{2\cdot N}}}{1-t\cdot e^{i\cdot(2\cdot k+1)\cdot\frac{\pi}{2\cdot N}}}\right]$$

(21.11)

$$N = 4 \qquad p = \begin{bmatrix} 2.427 + 1.447i \\ 0.797 + 1.147i \\ 0.409 + 0.588i \\ 0.304 + 0.181i \\ 0.304 - 0.181i \\ 0.409 - 0.588i \\ 0.797 - 1.147i \\ 2.427 - 1.447i \end{bmatrix} \qquad \begin{matrix} k \\[4pt] \boxed{0} \\ \boxed{1} \\ \boxed{2} \\ \boxed{3} \\ \boxed{4} \\ \boxed{5} \\ \boxed{6} \\ \boxed{7} \end{matrix}$$

$$\omega := 0, \frac{2\cdot\pi}{64} .. \, 2\cdot\pi$$

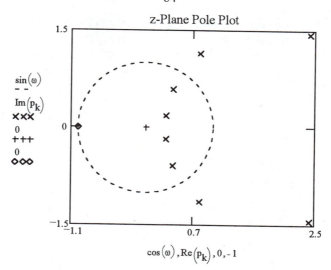

z-Plane Pole Plot

$$\cos(\omega), \text{Re}(P_k), 0, -1$$

It is clear from (21.5) that z=-1 is a zero of order 2N. Notice that T_s does not appear in the formulas for the singularities in the z-plane.

■ **EXERCISE 21.3** Verify that the singularities appear in reciprocal pairs, as is required by (21.2). Verify that the complex singularities appear in conjugate pairs, as is required for a real IR. ¤

For a stable digital filter we must take the poles inside the unit circle. We also take half the zeros (at z=-1). Placing them, in practice, just inside the unit circle results in zero total phase shift (**Chapter 19**). This should minimize the effect of the nonlinear phase.

PROBLEM 21.3

Verify that the index set that chooses the proper poles is [kmin,kmax] where

$$kmin := if\left(mod(N,2) \doteq 1, \frac{N+1}{2}, \frac{N}{2}\right)$$

$$kmax := if(mod(N,2) \doteq 1, 2 \cdot N - kmin, 2 \cdot N - kmin - 1)$$ ‡

Then the desired digital filter transfer function is

$$N = 4 \qquad G(z) := \left[\prod_{k=kmin}^{kmax} \left(\frac{z+1}{z-p_k}\right)\right] \qquad \begin{matrix} kmin = 2 \\ \\ kmax = 5 \end{matrix}$$ (21.12)

We know by direct inspection that (21.12) describes a stable, causal IIR filter. It remains to verify that the filter has the specified frequency response. To do so, we simply plot the squared magnitude $|G(e^{i\omega})|^2$ and compare it to the desideratum M.

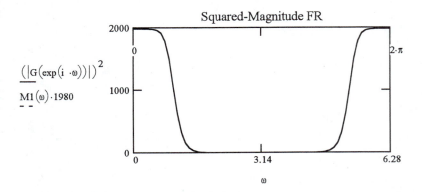

Squared-Magnitude FR

$$\frac{\left(|G(\exp(i \cdot \omega))|\right)^2}{M1(\omega) \cdot 1980}$$

Thus, with a gain adjustment, the constructed digital filter has the specified frequency response. We have, then, an interesting family of IIR filters parametrized by (ωc,N). We plot the frequency response magnitudes for this family.

$$FRM(\omega,N) := \cfrac{1}{1 + \left[\cfrac{\tan\left(\cfrac{\omega}{2}\right)}{\tan\left(\cfrac{\omega c}{2}\right)}\right]^{2\cdot N}}$$

(21.13)

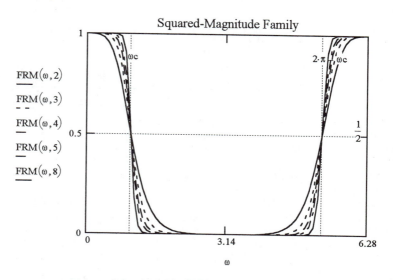

Squared-Magnitude Family

$\overline{FRM(\omega,2)}$

$\overline{FRM(\omega,3)}$ (- -)

$\overline{FRM(\omega,4)}$

$\overline{FRM(\omega,5)}$

$\overline{FRM(\omega,8)}$

Thus all members of the family have a frequency response magnitude with a common -3 db gain at ωc and are monotone decreasing for ω increasing from 0 to π. The parameter N controls, essentially, the width of the transition region from closely unity gain to a low gain. We could specify a frequency ωs at which the attenuation is to be A db. Then we choose the smallest N that meets this specification. We shall illustrate this design procedure later in specific cases.

Some Classical Squared-Magnitude Functions

Reviewing the above discussion, we see that we have used the bilinear transformation to map between the z-plane and an s-plane. This s-plane is the complex plane appropriate to discussing the system function Ha(s), the Laplace transform of the IR of an analog filter. In particular, we discussed the family defined by (21.7). But we could apply this transformation, or mapping, to other families of analog filters specified by the squared-magnitude of their frequency responses. We shall now discuss two such families. Fortunately we already know these functions do indeed correspond to the squared-magnitude of the frequency response of some causal, stable, real analog filter.

Butterworth Family

Suppose we specify the squared-magnitude to be

$$vc := 1000 \qquad M_B(v,N) := \frac{1}{1 + \left(\dfrac{v}{vc}\right)^{2 \cdot N}} \qquad (-\infty < v < \infty) \qquad (21.14)$$

$$v := -3 \cdot vc, \left(-3 \cdot vc + \frac{6 \cdot vc}{128}\right) .. \ 3 \cdot vc$$

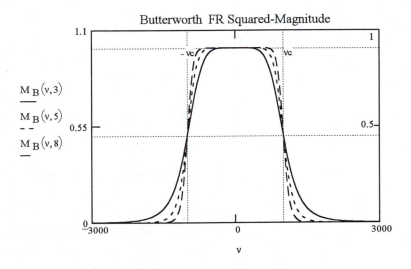

Butterworth FR Squared-Magnitude

$M_B(v,3)$ ——

$M_B(v,5)$ – –

$M_B(v,8)$ ——

This family is parametrized by (vc,N), where it is clear that vc is the -3 db frequency of the family and that N determines the width of the transition region from near unity gain to sufficiently low gain. As N is increased, $M_B(v,N)$ approaches the ideal low-pass filter characteristic.

For v sufficiently small, we have the Maclaurin series with terms of $[-(v/vc)^{2N}]^n$, n=0,1,..., and we can use it to show the following property.

PROBLEM 21.4

Show that the first (2N-1) derivatives of $M_B(v,N)$ are zero at v=0. ‡

This attribute of the Butterworth family is called **maximal flatness.** Its appeal as an optimality criterion presumably is that it gives us, at least near the origin, a best approximation to the flat ideal characteristic. Of course, such a criterion ignores the nature of the approximation except at $v=0$. Relative to the other family we discuss, the price of maximal flatness is a broad transition region. Still, it is a useful family.

 EXERCISE 21.4 Show that the family we have heretofore discussed is in fact the Butterworth family. ¤

Chebyshev Family

Type 1

Suppose that we wanted the squared-magnitude of the frequency response to be within a certain tolerance of unity in the passband. We might hope that we can trade off the Butterworth family's monotone behavior in the passband for a smaller transition region by allowing a ripple in the passband. And this turns out to be the case.

Recalling our discussion of the design of equiripple FIR filters (**Chapter 14**), we know the Chebyshev polynomial T(x,N) has the attractive attribute of equiripple with N zeros and N+1 extrema distributed, roughly uniformly, over (-1,1). Letting ε be a parameter, we can get an equiripple of adjustable magnitude over (-1,1) by either of the forms

$$f1 = 1 + (\varepsilon \cdot T(x,N))^2 \qquad \text{or} \qquad f2 = \frac{1}{1 + (\varepsilon \cdot T(x,N))^2}$$

The behavior of the Chebyshev polynomial for x outside (-1,1) - where it can be defined by its recursion (**14.4**) - controls our choice of form. As T(x,N) is an Nth-order polynomial in x, we know that |T(x,N)| will increase quite rapidly for |x|>1. This fortunate attribute directs us to use form f2.

$$T(x,m) := \cos(m \cdot a\cos(x)) \qquad vn := -1.1, -1.09 .. 1.1 \qquad N = 4$$

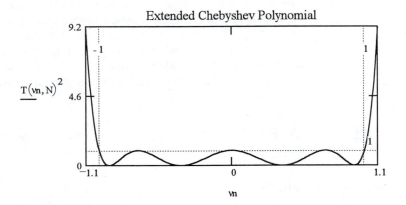

Note that Mathcad computes the required extension of the Chebyshev polynomial.

Thus we specify the squared-magnitude, scaled to a specified passband cutoff vc, as

$$\varepsilon := 0.25 \qquad M_T(v, N) := \frac{1}{1 + \left(\varepsilon \cdot T\left(\dfrac{v}{vc}, N\right)\right)^2} \qquad (21.15)$$

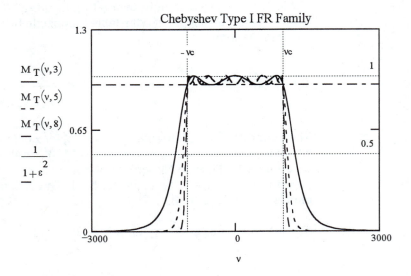

We notice that all members of the family cross through the point $(vc, 1/(1+\varepsilon^2))$ and that they do not have a common -3 db point.

▓ **EXERCISE 21.5** Vary ε and note the trade-off of ripple magnitude and width of the transition region. ¤

PROBLEM 21.5

Prove: (i) T(1,N)=1; (ii) for N odd, T(0,N)=0; for N even, T(0,N)=(-1)^N. These properties of the Chebyshev polynomials determine the behavior of $M_T(v,N)$ at $v=0$ and $v=vc$. ‡

Type II

Suppose that we wanted the squared-magnitude of the frequency response below a certain level in the stopband v>vs. We might hope that we can trade off the Butterworth family's monotone behavior in the stopband for a smaller transition region by allowing a ripple in the stopband. And this turns out to be the case.

A little thought shows that we can get the ripple in the stopband by inverting the argument of the Chebyshev polynomial so: T(vs/v,N). Now T(vs/v,N) will be very large for v<vs, but we can negate this and get the FR magnitude to be nearly constant thereby forming the ratio

$$f := \frac{T\left(\frac{vs}{v},N\right)^2}{\varepsilon^2 + T\left(\frac{vs}{v},N\right)^2} ∎$$

To keep the magnitude at the edge of the passband vc as 1/(1+ε^2), we modify our proposed form to

$$f := \frac{T\left(\frac{vs}{v},N\right)^2}{\varepsilon^2 \cdot T\left(\frac{vs}{vc},N\right)^2 + T\left(\frac{vs}{v},N\right)^2} ∎$$

Or, rewriting, we have the squared-magnitude function for a Chebyshev Type II filter:

$$vs := 1500 \quad \varepsilon := 0.1 \quad M_{TII}(v,N) := if\left[v=0,1,\frac{1}{1 + \left[\varepsilon \cdot \frac{T\left(\frac{vs}{vc},N\right)}{T\left(\frac{vs}{v},N\right)}\right]^2}\right] \quad (21.16)$$

$$v := -10 \cdot vc, \left(-10 \cdot vc + \frac{20 \cdot vc}{256}\right) .. \, 10 \cdot vc$$

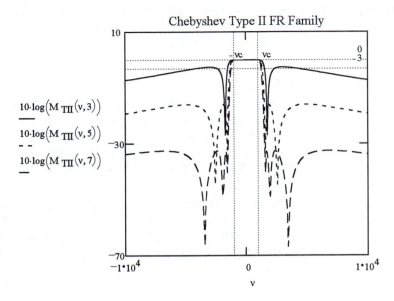

Chebyshev Type II FR Family

$10 \cdot \log\left(M_{TII}(v,3)\right)$ ——

$10 \cdot \log\left(M_{TII}(v,5)\right)$ - -

$10 \cdot \log\left(M_{TII}(v,7)\right)$ ——

EXERCISE 21.6 Vary ε and note the trade-off of ripple magnitude and width of the transition region. ¤

Bilinear Mapping

We have recognized the bilinear mapping, or transformation, between the s- and z-planes, (21.6):

$$s = \frac{z-1}{z+1} \qquad\qquad z = \frac{1+s}{1-s}$$

We now cite some properties of this invertible map.

Property 21.1 The bilinear transformation maps the left half of the s-plane onto the interior of the unit circle of the z-plane.

Note that, setting s=σ+iv,

$$(|z|)^2 = \frac{(1+\sigma)^2 + (v)^2}{(1-\sigma)^2 + (v)^2}$$

We see that , if σ<0, then |z|²<1. Also, if σ>1, then |z|²>1. And, if σ=0, |z|²=1.

Property 21.2 The bilinear transformation maps the iv–axis of the s-plane onto the unit circle $\exp(i\omega)$ of the z-plane.

When $z = \exp(i\omega)$, we have $s = iv$ purely imaginary and, after a little trigonometry,

$$v = \tan\left(\frac{\omega}{2}\right) \qquad\qquad \omega = 2 \cdot \operatorname{atan}(v) \qquad\qquad (21.17)$$

This mapping shows how the infinite-length v–axis is compressed onto the finite length unit circle $\exp(i\omega)$. This compression is called **frequency distortion** in this context. Note that when ω and v are small, we have

$$\omega = 2 \cdot v \qquad (\omega \ll 1) \qquad\qquad\qquad\qquad (21.18)$$

Remark

It has been common in the DSP context to define the bilinear transformation with a scaling involving the sampling period T_s. This is unfortunate because it plays no necessary role. Of course, in a particular application, the actual numerical choice of appropriate ωc and ωs can involve Ts - as when digitally processing a sampled analog signal.

Squared-Magnitude Specification

There are useful notational conventions for specifying common restraints on the squared-magnitude of a frequency response $M1(\omega)$.

(i) In a **passband**, $(1-\delta_1)^2 <= M1(\omega) <= 1$.

(ii) In a **stopband**, $M1(\omega) <= \delta_2^2$.

(iii) In a **transition band**, $M1(\omega) <= (1-\delta_1)^2$.

For the families discussed here, $M1(\omega)$ is also strictly monotone in a transition region.

For example, a low-pass filter would be specified by the parameters $\{\omega_c, \delta_1, \omega_s, \delta_2\}$ where

(i) In the **low-pass band** $0 <= \omega <= \omega_c$, $(1-\delta_1)^2 <= M1(\omega) <= 1$.

(ii) In the **stopband** $\omega_s <= \omega <= \pi$, $M1(w) <= \delta_2^2$.

(iii) In the **transition band** $\omega_c <= \omega <= \omega_s$, $M1(\omega) <= (1-\delta_1)^2$ and $M1(\omega)$ is strictly monotone decreasing.

A sketch of these requirements is given below.

$$\omega_c := \frac{2 \cdot \pi}{6.2} \qquad \delta_1 := 0.293 \qquad \omega_s := \frac{2 \cdot \pi}{4.55} \qquad \delta_2 := 0.2$$

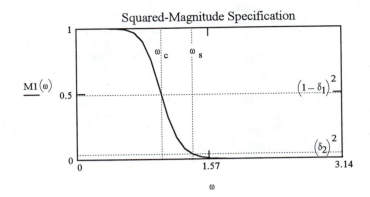

Squared-Magnitude Specification

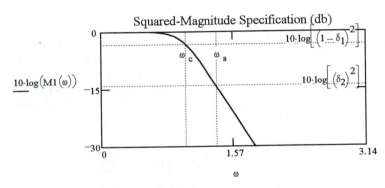

Squared-Magnitude Specification (db)

Project 21.1

Design a digital filter by selecting, by trial and error, a member of the Butterworth family that meets the following specifications: -3 db relative FRM at passband edge at $\omega_c = 1.0$ and at least -20 db relative FRM at $\omega_s = 1.25$. Plot the FRM and make a pole-zero plot. Find the realization as a linear difference equation, find its IR and then check its FR. ‡

References

Gold and Rader (1969), Sec. 3.9
Jackson (1996), Sec. 8.1
Oppenheim and Schafer (1989), Secs. 7.1, 7.3
Proakis and Manolakis (1996), Sec. 8.3

22 IIR Design: Butterworth Filters

We have already discussed the Butterworth family at some length. We now point out a procedure for routinely designing IIR filters by selecting a member of this family. We also complete our standard procedure (**Chapter 18**) for design by implementing the LDE.

Design Procedure

Suppose that we wanted a digital filter with a frequency response squared-magnitude that (i) was monotone decreasing for $0 <= |\omega| <= \pi$, (ii) had a maximum gain at $\omega = 0$, (iii) had a -3 db relative gain at a cutoff frequency ωc and (iv) had a relative gain less than Gs db for $\omega s <= \omega <= \pi$. Choosing the Butterworth family ensures (i) and (ii). We can satisfy (iii) by taking ωc as the ωc in (**21.3**). Finally, we can satisfy (iv) by choosing the least N such that, using (**21.3**), $M1(\omega s) <= 10^{-Gs/20}$.

Then the pole locations are determined by (**21.11**) and the IIR filter transfer function by (**21.12**).

Example 22.1 _____

Suppose we choose the following parameters.

-3 db passband cutoff frequency:	$\omega c := 2 \cdot \pi \cdot \dfrac{1}{8}$	$\omega c = 0.785$
stopband low frequency:	$\omega s := 2 \cdot \pi \cdot \dfrac{1}{5}$	$\omega s = 1.257$
relative gain (db) at stopband low frequency:	$Gs := -20$	

We find the minimum-order N sufficient to meet the stopband specification.

$$gs := 10^{-\frac{Gs}{10}} \qquad gs = 100 \qquad Nr := \frac{\ln(gs-1)}{2 \cdot \ln\left[\dfrac{\tan\left(\dfrac{\omega s}{2}\right)}{\tan\left(\dfrac{\omega c}{2}\right)}\right]}$$ (22.1)

minimum N:

$$Nr = 4.089 \qquad N := \text{ceil}(Nr) \qquad N = 5$$

Notice that, as N=4 nearly satisfies the specifications, one might reconsider the latter to see if N=4 is acceptable. ‡

PROBLEM 22.1

Derive the relation (22.1) for N. ‡

We plot the frequency response using (**21.12**) and verify that the specifications are met or exceeded.

$$FRM(\omega, N) := \frac{1}{1 + \left[\dfrac{\tan\left(\dfrac{\omega}{2}\right)}{\tan\left(\dfrac{\omega c}{2}\right)}\right]^{2 \cdot N}}$$

-3 db spec. met:

$$FRM(\omega c, N) = 0.5$$

-20 db spec. met:

$$FRM(\omega s, N) = 3.615 \cdot 10^{-3}$$

$$\omega := 0, \frac{2 \cdot \pi}{64} .. 2 \cdot \pi \qquad \delta\delta := 10^{-6}$$

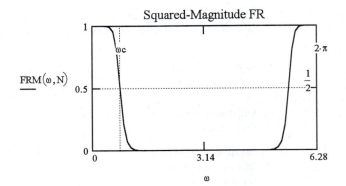

Squared-Magnitude FR

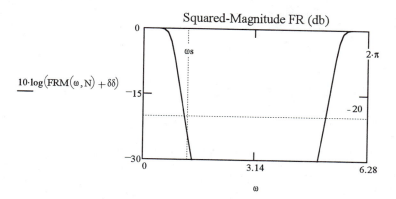

Squared-Magnitude FR (db)

$10 \cdot \log(\mathrm{FRM}(\omega, N) + \delta\delta)$

Thus the specifications are met or exceeded. We find that the corresponding z-plane pole locations are, using (**21.11**),

$$\mathrm{kmin} := \mathrm{if}\left(\mathrm{mod}(N, 2) \equiv 1, \frac{N+1}{2}, \frac{N}{2}\right)$$

$$\mathrm{kmax} := \mathrm{if}(\mathrm{mod}(N, 2) \equiv 1, 2 \cdot N - \mathrm{kmin}, 2 \cdot N - \mathrm{kmin} - 1) \qquad (22.2)$$

$$k := \mathrm{kmin} .. \mathrm{kmax}$$

$$t := \tan\left(\frac{\omega c}{2}\right) \qquad P_k := \mathrm{if}\left[\mathrm{mod}(N, 2) \equiv 1, \frac{1 + t \cdot e^{i \cdot k \cdot \frac{2 \cdot \pi}{2 \cdot N}}}{1 - t \cdot e^{i \cdot k \cdot \frac{2 \cdot \pi}{2 \cdot N}}}, \frac{1 + t \cdot e^{i \cdot (2 \cdot k + 1) \cdot \frac{\pi}{2 \cdot N}}}{1 - t \cdot e^{i \cdot (2 \cdot k + 1) \cdot \frac{\pi}{2 \cdot N}}}\right]$$

$$p = \begin{bmatrix} 0 \\ 0 \\ 0 \\ 0.58 + 0.552i \\ 0.45 + 0.264i \\ 0.414 \\ 0.45 - 0.264i \\ 0.58 - 0.552i \end{bmatrix} \qquad \begin{array}{c} k \\ \boxed{\begin{array}{c} 3 \\ 4 \\ 5 \\ 6 \\ 7 \end{array}} \end{array}$$

z-Plane Pole Plot

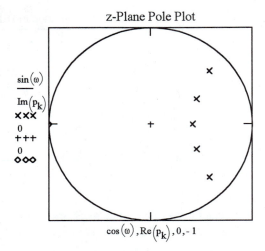

$\sin(\omega)$

$\text{Im}(p_k)$

The transfer function of the digital filter can now be formed and we verify that its frequency response meets the specifications.

$$H(z) := \prod_{k=kmin}^{kmax} \frac{z+1}{z-p_k}$$

Squared-Mag FR: Spec & Design

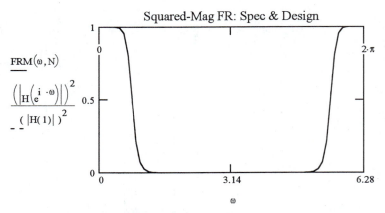

$\text{FRM}(\omega, N)$

$$\frac{\left(\left|H\left(e^{i \cdot \omega}\right)\right|\right)^2}{(|H(1)|)^2}$$

ω

Thus, within a gain constant, the digital filter H(z) has a frequency response squared-magnitude that meets or exceeds the specifications.

Real Second-Order Cascade Implementation

An important means of constructing an IIR filter is as a cascade of real filters of, at most, second order. One reason is that such filters are quite well understood when they are implemented in DSP chips using integer arithmetic, which introduces nonlinear effects. We group factors of the transfer function whose poles are complex conjugates and multiply them together to get a second-order transfer function with real coefficients. If N is even, we then have a cascade of such real, second-order transfer functions, each of which is the transfer function of an IIR filter with a real impulse response.

Example 22.2 _____

Continuing with Example 22.1, we display one such second-order IIR. Here p_3 and p_7 are a conjugate pair.

$$H3(z) := \frac{(z+1)^2}{(z-p_3)\cdot(z-p_7)} \qquad H3(z) := \frac{(z+1)^2}{z^2 - 2\cdot\text{Re}(p_3)\cdot z + (|p_3|)^2} \qquad \ddagger$$

When N is odd, we also will have a factor with a real pole corresponding to a first-order IIR filter with a real impulse response.

Example 22.3 _____

Continuing with Example 22.1, we display one such first-order IIR. Here p_5 is a real pole.

$$H5(z) := \frac{z+1}{z-p_5} \qquad \ddagger$$

We now rewrite the transfer function in terms of real second-order factors, with a real first-order factor for the case N odd. The index for the second-order factors is kr, now defined.

$$krmax := N - 1 \qquad\qquad kr := kmin .. krmax \qquad\qquad (22.3)$$

▨ **EXERCISE 22.1** Show that we now want to sum over [kmin,krmax], with krmax given by (22.3), to account for the second-order factors. ¤

It is convenient to form a first stage that is the first-order system if it is required and is otherwise the identity.

$$H_1(z) := if\left(mod(N,2)\!\!=\!\!1, \frac{z+1}{z-p_N}, 1\right) \qquad N=5$$

Now we compute the second-order stages as required. If N=1, then kmin=1 and krmax=0 so no computations will be made.

$$kmin = 3 \qquad\qquad krmax = 4$$

$$H_2(z) := \prod_{kr} \frac{(1+z)^2}{z^2 - 2\cdot Re(p_{kr})\cdot z + (|p_{kr}|)^2} \qquad H(z) := H_1(z)\cdot H_2(z)$$

We verify that this transfer function has the desired frequency response magnitude.

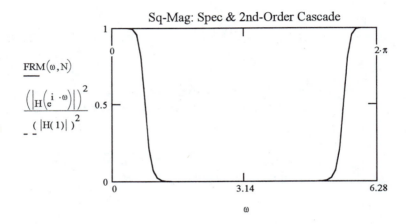

Sq-Mag: Spec & 2nd-Order Cascade

$$FRM(\omega, N)$$

$$\left(|H(e^{i\cdot\omega})|\right)^2 \qquad 0.5$$

$$(|H(1)|)^2$$

ω

LDE Implementation

We now realize the IIR filter as a cascade of LDEs (with real coefficients). To find the frequency response, we consider a unit impulse input.

$$M := 64 \qquad m := 0..M-1 \qquad x_m := \delta(m,0) \qquad n := 2..M-1$$

We compute the first stage, which is the first-order section if required (N odd); if not (N even), it is an identity operation.

$$\kappa := kmin - 1 \qquad\qquad p_\kappa := p_N$$

$$y_{0,\kappa} := x_0$$

$$y_{1,\kappa} := \text{if}\left(\text{mod}(N,2)\doteq1, \rho_\kappa \cdot y_{0,\kappa} + x_1 + x_0, x_1\right)$$

$$y_{n,\kappa} := \text{if}\left(\text{mod}(N,2)\doteq1, \rho_\kappa \cdot y_{n-1,\kappa} + x_n + x_{n-1}, x_n\right)$$

We now compute the subsequent second-order stages as required. When N=1, no second-order stages are required and Mathcad will give the error message "index out of bounds". Mathcad will not compute these recursions, so the message can be ignored.

$$\kappa := \text{kmin} .. \text{krmax}$$

$$y_{0,\kappa} := y_{0,\kappa-1}$$

$$y_{1,\kappa} := 2 \cdot \text{Re}\left(p_\kappa\right) \cdot y_{0,\kappa} + y_{1,\kappa-1} + 2 \cdot y_{0,\kappa-1}$$

$$y_{n,\kappa} := 2 \cdot \text{Re}\left(p_\kappa\right) \cdot y_{n-1,\kappa} - \left(\left|p_\kappa\right|\right)^2 \cdot y_{n-2,\kappa} + y_{n,\kappa-1} + 2 \cdot y_{n-1,\kappa-1} \cdots$$
$$+ y_{n-2,\kappa-1}$$

The output of the cascade is $\{y_{n,\text{krmax}}\}$. For the unit impulse input, the output is the IR of the LDE realization.

$$h_m := y_{m,\text{krmax}}$$

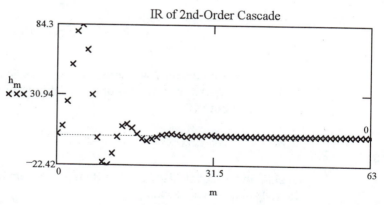

IR of 2nd-Order Cascade

We can now compute the frequency spectrum magnitude using the DFT/FFT and verify that it meets the specifications. We zero pad h for added detail in the FR magnitude (FRM).

$$\text{me} := 0 .. 8 \cdot M \qquad \text{he}_{\text{me}} := \text{if}\left(\text{me}<M, h_{\text{me}}, 0\right) \qquad \text{dft}(v) := \sqrt{8 \cdot M} \cdot \text{icfft}(v)$$

$$H := \text{dft}(\text{he}) \qquad \text{Hm}_{\text{me}} := \left(\left|H_{\text{me}}\right|\right)^2 \qquad \text{mx} := \max(\text{Hm}) \qquad \text{Hm}_{\text{me}} := \frac{\text{Hm}_{\text{me}}}{\text{mx}}$$

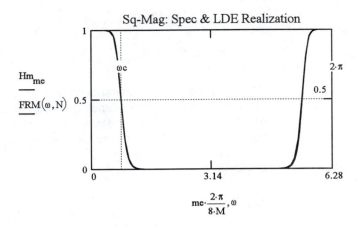

Sq-Mag: Spec & LDE Realization

$$\dfrac{Hm_{me}}{FRM(\omega,N)}$$

$$me \cdot \dfrac{2 \cdot \pi}{8 \cdot M}, \omega$$

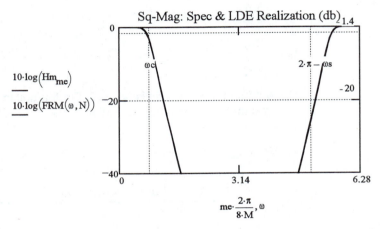

Sq-Mag: Spec & LDE Realization (db)

$$\dfrac{10 \cdot \log\left(Hm_{me}\right)}{10 \cdot \log\left(FRM(\omega,N)\right)}$$

$$me \cdot \dfrac{2 \cdot \pi}{8 \cdot M}, \omega$$

Note It has been noticed that numerical problems in this chapter may be encountered on some computers if the order N of the filter is greater than about 10.

Project 22.1

Design an IIR digital filter from the Butterworth family that satisfies the following specifications:

1. FRM between 0 db and -1.4 db from 0 to $2\pi/10$;
2. FRM no greater than -20 db at $2\pi/15$.

Completely detail your design considerations. In particular, show the pole-zero plot and plot the frequency response magnitude and phase. Implement your design as a cascade of real first- (if needed) and second-order IIRs, find its impulse response and from it the frequency response magnitude and phase. Verify that the cascade satisfies the specifications. Make a simulation. ‡

Project 22.2

Using Butterworth digital filters, design some filters for an **audio equalizer**.
(a) A low-pass filter for bass control over the band 20-500 Hz.
(b) A bandpass filter for midrange control over the band 500-1600 Hz.
(c) A high-pass filter for treble control over the band 1.6-16 kHz.
These filters will have separate gain controls.
(d) A low-stop filter for noise reduction over the range 0-20 Hz.
(e) A high-stop filter for noise reduction over the range 16-22.05 kHz.
Assume that the analog audio is adequately sampled at the rate of 44.1 kHz. ‡

Project 22.3

Recall the FM stereo receiver discussed in Projects 19.1 and 20.2. Design low- and high-pass filters that separate out the two stereo signals. ‡

References

Jackson (1996), Secs. 8.1, 8.3
Oppenheim and Schafer (1989), Sec.7.1
Proakis and Manolakis (1996), Sec. 8.3

23 IIR Design: Chebyshev Filters

We have already defined the Chebyshev analog filter frequency response magnitude. We can now design digital filters with a corresponding character by using the bilinear map. We do this by finding the s-plane singularities of the analog filter and mapping them to the z-plane singularities of the digital filter. The analog filter singularities are not quite as easy to find as those of the Butterworth family but still can be expressed in a convenient, computationally simple form. We will be using trigonometric functions with possibly complex arguments: these may be less familiar to you.

Type I Design

The Type I Chebyshev filter has an equiripple in the passband and a monotone decreasing frequency response elsewhere. We copy (**21.16**) and related forms from **Chapter 21**.

$$T(x, N) := \cos(N \cdot \mathrm{acos}(x))$$

$$M_I(v, N) = \frac{1}{1 + \left(\varepsilon \cdot T\left(\frac{v}{vc}, N\right)\right)^2} \tag{23.1}$$

Under the bilinear transformation between the z- and s-planes we have seen that the frequency is warped according to

$$v = \tan\left(\frac{\omega}{2}\right) \tag{23.2}$$

So the squared-magnitude of the FR of the digital filter is, substituting (23.2) into (23.1),

$$\omega c := 1 \qquad \varepsilon := 0.2 \qquad M1_I(\omega, N) := \frac{1}{1 + \left[\varepsilon \cdot T\left(\frac{\tan\left(\frac{\omega}{2}\right)}{\tan\left(\frac{\omega c}{2}\right)}, N\right)\right]^2} \tag{23.3}$$

$$\omega := 0, \frac{2 \cdot \pi}{128} \cdot\cdot \, 2 \cdot \pi$$

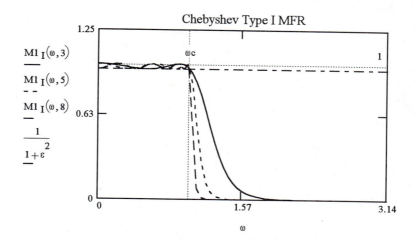

Chebyshev Type I MFR

You may wish to compare (23.3) with the corresponding form (21.3) for the Butterworth family.

EXERCISE 23.1 Show that $M1_I(\omega c, N) = 1/(1+\varepsilon^2)$ for all N. ¤

Continuing this function into the complex z-plane, as in Chapter 21, we have $\tan(\omega/2)$ replaced by

$$-i \cdot \left(\frac{z-1}{z+1}\right) \tag{23.4}$$

$$M_I(z, N) := \cfrac{1}{1 + \left[\varepsilon \cdot T\left[\cfrac{-i \cdot \left(\dfrac{z-1}{z+1}\right)}{\tan\left(\dfrac{\omega c}{2}\right)}, N\right]\right]^2} \tag{23.5}$$

EXERCISE 23.2 Compare (23.5) with the corresponding form (21.5) for the Butterworth family. ¤

Zeros

Examining (23.1), we see that $M1_I(\omega, N)$ will be zero at $\omega = \pi$, or z=-1. For as ω approaches π, $\tan(\omega/2)$ increases without bound. And hence the Chebyshev polynomial (N>0) increases without bound. As the Chebyshev polynomial T(x,N) is of degree N, the denominator of $M1I(\omega, N)$ is of degree 2N and so the zero at z=-1 is of order 2N.

Poles

To find the poles, the zeros of the denominator of $M_l(z,N)$, it is clearly advantageous to use the bilinear transformation

$$s = \left(\frac{z-1}{z+1}\right) \qquad (23.6)$$

$$Mb_I(z,N) = \cfrac{1}{1 + \left(\varepsilon \cdot T\left(\cfrac{-i \cdot s}{\tan\left(\cfrac{\omega c}{2}\right)}, N\right)\right)^2} \qquad (23.7)$$

We introduce the complex variable

$$sn = \cfrac{-i \cdot s}{\tan\left(\cfrac{\omega c}{2}\right)} \qquad (23.8)$$

Then

$$Mn_I(sn,N) = \cfrac{1}{1 + (\varepsilon \cdot T(sn,N))^2} \qquad (23.9)$$

> **EXERCISE 23.3** Compare (23.5-23.9) with the corresponding forms (21.5-21.9) for the Butterworth family. ¤

It is a bit involved to find the poles, which will be 2N in number, because T(sn,N) is a polynomial in sn of order N as already noted. The poles are such that

$$1 + (\varepsilon \cdot T(sn,N))^2 = 0 \qquad (23.10)$$

which implies that

$$\cos(N \cdot a\cos(sn)) = \beta \cdot \frac{i}{\varepsilon} \qquad (23.11)$$

where β is a *symbol* for +/-. We see that (23.10) requires that the cosine of an argument, say S, be purely imaginary. Then S itself must be complex: denote it S=u+iv. Using a familiar trigonometric identity and recalling the hypergeometric functions, we have

$$\cos(u + i \cdot v) = \cos(u) \cdot \cos(i \cdot v) - \sin(u) \cdot \sin(i \cdot v)$$

$$\cos(u + i \cdot v) = \cos(u) \cdot \cosh(v) - i \cdot \sin(u) \cdot \sinh(v)$$

EXERCISE 23.4 Graph the real functions cosh(x) and sinh(x) of real variable x. Note that cosh(x)>=1 and that sinh(x) is strictly monotone increasing. ¤

As cosh(v)>=1, the only way cos(u+iv) can be purely imaginary is for cos(u) to be zero. Therefore,

$$u = (2 \cdot k + 1) \cdot \frac{\pi}{2} \qquad\qquad k = \dots, -1, 0, 1, \dots$$

Then sin(u) is +/-1 and so

$$\cos(u + i \cdot v) = \beta \cdot i \cdot \sinh(v)$$

Thus we have established the following result.

Lemma cos(u+iv) is purely imaginary if and only if u=(2k+1)π/2, k=...,-1,0,1,... Then cos(u+iv)=+/- i sinh(v).

Applying this lemma to our problem, we have the two relations

$$i \cdot \phi \cdot \sinh(v) = \beta \cdot \frac{i}{\varepsilon} \tag{23.12}$$

$$N \cdot a\cos(sn) = (2 \cdot k + 1) \cdot \frac{\pi}{2} + i \cdot v \tag{23.13}$$

From (23.11), using the fact that sinh(x) is monotone increasing and hence has an inverse, denoted asinh(y), we have

$$v = \beta \cdot \mathrm{asinh}\left(\frac{1}{\varepsilon}\right) \tag{23.14}$$

Using (23.13) in (23.12), we obtain

$$a\cos(sn) = \frac{2 \cdot k + 1}{N} \cdot \frac{\pi}{2} + \beta \cdot \frac{i}{N} \cdot \mathrm{asinh}\left(\frac{1}{\varepsilon}\right) \tag{23.15}$$

Then, taking the cosine, of complex argument, of both sides of (23.14), we have

$$sn_k = \cos\left(\frac{2 \cdot k + 1}{N} \cdot \frac{\pi}{2} + \beta \cdot \frac{i}{N} \cdot \mathrm{asinh}\left(\frac{1}{\varepsilon}\right)\right)$$

$$sn_k = \cos\left(\frac{2 \cdot k + 1}{N} \cdot \frac{\pi}{2}\right) \cdot \cos\left(\frac{i}{N} \cdot \operatorname{asinh}\left(\frac{1}{\varepsilon}\right)\right) - \beta \cdot \left(\sin\left(\frac{2 \cdot k + 1}{N} \cdot \frac{\pi}{2}\right) \cdot \sin\left(\frac{i}{N} \cdot \operatorname{asinh}\left(\frac{1}{\varepsilon}\right)\right)\right)$$

We notice that k=0,...,2N-1 and β replaced by +1 produces all the unique values of the $\{s_n\}$. Thus all the 2N poles are given by

$$sn_k = \cos\left(\frac{2 \cdot k + 1}{N} \cdot \frac{\pi}{2}\right) \cdot \cosh\left(\frac{\operatorname{asinh}\left(\frac{1}{\varepsilon}\right)}{N}\right) - i \cdot \left(\sin\left(\frac{2 \cdot k + 1}{N} \cdot \frac{\pi}{2}\right) \cdot \sinh\left(\frac{\operatorname{asinh}\left(\frac{1}{\varepsilon}\right)}{N}\right)\right)$$

$$k = 0, ..., 2 \cdot N - 1 \tag{23.16}$$

▦ **EXERCISE 23.5** Show that $\{sn_k\}$ has period 2π. ¤

Finally, inverting the maps (23.8) and (23.6), we find the corresponding z-plane pole locations.

$$p_k = \frac{1 + \tan\left(\frac{\omega c}{2}\right) \cdot i \cdot sn_k}{1 - \tan\left(\frac{\omega c}{2}\right) \cdot i \cdot sn_k} \qquad k = 0, ..., 2 \cdot N - 1 \tag{23.17}$$

▦ **EXERCISE 23.6** Compare (23.17) with the corresponding form (21.11) for the Butterworth family. ¤

Example 23.1

We would like to verify our results thus far in a specific instance.

$$N := 5 \qquad k := 0..2 \cdot N - 1 \qquad \varepsilon = 0.2$$

$$sn_k := \cos\left(\frac{2 \cdot k + 1}{N} \cdot \frac{\pi}{2}\right) \cdot \cosh\left(\frac{\operatorname{asinh}\left(\frac{1}{\varepsilon}\right)}{N}\right) - i \cdot \left(\sin\left(\frac{2 \cdot k + 1}{N} \cdot \frac{\pi}{2}\right) \cdot \sinh\left(\frac{\operatorname{asinh}\left(\frac{1}{\varepsilon}\right)}{N}\right)\right)$$

$$t := \tan\left(\frac{\omega c}{2}\right) \qquad p_k := \frac{1 + t \cdot i \cdot sn_k}{1 - t \cdot i \cdot sn_k}$$

$$\omega := 0, \frac{2 \cdot \pi}{256} .. 2 \cdot \pi$$

Pole-Zero Plot

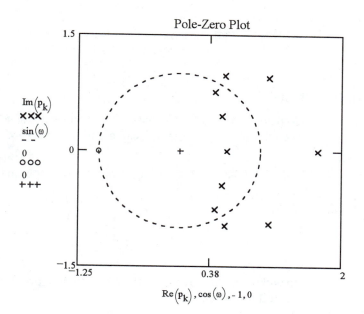

$$\text{Re}\left(p_k\right), \cos\left(\omega\right), -1, 0$$

‡

⊞ **EXERCISE 23.7** Show that the poles appear in quadruplets of complex conjugates and reciprocals. ¤

⊞ **EXERCISE 23.8** Compare this pole-zero pattern with that of the Butterworth filter of Chapter 21. ¤

We verify that we have correctly realized the specified squared-magnitude FR.

$$\text{Md}_I(z) := \prod_k \left(\frac{z+1}{z-p_k}\right) \qquad \text{M1d}_I(\omega) := \text{Md}_I\left(e^{i \cdot \omega}\right)$$

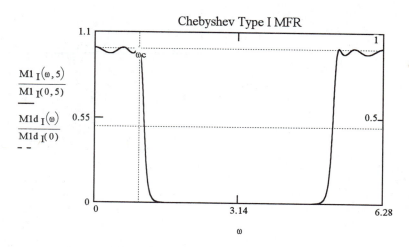

Chebyshev Type I MFR

EXERCISE 23.9 Compare this pole-zero pattern with that of the Butterworth squared-magnitude of Chapter 21. ¤

System Function

We now wish to form the system function of the digital filter. We take the poles inside the unit circle and half the zeros at z=-1.

EXERCISE 23.10 Show that the poles inside the unit circle have index k=N,...,2N-1. ¤

$$\kappa := N .. \, 2 \cdot N - 1 \qquad H_I(z) := \prod_\kappa \left(\frac{z+1}{z - p_\kappa} \right)$$

We verify that we have a digital filter with the specified squared-magnitude FR.

$$H1_I(\omega) := H_I\left(e^{i \cdot \omega}\right)$$

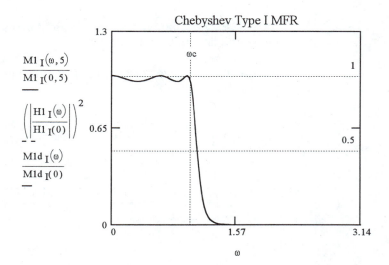

Chebyshev Type I MFR

$$\frac{M1_I(\omega, 5)}{M1_I(0, 5)}$$

$$\left(\left| \frac{H1_I(\omega)}{H1_I(0)} \right| \right)^2$$

$$\frac{M1d_I(\omega)}{M1d_I(0)}$$

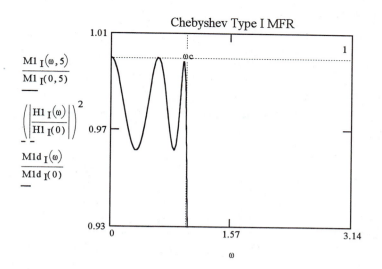

Chebyshev Type I MFR

$$\frac{M1_I(\omega,5)}{M1_I(0,5)}$$

$$\left(\left\|\frac{H1_I(\omega)}{H1_I(0)}\right\|\right)^2$$

$$\frac{M1d_I(\omega)}{M1d_I(0)}$$

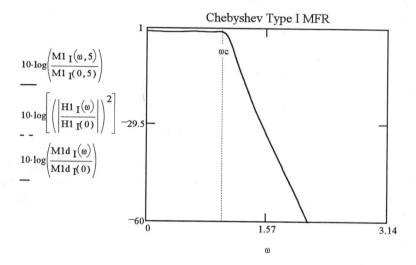

Chebyshev Type I MFR

$$10\cdot\log\left(\frac{M1_I(\omega,5)}{M1_I(0,5)}\right)$$

$$10\cdot\log\left[\left(\left\|\frac{H1_I(\omega)}{H1_I(0)}\right\|\right)^2\right]$$

$$10\cdot\log\left(\frac{M1d_I(\omega)}{M1d_I(0)}\right)$$

Thus the designed filter has the specified squared-magnitude.

Design

The design parameters outlined in Chapter 21 are $(\delta1,\omega c,\delta2,\omega s)$. For the Chebyshev Type I family, a specific filter is selected by specifying the parameters $(\varepsilon,\omega c,N)$. So we must relate the latter to the former. To carry along an example we specify a set of design parameters.

$\delta1 := 0.1 \qquad \delta2 := 0.01 \qquad \omega c := 1 \qquad \omega s := 1.5\cdot\omega c$

In view of Exercise 23.1, we have the following result.

**PROBLEM
23.1**

Show that ε is determined by δ1.

$$\varepsilon := \sqrt{\frac{1}{1-\delta 1^2} - 1} \qquad \varepsilon = 0.101 \qquad \ddagger$$

It remains to determine N by the condition

$$M1_I(\omega s, N) = \frac{1}{1 + \left[\varepsilon \cdot T\left[\frac{\tan\left(\frac{\omega s}{2}\right)}{\tan\left(\frac{\omega c}{2}\right)}, N\right]\right]^2} \le \delta 2^2 \qquad (23.18)$$

**PROBLEM
23.2**

Show that

$$\cos\left[N \cdot \text{acos}\left[\frac{\tan\left(\frac{\omega s}{2}\right)}{\tan\left(\frac{\omega c}{2}\right)}\right]\right] \ge \sqrt{\frac{\frac{1}{\delta 2^2} - 1}{\varepsilon^2}}$$

and that the argument of the cosine is generally complex. ‡

By again using the properties of trigonometric functions of a complex argument and an argument similar to that already used above to find the poles, we can find a bound on N.

**PROBLEM
23.3**

Show that

$$N := \text{ceil}\left[\frac{\text{acosh}\left[\sqrt{\frac{\frac{1}{\delta 2^2} - 1}{\varepsilon^2}}\right]}{\text{acosh}\left[\frac{\tan\left(\frac{\omega s}{2}\right)}{\tan\left(\frac{\omega c}{2}\right)}\right]}\right] \qquad N = 7 \qquad \ddagger$$

The defining parameters (ε, ωc,N) have now been determined, given a specification of the standard parameters (δ1,ωc,δ2,ωs).

Realization

The determination of the filter in factored form of at most second-order filters and the implementation as an LDE can now be carried out much as in Chapter 22.

Type II Design

The Type II Chebyshev filter has an equiripple in the stopband and a monotone-decreasing frequency response elsewhere. We copy (21.16) and related forms from **Chapter 21**.

$$T(x,m) := \cos(m \cdot \mathrm{acos}(x))$$

$$M_{II}(v,N) = \cfrac{1}{1 + \varepsilon \cdot \left[\cfrac{T\left(\cfrac{vs}{vc}, N\right)}{T\left(\cfrac{vs}{v}, N\right)} \right]^2} \qquad (23.19)$$

Under the bilinear transformation between the z- and s-planes, we have seen that the frequency is warped according to

$$v = \tan\left(\frac{\omega}{2}\right) \qquad (23.20)$$

So the squared-magnitude of the FR of the digital filter is, substituting (23.20) into (23.19),

$$N := 5 \qquad \omega c := 1 \qquad \omega s := 1.5 \qquad \varepsilon := 0.1$$

$$M1_{II}(\omega, N) := \mathrm{if}\left[\omega = 0, 1, \cfrac{1}{1 + \varepsilon \cdot \left[\cfrac{T\left(\cfrac{\tan\left(\cfrac{\omega s}{2}\right)}{\tan\left(\cfrac{\omega c}{2}\right)}, N\right)}{T\left(\cfrac{\tan\left(\cfrac{\omega s}{2}\right)}{\tan\left(\cfrac{\omega}{2}\right)}, N\right)} \right]^2} \right]$$

$$\omega := 0, \frac{2 \cdot \pi}{128} .. 2 \cdot \pi$$

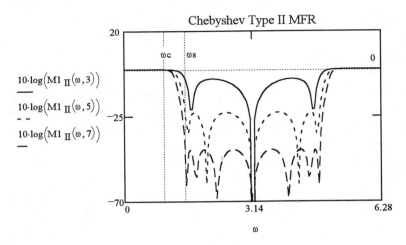

Chebyshev Type II MFR

$10 \cdot \log\left(M1_{\mathrm{II}}(\omega, 3)\right)$

$10 \cdot \log\left(M1_{\mathrm{II}}(\omega, 5)\right)$
- -

$10 \cdot \log\left(M1_{\mathrm{II}}(\omega, 7)\right)$

▧ **EXERCISE 23.11** Vary the parameters (N,ωc,ωs,ε) and observe the resulting plots. Show that M1$_{\mathrm{II}}$(ωc)=1/(1+ε²). ¤

It is helpful to simplify this expression.

$$TscN := T\left[\frac{\tan\left(\dfrac{\omega s}{2}\right)}{\tan\left(\dfrac{\omega c}{2}\right)}, N\right]$$

$$M1_{\mathrm{II}}(\omega, N) := \mathrm{if}\left[\omega = 0, 1, \cfrac{1}{1 + \left[\varepsilon \cdot \cfrac{TscN}{T\left[\cfrac{\tan\left(\dfrac{\omega s}{2}\right)}{\tan\left(\dfrac{\omega}{2}\right)}, N\right]}\right]^2}\right]$$

Continuing this function into the complex z-plane, as in Chapter 21, we have tan(ω/2) replaced by

$$-i \cdot \left(\frac{z-1}{z+1}\right)$$

$$M_{II}(z,N) = \cfrac{1}{1 + \left[\varepsilon \cdot \cfrac{TscN}{\left[T\left(\cfrac{\tan\left(\frac{\omega s}{2}\right)}{-i \cdot \left(\frac{z-1}{z+1}\right)} , N \right) \right]} \right]^2}$$

(23.21)

It is clearly advantageous to use the bilinear transformation

$$s = \left(\frac{z-1}{z+1} \right)$$

$$Mb_{II}(s,N) = \cfrac{1}{1 + \left[\varepsilon \cdot \cfrac{TscN}{\left[T\left(\cfrac{\tan\left(\frac{\omega s}{2}\right)}{-i \cdot \frac{T_s}{2} \cdot s} , N \right) \right]} \right]^2}$$

We introduce the complex variable

$$s1n = \cfrac{\tan\left(\frac{\omega s}{2}\right)}{-i \cdot \left(\frac{T_s}{2} \cdot s\right)} \qquad\qquad s = \cfrac{\tan\left(\frac{\omega s}{2}\right)}{-i \cdot \left(\frac{T_s}{2} \cdot s1n\right)}$$

(23.22)

Then,

$$Mn_{II}(z,N) = \cfrac{1}{1 + \left(\varepsilon \cdot \cfrac{TscN}{T(s1n,N)} \right)^2} = \cfrac{T(s1n,N)^2}{T(s1n,N)^2 + (\varepsilon \cdot TscN)^2}$$

(23.23)

Zeros

The zeros of $M_{II}(z)$ are the double-order zeros of $T(s1n,N)$. Recall from Chapter 14 that the zeros of $T(s1n,N)$ are

$$k := 0..\,2 \cdot N - 1 \qquad\qquad sino_{k,N} := \cos\left(\frac{2 \cdot k + 1}{N} \cdot \frac{\pi}{2} \right)$$

Inverting using (23.22), the zeros are

$$so_k = i \cdot \frac{\tan\left(\dfrac{\omega s}{2}\right)}{\cos\left(\dfrac{2 \cdot k + 1}{N} \cdot \dfrac{\pi}{2}\right)}$$

Notice that these zeros are purely imaginary. Therefore, under the bilinear transformation, they will map to the unit circle of the z-plane.

$$zo_k = \frac{1 + so_k}{1 - so_k} \qquad\qquad zo_k := \frac{1 + i \cdot \dfrac{\tan\left(\dfrac{\omega s}{2}\right)}{\cos\left(\dfrac{2 \cdot k + 1}{N} \cdot \dfrac{\pi}{2}\right)}}{1 - i \cdot \dfrac{\tan\left(\dfrac{\omega s}{2}\right)}{\cos\left(\dfrac{2 \cdot k + 1}{N} \cdot \dfrac{\pi}{2}\right)}} \qquad\qquad (23.24)$$

EXERCISE 23.12 Verify that these zeros all have unit magnitude. Verify that all zeros are of order 2. ¤

Poles

According to (23.23), the poles s1np are such that

$$0 = 1 + \left(\varepsilon \cdot \frac{TscN}{T(s1np, N)}\right)^2 = 1 + (\varepsilon 1 \cdot T(s1np, N))^2 \qquad\qquad (23.25)$$

$$\varepsilon 1 = \frac{1}{\varepsilon \cdot TscN} \qquad\qquad \varepsilon 1 := \frac{1}{\varepsilon \cdot T\left[\dfrac{\tan\left(\dfrac{\omega s}{2}\right)}{\tan\left(\dfrac{\omega c}{2}\right)}, N\right]}$$

We note that (23.25) is of the same form as (23.10). We can write down the solutions directly using (23.16) with ε replaced by $\varepsilon 1$.

$$slnp_k := \cos\left(\frac{2\cdot k+1}{N}\cdot\frac{\pi}{2}\right)\cdot\cosh\left(\frac{asinh\left(\frac{1}{\varepsilon 1}\right)}{N}\right) - i\cdot\left(\sin\left(\frac{2\cdot k+1}{N}\cdot\frac{\pi}{2}\right)\cdot\sinh\left(\frac{asinh\left(\frac{1}{\varepsilon 1}\right)}{N}\right)\right)$$

Inverting the mapping (23.22), the poles are (23.26)

$$sp_k = \frac{\tan\left(\frac{\omega s}{2}\right)}{-i\cdot(slnp)} = i\cdot\frac{\tan\left(\frac{\omega s}{2}\right)}{(slnp)}$$

Finally, inverting the bilinear mapping, the z-plane poles are

$$zp_k = \frac{1+sp_k}{1-sp_k} \qquad zp_k := \frac{1+i\cdot\dfrac{\tan\left(\frac{\omega s}{2}\right)}{slnp_k}}{1-i\cdot\dfrac{\tan\left(\frac{\omega s}{2}\right)}{slnp_k}}$$ (23.27)

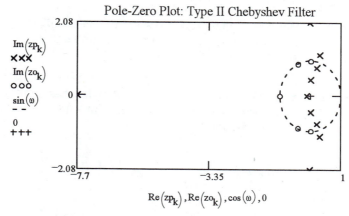

Pole-Zero Plot: Type II Chebyshev Filter

$\text{Im}(zp_k)$ ×××
$\text{Im}(zo_k)$ ○○○
$\sin(\omega)$ − − −
0 +++

2.08

0

−2.08

−7.7   −3.35   1

$\text{Re}(zp_k), \text{Re}(zo_k), \cos(\omega), 0$

Example 23.2 _____

We would like to verify our results thus far in a specific instance.

EXERCISE 23.13 Show that the poles appear in quadruplets of complex conjugates and reciprocals. Is there a degenerate case? ¤

EXERCISE 23.14 Compare this pole-zero pattern with that of the Butterworth filter of Chapter 21 and the Type I filter considered above. ¤

$$\text{Md}_{\Pi}(z) := \prod_k \left(\frac{z - zo_k}{z - zp_k} \right) \qquad \text{M1d}_{\Pi}(\omega) := \text{Md}_{\Pi}\left(e^{i \cdot \omega}\right)$$

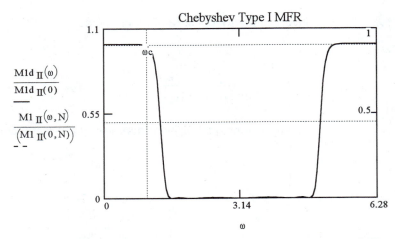

Chebyshev Type I MFR

We see that the specified squared-magnitude FR has been realized.

System Function

We now wish to form the system function of the digital filter. We take the poles inside the unit circle and one zero from each of the second-order zeros.

▨ **EXERCISE 23.15** Show that the poles inside the unit circle have index k=0,...,N-1. Show that this same indexing selects one zero of each second-order zero. ¤

$$\kappa := 0 .. N - 1 \qquad H_{\Pi}(z) := \prod_\kappa \left(\frac{z - zo_\kappa}{z - zp_\kappa} \right) \qquad (23.28)$$

▨ **EXERCISE 23.16** Compare this pole-zero pattern with that of the Butterworth filter of Chapter 21 and the Type I filter considered above. ¤

We verify that we have a digital filter with the specified squared-magnitude FR.

$$\text{H1}_{\Pi}(\omega) := H_{\Pi}\left[e^{i \cdot \left(\omega + 10^{-6}\right)} \right] \qquad (23.29)$$

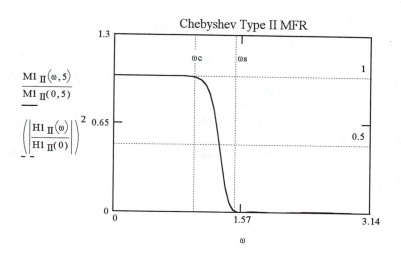

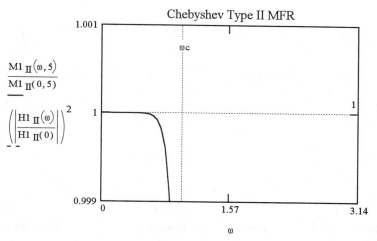

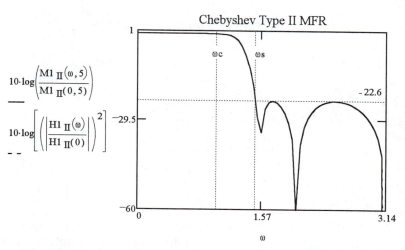

Thus the designed filter has the specified squared-magnitude.

Design

The design parameters outlined in Chapter 21 are $(\delta_1, \omega_c, \delta_2, \omega_s)$. For the Chebyshev Type II family, a specific filter is selected by specifying the parameters $(\varepsilon, \omega_c, N)$. So we must relate the latter to the former. To carry along an example, we specify a set of design parameters.

$$\delta_1 := 0.1 \qquad \delta_2 := 0.01 \qquad \omega_c := 1 \qquad \omega_s := 1.5 \cdot \omega_c$$

In view of Exercise 23.11, we have the following result.

PROBLEM 23.4

Show that ε is determined by δ_1.

$$\varepsilon := \sqrt{\frac{1}{1 - \delta_1^2} - 1} \qquad \varepsilon = 0.101 \qquad\qquad \updownarrow$$

It remains to determine N by the condition

$$\text{M1}_{\Pi}(\omega_s, N) = \frac{1}{1 + \left[\varepsilon \cdot \dfrac{\text{TscN}}{T\left(\dfrac{\tan\left(\dfrac{\omega_s}{2}\right)}{\tan\left(\dfrac{\omega_s}{2}\right)}, N \right)} \right]^2} \leq \delta_2^2$$

PROBLEM 23.5

Show that this is the same restraint on N as for the Type I filter. $\updownarrow$

Then we have also for the Type II filter

$$N := \text{ceil}\left[\frac{\text{acosh}\left[\sqrt{\dfrac{\dfrac{1}{\delta_2^2} - 1}{\varepsilon^2}} \right]}{\text{acosh}\left[\dfrac{\tan\left(\dfrac{\omega_s}{2}\right)}{\tan\left(\dfrac{\omega_c}{2}\right)} \right]} \right] \qquad N = 7$$

The defining parameters $(\varepsilon, \omega_c, N)$ have now been determined, given a specification of the standard parameters $(\delta_1, \omega_c, \delta_2, \omega_s)$.

Realization

The determination of the filter in factored form of at most second-order filters and the implementation as an LDE can now be carried out much as in Chapter 22.

Project 23.1

Design a Chebyshev Type I IIR digital filter with a frequency response squared-magnitude that satisfies the specifications $(\delta 1, \omega c, \delta 2, \omega s) = (0.293, \pi/4, 1/20, 2\pi/5)$. Completely detail your design considerations. In particular, show the pole-zero plot and graph the frequency response magnitude and phase. List all critical parameters. Implement your design as a cascade of real first- (if needed) and second-order LDEs, and find its impulse response and from it the frequency response magnitude and phase. Verify that the cascade satisfies the specifications. Make an interesting simulation of this filter. ‡

Project 23.2

Design a Chebyshev Type II IIR digital filter with a frequency response squared-magnitude that satisfies the specifications $(\delta 1, \omega c, \delta 2, \omega s) = (0.293, \pi/4, 1/20, 2\pi/5)$. Completely detail your design considerations. In particular, show the pole-zero plot and graph the frequency response magnitude and phase. List all critical parameters. Implement your design as a cascade of real first- (if needed) and second-order LDEs, and find its impulse response and from it the frequency response magnitude and phase. Verify that the cascade satisfies the specifications. Make an interesting simulation of this filter. ‡

Project 23.3

Recall the FM stereo receiver discussed in **Project 19.1** and also in **Project 20.2**. Design low- and high-pass Chebyshev filters that separate the two stereo signals. ‡

References

Jackson (1996), Secs. 8.1, 8.3
Oppenheim and Schafer (1989), Sec. 7.1
Proakis and Manolakis (1996), Sec. 8.3
Stearns and Hush (1990), Sec. 12.3

24 Stationary Random Sequences

Many signal processing algorithms are designed assuming that a statistical model of the signal and its environment are known. Typically a physical model is derived that involves unknown parameters. Knowledge of these parameters is obtained from experimental measurements, which are used to form estimates of the unknown parameters. We are especially interested in DSP in characterizing the typical time variation of a sequence - perhaps to enable prediction. The correlation sequence is the simplest such statistical knowledge. The DTFT of the correlation sequence is called the spectral density and gives the equivalent information in the frequency domain, which is very agreeable to us in view of our earlier studies.

We will now be dealing with random sequences in place of the deterministic sequences we have considered previously. The previous discussion emphasizing the frequency domain description is called **harmonic analysis**. The subject we now discuss is called **generalized harmonic analysis**. We will see that there are comfortable parallels between the two subjects. They are different, however, because we will be using models of sequences of infinite length that are not absolutely summable and therefore do not have a DTFT as we have discussed it. Of course, in practice, we only have finite-length sequences available for purposes such as estimating statistical parameters.

We thus need to first recall some basic statistical descriptions, define the class of sequences that are the subject of our study, determine how they are affected by digital filtering and hence determine how we can generate sample sequences on the digital computer.

Sequences of Random Variables

We build up the descriptions we will need from the simplest case.

Univariate Case

Recall first the concept of a **random variable**, X, which can describe the outcome of a random experiment that has a numerical outcome x on any particular trial. The basic statistical description of X is the probability $F_X(b)$ that the event $\{x:-\infty<x<=b\}$ occurs, called the **distribution function** of the random variable X. Our discussion here assumes that X has a **density function** $f_X(b)$ such that

$$F_X(b)=\int_{-\infty}^{b} f_X(x)\,dx \qquad\qquad f_X(x)=\frac{d}{dx}F_X(x) \qquad (24.1)$$

A density function is nonnegative and of integral 1.

Example 24.1

A simple random variable U is **uniformly distributed** over an interval (0,a).

$$a := 3 \qquad\qquad u := 0,0.01..\,a \qquad\qquad f_U(u) := if\left[(u>0)\cdot(u<a),\frac{1}{a},0\right]$$

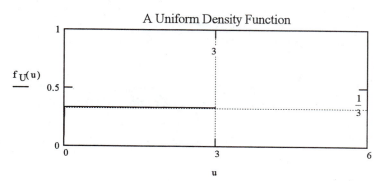

A Uniform Density Function

Mathcad has a built-in function **rnd(a)** that can draw a random sample u of such a random variable U.

$$u := rnd(a) \qquad\qquad u = 3.805\cdot 10^{-3} \qquad\qquad \updownarrow$$

▨ **EXERCISE 24.1** To make repeated draws, click on the declaration for u and repeatedly push F9. ¤

PROBLEM 24.1

Devise a counter for the number of random draws in (0,a/2) and the number of random draws in (a/2,a). For a large number of trials N, what should these counts, divided by N, be near? This idea, refined and generalized, leads to the histogram estimator of a density function. We discuss it later (**Chapter 27**). ‡

Example 24.2

Probably the most famous example of such a random variable, and perhaps the most important one in DSP modeling, is the **Gaussian**, or **normal**, random variable. ‡

mean: $m_X := 1$

standard deviation: $\sigma_X := 0.5$

normal density function: $f_X(x) := \dfrac{e^{-\dfrac{(x - m_X)^2}{2 \cdot \sigma_X^2}}}{\sqrt{2 \cdot \pi \cdot \sigma_X}}$

$x := m_X - 3 \cdot \sigma_X, m_X - 2.9 \cdot \sigma_X .. m_X + 3 \cdot \sigma_X$

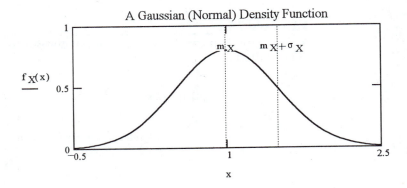

A Gaussian (Normal) Density Function

We can use the built-in random number generator rnorm(N,μ,σ) to draw one **sample** of a normal random variable.

$x := \text{rnorm}(1, m_X, \sigma_X)$ $x = 1.377$

EXERCISE 24.2 To make repeated draws, click on the declaration for x and repeatedly push F9. ¤

PROBLEM 24.2

Devise a counter for the number of random draws in (0,σ_X) and the number of random draws in (-σ_X,0). For a large number of trials N, what should these counts, divided by N, be near? ‡

The density function of a random variable has some important properties that are defined as averages, or expectations, that summarize certain statistical properties of the random variable. **Expectations** are integrals, with the density function as a weighting, of functions of the random variable. The most well-known expectations are the **mean**, m, and the **variance**, σ^2; σ is the **standard deviation**.

$$\text{inf} := 10 \qquad m := \int_{m_X - \text{inf}}^{m_X + \text{inf}} x \cdot f_X(x)\, dx \qquad m = 1$$

$$\sigma := \sqrt{\int_{m_X - \text{inf}}^{m_X + \text{inf}} \left(x - m_X\right)^2 \cdot f_X(x)\, dx} \qquad \sigma^2 = 0.25$$

The numerical integration of an exponential can encounter numerical overflow. We help Mathcad out by choosing limits just sufficiently large so that, at these limits, the density function is negligibly small or, better, its integral within the limits is sufficiently close to 1.

Example 24.2 (continued) _____

We see, empirically, that the normal density function is explicitly characterized by two parameters (m_X, σ_X^2), which are in fact the mean and variance. ‡

PROBLEM 24.3

Compute the mean and variance of a random variable U uniformly distributed over (0,a). ‡

PROBLEM 24.4

Given a random variable X with mean m_X and variance σ_X^2, show that the **standardized** random variable $Xs = (X - m_X)/\sigma_X$ has zero mean and unit variance. ‡

What does the mean mean? Here is an answer that, suitably generalized, is of great interest in DSP. Suppose that the outcome of an experiment is described by a random variable X, whose density function we know. Prior to running the experiment we wish to predict the outcome x using an estimator, or predictor, Xp, that minimizes the mean-square error

$$MSE = \int_{-\infty}^{\infty} (x - Xp)^2 \cdot f_X(x)\, dx$$

Our a priori knowledge is the density function f_X. We can show that we should take Xp=m_X: this is the meaning of the mean. Note that to build this estimator we need to know only the mean: we do not need to know the entire density function. The resultant minimum MSE is, perhaps not surprisingly, the variance σ_X^2 of the random variable X.

PROBLEM 24.5

By setting the derivative of the above MSE with respect to Xp equal to zero, show that Xp=m_X. Find the corresponding MSE. ‡

Bivariate Case

The density function of one random variable is called a **univariate** density function. When we are concerned with two random variables, say X and Y, their statistical nature is described by a **bivariate** density function, $f_{X,Y}(x,y)$.

Example 24.3 _____

The Gaussian, or normal, bivariate density is defined by five parameters.

$$m_X := 1 \quad m_Y := 2 \quad \sigma_X := 0.5 \quad \sigma_Y := 1 \quad \rho_{XY} := 0.33$$

$$f_{XY}(x,y) := \frac{\exp\left[-\frac{\left(\frac{x-m_X}{\sigma_X}\right)^2 - 2 \cdot \rho_{XY} \cdot \left(\frac{x-m_X}{\sigma_X}\right) \cdot \left(\frac{y-m_Y}{\sigma_Y}\right) + \left(\frac{y-m_Y}{\sigma_Y}\right)^2}{2 \cdot \left(1 - \rho_{XY}^2\right)}\right]}{2 \cdot \pi \cdot \sigma_X \cdot \sigma_Y \cdot \sqrt{1 - \rho_{XY}^2}}$$

$$M := 32 \qquad m := 0..M-1 \qquad x_m := m_X + \left(-3 \cdot \sigma_X + m \cdot \frac{6 \cdot \sigma_X}{M}\right)$$

$$N := 32 \qquad n := 0..N-1 \qquad y_n := m_Y + \left(-3 \cdot \sigma_Y + n \cdot \frac{6 \cdot \sigma_Y}{N}\right)$$

$$f_{m,n} := f_{XY}(x_m, y_n)$$

Bivariate Normal Density Function

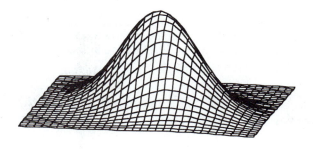

f

‡

Two random variables X and Y are **independent** if their bivariate density function is the product of two univariate density functions: $f_{XY}(x,y)=f_X(x)\,f_Y(y)$.

Example 24.4 _____

It is easy to generate independent random variables in Mathcad with the built-in random number generators. Every time one is called it generates a random sequence independent of previous and future calls. We can draw samples of two independent, standard normal random variables, X and Y, as follows.

$$\begin{pmatrix} x \\ y \end{pmatrix} := rnorm(2,0,1) \qquad\qquad x = 1.581 \qquad y = 2.074$$

(One does need to be careful when using random variable generators in software. It is difficult to devise an algorithm that generates sufficiently independent random variables. Some poor algorithms have been used in the past, and the design of such generators is a complicated subject!) ‡

A bivariate density function has parameters that summarize attributes of the distribution. Four are the means and variances of the two random variables, expectations that are computed as integrals with the bivariate density function as the weighting. For example,

$$meanofX := \int_{m_X - \inf}^{m_X + \inf} \int_{m_Y - \inf}^{m_Y + \inf} x \cdot f_{XY}(x,y)\ dx\ dy$$

These numerical integrals take a long time to compute!

Example 24.3 (continued) _____

We see, empirically, that the normal bivariate density function's four parameters $(m_X, m_Y, \sigma_X^2, \sigma_Y^2)$ are in fact the means and variances of X and Y, respectively. ‡

A new parameter appropriate to a bivariate density function is the **covariance, cov(X,Y).**

$$\mathrm{cov}(X,Y) = \int_{m_X - \inf}^{m_X + \inf} \int_{m_Y - \inf}^{m_Y + \inf} (x - m_X) \cdot (y - m_Y) \cdot f_{XY}(x,y) \, dx \, dy$$

The **correlation coefficient,** ρ_{XY}, of random variables X and Y is

$$\rho_{XY} = \int_{m_X - \inf}^{m_X + \inf} \int_{m_Y - \inf}^{m_Y + \inf} \left(\frac{x - m_X}{\sigma_X}\right) \cdot \left(\frac{y - m_Y}{\sigma_Y}\right) \cdot f_{XY}(x,y) \, dx \, dy$$

Example 24.3 (continued) _____

We see, empirically, that the normal bivariate density function's parameter ρ_{XY} is in fact the correlation coefficient of X and Y. ‡

Two random variables X and Y are **uncorrelated** if their correlation coefficient ρ_{XY} equals 0. Examining the bivariate normal density function, we see that uncorrelated normal random variables are independent random variables.

Example 24.5 _____

We can generate samples x and y of two standard normal random variables X and Y with correlation ρ as follows. First we generate two samples, x_1 and x_2, of independent standard normal random variables, X_1 and X_2, as described in Example 24.4. Then we form

$$\rho := 0.33 \qquad\qquad y = \rho \cdot x_1 + \sqrt{1 - \rho^2} \cdot x_2 \qquad\qquad ‡$$

What is the significance of the correlation coefficient? Here is an answer that generalizes the problem that gave us an interpretation of the mean and, in more general contexts, is of great importance in DSP. Suppose X and Y are two random variables with a known bivariate density function. We run an experiment whose outcomes are given by samples x and y, respectively, of X and Y. However, we can only observe x and must estimate y. We decide to use a linear estimator Ye(x) of the form (aX+b) and choose a and b to minimize the mean-square error

$$Ye(x) = a \cdot X + b$$

$$MSE = \int_{-\infty}^{\infty} \int_{-\infty}^{\infty} (y - Ye(x))^2 \cdot f_{XY}(x,y) \, dx \, dy$$

Since we know the means and variances of X and Y, we can, without loss of generality, assume that X and Y are standardized random variables. (We can form the standardized data, a sample of Xs=(X-m_X)/σ_X, estimate (with Yse) the standardized random variable Ys=(Y-m_Y)/σ_Y and then destandardize to Ye=σ_YYse+m_Y.) Thus the class of estimators we need to consider are of the simpler form

$$Ye(x) = a \cdot x \qquad\qquad (24.2a)$$

It is easy to show that

$$a = \rho_{XY} \qquad\qquad (24.2b)$$

and that the minimum mean-square error is

$$MMSE = 1 - \rho_{XY}^2 \qquad\qquad (24.2c)$$

Note that the a priori information required to construct the estimator is the correlation coefficient: knowledge of the entire bivariate density function is not required.

PROBLEM 24.6

Prove equations (24.2). ‡

N-Variate Case

Suppose we have N random variables that are very conveniently arranged into a vector. For our purposes we can imagine these random variables as members of a finite sequence.

$$N := 8 \qquad n := 0 .. N - 1 \qquad X = \begin{pmatrix} X_0 & X_1 & X_2 & X_3 & X_4 & X_5 & X_6 & X_7 \end{pmatrix}^T$$

The statistical nature of the random vector **X** is given by the N-variate density function of the random variables $(X_0,...,X_7)$, which we denote $f_X(x)$, the N-vector x denoting a sample of **X**. This could be a very complicated expression, determined by a large number of parameters, all of which would have to be known or estimated. However, there is a special case when the means, variances and covariances suffice to determine the N-variate density function: the normal, or Gaussian, case.

Example 24.6

The N-variate normal density function has the following form. Define a **mean vector** m of the means for the component random variables, denoted $m_0,...,m_{N-1}$. Also define the **covariance matrix** C of elements $Cov(X_i,X_j)$. Then

$$f_X(x) = \frac{\exp\left[-\dfrac{1}{2} \cdot (x - m)^T \cdot C^{-1} \cdot (x - m)\right]}{(2 \cdot \pi)^{\frac{N}{2}} \cdot (|C|)^{\frac{1}{2}}}$$

Thus, the N-vector of means, m, and the N-by-N matrix C of covariances completely determines the N-variate normal density function. We may still have a large number of parameters but their estimation can be tractable. Often m is the zero vector. And we shall see that C, in the stationary case discussed next, can be closely related to the spectral density, an object of ultimate interest here. ‡

 EXERCISE 24.3 Show that if the N normal variates are uncorrelated, then they are independent. ¤

Statistical Stationarity

We consider a random vector, or sequence, $X=\{X_n, n=0,+/-1,....\}$, of indefinitely large length. Such a sequence is statistically described by the family of N-variate joint density functions for arbitrarily large N. Such a general description is unmanageably complex in both theory and practice. It is necessary to simplify matters.

The concept of stationarity is crucial to eventually obtaining a frequency domain description of the random sequence. We define **(statistical, strict sense) stationarity** to mean the following. Given any subset $Xs=\{X_{n1},...,X_{nN}\}$ of X and an integer nt, the random vector $Xst=\{X_{n1+nt},...,X_{nN+nt}\}$ has the same joint density function as Xs. Roughly speaking, the random sequence looks (statistically) the same today as it did yesterday.

With this definition in mind, suppose we look at the case of a Gaussian random sequence, defined by having for every N a Gaussian or normal joint density function. Suppose the mean value vector, or sequence, m is zero. Then the joint density functions are completely determined by the covariances $Cov(X_{ai},X_{aj})$. If these equal $Cov(X_{ai+nt},X_{aj+nt})$ then the normal random sequence will be stationary. But for this to be true it is sufficient that $Cov(X_n,X_m)$ depend on n and m only as their difference (n-m).

This property of the covariance turns out to be the property of main interest to us here, whether or not the random sequence is normal. We define the class of random sequences that are of interest to us here as follows. A random sequence $\{X_n, n=0,+/-1,...\}$ whose mean value sequence $\{m_n, n=0,+/-1,...\}$ is independent of n and whose covariance $Cov(X_m,X_n)$ depends on m and n only as (m-n) is called **wide-sense stationary (WSS)** or **second-order stationary**. The meaning of a property with strict and wide senses is precisely the following: the wide-sense property plus the normal property implies the strict-sense property. (We saw a similar relation between uncorrelatedness and independence.) We introduce a more compact notation for the covariance when discussing WSS random sequences. The **covariance sequence** is

$$R_X(n)=Cov\left(X_{m+n},X_m\right) \tag{24.3}$$

Filtering WSS Random Sequences

Why is this family of random sequences of such interest to us? If a sample sequence of a WSS random sequence is passed through a digital filter, the output sequence is a sample sequence of a WSS random sequence. We shall relate the covariances of the input and output random sequences in a kind of double convolution. We will not be surprised that an equivalent description in the frequency domain is much simpler. It is there that the spectral density appears.

So once more consider a digital filter with impulse response $\{h_n,$ $n=0,+/-1,...\}$. Let the input sequence be a sample sequence $\{x_n,$ $n=0,+/-1,...\}$ of a WSS random sequence $\{X_n, n=0,+/-1,...\}$ with zero mean value sequence and covariance sequence $R_X(n)$. The output sample sequence $\{y_n, n=0,+/-1,...\}$ is given by the convolution

$$y_n = \sum_{m=-\infty}^{\infty} h_m \cdot x_{n-m}$$

It is easy to show that the output random sequence $\{Y_n,$ $n=0,+/-1,...\}$ has a zero mean value sequence. The mean of a sum is the sum of the means - which are all zero. (We do need for the sequence $\{h_n, n=0,+/-1,...\}$ to be absolutely summable.) The covariance of the output random sequence is

$$\text{Cov}\left(Y_m, Y_n\right) = \sum_{i=-\infty}^{\infty} \sum_{j=-\infty}^{\infty} h_i \cdot h_j \cdot \text{Cov}\left(X_{m-i}, X_{n-j}\right) \tag{24.4}$$

But $\text{Cov}(X_{m-i}, X_{n-j}) = R_X(m-n)$ so that the right side of (24.4) only depends on m and n as (m-n). Thus we have proved that $\{Y_n,$ $n=0,+/-1,...\}$ is a WSS random sequence and we set

$$R_Y(n) = \text{Cov}\left(Y_{m+n}, Y_m\right) \tag{24.5}$$

Thus we see that digital filtering leaves invariant the WSS property. Using (24.5) in (24.4), we have

$$R_Y(n) = \sum_{i=-\infty}^{\infty} \sum_{j=-\infty}^{\infty} h_i \cdot h_j \cdot R_X(n-i+j) \tag{24.6}$$

The form of (24.6) suggests a convolution type of operation that may be more simply described in the frequency domain. So we take the DTFT of both sides of (24.6). If we define the **spectral density** as the DTFT of the covariance sequence,

$$Sl_X(\omega) = \sum_{n=-\infty}^{\infty} e^{-i \cdot \omega \cdot n} \cdot R_X(n) \tag{24.7}$$

then we get, in an alternative to (24.6), the simpler description

$$Sl_Y(\omega) = (|H1(\omega)|)^2 \cdot Sl_X(\omega) \tag{24.8}$$

Notice that the phase of the frequency response, H1(ω), of the filter does not enter into the relation (24.8).

Recall that in the case of nonrandom sequences, we related the DTFTs of the input and output sequences as

$$Y1(\omega) = H1(\omega) \cdot X1(\omega)$$

We cannot do this for WSS random sequences because their DTFTs do not exist. Instead, we are able to relate the DTFTs of the input and output covariance sequences as in (24.8).

Example 24.7 _____

Suppose that $\{x_n, n=0,+/-1,...\}$ is a sequence of uncorrelated random variables with zero mean and variance σ^2. Then it is easy to see that the associated covariance sequence is $\sigma^2 \delta(n)$ and hence that the spectral density is the constant σ^2 for ω in $(0, 2\pi)$. Such a random sequence is termed a **white** random sequence, in analogy to the spectrum of white light, where all spectral components are present equally. ‡

Generating WSS Random Sequences

The relation (24.8) shows us a way to generate a WSS random sequence with a known spectral density. Suppose that we have a digital filter with known frequency response H1(ω) and provide as input a sample sequence of a zero mean white sequence with variance σ^2. Then we now know that the output random sequence will be WSS and of zero mean value sequence and spectral density $\sigma^2 |H1(\omega)|^2$.

Example 24.8 _____

We illustrate the generation of a sample sequence of a WSS random sequence with a specified spectral density. We can do this efficiently with a linear difference equation realization of the filter with a specified frequency response. We first define a white sequence for the filter input.

$$N := 128 \qquad n := 0 .. N - 1 \qquad \sigma := 1 \qquad x := \text{rnorm}(N, 0, \sigma)$$

We define a second-order resonator's system function (**Chapter 19**) and plot its frequency response.

$$\rho := 0.75 \qquad \theta := \frac{\pi}{4} \qquad H(z) := \frac{z^2 - 1}{z^2 - 2 \cdot \rho \cdot \cos(\theta) \cdot z + \rho^2} \cdot 0.218$$

$$z(\omega) := e^{i \cdot \omega} \qquad \omega_n := -\pi + n \cdot \frac{2 \cdot \pi}{N}$$

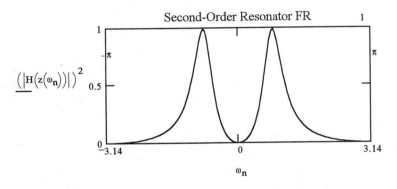

$$\left(\left| H(z(\omega_n)) \right| \right)^2$$

Second-Order Resonator FR

We compute the output random sequence using the associated linear difference equation.

$$\alpha := 2 \cdot \rho \cdot \cos(\theta) \qquad \beta := \rho^2 \qquad y_0 := x_0 \qquad y_1 := \alpha \cdot y_0 + x_1$$

$$y_n := \text{if}\left(n \geq 2, \alpha \cdot y_{n-1} - \beta \cdot y_{n-2} + x_n - x_{n-2}, y_n \right)$$

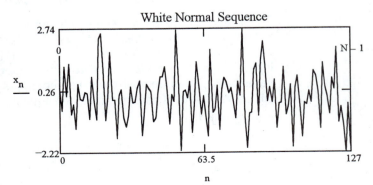

White Normal Sequence

$$\frac{x_n}{}$$

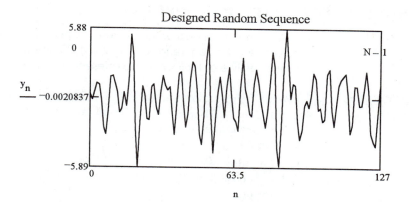

Designed Random Sequence

$\dfrac{y_n}{}$

Optimal Filtering

We now point out an important use of the spectral density. Suppose that the data is modeled as an indefinitely long sequence composed, additively, of a signal random sequence $\{S_n, n=0,+/-1,...\}$ with spectral density $S1_s(\omega)$ and zero mean and an uncorrelated noise random sequence $\{w_n, n=0,+/-1,...\}$ with spectral density $S1_w(\omega)$ and zero mean. After observing the data, suppose we wish to estimate the contained sample function $\{s_n, n=0,+/-1,...\}$ with minimum mean-square error and with a linear filter. What should the filter's frequency response be? We can show, without much difficulty, that it should be

$$H1(\omega)=\frac{S1_s(\omega)}{S1_w(\omega)+S1_s(\omega)}$$

(24.9)

Note that to construct this filter, we must know the spectral densities of the signal and noise random sequences. As this estimation problem is a very important prototype in DSP, we will want to study how, given a sample sequence of a WSS random sequence, we can estimate its spectral density.

Spectral Density Properties

We list some properties of the covariance sequence and spectral density of a WSS real random sequence. The proofs are left to the reader to devise or look up in the references below.

PROBLEM 24.7
Prove the following properties of the covariance sequence R(n) and spectral density S1(w) for a WSS real random sequence.
For the covariance sequence, prove
(a) symmetry: R(-n)=R(n),

(b) boundedness: $|R(n)|^2 <= \sigma^2$.
For the spectral density, prove
(c) symmetry: S1(-w)=S1(w),
(d) realness: S1(w)*=S1(w),
(e) positivity: S1(w)>=0,
(f) power density:

$$\sigma^2 = \frac{1}{2 \cdot \pi} \cdot \int_{-\pi}^{\pi} S1(\omega) \, d\omega \qquad \ddagger$$

Project 24.1

Illustrate the action of the optimal filter (24.9). This filter is called the **Wiener (infinite lag) filter** after its discoverer. ‡

Reference

Hayes (1996), Chap. 3
Oppenheim and Schafer (1989), Sec. 2.10, App. A
Oppenheim and Schafer (1975), Chap. 8

25 Estimating Random Sequences

In DSP a signal is commonly modeled by a random sequence and, in practice, our knowledge about its statistical description is often incomplete. As we have just seen (**Chapter 24**), a zero mean WSS random sequence is usefully characterized by its covariance sequence or, equivalently, by its spectral density. This knowledge is sufficient for some important signal processing problems. We wish to discuss the estimation of the covariance sequence and the spectral density when given the observation of a finite-length (N) sequence of the random sequence.

We note the appearance and usefulness of sample averaging in estimating statistical parameters, first in simple examples. In the context of random sequences, sample averages are called **time averages**. The averages we discussed in **Chapter 24**, which were computed using the joint density functions, are called **ensemble averages**. Giving conditions under which these two averages are equal in some sense is well beyond the bounds of our present discussion. In practice, we would rarely have sufficient information to verify the conditions anyway. Stationarity is a necessary, but not sufficient, condition. We are going to discuss merely WSS random sequences.

To gauge the performance of the estimators we consider, which are all sample averages, we compute the mean and variance of the error between the estimate and the true value using *ensemble* averages. If the mean of the error is zero, then the estimate is called an **unbiased** estimator. If the mean of the error tends to zero as N tends to infinity, then the estimate is called **asymptotically unbiased**.

Mean, Variance, and Covariance Estimation

We begin with some simple examples that show the usefulness of sample averages.

Estimating the Mean

Suppose that $\{X_n, n=0,+/-1,...\}$ is a white WSS random sequence with an unknown, constant mean value sequence $\{m_X, n=0,+/-1,...\}$ and we are given a sample sequence observation of finite length, $\{x_n, n=0,...,N-1\}$ from which we wish to estimate the unknown mean m. An estimator of the mean is the **sample mean**, which is just the arithmetic average of the observed samples. We carry along an illustration with normal random variables, denoting the sample mean by **smean**.

$$N := 64 \qquad n := 0 .. N - 1 \qquad\qquad m_X := 4 \qquad \text{var}_X := 2$$

$$x := \text{rnorm}\left(N, m_X, \sqrt{\text{var}_X}\right)$$

$$\text{smean} := \frac{1}{N} \cdot \sum_n x_n \qquad\qquad \text{smean} = 3.947 \qquad\qquad (25.1)$$

The sample mean, which we denoted smean, is a built-in function, **mean**, in Mathcad.

$$\text{mean}(x) = 3.947$$

▨ **EXERCISE 25.1** Make repeated runs of this illustration by clicking on the x_n declaration and repeatedly pushing F9. Repeat for several N and note the degree of approximation. ¤

PROBLEM 25.1
Compute the (ensemble) mean of the error of the sample mean smean. Is it an unbiased estimator? Show that the error variance is var_X/N. How should one choose N? ‡

Estimating the Variance

Known Mean Similarly, the variance may be unknown and the mean known. An estimator of the variance is the **sample variance**, denoted in our illustration by svar1.

$$\text{svar1} := \frac{1}{N} \cdot \sum_n \left(x_n - m_X\right)^2 \qquad\qquad \text{svar1} = 1.737 \qquad\qquad (25.2)$$

EXERCISE 25.2 Make repeated runs of this illustration by clicking on the x_n declaration and pushing F9 repeatedly. Repeat for several N and note the degree of approximation. ¤

PROBLEM 25.2

Compute the (ensemble) mean of the error of sample variance svar1. Is it an unbiased estimator? Show that the error variance is $2var_X^2/N$ for a normal sequence. How should one choose N? ‡

Unknown Mean If both the mean and variance are unknown, we can use the sample variance estimate with the sample mean estimate replacing the unknown mean in (25.2). We denote this estimator svar2.

$$svar2 := \frac{1}{N} \cdot \sum_n \left(x_n - smean \right)^2 \qquad svar2 = 1.735 \qquad (25.3)$$

The sample variance, using the sample mean, which we denoted svar2, is a built-in function, **var**, in Mathcad.

$$var(x) = 1.735$$

EXERCISE 25.3 Make repeated runs of this illustration by clicking on the x_n declaration and pushing F9 repeatedly. Repeat for several N and note the degree of approximation. ¤

PROBLEM 25.3

Compute the (ensemble) mean of the error of sample variance svar2. Is it an unbiased estimator? Is it an asymptotically unbiased estimator? Show that the error variance is, to highest order in N, $2var_X^2/N$, for a normal sequence. How should one choose N? ‡

Estimating the Covariance

Now suppose that $\{X_n, n=0,+/-1,...\}$ and $\{Y_n, n=0,+/-1,...\}$ are both white sequences with unknown but constant means and variances. X_m and Y_n are uncorrelated except when m=n they have an unknown covariance ρ. Given an N-length sample of each random sequence, we estimate the covariance. Again we pose a **sample covariance, scov**, as the estimate.

$$scov_{XY} = \frac{1}{N} \cdot \sum_n \left(x_n - mean(x) \right) \cdot \left(y_n - mean(y) \right)$$

Example 25.1

We illustrate this estimator, generating correlated random variables as described in **Example 24.5**.

correlation model:

$$m_W := 3 \qquad var_W := 3 \qquad \rho := 0.75$$

$$w := morm\left(N, m_W, \sqrt{var_W}\right)$$

$$y_n := \rho \cdot x_n + \sqrt{1 - \rho^2} \cdot w_n$$

$$mean(y) = 4.771 \qquad var(y) = 2.063$$

sample covariance:

$$scov_{XY} := \frac{1}{N} \cdot \sum_n \left(x_n - mean(x)\right) \cdot \left(y_n - mean(y)\right)$$

$$scov_{XY} = 1.10^{\frac{1}{2}}$$

The sample covariance, using the sample means, is a built-in function, **cvar**, in Mathcad.

$$cvar(x, y) = 1.101 \qquad\qquad cvar(x, w) = -0.302$$

If we standardize the random variables then we estimate the correlation coefficient of X_n and Y_n with the **sample correlation coefficient**, sρ. We use Mathcad's built-in functions for the variance and covariance, which employ the centered random variables and explicitly normalize by the standard deviations.

$$s\rho := \frac{cvar(x, y)}{\sqrt{var(x) \cdot var(y)}} \qquad\qquad s\rho = 0.582$$

We see that the estimated correlation coefficient is accurate for this set of parameters. ‡

EXERCISE 25.4 Make repeated runs of this illustration by clicking on the w declaration and pushing F9 repeatedly. Compare the estimated correlation coefficient with the known value ρ. Repeat for several N and ρ. ¤

PROBLEM 25.4

Show that the mean and variance of Y, in the correlation model above, are

$$m_Y := \rho \cdot m_X + \sqrt{1 - \rho^2} \cdot m_W$$

$$\mathrm{var}_Y := \rho^2 \cdot \mathrm{var}_X + \left(1 - \rho^2\right) \cdot \mathrm{var}_W$$ ‡

PROBLEM 25.5

Show that scov_{XY} is an asymptotically unbiased estimator of cov_{XY}. ‡

Example 25.2 _____

Suppose that we observe, in fact, the just-defined finite-length sample sequence {y_n, n=0,...,N-1} and wish to estimate the correlated sequence {x_n, n=0,...,N-1}. We use a linear estimator and adopt the minimum mean-square error criterion. Suppose, for a given n, we estimate x_n: the only random variable that has nonzero correlation with x_n is y_n and thus we have already stated the optimal estimator and its attained MSE in **Chapter 24**. To implement this estimator, we need to know the means, variances and correlation coefficient. The attained MMSE is

$$\rho_{XY} := \rho \qquad \mathrm{MMSE} := \mathrm{var}_X \cdot \left(1 - \rho_{XY}^2\right) \qquad \mathrm{MMSE} = 0.875$$

We can now implement the optimal estimator and compute the **sample MSE**, defined as the arithmetic average of the MSE for each x_n and denoted **smse**.

optimal estimator:

$$\mathrm{xest}_n := m_X + \rho_{XY} \cdot \sqrt{\frac{\mathrm{var}_X}{\mathrm{var}_Y}} \cdot \left(y_n - m_Y\right)$$

optimal estimator's MSE:

$$\mathrm{smse} := \frac{1}{N} \cdot \sum_n \left(x_n - \mathrm{xest}_n\right)^2 \qquad \mathrm{smse} = 1.199$$

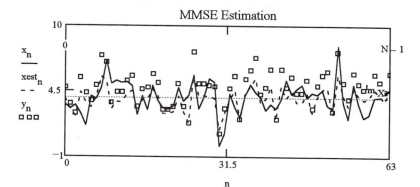

MMSE Estimation

We see that xest is a fairly accurate estimate of x for this value of the correlation coefficient. ‡

![icon] **EXERCISE 25.5** Vary the correlation coefficient $\rho_{XY}=\rho$ from 1 to -1 and observe xest. What is the MMSE estimate of X_n when $\rho_{XY}=0$?
¤

Estimating the Covariance Sequence

The examples considered thus far in this section have concerned white sequences. We may say that they have the simplest possible statistical structure in time. We now wish to consider estimation examples that can exploit correlation structure in time, when present. We consider a WSS random sequence $\{X_n, n=0,+/-1,...\}$ with zero mean value sequence and an unknown covariance sequence $\{R_n, n=0,+/-1,...\}$. We observe a finite-length sample sequence $\{x_n, n=0,...,N-1\}$ and wish to estimate the covariance sequence.

To advance an estimator of R_n for a specific n, sometimes called the **lag**, we first note that in the above examples we formed estimators that employed sample averages. Given the N-length sequence $\{x_m, m=0,...,N-1\}$ and a lag n, we can translate a copy of the sample sequence by n and multiply it point by point against the sample sequence. Then N-n overlapping values, called **lag products**, will result. These can be arithmetically averaged to provide an estimate of R_n. Call the estimate $Rest_n$. Then, for nonnegative lag n less than N,

$$Rest_n = \frac{1}{N-n} \cdot \sum_{m=0}^{N-n-1} x_m \cdot x_{n+m} \qquad (0<=n<=N-1)$$

![icon] **EXERCISE 25.6** Make a sketch of the N-length sequences x_m and x_{n+m} as a function of m and verfiy the above form for n in [0,N-1]. Make a similar sketch for n in [0,-(N-1)] and show that then

$$Rest_n = \frac{1}{N+n} \cdot \sum_{m=-n}^{N-1} x_m \cdot x_{-n+m} \qquad (-(N-1)<=n<=0)$$

Now show that we can combine these forms to have

$$\text{Rest}_n = \frac{1}{N - |n|} \cdot \sum_{m=0}^{N-|n|-1} x_m \cdot x_{|n|+m} \qquad (0 <= |n| <= N-1) \qquad (25.4)$$

Then note that Rest is a real and even sequence. Why is this a desirable property of the estimate? ¤

Example 25.3 _____

We consider the simplest example of a white sequence. Then the covariance sequence is the delta sequence $\delta(n,0)$.

**white
sequence:** $\qquad x := \text{rnorm}(N,0,1)$

**covariance
sequence
estimate:** $\qquad \text{Rest}_n := \frac{1}{N - |n|} \cdot \sum_{m=0}^{N-|n|-1} x_m \cdot x_{|n|+m}$

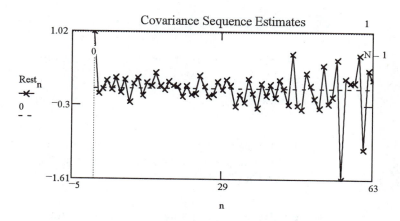

Note that we have plotted the estimate only for nonnegative n. For small n, the sequence well approximates the exact delta sequence. How well depends on how large N is: this is approximately the size of the sample average. But note that as n approaches N-1, few lagged products are averaged. The expected, increased variability of the estimate of R_n is evident in the plot. ‡

Example 25.4 _____

As a more interesting example, suppose we generate a nonwhite random sequence by passing a white random sequence through a simple low-pass FIR filter, as exemplified in **Example 24.8**. We will compute the covariance sequence and also estimate it from a sample sequence.

We define the FIR filter by placing its zeros in the z-plane.

$$p := 0.9 \qquad\qquad \theta := \frac{\pi}{2}$$

generation:
filter system
function:
$$H(z) := \frac{\left(z - p \cdot e^{i \cdot \theta}\right) \cdot (z + p) \cdot \left(z - p \cdot e^{-i \cdot \theta}\right)}{z^3}$$

▨ **EXERCISE 25.7** What type of filter is this: low-, band- or high-pass? ¤

We can use Mathcad's symbolic algebra capability to expand this form.

generation:
filter system
function:
$$H(z) := 1 + \frac{1}{z} \cdot p + \frac{1}{z^2} \cdot p^2 + \frac{1}{z^3} \cdot p^3$$

from which we can read out the FIR.

▨ **EXERCISE 25.8** What is the FIR? ¤

We can also ask Mathcad to symbolically compute the IZT, and we get

generation:
filter IR:
$$h_n := \delta(n - 3, 0) \cdot p^3 + \delta(n - 2, 0) \cdot p^2 + \delta(n - 1, 0) \cdot p + \delta(n, 0)$$

The Maple symbolic engine employs the symbol $\Delta(n)$ for the unit impulse sequence; for numerical computation in Mathcad, we edit it to read $\delta(n,0)$.

▨ **EXERCISE 25.9** Verify this symbolic computation ¤

We compute the covariance sequence. Referring to (**24.6**) with $R_x(n) = \sigma^2 \delta(n,0)$, we find

exact
covariance
sequence:
$$\sigma := 1 \quad R_{Y_n} := \sigma^2 \cdot \sum_{k=0}^{N-1} h_k \cdot \mathrm{if}\left(k - n < 0, 0, h_{k-n}\right) \quad (25.5)$$

PROBLEM
25.6
Derive (25.5) from (**24.6**). ‡

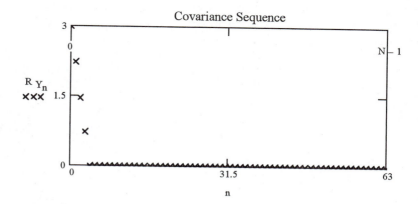

Covariance Sequence

We now generate the white random sequence.

generation:
white input:
$$w := \text{morm}(N, 0, \sigma)$$

We next compute the output random sequence and estimate its covariance sequence.

generation:
output
sequence:
$$y_n := \sum_{m=0}^{N-1} h_m \cdot \text{if}\left(n - m < 0, 0, x_{n-m}\right)$$

covariance
sequence
estimate:
$$\text{Ryest}_n := \frac{1}{N - |n|} \cdot \sum_{m=0}^{N-|n|-1} y_m \cdot y_{n+m}$$

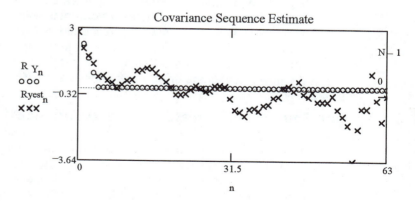

Covariance Sequence Estimate

We see that the estimate of the covariance sequence is an accurate estimate of the true covariance for small n where a fairly large number of lag products are sample averaged. However, for large n, fewer lag products are sample averaged. This results in the increased variability and decreased accuracy in this regime.

Out of curiosity we compute the spectral density of the $\{y_n\}$ random sequence using its exact covariance sequence. Since it is of finite duration we can use the DFT/FFT to compute as dense a sampling of the exact spectral density as we like. We then check that it is the same as the magnitude-squared of the FR of the generating filter.

$$R_{Ym_n} := if\left(n \le \frac{N}{2}, R_{Y_n}, R_{Y_{N-n}}\right) \qquad dft(v) := \sqrt{N} \cdot icfft(v)$$

$$S_Y := dft\left(R_{Ym}\right) \qquad \omega_n := n \cdot \frac{2 \cdot \pi}{N}$$

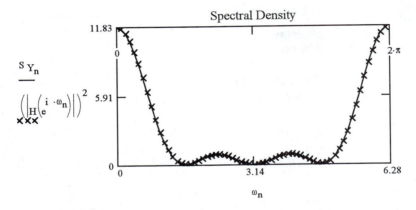

Spectral Density

So we get the expected agreement. This spectral density shows the low-pass character of the random sequence. ‡

In practice, often the covariance sequence becomes negligible beyond some lag, say L. Suppose we want to estimate the significant values of the covariance sequence. Our experience with our covariance sequence estimator thus far leads us to the conclusion that we can get an accurate estimate provided N>>L. We now consider the error mean and variance of this estimator.

Covariance Sequence Estimate Mean and Variance

From the definition (25.4) of the covariance sequence estimate and its evenness, it is easy to see that the mean sequence of the covariance sequence estimate of the covariance sequence of a random sequence $\{y_n\}$, $\{mRYest_n\}$, is R_Y itself. Thus the estimate is **unbiased**.

PROBLEM 25.7

Show that the covariance sequence estimator (25.4) is unbiased. ‡

It is a little harder to compute the variance of the error of this estimate. A fourth-order moment appears in the calculation but it is customary to assume that the random sequence is normal so that the moment may be expressed in terms of the second-order moments - i.e., the covariance sequence. A useful diagonalization trick is also used: it reduces a double sum, whose summand depends on the summing indices only as their difference, to a single sum. We find that this variance is an even function of n and is, for nonnegative n,

$$T_n = \sum_{m = -(N-n-1)}^{N-n-1} (N - n - |m|) \cdot \left(R_{Y_m} + R_{Y_{m-n}} \cdot R_{Y_{m+n}} \right)$$

$$\text{varerr}_n = \left(\frac{1}{N-n} \right)^2 \cdot T_n \tag{25.6}$$

PROBLEM 25.8

Derive (25.6). ‡

To compute this form in Mathcad, we must modify it to avoid negative indices.

PROBLEM 25.9

Show that we can write (25.6) in the form

$$V1_n := \sum_{m=0}^{N-n-1} (N - n - m) \cdot \left[\left(R_{Y_m} \right)^2 \right]$$

$$V2_n := \sum_{m=0}^{N-n-1} (N - n - m) \cdot \left(R_{Y_{m+n}} \cdot \text{if} \left(m - n > 0, R_{Y_{m-n}}, R_{Y_{n-m}} \right) \right)$$

$$V3_n := (N - n) \cdot \left[\left(R_{Y_0} \right)^2 + \left(R_{Y_n} \right)^2 \right]$$

$$\text{varerr}_n := \left(\frac{1}{N-n} \right)^2 \cdot \left(2 \cdot V1_n + 2 \cdot V2_n + V3_n \right) \qquad ‡ \tag{25.7}$$

Example 25.5

We graph the variance of the error of the estimate of the covariance sequence of the random sequence $\{y_n\}$ of Example 25.2, which we have just computed.

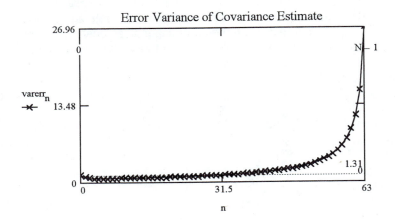

Error Variance of Covariance Estimate

As we expect, in view of our earlier study of the estimate, the variance of the error generally increases with n. ‡

Project 25.1

An alternate estimator for the covariance sequence of the random sequence $\{y_n\}$ is

$$\text{rest}_n := \frac{1}{N} \cdot \sum_{m=0}^{N-|n|-1} y_m \cdot y_{|n|+m} \qquad (25.8)$$

(a) Compare the definitions of the estimators $\{\text{Rest}_n\}$, (25.4), and $\{\text{rest}_n\}$, (25.8).

(b) Show that the estimator (25.8) has a mean value sequence

$$\text{mrest}_n := \left(1 - \frac{|n|}{N}\right) \cdot R Y_n \qquad (25.9)$$

and is therefore a biased estimator of RY_n. Graph $\{\text{mrest}_n\}$ and $\{RY_n\}$.

(c) Show that the estimator (25.8) has an error variance sequence

$$\text{varerr1}_n := \left(1 - \frac{|n|}{N}\right)^2 \cdot \text{varerr}_n$$

Graph this sequence and also $\{\text{varerr}_n\}$.

(d) Which estimator do you prefer? To help in your assessment, you can graph the true covariance sequence $\{RY_n\}$, the sequence $\{RY_n + \text{sqrt}[\text{var}_{\text{errn}}]\}$ and the sequence $\{\text{mrest}_n + \text{sqrt}[\text{varerr1}_n]\}$. Why are these graphs useful? ‡

Project 25.2

In Example 25.4 and some of the following analysis we assumed an FIR filter. Repeat these considerations with an IIR filter. You might consider a unity gain resonator. ‡

References

Oppenheim and Schafer (1975), Sec. 11.1, 11.2

26 Spectral Density Estimation

Let $\{X_n, n=0,+/-1,...\}$ be a zero mean WSS random sequence with an unknown covariance sequence $\{R_n, n=0,+/-1,...\}$. Then its spectral density $S1(\omega)$, $-\pi <= \omega < \pi$, is unknown, being the DTFT of the covariance sequence. We have aready discussed the estimation of the covariance sequence in **Chapter 25**. Now we wish to discuss directly estimating the spectral density. We have seen that the spectral density can be a more informative quantity in describing, e.g., the filtering of WSS random sequences.

The spectral density is to be estimated from a finite-length sample sequence $\{x_n, n=0,...,N-1\}$. We introduce first a reasonable estimator of the spectral density called the periodogram. However, its error variance is large and we are led to consider a sample average of periodograms to reduce the variability of the spectral estimate. We also consider the efficient computation of the estimate.

Periodogram

We have considered the covariance sequence estimators $Rest_n$, **(25.4)**, and $rest_n$, **(25.8)**. Both are accurate estimators of the true covariance R_n when $n<<N$. And both are inaccurate when the lag n is near N. Having an estimate of the covariance sequence, it is reasonable to consider its DTFT as an estimate of the spectral density. This does mean that we are using a segment of the covariance sequence where estimation accuracy is poor and we should not be surprised if this leads to problematic accuracy in estimating the spectral density.

We will proceed with the covariance sequence estimator $\{rest_n, n=-(N-1),...,(N-1)\}$, **eq. (25.8)**. Its DTFT - call it $Sper(\omega)$ - is an estimator of the true spectral density $S1(\omega)$ called the **periodogram**.

periodogram estimator:
$$Sper(\omega)= \sum_{n=-(N-1)}^{N-1} rest_n \cdot e^{-i \cdot \omega \cdot n} \qquad (26.1)$$

EXERCISE 26.1 Using the fact that $\{rest_n\}$ is real and even, show that Sper(ω) is real and even. Why is this desired? ¤

It is also true that Sper(ω) is nonnegative - as is the true spectral density - as we now show. We rewrite the estimator (**25.8**) using a rectangular window $w_{N,n}$ of length N to truncate the unlimited length data x_n to n in [0,N-1].

PROBLEM 26.1

Show that (25.8) may be written in the form

$$rest_n = \frac{1}{N} \cdot \sum_{m=-\infty}^{\infty} \left(w_{N,m} \cdot x_m\right) \cdot \left(w_{N,m-n} \cdot x_{m-n}\right) \qquad \ddagger \qquad (26.2)$$

We recognize that (26.2) is 1/N times the convolution of $\{w_{N,n} x_n\}$ with the reversed sequence $\{w_{N,-n} x_n\}$. This is a useful observation as we have had a lot of experience now with the convolution.

We would like to express the periodogram directly in terms of the data. Using (26.2) in (26.1), this is not difficult to do.

periodogram estimator:

$$Sper(\omega) = \frac{1}{N} \cdot \left[\left| \sum_{n=0}^{N-1} \left(w_{N,n} \cdot x_n\right) \cdot e^{-i \cdot \omega \cdot n} \right|\right]^2 \qquad (26.3)$$

This is clearly a nonnegative form.

EXERCISE 26.2 Write down the details of the derivation of (26.3). ¤

Further, (26.3) suggests an efficient computation of the spectral density estimate. We can use the DFT/FFT of the finite-length sample sequence to compute Sper(ω) as accurately as we desire. And we are mindful of the possibility of using windows other than rectangular if this should prove to be advantageous.

Periodogram Mean

Taking the expectation of (26.1), and using the expectation (**25.9**) of $\{rest_n\}$, we find that the average spectral density estimate is

$$mSper(\omega) = \sum_{n=-(N-1)}^{N-1} \left(1 - \frac{|n|}{N}\right) \cdot R_n \cdot e^{-i \cdot \omega \cdot n} \qquad (26.4)$$

which can be written as

$$mSper(\omega) = \sum_{n=-(N-1)}^{N-1} R_n \cdot e^{-i \cdot \omega \cdot n} - \sum_{n=-(N-1)}^{N-1} \frac{|n|}{N} \cdot R_n \cdot e^{-i \cdot \omega \cdot n}$$

(26.5)

Thus the periodogram estimator is a biased estimator of the spectral density. However, as N becomes arbitrarily large, the first term goes to the DTFT of R_n - that is, the spectral density $S1(\omega)$, while, if $\{nR_n\}$ is absolutely summable, the second term on the right side of (26.6) goes to zero. Then the periodogram is an asymptotically unbiased estimator of the spectral density.

PROBLEM 26.2

Show that for a more general N-length window w_n,

$$mSper(\omega) = \sum_{k=-\infty}^{\infty} \left(\frac{1}{N} \cdot wc_k \right) \cdot R_k \cdot e^{-i \cdot \omega \cdot k}$$

(26.6)

where wc_n is the convolution of w_n and w_{-n}. ‡

Thus, in general, the mean periodogram is the DTFT of a windowing of the true covariance sequence. The window is (1/N)wc.

In the particular case of a rectangular window, we see that the mean periodogram estimate is the DTFT of a windowed covariance sequence with a window called the **Bartlett window**

$$w_{BN_n} = if\left(|n| < N, 1 - \frac{|n|}{N}, 0 \right)$$

This triangular shape is to be expected, as it is the convolution of a rectangular window with itself reversed.

We would like to express the mean periodogram directly in terms of the true spectral density. We see from (26.6) that the mean periodogram is the DTFT of a product of the true covariance function and a windowing sequence. As we know (**Chapter 7**), this means that the mean periodogram is expressible as a periodic convolution of the DTFTs, in this case the true spectral density and the DTFT of the windowing sequence.

Furthermore, the DTFT of the windowing sequence, (1/N)wc_n, being the convolution of the data window w_n with w_{-n}, is just (1/N) times the magnitude-squared of the DTFT $W1(\omega)$ of the data window. Thus

mean periodogram:

$$mSper(\omega) = \frac{1}{2 \cdot \pi} \cdot \int_{-\pi}^{\pi} \frac{1}{N} \cdot \left(|W1(\omega - v)| \right)^2 \cdot S1(v) \, dv$$

(26.7)

In the case of a rectangular window, we have computed its DTFT many times (e.g., **Chapter 6**). Thus, we can write (26.7) specifically as

$$N := 16 \qquad W1_{BN}(\omega) := \text{if}\left[\omega = 0, N, \frac{1}{N} \cdot \left[\frac{\sin\left(\omega \cdot \dfrac{N}{2} \right)}{\sin\left(\omega \cdot \dfrac{1}{2} \right)} \right]^2 \right]$$

mean periodogram:

$$mSper(\omega) = \frac{1}{2 \cdot \pi} \cdot \int_{-\pi}^{\pi} W1_{BN}(\omega - v) \cdot S1(v) \, dv \qquad (26.8)$$

PROBLEM 26.3

Write down the details of the derivation of (26.7) and (26.8). ‡

We graph this weighting function for a particular N.

$$K := 128 \qquad k := 0 .. K \qquad \omega_k := -\pi + k \cdot \frac{2 \cdot \pi}{K}$$

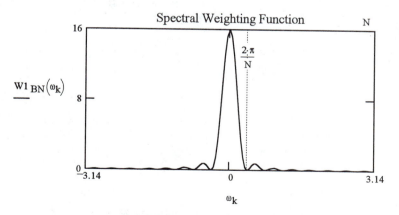

Spectral Weighting Function

Thus, on average, the periodogram value at a particular frequency ω is not a sample of the spectral density at ω, but rather a weighted sum of all the values of the latter. The weighting does give preference to spectral values near ω. The **spectral resolution** of the estimate can be defined as half the distance between the first nulls - $2\pi/N$ in this case.

The mean periodogram would equal the true spectral density if $(1/N)|W1(\omega)|^2$ were a delta function. This is not possible as W1 is a rational function of $\exp(i\omega)$. But we can at least arrange to have $(1/2\pi)|W1(\omega)|^2$ be of integral N. By Plancherel's Theorem (**Chapter 7**) we then want the sum of the squares of the weights of the data window w to be N. Note that the rectangular window naturally has this property. We shall impose this restraint on more general windows.

The particular weighting function we have exhibited, the Bartlett window, results when we truncate the sample sequence with a rectangular window. We have discussed this type of frequency weighting before, and do not favor it because of its high sidelobe level. We have already discussed the use of other windows to get better confinement of the DTFT, in the sense of lower sidelobes or greater energy content in a specified frequency band. The cost of such confinement was a broader mainlobe, which could be ameliorated if we choose a greater window length. This requires a longer sample sequence, which may be available in practice. Optimal energy windows are especially appealing for FIR filter design by the method of windows and DTFT estimation, as we have already discussed. *Note that there is no reason to use the Kaiser approximation as the optimal energy window is easily found with Mathcad.*

Example 26.1 _____

To see the effect of the convolution, we recall **Chapter 24**'s discussion of the generation of a sample function of a WSS random sequence.

generating filter:
$$p := 0.75 \qquad \theta := \frac{\pi}{4} \qquad z(\omega) := e^{i \cdot \omega}$$

$$H(z) := \frac{z^2 - 1}{z^2 - 2 \cdot p \cdot \cos(\theta) \cdot z + p^2}$$

true spectral density:
$$S1(\omega) := \left(\left| H(z(\omega)) \right| \right)^2$$

mean periodogram:
$$mSper(\omega) = \frac{1}{2 \cdot \pi} \cdot \int_{-\pi}^{\pi} W1_{BN}(\omega - v) \cdot S1(v)\, dv$$

As the calculation of this convolution is slow, we do it for a reasonably dense set of ω's and store the calculations in an array.

$$mSpers_k := \frac{1}{2 \cdot \pi} \cdot \int_{-\pi}^{\pi} W1_{BN}(\omega_k - v) \cdot S1(v) \, dv$$

**compute time about
8 s on a 300 MHz
Pentium II**

We graph both S1(ω) and mSper(ω).

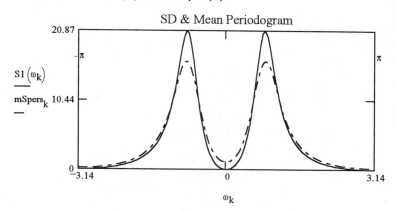

We see the effect of the convolution in computing the mean periodogram: it is a smeared version of the true spectral density. ‡

EXERCISE 26.3 Decrease p in Example 26.1 by steps and observe the merging of the two modes of the spectral density and its estimate. ¤

Periodogram Error Variance

The mean of the periodogram exhibits the "smearing" of the spectral density due to truncation, as expected. The property of the periodogram that renders it problematic is the error variance. One can show that, again assuming the fourth-moment factorization property for the subject WSS random sequence, the error variance is bounded away from zero for any N: indeed, it is lower bounded by the square of the estimate's mean.

Thus, the periodogram's error has a standard deviation at least as large as its mean. The periodogram is therefore not a very desirable estimator of the spectral density, and we will look for a way to improve it. But first we consider an example.

Chapter 26   Spectral Density Estimation   6

Example 26.2

We compute the periodogram estimator of the spectral density for Example 26.1, generating a finite-length sample sequence as described in **Chapter 24**.

$$n := 0 .. N - 1 \qquad u := \text{rnorm}(N, 0, 1)$$

$$\alpha := 2 \cdot p \cdot \cos(\theta) \qquad \beta := p^2 \qquad x_0 := u_0 \qquad x_1 := \alpha \cdot x_0 + u_1$$

$$x_n := \text{if}\left(n \geq 2, \alpha \cdot x_{n-1} - \beta \cdot x_{n-2} + u_n - u_{n-2}, x_n\right)$$

$$\text{Sper}(\omega) := \frac{1}{N} \cdot \left(\left\| \sum_{n=0}^{N-1} x_n \cdot e^{-i \cdot \omega \cdot n} \right\| \right)^2$$

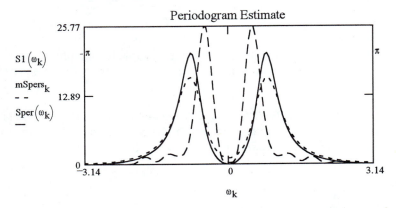

Periodogram Estimate

$S1\left(\omega_k\right)$ ——

$mSpers_k$ - -

$Sper\left(\omega_k\right)$ ——

ω_k

Note that Sper(ω) is not particularly accurate. We observe, through a number of trials, that this periodogram does convey the important information that the spectral density is of a bandpass nature and the general shape is roughly accurate. ‡

EXERCISE 26.4 Click on the equation defining u and repeatedly push F9. Note the wide variability in the periodogram estimate Sper. What do you think of its worth? ¤

Modified Periodogram

Again, we may try to use the basic technique of forming sample averages to reduce the estimate's variability. How can that be done here? Suppose we can form a number of periodograms: then we can form their sample average. We can hope that this will reduce the variability of the resulting estimate; in fact it will, and the error mean will remain unchanged.

Given a finite-length sample sequence, we can subdivide it into a number, J, of disjunct subsequences. We form the periodogram of each subsequence and then form their arithmetic average.

$$Aper(\omega) = \frac{1}{J} \cdot \sum_{j=0}^{J-1} Sper(\omega)^{<j>} \qquad (26.9)$$

To note the properties of this sample average of the periodograms, we recall two facts from elementary probability theory which, in fact, we discussed in **Chapter 24**. If $\{X_j, j=0,...,J-1\}$ is a sequence of uncorrelated random variables with mean m and variance σ^2, then:

(i)   Their sample average is m.

(ii) Their sample variance is σ^2/J.

Since the average of each periodogram is identical, the average of the arithmetic mean is the average of any one periodogram and therefore this technique does not change the average periodogram's properties. However, if the disjunct subsequences are nearly independent, then the sample averaged periodogram will have approximately the error variance of any one of the subperiodograms, multiplied by 1/J, where J is the number of periodograms used in the sample average. This scheme will reduce the variability of the estimate, albeit only inversely to the number of periodograms averaged, a rather slow dependence.

Example 26.3

We try our scheme.

$$J := 32 \quad j := 0 .. J - 1 \qquad\qquad u^{<j>} := \text{morm}(N, 0, 1) \qquad (26.10)$$

$$\alpha := 2 \cdot p \cdot \cos(\theta) \qquad \beta := p^2 \qquad X_{0,j} := u_{0,j} \qquad X_{1,j} := \alpha \cdot X_{0,j} + u_{1,j}$$

$$X_{n,j} := \text{if}\left(n \geq 2, \alpha \cdot X_{n-1,j} - \beta \cdot X_{n-2,j} + u_{n,j} - u_{n-2,j}, X_{n,j}\right)$$

$$Sper_{k,j} := \frac{1}{N} \cdot \left(\left\| \sum_{n=0}^{N-1} x_{n,j} \cdot e^{-i \cdot \omega_k \cdot n} \right\| \right)^2 \qquad (26.11)$$

$$Aper_k := \frac{1}{J} \cdot \sum_j \left(Sper^{<j>} \right)_k$$

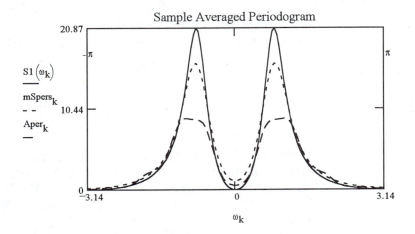

Sample Averaged Periodogram

It is evident that a more accurate estimate of the spectral density is obtained using the sample average of multiple periodograms. ‡

EXERCISE 26.5 Make numerous estimates by clicking on (26.10) and pushing F9. Vary J in Example 26.3 and observe the quality of the spectral density estimate. ¤

Application with Optimal Window

We now review the above discussion and outline an efficient computation of the modified periodogram. We will use the optimal energy window and the DFT/FFT algorithm.

Suppose that we have a sufficiently long sample sequence. First, we decide on the resolution bandwidth Ω that we need and the fraction of energy of the truncation window that we desire in this bandwidth. Then, using the plot of fractional energy r in the specified band versus TBP derived in **Chapter 13**, we can determine the required TBP of the optimal window. Then we can determine the required window length as follows.

optimal
window
parameters:

$$\Omega := \frac{2 \cdot \pi}{32} \qquad r := 0.999943 \qquad TBP := 4$$

$$N := ceil\left(\frac{2 \cdot \pi}{\Omega} \cdot TBP\right) \qquad N = 128$$

Optimal Window We now determine the optimal window as discussed in **Chapter 13**.

$$n := 0 .. N - 1 \qquad\qquad m := 0 .. N - 1$$

$$\gamma(y) := if\left[y=0, \frac{\Omega}{2 \cdot \pi}, \frac{\Omega}{2 \cdot \pi} \cdot \frac{sin\left(\frac{\Omega}{2} \cdot y\right)}{\frac{\Omega}{2} \cdot y}\right] \qquad \Gamma_{m,n} := \gamma(m - n)$$

We now find the maximum characteristic value and its associated characteristic vector, which we normalize to have norm N.

$$\lambda := eigenvals(\Gamma) \qquad\qquad L := reverse(sort(\lambda))$$

$$L_0 = 0.999943 \qquad wopt := eigenvec\left(\Gamma, L_0\right) \qquad wopt := \sqrt{N} \cdot wopt$$

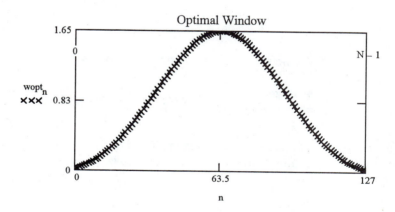

Optimal Window

We now decide on the number, L, of periodograms we wish to average. The total length of the sample sequence required is M=LN.

$$L := 64 \qquad\qquad l := 0 .. L - 1 \qquad\qquad M := L \cdot N \qquad\qquad m := 0 .. M - 1$$

data
generation
by LDE:

$$v := rnorm(M, 0, 1) \qquad\qquad\qquad\qquad\qquad (26.12)$$

$$\alpha := 2 \cdot p \cdot cos(\theta) \qquad \beta := p^2$$

$$z_0 := v_0 \qquad z_1 := \alpha \cdot z_0 + v_1$$

$$z_m := \mathrm{if}\left(m \geq 2, \alpha \cdot z_{m-1} - \beta \cdot z_{m-2} + v_m - v_{m-2}, z_m\right)$$

We form the L subsequences and weight them separately with the optimal window.

windowed
subsequences: $\qquad zz_{n,1} := wopt_n \cdot z_{n+1\cdot N}$

We now wish to compute the L periodograms and their sample average as in the form (26.11). But note that if the number of points at which the modified periodogram is computed is N, then we may implement the sampled DTFT as a DFT/FFT. The resulting sample spacing in ω will be $\delta\omega = 2\pi/N$.

periodogram $\qquad \mathrm{dft}(v) := \sqrt{N} \cdot \mathrm{icfft}(v)$
calculation
with DFT/FFT:

$$zft^{<1>} := \mathrm{dft}\left(zz^{<1>}\right)$$

$$Sper_{n,1} := \frac{1}{N} \cdot \left(\left|zft_{n,1}\right|\right)^2$$

We now form the sample average of the periodograms.

average $\qquad Aper_n := \frac{1}{L} \cdot \sum_1 Sper_{n,1}$
periodogram:

We place the estimate in FT order, rather than DFT order, to plot comparisons with our earlier results.

$$Aperq_n := \mathrm{if}\left(n < \frac{N}{2}, Aper_{n+\frac{N}{2}}, Aper_{n-\frac{N}{2}}\right)$$

We recompute the mean periodogram using the optimal window.

$$\delta\omega := \frac{2 \cdot \pi}{N} \qquad\qquad\qquad \omega_n := -\pi + n \cdot \frac{2 \cdot \pi}{N}$$

$$Wopt := \mathrm{dft}(wopt)$$

$$WW_n := \frac{1}{N} \cdot \left(\left| Wopt_n \right| \right)^2$$

$$mSper_n := \left(\frac{1}{2 \cdot \pi} \right) \cdot \sum_{m=0}^{N-1} if\left(n - m < 0, 0, WW_{n-m} \cdot S1\left(\omega_n\right)\right) \cdot \delta\omega$$

We plot the true spectral density, S1(ω), the mean periodogram, mSper(ω), and the averaged, optimally weighted periodogram, Aper(ω).

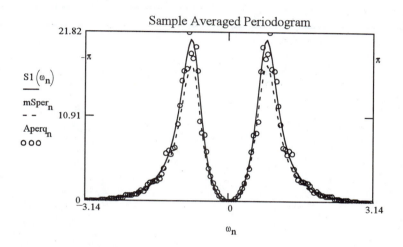

Sample Averaged Periodogram

We see that the averaged periodogram, with the optimal window, can be a quite accurate estimate of the spectral density. It appears to converge to the average periodogram as L increases. This we predicted.

EXERCISE 26.6 Vary the number L of periodograms averaged and note the general decrease in variability with increasing L. Note, however, that the decrease is slow with increasing L. For each L make repeated runs by clicking on (26.12) and repeatedly pushing F9, and note the variability of the estimates. ¤

Project 26.1

Repeat the considerations discussed in the Application with Optimal Window section of this chapter with a different data model. You could, e.g., use a different filter to generate the random data. Better, you may be able to import a data file of interest to you, about which you may or may not have a priori knowledge. ‡

References

Hayes (1996), Secs. 8.1, 8.2
Jackson (1996), Sec.7.6
Oppenheim and Schafer (1989), Secs. 11.2, 11.6
Oppenheim and Schafer (1975), Secs. 11.3, 11.4

27 Digital Images

One of the most important areas of application of digital processing, with its great flexibility, is image processing. A digital image may be generated by sampling an analog image, such as a photograph, or it may be generated directly by a digital computer. Scanning systems, including imaging radar, are a very important source of images. A digital image typically consists of a square array of pixels that take on values in a restricted set (for example, 0 to 255), which allows fast integer arithmetic. The size of the array, N by N, can have values N of tens or hundreds or a few thousand. The desire to increase this number has been a driver of new developments of hardware, software and processing algorithms.

The tractable number and size of images in a Mathcad document varies with the computer. To minimize the requirements, we shall work with two 64-by-64 images, placed near the end of this chapter. We also try to minimize the memory required by reusing image definitions. These steps will require toggling equations between active and inactive states.

We define a set of **sites**, or **pixels**, $L=\{(m,n), m=0,...,N-1, n=0,...,N-1\}$ called a **lattice.** A function $\{x(m,n)\}$ defined on the lattice is called a **digital image** or, simply, **image**. Digital images commonly take on a discrete set of values, but we shall assume here that they are real-valued. An image is naturally described by a **matrix array**. In Mathcad, an image is an N-by-N matrix. Later we will have use for complex arrays. The two-dimensional discrete Fourier transform of an image (defined later) is an array of complex values that can be informatively displayed as an image, especially its magnitude.

Mathcad can plot images with its **surface plot** capability. We set the tilt at 90, the rotation at 270, and select gray scale. The larger the pixel value, the brighter the plotted intensity. Mathcad plots only square arrays. One can always zero pad a rectangular array, but the resulting plot may be disconcerting.

With a rotation of 270, Mathcad plots the image coordinate m as the abscissa, increasing to the right, and the image coordinate n as the ordinate, increasing upward. This choice is agreeable when an analog image i(x,y) is sampled with m indexing the x-coordinate samples and n indexing the y-coordinate samples.

Tip When scrolling in a document, the delay due to replotting images can be avoided by temporarily removing the array name from the placeholder.

Data Files Images can be written to data files and read with the WRITEPRN and READPRN commands. Mathcad can read and write between *.bmp bit map files and data files. **Create Picture** under the **Graphics** menu displays a *.bmp image much more quickly than a Surface Plot.

Digital Image Examples

Example 27.1 _____

The unit impulse image will play the same role in image processing as the unit impulse sequence did in one-dimensional signal processing. When it is the input to a two-dimensional filter, the resulting image will be called the **impulse response** of the filter.

unit impulse image: $\quad N := 32 \qquad m := 0..\,N-1 \qquad\qquad n := 0..\,N-1$

$$x_{m,n} := 0 \qquad\qquad x_{0,0} := 1 \qquad\qquad \ddagger \qquad (27.1)$$

▨ **EXERCISE 27.1** Plot the unit impulse image at location (m_o, n_o). It may be hard to see! ¤

If an image is such that $\{x_{m,n} = x_{m+M,n+N}\}$, we say that the image $\{x_{m,n}\}$ has **period** (M,N). Note that the period is a vector of two dimensions.

Example 27.2 _____

The sinusoids are fundamental in image representation and processing. We give a simple illustration of an image with a **sinusoidal** variation.

sinusoidal image: $\quad x_{m,n} := \cos\!\left(\dfrac{2\cdot\pi}{N}\cdot 2\cdot m + \dfrac{2\cdot\pi}{N}\cdot 3\cdot n\right) \qquad (27.2)$

The vector $k = (2\pi/N)(2,3)^{\mathsf{T}}$ is called the **wavenumber**; its components k_m and k_n are the **spatial frequencies** of the sinusoidal variation. $\ddagger$

EXERCISE 27.2 Plot the sinusoidal image for various spatial frequencies. (Toggle (27.1) active, then go to page 11 of the document and note the image for each wavenumber chosen; finally, toggle (27.1) inactive.) Given a sinusoidal image with wavenumber $k=(k_m,k_n)$, when is the sinusoidal image periodic? ¤

Example 27.3 _____

We generalize Example 27.2 to a weighted sum of sinusoids.

spatial
frequencies: $\quad k := 0 .. \dfrac{N}{2} \qquad u_k := \dfrac{2 \cdot \pi}{N} \cdot k \qquad \kappa := 0 .. \dfrac{N}{2} \qquad v_\kappa := \dfrac{2 \cdot \pi}{N} \cdot \kappa$

arbitrary
weights: $\quad c_{k,\kappa} := 1$

a very slow
computation: $\quad X_{m,n} := \displaystyle\sum_{k}\sum_{\kappa} c_{k,\kappa} \cdot \cos\left(u_k \cdot m + v_\kappa \cdot n\right)$ ▯

It is possible to show that any real image defined over an N-by-N region has a unique representation as a weighted sum of sinusoids. It is a two-dimensional Fourier series representation, which we will also call a two-dimensional inverse discrete Fourier transform. We need a fast algorithm to compute this form, even more so than in the one-dimensional case. ‡

EXERCISE 27.3 Choose other amplitudes $\{c_{k,k}\}$ and plot the resulting images. You may need to adjust N to render this computation feasible. ¤

Example 27.4 _____

We can construct an image of an object that is modeled by a truncated Gaussian shape at location (m_o, n_o) and of radius of gyrations σ and v in, respectively, the m-coordinate direction and the n-coordinate direction.

$$m_o := 12 \qquad n_o := 16 \qquad \sigma := 1 \qquad v := 2 \qquad a_o := 5$$

Gaussian
image: $\quad X_{m,n} := a_o \cdot \exp\left[-\dfrac{1}{2} \cdot \dfrac{(m - m_o)^2}{\sigma^2} - \dfrac{1}{2} \cdot \dfrac{(n - n_o)^2}{v^2} \right] \qquad$ ‡ (27.3)

EXERCISE 27.4 Plot the Gaussian image for various values of σ and v. This signal has a factored form: we can write it as the product of a factor dependent on m and a factor dependent on n. Do so. ¤

PROBLEM 27.1 Can you construct a Gaussian-shaped image that is not of factorable form? ‡

Random models of digital images are useful in representing the image of many classes of scenes and are widely used. We give a simple example next.

Example 27.5

We can construct a normal **random field** or image. For simplicity, we construct a white random field that has no correlation between the pixel values. We add this field to the signal of Example 27.3.

normal
random $\text{var} := 1 \qquad \text{no}^{<n>} := \text{rnorm}\left(N, 0, \sqrt{\text{var}}\right)$
image:

noisy
image: $x := x + \text{no} \blacksquare$

$$(27.4)$$

Note that we filled the matrix array no column by column using the built-in random generator, which draws a random vector. ‡

EXERCISE 27.5 Plot this random field for various choices of signal-to-noise ratio (SNR), a_o^2/var. ¤

Basic Operations on Images

There are a number of important simple algebraic operations on images. Many can be done with expeditious commands in Mathcad. To illustrate these operations, we define two images.

$$x_{m,n} := \cos\left(\frac{2\cdot\pi}{N}\cdot 2\cdot m + \frac{2\cdot\pi}{N}\cdot 3\cdot n\right)\blacksquare$$

$$y^{<n>} := \text{rnorm}\left(N, 0, \sqrt{\text{var}}\right)$$

Image Addition

Image addition/subtraction is the addition/subtraction of same-indexed pixels in two images to form a new image.

$$z_{m,n} := x_{m,n} + y_{m,n}\blacksquare \qquad\qquad z := x + y\blacksquare \qquad\qquad z := \overrightarrow{(x+y)}\blacksquare$$

The definition is explicitly implemented in the first form; Mathcad understands the intent of the second form and its computation is speeded up by using Mathcad's **vec** operation in the third form.

Image Multiplication

Image multiplication is the multiplication of same-indexed pixels in two images to form a new image.

$$z_{m,n} := x_{m,n} \cdot y_{m,n} \qquad z := \overrightarrow{(x \cdot y)}$$

The definition is explicitly implemented in the first form and its computation is speeded up by using the vec operation in the second form. Note that we would not form x*y, which is rather a matrix multiply.

Scalar Multiplication

Scalar multiplication is the multiplication of every pixel value of the image by a scalar to form a new image.

$$a := \pi \qquad z_{m,n} := a \cdot x_{m,n} \qquad z := a \cdot x$$

The definition is explicitly implemented in the first form; Mathcad understands the intent of the second form.

Basic Image Processing Operations

Value Range

We can use the Mathcad built-in functions max( ) and min( ) to find the maximum and minimum values and hence find the range of values in an image.

$$\text{supx} := \max(x) \qquad \text{supx} = 5$$

$$\text{infx} := \min(x) \qquad \text{infx} = 0 \qquad \text{rngx} := \text{supx} - \text{infx} \qquad \text{rngx} = 5$$

Rescaling

After we have found the range of values in an image, we can rescale it. Suppose we wanted to rescale the image to values in [0,255].

$$z_{m,n} := \left(x_{m,n} - \text{infx}\right) \cdot \frac{255}{\text{rngx}} \qquad \min(z) = 0 \qquad \max(z) = 255$$

Histogram

The **histogram** of an image is a vector **f** of the relative frequency of image values in a specified set of subintervals, defined by a vector **pt** of points. It provides, when normalized, an estimate of the univariate density function of the image. Mathcad has a built-in function, **hist(,)**, to compute the histogram.

Example 27.6

We generate an image composed of J pixels drawn independently from a Rayleigh distribution to see if the histogram approximates a Rayleigh density function. We define uniform intervals, U in number and of size δu. We assume we have an estimate of the variance var (it can be obtained from the data itself as discussed in **Chapter 25**) so that we can choose the subinterval size δu reasonably. Since Mathcad does not generate Rayleigh random variables, we do so by transforming uniformly distributed random variables.

sample index:
$$J := 10000 \quad j := 0.. J - 1 \quad var := 1.0$$

Rayleigh samples:
$$w_j := \sqrt{-2 \cdot var \cdot \ln(rnd(1))}$$

interval number, size and points:
$$U := 100 \quad i := 0.. U \quad \delta u := \frac{5 \cdot \sqrt{var}}{U} \quad pt_i := i \cdot \delta u$$

histogram:
$$f := hist(pt, w)$$

The number of histogram values, equal to the number of intervals, is one less than the number of points in the vector pt. The locations of the intervals are

interval locations:
$$ii := 0.. U - 1 \quad r_{ii} := 0.05 \cdot ii$$

How can we fit a Rayleigh density function f_{RAY} to the histogram? Note that, if the Rayleigh density function changes little over a subinterval (pt_i, pt_{i+1}), then the probability of a Rayleigh random variable falling in the interval is about $\delta u * f_{RAY}(pt_i)$. This probability is approximated by the relative frequency f_i/J. Therefore, from the histogram we obtain the estimate of the density function, namely,

estimated density function:
$$f_{RAYest_{ii}} := \frac{f_{ii}}{\delta u \cdot J}$$

We can also plot on the same graph the true Rayleigh density with a variance we choose to render a good fit.

$$\text{var} := 1.0 \qquad\qquad \text{Raydf}_{ii} := \frac{r_{ii}}{\text{var}} \cdot \exp\left[-\frac{\left(r_{ii}\right)^2}{2 \cdot \text{var}} \right]$$

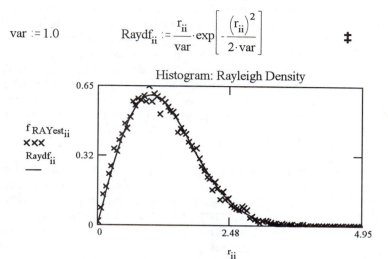

Histogram: Rayleigh Density

$f\,\text{RAYest}_{ii}$
×××
Raydf_{ii}
——

We see that the estimated density function, based on the histogram, gives a fairly close approximation to the true density function.

EXERCISE 27.6 Vary the number of samples J and the number of intervals U, and observe the approximation. ¤

Extension

In operations such as filtering, which we will discuss in **Chapter 28**, the direct implementation requires definition of the finite extent image outside its given domain. We have two options. We can zero pad the image or we can make a periodic extension. We will see that a fast algorithm, the two-dimensional DFT/FFT, is almost mandatory. The frequency domain method, extended now to two dimensions, naturally uses the periodic extension. It is fairly clear how to make the aperiodic and periodic convolutions agree given our experience in the one-dimensional case (**Chapter 2**).

The N-by-N image has a natural periodic extension of period N in both m and n. The periodic extension can again be implemented by the pod function defined by (**2.3**).

$$\text{pod}(n, N) := \text{mod}(N + \text{mod}(n, N), N)$$

$$nn := 0 .. 2 \cdot N - 1_\square \qquad mm := 0 .. 2 \cdot N - 1_\square$$

$$\text{ype}_{mm, nn} := y_{\text{pod}(mm, N), \text{pod}(nn, N)}{}^\square$$

Symmetric Arrays

The impulse response of a filter appropriate for an image is a two-dimensional array. We don't need to extend the idea of causality from the one-dimensional situation. In fact, it is natural to specify such an IR as $\{h_{m,n}, m=-M,...,M, n=-M,...,M\}$, where M<N. Real, symmetric, two-dimensional IRs are especially interesting to us because their two-dimensional FRs are real: that is, they have no phase and so their filtering has no translation and dispersive effects. For implementation in Mathcad, however, we need to find a way to accommodate the fact that the indices must be nonnegative.

For simplicity, let us first consider the case of M=N and suppose that the FIR is given to us in a form symmetric about (0,0), which we call **FT order**. We need to convert it to the asymmetric form, which we call **DFT order**. Now four rectangular regions are involved and it is fairly involved to use the if( ) structure as in the one-dimensional case. The following alternative, due to Eylon Caspi, is more concise. It uses the fact that, whereas we cannot define negative array (range) indices in Mathcad, we can resort, albeit temporarily, to a function that does not have such a limit on its arguments. We can then use the periodicity of the DFT to define the array. We illustrate this now.

Example 27.7 _____

Suppose that a low-pass FIR $\{h_{m,n}\}$ is modeled by a (truncated to N by N) Gaussian shape centered on (0,0) and of radius of gyrations σ and v, respectively, in the m- and n-coordinates. Then we define $\{h_{m,n}\}$ in DFT order as follows.

$$f(x,y) := 5 \cdot \exp\left(-\frac{1}{2} \cdot \frac{x^2}{\sigma^2} - \frac{1}{2} \cdot \frac{y^2}{v^2}\right) \qquad xm := -\frac{N}{2}..\frac{N}{2} - 1 \qquad yn := -\frac{N}{2}..\frac{N}{2} - 1$$

$$pod(n, N) := mod(N + mod(n, N), N)$$

$$x_{pod(xm,N),pod(yn,N)} := f(xm, yn) \qquad\qquad \ddagger \qquad\qquad (27.5)$$

EXERCISE 27.7 Plot this IR. Vary σ and v and note the resulting variation in the nature of $\{h_{m,n}\}$. Carefully note the location of the support of this low-pass filter: it is at the corners of the region of one (asymmetric) period. ¤

PROBLEM 27.2   It is helpful to now review how we would analogously define a noncausal FIR in the one-dimensional case. ‡

To deal with the case M<N, we first zero pad the FIR description.

Example 27.8

Suppose that a low-pass FIR $\{h_{m,n}\}$ is modeled by a (truncated to M by M, M<N) normal, or Gaussian, shape, centered on (0,0) and of radius of gyrations σ and ν, respectively, in the m- and n-coordinates.

$$M := 8$$

$$f(xm, yn) := \text{if}\left[\left(|xm| \leq \frac{M}{2}\right) \cdot \left(|yn| \leq \frac{M}{2}\right), 5 \cdot \exp\left(-\frac{1}{2} \cdot \frac{xm^2}{\sigma^2} - \frac{1}{2} \cdot \frac{yn^2}{\nu^2}\right), 0\right]$$

$$X_{\text{pod}(xm,N),\,\text{pod}(yn,N)} := f(xm, yn)\,_{\square}$$ ‡

▨   **EXERCISE 27.8**   Plot this IR as an image and carefully examine its support. ¤

Alternatively, we can first rearrange into DFT order of size M by M and then zero pad appropriately. This is perhaps more difficult because the zeros must be added in the middle to preserve the symmetry.

Two-Dimensional DFT

In analyzing, synthesizing and processing digital images, a description of the image's frequency content is very helpful, as we would expect from our experience with digital signals. For a finite-size image, the two-dimensional Fourier series gives us the desired information: the frequency content is given by the coefficients of the Fourier series. This N-by-N array of coefficients is the two-dimensional DFT. This DFT and its inverse naturally introduce the periodic extension of the image. In our case, the DFT and the IDFT have period N in m and n. Conventionally, the choice of index set is the asymmetric one we are now using. As in the case of one-dimensional digital signals, these facts must be kept in mind.

The **two-dimensional DFT** and **IDFT** are defined as, respectively,

$$k := 0 .. N - 1 \qquad \kappa := 0 .. N - 1$$

DFT: $\qquad X_{k,\kappa} = \displaystyle\sum_{m=0}^{N-1} \sum_{n=0}^{N-1} x_{m,n} e^{-i \cdot m \cdot k - i \cdot n \cdot \kappa}$ $\qquad$ (27.6)

IDFT: $\qquad x_{m,n} = \dfrac{1}{N^2} \cdot \displaystyle\sum_{k=0}^{N-1} \sum_{\kappa=0}^{N-1} X_{k,\kappa} e^{-i \cdot m \cdot k + i \cdot \kappa}$ $\qquad$ (27.7)

These direct calculations, requiring about N^4 complex multiply-adds, are so slow that they are likely useless. We desperately need a fast algorithm! But we recognize that the two-dimensional DFT can be regarded as a two-step procedure employing the one-dimensional DFT (**Chapter 3**). First, the one-dimensional DFT of each column of the array, N total DFTs, are computed. Second, the one-dimensional DFT of each row of the resultant matrix, N more total DFTs, are computed. The FFT, requiring about $(1/2)N \log_2 N$ complex multiply-adds, is used to implement the DFT, of course. Then the algorithm uses the order of $N^2 \log_2 N$ complex multiply-adds versus N^4 for either (27.6) or (27.7). (Some further reduction is possible: see Dudgeon and Mersereau (1984).)

For example, suppose $N=512=2^9$. Then $N^4=2^{36}$, which is about 6.4×10^{10}, while $N^2 \log_2 N = 9 \times 2^{18}$, which is about 2×10^6. The fast algorithm reduces the required number of complex multiply-adds by more than four orders of magnitude.

Mathcad computes the two-dimensional DFT/FFT when the argument is a matrix array. The constant N accounts for the difference between Mathcad's definition and our definition of the DFT.

$$\text{dft}(A) := N \cdot \text{icfft}(A) \qquad\qquad \text{idft}(A) := \frac{1}{N} \cdot \text{cfft}(A)$$

We will also denote both the one- and two-dimensional discrete Fourier transforms by the same symbol and note which is intended from the context.

An informative way to present the two-dimensional DFT is as an image. As it is generally complex, the magnitude is usually plotted.

DFT Examples

Example 27.9 _____

We compute and plot the DFT of the two-dimensional unit impulse sequence, expecting it to be a constant array.

$$x_{m,n} := 0 \quad\quad\quad x_{0,0} := 1 \quad\quad\quad\quad X := dft(x) \quad\quad\quad \ddagger$$

EXERCISE 27.9 Continuing the illustration of a sinusoidal image, compute its DFT. Vary the wavenumber in the sinusoidal image of Example 27.1 and note the corresponding DFTs. Choose a noncommensurable wavenumber and note the "leakage" effect. ¤

Recall again that, because we chose an asymmetric period (n=0,...,N-1) for the DFT, the low frequencies will appear near the corners of this DFT image. Similarly, high frequencies will appear near the center of this DFT image. Some time may be required to become comfortable with this display of the frequency information.

Example 27.10 _____

We compute and plot the DFT of the signal/image of Example 27.4. If we carefully examine the DFT magnitude, we see that the signal's DFT magnitude is more extended in the m-coordinate than in the n-coordinate, an inversion of the relationship between the extents in the signal itself. Of course, the signal is low-pass and so its DFT has major support near the corners of the DFT image.

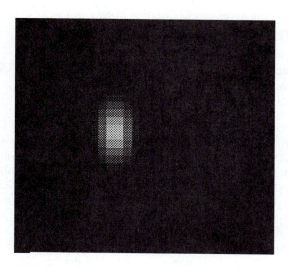

X

Image

$$X := dft(x) \qquad X_{m,n} := |X_{m,n}|$$

X

2-Dimensional DFT

‡

DFT Properties

Generally the properties of the two-dimensional DFT are fairly obvious extensions of those of the one-dimensional DFT (**Chapter 4**), so we shall just list them without proof. Neither will we here prove the inversion (27.5). For brevity, we write $\exp[i(2\pi/N)kn]$ as $ec_{n,k}$.

Property 27.1: Periodicity As already noted, the DFT and IDFT have period N in m and in n.

Property 27.2: Symmetries If $\{X_{m,n}\}$ is a (real) image with DFT $\{X_{k,k}\}$, then the DFT is Hermitian symmetric: $X_{-m,-n}=X_{m,n}^*$. By Property 27.1 this may be expressed as $X_{m,n}^*=X_{N-m,N-n}$. Also, the real and imaginary parts are, respectively, even and odd. By Property 27.1, these may be expressed as $XR_{m,n}=XR_{N-m,N-n}$ and $XI_{m,n}=-XI_{N-m,N-n}$, respectively.

Property 27.3: Periodic Spatial Translation If an image $\{x_{m,n}\}$ has DFT $\{X_{k,k}\}$, then the translated image $\{x_{m-mo,n-no}\}$ has DFT $\{X_{k,k}(ec_{mo,k})^*(ec_{no,k})^*\}$.

Property 27.4: Periodic Frequency Translation If a DFT $\{X_{k,\kappa}\}$ has IDFT (image) $\{x_{m,n}\}$, then the translated DFT $\{X_{k-ko,\kappa-\kappa o}\}$ has IDFT (image) $\{x_{m,n}\ ec_{ko,m}\ ec_{\kappa o,m}\}$.

Property 27.5: Plancherel's Identity If an image $\{x_{m,n}\}$ has DFT $\{X_{k,\kappa}\}$, then

$$\sum_{m=0}^{N-1}\ \sum_{n=0}^{N-1} \left(|x_{m,n}|\right)^2\ :=\ \frac{1}{N^2}\cdot \sum_{k=0}^{N-1}\ \sum_{\kappa=0}^{N-1} \left(|X_{k,\kappa}|\right)^2\ \ \square$$

Property 27.6: Parseval's Identity If images $\{x_{m,n}\}$ and $\{y_{m,n}\}$ have DFTs $\{X_{k,\kappa}\}$ and $\{Y_{k,\kappa}\}$, respectively, then

$$\sum_{m=0}^{N-1}\ \sum_{n=0}^{N-1} x_{m,n}\cdot y_{m,n}\ :=\ \frac{1}{N^2}\cdot \sum_{k=0}^{N-1}\ \sum_{\kappa=0}^{N-1} X_{k,\kappa}\cdot \overline{Y_{k,\kappa}}\ \ \square$$

Property 27.7: IDFT of Product of DFTs If images $\{x_{m,n}\}$ and $\{y_{m,n}\}$ have DFTs $\{X_{k,\kappa}\}$ and $\{Y_{k,\kappa}\}$, respectively, then the IDFT of the product $\{X_{k,\kappa}\ Y_{k,\kappa}\}$ is the periodic convolution of $\{x_{m,n}\}$ and $\{y_{m,n}\}$. (The periodic convolution in two dimensions is defined in **Chapter 28**.)

PROBLEM 27.3   Illustrate and verify the above properties with specific images. ‡

Project 27.1

Various noise sources in image processing can be modeled by a multiplicative noise. Heretofore we have mainly considered additive noise and so we face a new image processing problem in attempting to restore the image. Suppose that $s_{m,n}$ is the noise-free image and is nonnegative. And suppose that $p_{m,n}$ is a random field of independent, identically distributed Poisson random variables with parameter λ. (Mathcad has a built-in generator for such random variables.) The image data available for processing is the pixel-by-pixel product of s and p.

$$x = \overrightarrow{(s\cdot p)}$$

Propose and demonstrate some ideas for processing this image data. Some ideas you may wish to consider could include the following. First, if we have multiple images available, we can consider sample averaging. Second, for one image we can consider a simple spatial (moving) average. Third, we can consider combining sample and spatial averaging.

As an example of a different kind of idea, note that if we took the natural logarithm of the image data then we would have the log(noise-free image) plus a noise field. We have had experience with additive noise and we can, e.g., perform a spatial average to reduce this noise. Then, we can form exp(filtered data) to hope to recover a good estimate of the noise-free image.

Compare such methods and any other ideas that you have. ‡

References

Dudgeon and Mersereau (1984), Secs. 1.1, 2.2
Jain (1989), Chap. 2
Oppenheim and Schafer (1975) , Secs. 1.8, 3.9

28 Digital Image Filtering

A digital image filter is a generalization of the digital signal filter. The IR of a two-dimensional filter is represented as an array - i.e., a doubly indexed sequence. We consider filters with IRs of finite extent, which we call **finite impulse response (FIR)** filters. An FIR filter is especially attractive for image processing because (i) it is represented by a matrix; (ii) its frequency response can be real and hence nondispersive; (iii) it is, in principle and in practice, easily implemented; (iv) there are efficient design methods; and, of course, (v) the images themselves are of finite extent.

An FIR filter $\{h_{m,n}\}$ is naturally defined with a symmetric support over [-M,M] by [-M,M]. We have already discussed, in **Chapter 27**, implementing a representation of such a sequence in Mathcad by zero padding and periodic extension. Thus we have in mind application to images of a given size N by N. We assume 2M+1<=N.

An **FIR filtering** of a digital image is defined as the two-dimensional periodic convolution

$$y_{m,n} := \sum_{\mu=-M}^{M} \sum_{\eta=-M}^{M} h_{\text{pod}(\mu,N),\,\text{pod}(\eta,N)} \cdot x_{\text{pod}(m-\mu,N),\,\text{pod}(n-\eta,N)} \quad \blacksquare$$

(28.1)

Note that the periodic extension of two-dimensional arrays solves two problems. First, it defines the image when the convolution operation indices m-μ and n-η do not lie in [0,N]. Second, it allows us to, in effect, handle negative indices defining the FIR.

This direct computation is so slow that we reduce N to 32 and consider only very small M. As in Chapter 27, we use few image plots, labeling them and toggling equations as required.

The interpretation of this operation is this. At each point $(m,n) \in L$, the filtered image is a weighted sum of the values of the input image, periodically extended as necessary. For FIRs of sufficiently limited extent, the definition (28.1) can be directly implemented. Indeed, for some digital processors of limited computational power, such filterings may be the only practical ones. These filters are called **masks**.

We define the image size, indices and pod function at this point.

$$N := 32 \qquad m := 0..N-1 \qquad n := 0..N-1$$

$$pod(n,N) := mod(N + mod(n,N),N)$$

FIR Filter Masks

We can specify the FIR directly and, if it is simple enough, compute the filtering directly by (28.1). We discuss some simple examples.

Example 28.1: Simple Spatial Averaging _____
A two-dimensional generalization of the one-dimensional, simple (uniform weights) moving average filter has a constant FIR over a region (-M,M) by (-M,M) and zero elsewhere. It is a low-pass filter that smoothes the image, reducing noise but blurring the image. Its direct calculation is slow, so we choose a small M.

$$M := 2 \qquad f(x,y) := if\left[(|x| \le M) \cdot (|y| \le M), \frac{1}{(2 \cdot M + 1)^2}, 0 \right] \qquad (28.2a)$$

$$xm := -\frac{N}{2}..\frac{N}{2} - 1 \qquad yn := -\frac{N}{2}..\frac{N}{2} - 1$$

$$h_{pod(xm,N), pod(yn,N)} := f(xm,yn) \qquad\qquad \ddagger \qquad (28.2b)$$

EXERCISE 28.1 Graphically display the FIR as both a surface plot (with a rotation of 270 degrees) and as an image plot. Carefully note where its support lies. (For this exercise you may want to adjust M.) ¤

We define a simple, square signal of side (2L+1), centered at (m_o, n_o) and entirely contained in the N-by-N image lattice.

$$L := 4 \qquad\qquad sf(m,n) := if((|m| \le L) \cdot (|n| \le L), 1, 0)$$

$$m_o := 6 \qquad\qquad n_o := 10 \qquad\qquad x_{m,n} := sf\left(m - m_o, n - n_o\right)$$

The image data is a noisy version of the signal.

$$var := 0.01 \qquad\qquad noise^{<n>} := rnorm(N, 0, var)$$

$$x := x + noise$$

We now filter the image data by direct implementation of the definition as a convolution.

slow calculation:

$$y_{m,n} := \sum_{\mu = -M}^{M} \sum_{\eta = -M}^{M} h_{pod(\mu, N), pod(\eta, N)} \cdot x_{pod(m - \mu, N), pod(n - \eta, N)}$$

▦ **EXERCISE 28.2** For several (small!) values of M, compute and plot the smoothed image. Note the time required for the calculation, the noise suppression and the blurring of the signal. ¤

Example 28.2: High-Pass Filtering _____

High-pass filters are used to sharpen images and extract edges, at the cost of emphasizing the noise. A simple high-pass filter can be formed by subtracting the low-pass filtered image from the image. For this example we use a noise-free image.

$$z_{m,n} := x_{m,n} - y_{m,n_0} \qquad\qquad\qquad ‡$$

▦ **EXERCISE 28.3** For several small values of M, compute and plot the high-pass filtered image. You will note emphasized edges. ¤

Example 28.3: Edge Crispening _____

By adding a high-pass filtered version of the image to the image itself, edges are enhanced. This technique is commonly used in printing.

$$z_{m,n} := z_{m,n} + x_{m,n_0} \qquad\qquad\qquad ‡$$

▦ **EXERCISE 28.4** Illustrate this edge-crispening algorithm. How does the processed image differ from that of Exercise 28.3? ¤

Example 28.4: Bandpass Filtering _____

A bandpass filter can be a compromise between the features of low- and high-pass filters. A simple bandpass filter can be formed by subtracting the images formed by two simple spatial averaging filters, one of greater spatial extent in its IR. ‡

**PROBLEM
28.1**

Illustrate bandpass filtering with the technique mentioned in Example 28.4. ‡

Frequency Response

For other than FIRs of quite small extent, the direct calculation of (28.1) is likely to be too slow. (We may be quite exasperated at this point with the slow speed of (28.1), even for the small extent FIRs we have considered!) We therefore have an interest in a fast algorithm to implement the filtering (28.1). We expect that there should again be a "frequency domain" method using a DFT/FFT, suitably generalized to two dimensions.

Example 28.5 _____

It is easy to show, by direct substitution, that the two-dimensional sinusoid ec(m,k)*ec(n,k), where k and k are integers in [0,...,N-1], is invariant under (28.1).

**input
image:**
$$k := 0..N-1 \qquad \kappa := 0..N-1 \qquad ec_{n,k} := \exp\left(i \cdot \frac{2\cdot\pi}{N} \cdot k \cdot n \right)_{\mathbb{0}}$$

slow calculation:
$$H_{k,\kappa} := \sum_{\mu=0}^{N-1} \sum_{\eta=0}^{N-1} h_{\mu,\eta} \cdot \overline{ec_{\mu,k} \cdot ec_{\eta,\kappa}}_{\mathbb{0}} \qquad (28.3)$$

**output
image:**
$$y_{m,n} := H_{k,\kappa} \cdot ec_{m,k} \cdot ec_{n,\kappa\mathbb{0}} \qquad\qquad ‡$$

▨   **EXERCISE 28.5** Illustrate the invariance of sinusoids under FIR filtering defined by (28.1). ¤

The right side of (28.3) is a two-dimensional Fourier series we have already defined (**Chapter 27**) as the two-dimensional discrete Fourier transform. In image processing, {$H_{k,\kappa}$} is called the **frequency response** of the FIR filter. Thus, the DFT representation of an image is very convenient when describing its linear, invariant filtering: the DFT of the output, or processed, image is the element-by-element product of the frequency response and the DFT of the input image. This is again called the **frequency method** of performing the convolution, or filtering, operation. It is often much faster than the direct implementation (28.1).

We examine the frequency responses of the above mask examples: indeed, we have already named some of them, to indicate the nature of their frequency response.

$$dft(v) := N \cdot icfft(v)$$

Example 28.6 _____

We compute and display the FR of the simple averaging filter of Example 28.1.

$$H := dft(h)\square \qquad\qquad\qquad\qquad ‡$$

EXERCISE 28.6 Choose various M in Example 28.6 and note the reciprocal behavior of the FIR and the FR. ¤

Example 28.7 _____

We compute and display the FR of the high-pass filter of Example 28.2. Its IR and FR are

$$h_{m,n} := \delta(m,0) \cdot \delta(n,0) - h_{m,n}\square \qquad H := dft(h)\square \qquad ‡$$

EXERCISE 28.7 Choose various M in Example 28.7 and note the reciprocal behavior of the low-pass and high-pass filter FRs. ¤

PROBLEM 28.2 Show that the IR of the edge-crispening operation of Example 28.3 is

$$h_{m,n} := 2 \cdot (\delta(m,0) \cdot \delta(n,0)) - h_{m,n}\square \qquad H := dft(h)\square$$

Display the FR as a surface plot and as an image. ‡

PROBLEM 28.3 Create a bandpass filter as the difference of two low-pass filters and display its FR. ‡

Filtering with the DFT/FFT

Computation with simple, mask-type FIR filter outputs by the direct method (28.1) can be painfully slow. We now redo some of these computations using the frequency method. We will observe a dramatic speed increase.

We will now need the two-dimensional IDFT.

$$idft(v) := \frac{1}{N} \cdot cfft(v)$$

Example 28.8

Suppose we repeat Example 28.1, but now compute the processed image by the frequency method.

$$H := dft(h)\square \qquad X := dft(x)\square \qquad Y_{m,n} := \overrightarrow{\left(H_{m,n} \cdot X_{m,n}\right)}\square \qquad y := idft(Y)\square$$

The greatly increased computational speed in Example 28.8 illustrates the great worth of the FFT and makes possible increased image and mask size. ‡

EXERCISE 28.8 Position the signal in Example 28.8 near the edge and/or corner of the image. Observe the effect of the periodic convolution. How could this periodic effect be avoided? (This effect is most clearly observed with low noise level.) ¤

h

Image Plot

y

Image Plot

FIR Filter Design

We have discussed some relatively simple filters with directly specified FIRs. They were not designed by applying criteria to their FR. They are appealing because the limited support of their IR lends simplicity in directly computing the convolution (28.1).

If the computational resources allow the entire N-by-N image to be read into memory and its DFT computed, then the frequency method of filtering is feasible. The N-by-N FR of the filter must be made available, perhaps by storing it in an N-by-N array. These N^2 values of the FR may be arbitrarily chosen. If we want a real FR and a real FIR, we impose the appropriate symmetries. But otherwise the FR is arbitrary. There is no approximation problem!

It may be true in some applications that the image is too large to be read into memory and its DFT computed. Then we may consider importing the image in blocks and filtering each block using a smaller size DFT. This must be arranged so that the desired processed image can be reassembled. This scheme is a two-dimensional generalization of the fast convolution discussed in **Chapter 5**. If we wish to design an M-by-M FIR to be used in a "fast convolution" of an image of size N-by-N, the FIR behavior on the frequencies (m2π/N,n2π/N) determines the filtering. If N is very much larger than M, then these frequencies become quite dense and we could reasonably design for satisfactory response at all frequencies $\{(k,\kappa), k \varepsilon [0,2\pi], \kappa \varepsilon [0,2\pi]\}$. Such a procedure does make the filter acceptability independent of image size.

Now we shall further discuss FIR design for image processing under the assumption that a fast convolution method will be employed for a relatively large image. We want to profit from our experience in designing one-dimensional FIR filters as much as possible.

We may assume that the desired FIR $\{h_{m,n}\}$ is of the factored form $\{h1_m h2_n\}$ and that the design specifications can be placed separately on $\{h1_m\}$ and $\{h2_n\}$. Then, in principle, any of the one-dimensional design techniques are available. There is, however, no reason to place a causality restraint on the FIR. Alternatively, we can apply the technique of design by frequency sampling to the two-dimensional case. Then we no longer require the assumption of a factored form - which most images do not have, of course!

We shall discuss both methods here, assuming design by frequency sampling in both cases. Thus, in the first case, we will carry over our discussion of **Chapter 10**, removing the causality requirement. In the second case, we generalize the frequency sampling method to two dimensions.

Factored Form FIR

Suppose that the image filter is to have a frequency response that passes spatial frequencies $|k|<\pi/4$ and $|\kappa|<\pi/4$. Then it is allowable to assume that the FR has a factored form and to design each FR factor as a one-dimensional FR. We assume M=32.

We directly carry over the discussion of **Chapter 10**; we can copy and paste here the Mathcad statements. We do not need the linear phase that provides causality: the FR is real and, for a real IR, even. (We have to distinguish our DFT definition in the one-dimensional case.)

$$M := 32 \qquad k := 0 .. M - 1 \qquad H1_k := 0$$

desired response:
$$H1_0 := 1 \qquad H1_1 := 1 \qquad H1_2 := 1 \qquad H1_3 := 1$$

transition samples:
$$H1_4 := 0.97 \qquad H1_5 := 0.7 \qquad H1_6 := 0.2$$

imposing evenness:
$$H1_k := \mathrm{if}\!\left(k \le \frac{M}{2}, H1_k, H1_{M-k}\right)$$

We compute the IR and verify that it is real.

$$\mathrm{idft1}(v) := \frac{1}{\sqrt{M}} \cdot \mathrm{cfft}(v) \qquad\qquad h1 := \mathrm{idft1}(H1)$$

FIR Factor

Plot: $h1_k$ (×××) and $\mathrm{Im}\!\left(h1_k\right)$ (- -) versus k. Vertical axis from -0.0603 to 0.34 (with 0.14 marked). Horizontal axis from 0 to 31 (with 15.5 marked).

The IR is naturally computed in DFT order. We now zero pad the IR to interpolate the FR: because it is in DFT order, the zeros must be inserted into the center of the sequence. We inspect the FR to see whether it is agreeable - and real.

$$MM := 16 \cdot M \qquad mm := 0 .. MM - 1 \qquad dft1(v) := \sqrt{MM} \cdot icfft(v)$$

$$hle_{mm} := if\left(mm \leq \frac{M}{2}, h1_{mm}, if\left(mm \geq 16 \cdot M - \frac{M}{2}, h1_{MM-mm}, 0\right)\right)$$

$$Hle := dft1(hle) \qquad\qquad \omega_{mm} := mm \cdot \frac{2 \cdot \pi}{MM}$$

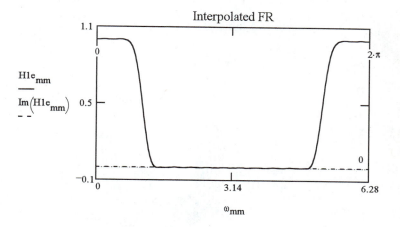

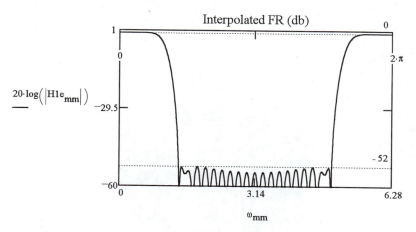

The two-dimensional IR is

$$m := 0 .. M - 1 \quad n := 0 .. M - 1 \qquad h2_{m,n} := h1_m \cdot h1_n$$

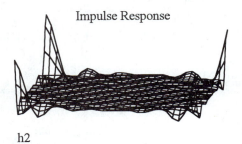

Impulse Response

h2

The two-dimensional FR is

$$H2_{m,n} := H1_m \cdot H1_n \qquad\qquad lH2_{m,n} := 20 \cdot \log\left(\left|H2_{m,n}\right| + 0.00001\right)$$

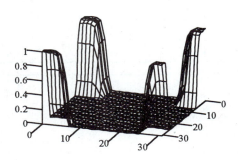

H2

Frequency Response

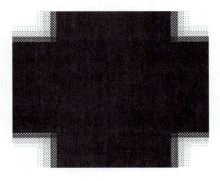

lH2

Frequency Response

Filter Design by Frequency Sampling

We can avoid the assumption of a factored form and directly choose the frequency samples of the two-dimensional FR. With some experience, we will be able to design reasonably good filters. We have restraints on the frequency samples. They are real and obey a symmetry so that the IR is real, namely, $H_{k,\kappa}=H_{N-k,N-\kappa}$.

We design a low-pass FIR filter that depends on the frequencies (k,κ) as $k^2+\kappa^2$, an **isotropic** dependence. We use two transition samples.

$$N := 32 \qquad km := -\frac{N}{2}..\frac{N}{2}-1 \qquad kn := -\frac{N}{2}..\frac{N}{2}-1$$

$$F(km,kn) := if\left[km^2 + kn^2 \le \left(\frac{N}{8}\right)^2, 1, if\left[km^2 + kn^2 \le \left(\frac{N}{8}+1\right)^2, 0.7, 0.2\right]\right]$$

$$F3(km,kn) := if\left[km^2 + kn^2 \le \left(\frac{N}{8}+2\right)^2, F(km,kn), 0\right]$$

$$pod(n,N) := mod(N + mod(n,N),N)$$

$$H3_{pod(km,N),pod(kn,N)} := F3(km,kn)$$

H3

Frequency Response Samples

H3

Frequency Response Samples

Next we find the corresponding two-dimensional FIR.

$$h3 := \frac{1}{M} \cdot icfft(H3)$$

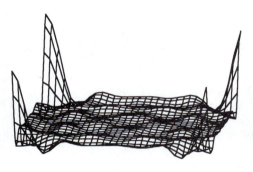

h3

Impulse Response

h3

Impulse Response

To find the interpolated FR, we zero pad the IR h3. Again, the zeros must be inserted into the middle of the array to preserve symmetry. We employ a temporary function again to use the periodicity. We define a function from h3 and then extend it. Then, as in Chapter 27, we define the zero-padded h3e. As these calculations are time-consuming, we interpolate by a factor of 4.

$$f3(xm, yn) := h3_{pod(xm, N), pod(yn, N)}$$

$$Ne := 4 \cdot N \qquad xme := -\frac{Ne}{2} .. \frac{Ne}{2} - 1 \qquad yne := -\frac{Ne}{2} .. \frac{Ne}{2} - 1$$

$$f3e(xme, yne) := if\left[\left(|xme| \le \frac{N}{2}\right) \cdot \left(|yne| \le \frac{N}{2}\right), f3(xme, yne), 0\right]$$

**slow
computation:** $$h3e_{pod(xme, Ne), pod(yne, Ne)} := f3e(xme, yne)$$

$$H3e := Ne \cdot icfft(h3e)$$

H3e

Interpolated FR

H3e

Interpolated FR

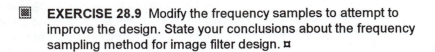

EXERCISE 28.9 Modify the frequency samples to attempt to improve the design. State your conclusions about the frequency sampling method for image filter design. ¤

Project 28.1

Another way to derive a two-dimensional FIR from a one-dimensional FIR is conceptually conveyed as follows. For a given one-dimensional FIR, visualize its FR plotted as a cross section of a surface along one axis in a plane. Now rotate the cross section through 2π radians, creating a surface. This surface defines a two-dimensional FR that is **isotropic**; that is, the FR depends only on the radial distance from the origin in the plane. This may be an appropriate design in some applications. We pose one here.

 Suppose an image, comprising the available data, contains a sinusoidal wave and additive noise. We know only the magnitude of the wavenumber k of the wave. That is, we do not know the direction of the wave but we know its wavelength k - practically, to some degree of accuracy that you can specify. Design a reasonable filter to remove some of the noise and simulate your filter design. Be clear about the design specifications. ‡

Project 28.2

When images are formed there are many sources of degradation, and one area of digital signal processing is called image restoration. One such degradation is **blurring** due to relative motion between the camera, or sensor, and the object. A simple model for blurring along the x-y diagonal, implemented by Elyon Caspi, is

$$N := 64 \qquad x := -\frac{N}{2} .. \frac{N}{2} - 1 \qquad y := -\frac{N}{2} .. \frac{N}{2} - 1$$

$$h\_umb_{pod(x,N),pod(y,N)} := (x=y) \cdot \left(|x| < \frac{N}{14} \right)$$

h_umb

Blurring Model

An example of this blurring is shown below. It was computed by finding the DFTs of the image and blurring FIR, multiplying them together and inverting with the IDFT.

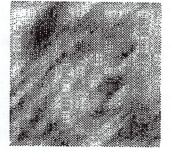

f   g_umb

Image   Blurred Image

 We would like to restore the unblurred image as well as possible. Construct a blurred image. Design a linear filter to restore the unblurred image. The above image is in the data file cat_64.prn. It can be read into the matrix array catt with

catt := READPRN(cat_64)⬛

(Use rotation=0.) ‡

References

Dudgeon and Mersereau (1984), Secs. 3.2, 3.3
Jain (1989), Sec. 7.4

29 Adaptive FIR Filters

The common FIR design techniques, such as the frequency sampling method, assume that the designer has enough knowledge about the ensemble of signals to be processed that he or she can specify the design parameters: the passband and stopband frequencies, stopband attenuation and so on. The interpolation FIR filter of **Chapter 16** is so specified.

More sophisticated design techniques using optimization criteria of a probability nature, such as minimum mean square error, assume prior knowledge of the requisite statistical parameters of the signal ensemble. The Wiener optimal filter of **Chapter 24** was specified by the spectral densities of the signal and noise random processes. It may be necessary to perform preliminary analysis and/or experimentation to garner this knowledge. These procedures can be expensive and time-consuming, and the knowledge obtained may be soon outdated if there are temporal changes, or statistical nonstationarity, in the ensemble.

Recently there has been great interest in and wide-spread application of systems that can learn the requisite characteristics of the signal ensemble and adapt to its subsequent changes. These systems lessen the need for prior knowledge by (often implicitly) estimating the required characteristics.

System Identification

One of the earliest such systems was the adaptive FIR filter. We shall base our discussion on an application to the specific problem of learning and adapting to changes to a model for an unknown system. This is a **system identification problem**. As is typical of a wide and interesting class of applications, we assume that the actual system's input and output are available to the system that will learn and adapt the parameters of an FIR model for the unknown system. Of course, we assume we have some a priori knowledge that leads us to believe such a simple model has validity - we can of course always try it, if the cost is not prohibitive!

These ideas can be generalized greatly. For example, one may have a very complex computer model of an actual, on-line, system - say, a package delivery system. Then trial-and-error changes can be made in the computer model that would be of prohibitive cost in the actual system. If the changes produce greater efficiencies in the model, they can then be implemented in the actual system.

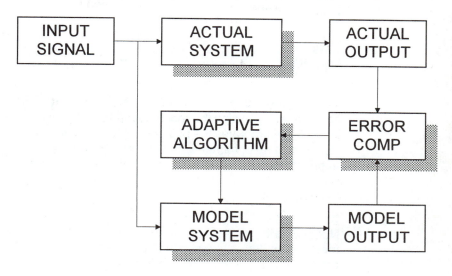

LMS Algorithm

There are many criteria under which adaptive systems can be designed. The resulting solutions are often computational algorithms in the form of an iterative scheme or recursive equation, which can be implemented on a digital computer. Such algorithms may be simplified on an ad hoc or trial-and-error basis to reduce the required computation to the minimum, allowing practical application.

One of the earliest such algorithms is the LMS (least mean square) algorithm of Widrow and Hoff; see Widrow and Winter (1988) for a recent, informative and accessible discussion. We now consider this algorithm. (We will derive it in **Chapter 30**.)

Let the actual system's input and output be the sequences $\{x_n\}$ and $\{d_n\}$, respectively, and let the model system's output be $\{y_n\}$. Then the error sequence is $\{e_n = d_n - y_n\}$. It is convenient to define the (M+1)-length vector X^n of the M+1 most recent (at time n) input data; similarly, let h^n be the (M+1)-length vector representing the model's FIR at time n. Then $y_n = \text{transpose}(h^n)X^n$ and the **LMS algorithm** may be written

$$h^{<n+1>} = h^{<n>} + \alpha \cdot \left(d_n - h^{<n>\,T} \cdot X^{<n>} \right) \cdot X^{<n>} \qquad (29.1)$$

Mathcad is not able to process the algorithm in this vector form. We shall have to write it out in terms of the components of the vectors. We can express the **LMS algorithm** in Mathcad as follows.

LMS algorithm:
$$h_{m,n+1} = h_{m,n} + \alpha \cdot \left(d_n - \sum_{\mu} h_{\mu,n} \cdot x_{n-\mu} \right) \cdot x_{n-m} \qquad (29.2)$$

The LMS algorithm is typical of adaptive algorithms in that the iteration is done using the most recent data. Its recursive nature implicitly incorporates the past data. Thus, with increasing amounts of data, hopefully the model's IR converges to an approximation to the actual system's IR. The rate of convergence will determine how rapidly the filter can adapt to changes in the modeled system.

Notice that the correction at time n is in the direction of the vector of most recent data; the magnitude of the correction depends on the error at time n (the quantity in parentheses in (29.1) or (29.2)) and a constant α that is selected, in part, by trial and error. Since h^{n+1} depends on h^n, we can expect that divergence can occur for an improper choice of α. It is a complicated matter to analyze the convergence of the LMS algorithm, and choosing α is part of the art of applying the algorithm.

Here we shall implement the LMS algorithm and, by trial and error, gain an understanding of the nature of this famous algorithm.

Example 29.1 _____

We characterize the actual system as a third-order, low-pass FIR filter defined by zeros at $i\rho$, $-i\rho$ and $-\rho$, which therefore has a system function

$$\rho := 0.9 \qquad H(z) := \frac{(z - i \cdot \rho) \cdot (z + i \cdot \rho) \cdot (z + \rho)}{z^3}$$

We use Mathcad's symbolic algebra capability to write H(z) in the form

$$H(z) := 1 + \frac{1}{z} \cdot \rho + \frac{1}{z^2} \cdot \rho^2 + \frac{1}{z^3} \cdot \rho^3$$

from which we read out the FIR sequence p=(1,ρ,ρ²,ρ³).

$$M := 3 \qquad m := 0 .. M \qquad P_m := \rho^m \qquad \mu := 0 .. M$$

We shall use a simple, uncorrelated sequence of normal random variables as the plant input, which will be very long relative to the plant's FIR length M+1.

$$N := 512 \qquad n := 0 .. N \qquad var1 := 1.0$$

$$x := morm(N + 1, 0, var1)$$

We compute the plant's actual output from time M that the system is fully loaded with input.

$$k := M + 1 .. N \qquad\qquad d_k := \sum_m P_m \cdot x_{k-m}$$

We now implement the LMS algorithm, choosing the LMS constant α by trial and error and a zero initial IR for the model FIR. The sequence of model IR estimates will be arrayed in a (M+1)-by-N matrix h; the nth column is the estimated IR at time n.

$$\alpha := 0.01 \qquad h_{m,M} := 0 \qquad h_{m,k+1} := h_{m,k} + \alpha \cdot \left(d_k - \sum_\mu h_{\mu,k} \cdot x_{k-\mu} \right) \cdot x_{k-m}$$

We display the evolving estimate of the model FIR.

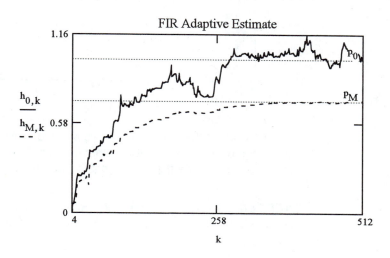

We are ultimately interested in how well the output of the actual and model systems agree. We compute them and their error $\{\varepsilon_k\}$.

$$y_k := \sum_m h_{m,k} \cdot x_{k-m} \qquad\qquad \varepsilon_k := d_k - y_k$$

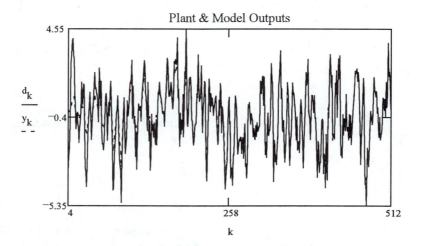

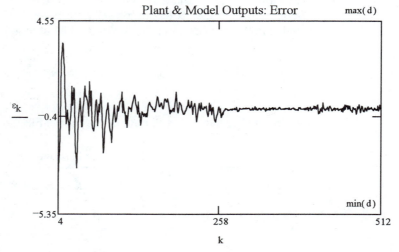

We observe that the model filter does a reasonably good job of estimating, or reproducing, the output of the actual plant. We can, at the least, conclude that the algorithm can be useful. ‡

EXERCISE 29.1 (i) Adjust the parameter α and observe the resulting behavior. (ii) Adjust the parameter M and observe the resulting behavior. ¤

PROBLEM 29.1 Suppose our a priori knowledge about the order of the actual system was wrong. Modify the above example so that the order M is different for the model. What are some consequences? ‡

Noisy Measurements

A common problem in system modeling, or system identification, is that the data can be corrupted in various ways. For example, the system output may be observed in the presence of additive noise modeling measurement errors.

Exercise 29.2 Assume that the output of the actual system is available to the adaptive system only in a noisy form. Specifically assume that

$$varn := 0.1 \qquad\qquad d := d + rnorm(N, 0, varn)▯$$

Repeat Exercise 29.1 for several values of the "signal-to-noise ratio" var/varn. Observe the accuracy after convergence. ¤

PROBLEM 29.2 Devise an argument showing that, when noise is present in the measurements, the LMS algorithm cannot converge with zero error. ‡

Adaptivity

We now wish to see if this scheme in fact allows the estimated system model to adapt to changes in the actual system. We assume a simple model in which the system's IR changes with time.

$$NP := 4 \qquad \omega := \frac{2 \cdot \pi}{N} \cdot NP \qquad a := 0.1 \qquad \rho_n := 0.9 + a \cdot \cos(\omega \cdot n)$$

The system FIR is now time-dependent with IR $(1, \rho_n, \rho_n^2, \rho_n^3)$.

$$P_{m,n} := \left(\rho_n\right)^m$$

We compute the system's actual output from time M that the plant is fully loaded with input. The output at time k is the weighted sum of the present and past M values of the input, where the weighting is the plant's IR at time k.

$$k := M.. N \qquad\qquad d_k := \sum_m P_{m,k} \cdot x_{k-m}$$

We again implement the LMS algorithm, choosing the LMS constant α by trial and error and a zero initial IR for the model FIR. Again, the sequence of model IR estimates will be arrayed in a (M+1)-by-N matrix h; the nth column the estimated IR at time n.

$$\alpha := 0.075 \quad h_{m,M} := 0 \quad h_{m,k+1} := h_{m,k} + \alpha \cdot \left(d_k - \sum_{\mu} h_{\mu,k} \cdot x_{k-\mu} \right) \cdot x_{k-m}$$

We display the model's IR, along with the system's IR, up to time N.

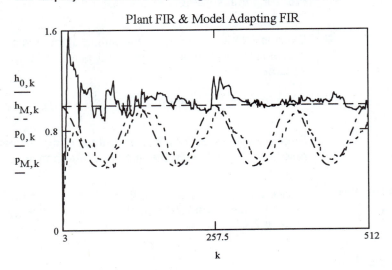

Plant FIR & Model Adapting FIR

To have a simple measure of performance, we can compare the time-averaged FIRs.

$$\text{have} := \frac{1}{N-M} \cdot \sum_{k} h^{<k>} \qquad \frac{\text{have}}{\max(\text{have})} = \begin{bmatrix} 1 \\ 0.877 \\ 0.788 \\ 0.695 \end{bmatrix}$$

$$\text{pave} := \frac{1}{N-M} \cdot \sum_{k} p^{<k>} \qquad \frac{\text{pave}}{\max(\text{pave})} = \begin{bmatrix} 1 \\ 0.9 \\ 0.814 \\ 0.741 \end{bmatrix}$$

We note that the agreement on average is good. However, we need to know if the model and actual outputs agree well.

$$y_k := \sum_{m} h_{m,k} \cdot x_{k-m} \qquad \varepsilon_k := d_k - y_k$$

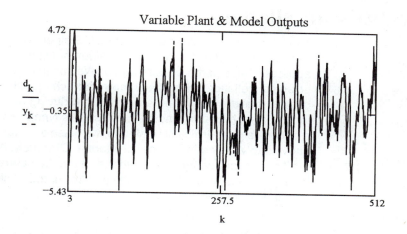

Variable Plant & Model Outputs

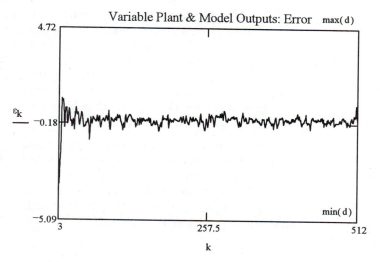

Variable Plant & Model Outputs: Error   max(d)

We observe that, even when the system's FIR is time-dependent, the model filter can do a good job of estimating or producing the output of the actual system. We can at least conclude that the algorithm can be useful.

Exercise 29.3 Adjust the parameter α and observe the resulting behavior. Can you observe a trade-off between adaptability and accuracy? ¤

PROBLEM 29.3

Suppose our a priori knowledge about the order of the actual system was wrong. Modify the above example so that the order M is different for the model. What are some consequences? ‡

Exercise 29.4 As in Exercise 29.2, assume a noisy measurement of the output of the actual system. Repeat the consideration of the topics of Exercise 29.3. ¤

Noise Cancellation

There are many applications for the LMS algorithm. It is not necessarily obvious how to use the algorithm in a particular application and some art is required. We consider the problem of noise cancellation, which has received much attention. There are commercial devices for personal use in reducing noise in restricted localities such as noisy industrial sites. This type of scheme uses a noise that is statistically related to the noise that has been unavoidably added to a signal of interest. Obviously, if the noise itself can be separately observed then it can be subtracted from the signal-plus-noise data, leaving just the signal. A sketch of the scheme is given below.

We see how this scheme works. Referring to the sketch, assume that the signal $\{s_n\}$ and noise $\{n1_n\}$ are uncorrelated. The unknown operation generates a random sequence $\{n2_n\}$ that is correlated with $\{n1_n\}$ and uncorrelated with $\{s_n\}$. The error is $\{\varepsilon_n = s_n + (n1_n - n2_n)\}$. The LMS algorithm strives to minimize the square of this error: it can only reduce the squared error by exploiting the correlation between $\{n1_n\}$ and $\{n2_n\}$ to make $\{n1_n - n2_n\}$ small. The residual error is, then, the signal estimate. This may seem a bit strange!

The structural form of the estimator of the noise $\{n1_n\}$, given the data $\{n2_n\}$, is a linear filter - an FIR filter. The output of the adapted FIR filter is an estimate of the noise $\{n1_n\}$; its input is the noise $\{n2_n\}$. We may expect that the scheme may work well if $\{n2_n\}$ is itself derived from $\{n1_n\}$ by a linear filtering - that is, if the unknown operation in the figure is a linear filter.

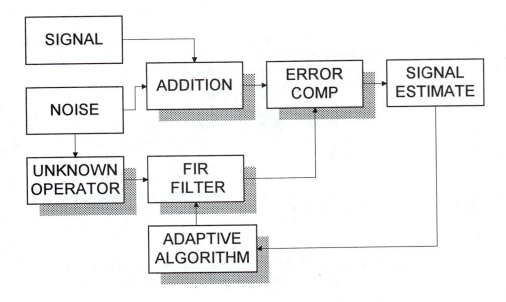

Example 29.2

We shall see if this scheme, which may be unexpected in its form, can work at all. We take a very simple case for the unknown operator: it generates, at each time n without regard to any other values of $\{x1_n\}$, a random variable $x2_n$ which has a correlation ρ with $x1_n$. We also assume a simple sinusoidal signal.

$$N := 512 \qquad\qquad n := 0 .. N - 1$$

$$NP := 4 \qquad\qquad \omega := \frac{2 \cdot \pi}{N} \cdot NP \qquad\qquad s_n := \cos(\omega \cdot n)$$

We allow different variances on the two noise sequences. We begin with the correlation as 1: we expect this to be the most favorable value for the scheme.

$$var1 := 1.0 \qquad\qquad var2 := 1.0 \qquad \rho := 1.0$$

$$n1 := \text{rnorm}(N, 0, var1) \qquad\qquad n2 := \text{rnorm}(N, 0, var2)$$

$$n2 := \rho \cdot n1 + \sqrt{1 - \rho^2} \cdot n2$$

In the notation above, the signal-plus-noise sequence is the desideratum $\{d_n\}$.

$$d_n := s_n + n1_n$$

We choose filter length M+1 and the initial estimate for the filter.

$$M := 4 \qquad m := 0 .. M \qquad\qquad h_{m,0} := 0 \qquad\qquad \mu := 0 .. M$$

We now implement the LMS algorithm, choosing the LMS constant α by trial and error. The sequence of model IR estimates will be arrayed in a (M+1)-by-N matrix h; the nth column is the IR at time n.

$$\alpha := 0.008 \qquad\qquad h_{m,M} := 0 \qquad\qquad k := M .. N - 1$$

$$h_{m,k+1} := h_{m,k} + \alpha \cdot \left(d_k - \sum_{\mu} h_{\mu,k} \cdot n2_{k-\mu} \right) \cdot n2_{k-m}$$

We display the evolving IR.

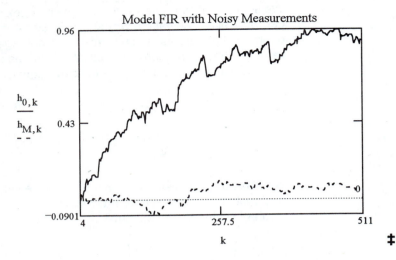

Model FIR with Noisy Measurements

$\dfrac{h_{0,k}}{h_{M,k}}$
- -

0.96

0.43

−0.0901

4   257.5   511

k

‡

⬛ **EXERCISE 29.5** Using the above graph, observe the evolution of all components of the IR. Vary the LMS constant α and observe the accuracy and rate of convergence. ¤

This evolution of the FIR is agreeable. Since there is no correlation in time in the noise processes, the FIR can only use the present value $n2_n$ to estimate $n1_n$. We expect the FIR to be zero except for its first value.

We now see how well the signal is recovered.

$$y_k := \sum_m h_{m,k} \cdot n2_{k-m} \qquad\qquad \varepsilon_k := d_k - y_k$$

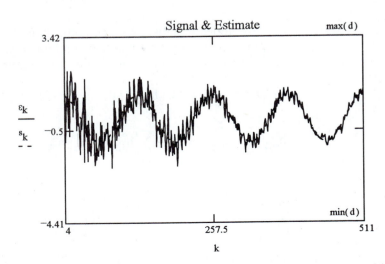

Signal & Estimate   max(d)

$\dfrac{\varepsilon_k}{s_k}$
- -

3.42

−0.5

−4.41

min(d)

4   257.5   511

k

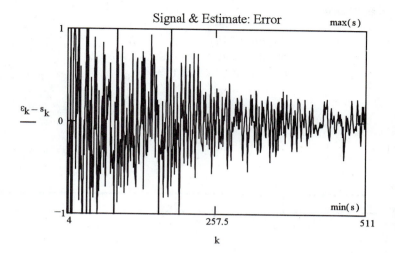

Signal & Estimate: Error

$\dfrac{\varepsilon_k - s_k}{}$

And so we find that the scheme does reduce the noise accompanying the signal after the FIR converges reasonably well. ‡

 EXERCISE 29.6 Vary ρ over the range (-1,1) in Example 29.2 and observe the performance. ¤

Project 29.1

In the noise cancellation problem discussed in Example 29.2, the noises $\{n1_n\}$ and $\{n2_n\}$ were correlated only at the same instant of time. Devise a correlation model that is more general and repeat the noise cancellation analysis. ‡

Project 29.2

A common use of an adaptive filter is in **echo cancellation**. Consult a communication systems book to obtain a simple model. Design the adaptive echo canceller and simulate it. ‡

Project 29.3

The LMS algorithm is very popular because of its minimal computational requirement. Its convergence can be somewhat slow and can be improved, at the cost of more computation. The RLS algorithm is one such algorithm. Apply this algorithm to the system identification problem and compare its performance with that of the LMS algorithm. ‡

References

Haykin (1991), Chaps. 9, 13
Ifeachor and Jervis (1993), Chap. 9
Widrow and Winter (1988)

30 Adaptive Equalization

Digital communication systems are a primary application area of digital signal processing. Designers are rapidly modifying and inventing communication systems to transmit information in the standard form of a binary-valued sequence. For example, a **pulse amplitude modulation (PAM)** communication system transmits a sequence of pulses whose amplitudes are determined by the binary sequence. After transmission through a communication medium, or **channel**, a system samples the received analog waveform, producing a binary sequence which, if all goes well, replicates the transmitted binary sequence. There are, of course, many phenomena that conspire to prevent perfect transmission.

PAM Communication

The most important channels are, not surprisingly, of limited bandwidth. This is true of telephone channels and microwave radio channels, which together carry the majority of the world's communication traffic. Finite channel bandwidth implies that the received pulses are of finite bandwidth and hence are not confined, even practically, to a time extent comparable to the interval allotted to transmit one binary symbol. Thus many pulses can affect each sample value; **intersymbol interference (ISI)** produces errors, and minimization of such errors is a central practical system design problem. The limited bandwidth channel is often well-modeled as a linear filter. Here we will assume it is a low-pass filter and thus ignore the usual heterodyning, or frequency translation, that occurs in many actual systems. A block diagram of such a system is shown below.

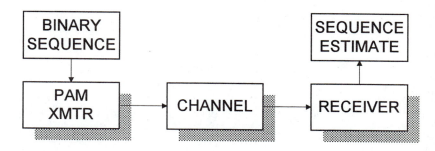

It is possible to design a pulse so that there is no ISI. For example, suppose that the pulse has the shape $[\sin(\pi t/T)/(\pi t/T)]^2$, which is unity at t=0 and zero at all other sample times nT, n=+/-1,+/-2,.... The bandwidth is finite as $\sin(\pi t/T)/(\pi t/T)$ has a rectangular Fourier transform supported over $(-\pi/T,\pi/T)$. (There are other pulses with this property, as well as the desirable property of faster decay than 1/t.) Note that, if the channel filter is known, then one could design the transmitted pulse so that the received pulse at the output of the channel is free from ISI. In practice, the problem is that the channel is often unknown. For example, each time a telephone communication occurs, it likely follows a different route.

We obtain a discrete-time or digital model of this communication system as follows. Let $\{r_n\}$ be the binary-valued sequence to be transmitted. The encoded binary symbols occur at a rate 1/T symbols per second. The PAM transmitter generates a sequence of pulses $\{p(t-nT)\}$ that are modulated by the binary sequence to give the transmitted analog waveform

$$a(t)=\sum_n r_n \cdot p(t - n \cdot T)$$

Let c(t) be the impulse response of the linear filter modeling the channel. Then the channel output is the analog waveform

$$sc(t)=\sum_n r_n \cdot \int_{-\infty}^{\infty} c(\tau) \cdot p(t - \tau - n \cdot T)\, d\tau$$

The receiver filters this analog waveform, with impulse response g(t), and then samples the filter output every T seconds. The channel and receiver cascade has an impulse response q(t) equal to the convolution of c(t) and g(t). If s(t) is the receiver output prior to sampling and $\{s_n=s(nT)\}$, we have the discrete model

$$s_n=\sum_m r_m \cdot h_{n - m} \tag{30.1}$$

EXERCISE 30.1 Show that

$$h_{n - m} = \int_{-\infty}^{\infty} q(\tau) \cdot p((n - m) \cdot T - \tau)\, d\tau \qquad ¤$$

Known Channel

We do remark that, in the special case of a fixed communication link, we could measure the channel frequency response. Suppose its frequency response is $C(v) > 0$ over its frequency band. Then, over this band, the frequency response $G(v)$ of the receiver could be taken as $G(v) = 1/C(v)$, with the result that the receiver output pulse is $p(t)$, which has presumably been designed for no ISI. This scheme is called **fixed equalization**.

Unknown, Invariant Channel

If the channel is unknown - for example, if it is the result of dialing a number on the telephone system - and of a time-invariant nature, then, prior to message transmission, the transmitter could send a special sequence that the receiver can use to measure the frequency response of the channel. Such a scheme is called **automatic equalization**. We can implement it as follows.

We assume that the receiver filter is an FIR filter of length $(2M+1)$. If $\{y_n\}$ is the input to the receiver filter, then the output samples are

$$s_n = \sum_{m=-M}^{M} h_m \cdot y_{n-m} \tag{30.2}$$

At the initialization of a communication, the known sequence of length $(2K+1)$, $K >> M$, is transmitted, which results in a sequence $\{s_n\}$. We choose the **tap weights** $\{h_m\}$ so as to minimize the total mean-square error

$$E_T = \sum_{k} \left(r_k - s_k \right)^2 \tag{30.3}$$

We can find necessary conditions for the tap weights $\{h_m\}$ by differentiating (30.3), in which (30.2) has been used for s_k, with respect to each tap weight, and setting the derivative equal to zero.

$$n = (-M..M)$$

$$\sum_{m=-M}^{M} h_m \cdot \left(\sum_{k=-K}^{K} y_{k-m} \cdot y_{k-n} \right) = \sum_{k=-K}^{K} r_k \cdot y_{k-n} \tag{30.4a}$$

Derive eqs. (30.4). ‡

We may compactly describe these necessary conditions by introducing the matrix Γ of elements $\{\Gamma_{m,n}\}$, the vector ρ of elements $\{\rho_m\}$ and the tap weight vector h of elements h_m, where

$$\Gamma_{m,n}= \sum_{k=-K}^{K} y_{k-m} \cdot y_{k-n} \qquad\qquad \rho_m= \sum_{k=-K}^{K} r_k \cdot y_{k-m}$$

Now (30.4) reads

$$\Gamma h = \rho \qquad\qquad\qquad (30.4b)$$

which has the solution - assuming the inverse exists -

$$h = \Gamma^{-1} \cdot \rho \qquad\qquad\qquad (30.5)$$

The equations (30.4) are the **normal equations** and Γ is the **Gramm matrix**. The normal equations arise frequently because the miminum mean-square error criterion is often used. It is mathematically tractable and leads to solutions that are robust - that is, relatively insensitive to parameter variations - in application. In DSP practice we rarely compute the inverse directly. Rather, it may be computed, in effect, indirectly by approximate, iterative schemes that are able to adapt under changing circumstance. We will discuss two such schemes below.

Example 30.1 _____
Suppose that the channel model is in fact an autoregressive, AR, model (**Chapter 18**). Then its frequency response is the reciprocal of a polynomial in $\exp(i\omega)$. Its inverse filter is simply the same polynomial in $\exp(i\omega)$, which is the frequency response of an FIR filter. Thus, if our scheme, which has an FIR filter in the receiver, is going to work at all, it should work now.

We make a random choice for the known sequence.

$$K := 512 \qquad k := 0 .. 2 \cdot K \qquad\qquad r_k := \text{if}(\text{rnd}(1)<0.5,0,1)$$

The output of the channel, modeled by a simple first-order AR filter, is easily computed by its corresponding first-order LDE.

$$a := 0.1 \qquad\qquad y_0 := r_0 \qquad\qquad y_k := \text{if}\left(k=0,y_0,a \cdot y_{k-1}+r_k\right)$$

We now determine the equalization filter assuming M=1.

$$M := 1 \qquad\qquad m := 0..\,2 \cdot M \qquad\qquad n := 0..\,2 \cdot M$$

$$\Gamma_{m,n} := \sum_k \text{if}\left[(k - m \geq 0) \cdot (k - n \geq 0), y_{k-m} \cdot y_{k-n}, 0 \right]$$

$$\rho_m := \sum_k \text{if}\left(k - m \geq 0, r_k \cdot y_{k-m}, 0 \right)$$

$$h := \Gamma^{-1} \cdot \rho \qquad\qquad\qquad h = \begin{bmatrix} 1 \\ -0.1 \\ -1.221 \cdot 10^{-15} \end{bmatrix}$$

Thus the FIR equalization filter is indeed the inverse filter.

To verify that the equalization filter is effective, we simulate the discrete-time model by putting the known sequence through the channel and equalization filters, in turn.

$$j := 2..\,2 \cdot K \qquad\qquad s_0 := h_0 \cdot y_0 \qquad\qquad s_1 := h_0 \cdot y_1 + h_1 \cdot y_0$$

$$s_j := h_0 \cdot y_j + h_1 \cdot y_{j-1} + h_2 \cdot y_{j-2}$$

$$e_k := r_k - s_k \qquad\qquad E_T := \sum_k \left(e_k \right)^2 \qquad\qquad E_T = 0$$

We graph these various sequences. Clearly the equalization filter is working well. ‡

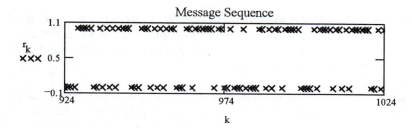

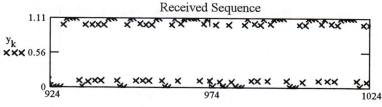

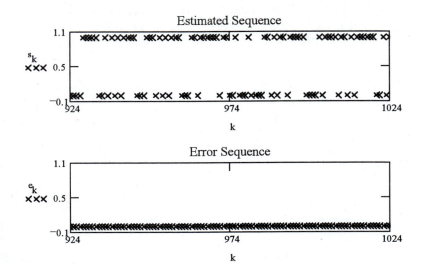

Estimated Sequence

Error Sequence

▨ **EXERCISE 30.2** Vary the parameter a of the AR channel model and observe the results. Vary the parameter M for the equalization filter and observe the results. Vary the length parameter K for the known sequence and observe the results. ¤

PROBLEM 30.2 Model the channel with an FIR filter of length Lc and repeat the above analysis. Can the FIR equalization filter be the inverse filter in this case? ‡

PROBLEM 30.3 Modify the channel model to include a sequence of white normal noise, additive to {y_n}. Repeat the above analysis. Is the inverse filter still a reasonable filter? ‡

Iterative Solution of the Normal Equations

It is interesting to consider an iterative approximation method to the solution of the normal equations based on a method of steepest descent, in part because it leads us to the idea of an adaptive equalization scheme.

Rather than wait until the entire known sequence {r_n} has been transmitted, we attempt to improve the estimate of the filter tap weights as each r_k, at time k, is received. At time k we minimize, over the choice of the tap weights, the squared error e_k^2, where

$$e_k = r_k - s_k$$

where s_k is given by (30.2). The gradient of e_k^2, with respect to h_m is

$$\frac{d}{dh_m}\left(e_k\right)^2 = 2\cdot\left(r_k - s_k\right)\cdot y_{k-m}$$

The (2M+1)-dimensional vector of these gradients gives the direction of most rapid increase of the squared error so its negative gives the direction of most rapid decrease, or the direction of **steepest descent**. So, to decrease the mean-square error we can decrease each tap weight proportionally to the gradient with respect to that tap weight. This gives us a method of incrementally improving the tap weights as each known symbol is received. The updating relation is, then,

$$h_{m,k+1} = h_{m,k} - \alpha\cdot\left(r_k - s_k\right)\cdot y_{k-m} \tag{30.6}$$

This recursion is called the **LMS algorithm** and is a very popular algorithm with a variety of applications. We used it in **Chapter 29**.

Example 30.2

We consider the same channel modeled above, a simple first-order AR filter, and now we apply the LMS algorithm (30.6) to determine, at least approximately, the optimal tap weights. We have already selected the known input sequence and computed the sequence $\{y_n\}$ at the input to the equalizing receiver. It only remains to implement the LMS algorithm - as in **Chapter 29**.

We choose a trial α and make an initial guess for the filter tap weight vector h.

$$\alpha := -0.01 \qquad\qquad h^{<0>} := \begin{pmatrix} 1.0 \\ 0.5 \\ 0.0 \end{pmatrix}$$

$$h_{m,k+1} := h_{m,k} - \alpha\cdot\left[r_k - \sum_n (k-n\geq 0)\cdot h_{n,k}\cdot y_{k-n}\right]\cdot(k-m\geq 0)\cdot y_{k-m}$$

$$h^{<2\cdot K>} = \begin{bmatrix} 0.938 \\ -0.063 \\ 8.413\cdot 10^{-3} \end{bmatrix} \qquad\qquad a = 0.1$$

With quite a long known sequence, the filter estimate becomes a reasonable approximation to (1,-a,0).

We now simulate the entire scheme.

$$h := h^{<2 \cdot K>} \qquad j := 2..2 \cdot K \qquad s_0 := h_0 \cdot y_0 \qquad s_1 := h_0 \cdot y_1 + h_1 \cdot y_0$$

$$s_j := h_0 \cdot y_j + h_1 \cdot y_{j-1} + h_2 \cdot y_{j-2}$$

$$e_k := r_k - s_k \qquad\qquad E_T := \sum_k \left(e_k\right)^2 \qquad E_T = 1.314$$

We graph these various sequences for the final stages of the iteration. Clearly the equalization filter is working well. ‡

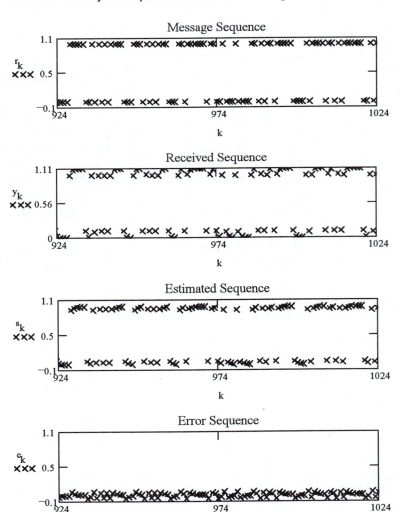

Message Sequence

Received Sequence

Estimated Sequence

Error Sequence

PROBLEM 30.4   The ultimate output of the communication system is a decision about the transmitted binary symbol. Implement a "decision rule" to complete the above receiver. Plot the sequence of decisions, $\{rest_k\}$, and the error sequence, $\{r_k-rest_k\}$. ‡

Unknown, Varying Channel

If the channel is unknown and is also slowly changing, then the above scheme of transmitting a known sequence and adjusting the equalization filter according to the LMS algorithm could be repeated at appropriate times. But this process requires time better spent on actual message transmission, and the equalization becomes less effective in the interim.

Here is a clever solution. Suppose that the equalization filter has been determined sufficiently well by the above scheme employing the LMS algorithm so that the message symbols $\{r_n\}$ are nearly always correctly estimated. Then in the LMS algorithm we can, at time k, try replacing r_k with its estimate, which again is probably in agreement. Then, in effect, we always have the desired sequence available, with large probabilty, and the algorithm - now called a **decision-directed algorithm** - can adapt to slow changes in the channel.

Example 30.3

The necessary modification to the Mathcad implementation of the LMS algorithm is rather simple: we replace r_k by its estimate. The decision rule for the symbol estimate is taken to be this: if $s_k<0.5$, then decide a "0" was transmitted; if $s_k>=0.5$, decide a "1" was transmitted. We may implement this decision rule in Mathcad as

$$rest_k = \text{if}\left(s_k < \frac{1}{2}, 0, 1\right)$$

or, taking advantage of Mathcad's logical variables, more simply as

$$rest_k = \left(s_k > \frac{1}{2}\right)$$

Recall that

$$s_n = \sum_n \text{if}\left(k - n \geq 0, h_{n,k} \cdot y_{k-n}, 0\right)$$

or, more simply,

$$s_k = \sum_n (k - n \geq 0) \cdot \left(h_{n,k} \cdot y_{k-n} \right)$$

Thus

$$rest_k = \left[\sum_n (k - n \geq 0) \cdot \left(h_{n,k} \cdot y_{k-n} \right) > \frac{1}{2} \right]$$

Note that the kth iterate of h is required to compute $rest_k$, and the Mathcad implementation becomes a bit more complex.

$$\alpha := -0.01 \qquad\qquad d := -\alpha \qquad\qquad h^{<0>} := \begin{pmatrix} 1.0 \\ 0.5 \\ 0.0 \end{pmatrix}$$

$$h_{m,k+1} := h_{m,k} \cdots$$
$$+ d \cdot \left[\left[\sum_n (k - n \geq 0) \cdot \left(h_{n,k} \cdot y_{k-n} \right) > \frac{1}{2} \right] - \sum_n (k - n \geq 0) \cdot \left(h_{n,k} \cdot y_{k-n} \right) \right] \cdot (k - m \geq 0) \cdot y_{k-m}$$

$$h^{<2 \cdot K>} = \begin{pmatrix} 0.938 \\ -0.053 \\ -0.014 \end{pmatrix} \qquad\qquad -a = -0.1$$

The filter does seem to approximate the inverse filter well and we will see that the communication of the binary symbols can be error-free.

We now simulate the entire scheme using the equalization filter of the (2K)th iterate.

$$h := h^{<2 \cdot K>} \qquad j := 2 .. 2 \cdot K \qquad s_0 := h_0 \cdot y_0 \qquad s_1 := h_0 \cdot y_1 + h_1 \cdot y_0$$

$$s_j := h_0 \cdot y_j + h_1 \cdot y_{j-1} + h_2 \cdot y_{j-2}$$

$$rest_k := \left(s_k > \frac{1}{2} \right) \qquad\qquad er_k := r_k - rest_k$$

$$Ter := \sum_k er_k \qquad\qquad Ter = 0$$

We graph these various sequences after a number of iterations of the scheme. Clearly the equalization filter is working well. ‡

Message Sequence

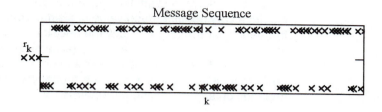

Received Sequence

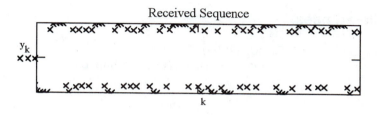

Estimated Sequence

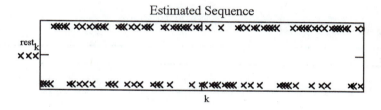

Error Sequence

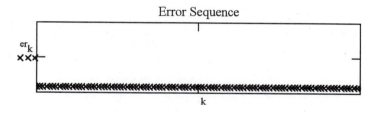

Project 30.1

Introduce a slow time variation into the channel. For example, you can let a vary about a mean value in a sinusoidal manner with a frequency parameter ωa. Study the decision-directed algorithm for variations in each of the parameters (a,ωa,K,M). Add normal noise to the input of the equalization filter and note its effect on error performance. Can you estimate the probability of error as it depends on some of these parameters? ‡

References

Gibson (1993), Chap. 8
Proakis and Salehi (1994), Chap. 8

31 Radar Processing

Processing radar signals was one of the earliest applications of DSP and it remains an important spur to DSP development. The early radar systems transmitted a pulse p(t) and then received the scaled and delayed pulse, σ p(t-τ_o), reflected by an isolated object. The measurement of the **delay** τ_o gives the **range** R_o by the relation τ_o=2R_o/c, where c is the velocity of light. The scale σ also depends on range, but less sensitively.

For a variety of reasons - such as efficiency of antennas and spectrum availability - the **pulse** is a **narrowband signal** of the form

$$p(t) = f_m(t) \cdot \cos\left(v_c \cdot t + \phi(t)\right)$$

where v_c is the **radiation frequency**, **RF**, and $f_m(t)$ and $\phi(t)$ are, respectively, the pulse **amplitude** and **phase modulations**.

Radar Model for Range Estimation

To process the received radar signal, it is (i) translated in frequency by multiplying it by cos(v_ct) and a copy of it by sin(v_ct), the **in-phase** and **quadrature carriers** generated by a **coherent local oscillator (LO)**, and (ii) each resulting waveform is low-pass filtered to remove the double harmonic. The result is that the radar data is now the pair of waveforms (σ f_m(t-τ_o)cos(ϕ(t-τ_o)-θ), σ f_m(t-τ_o)sin(ϕ(t-τ_o)-θ)), where θ=$v_c\tau_o$ is a phase and σ is an amplitude. Any such ordered pair of real functions can be taken as the real and imaginary parts of a **complex representation**

$$f_c\left(t - \tau_o\right) = \sigma \cdot f_m\left(t - \tau_o\right) \cdot e^{i \cdot \phi\left(t - \tau_o\right) - i \cdot \theta}$$

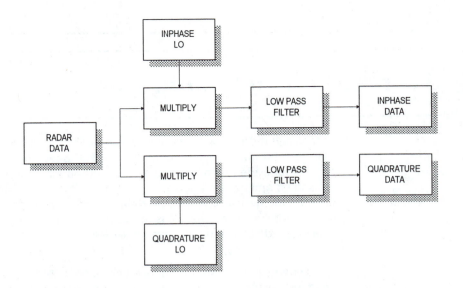

Whereas the phase θ does depend on range, many radar systems do not control knowledge of phase with sufficient accuracy to make this dependence useful, so we consider θ, along with σ and τ_o, as unknown parameters. We therefore write the radar data in the form

$$b = \sigma \cdot e^{-i \cdot \theta} \qquad b \cdot f\left(t - \tau_o\right) = b \cdot f_m\left(t - \tau_o\right) \cdot e^{i \cdot \phi\left(t - \tau_o\right)} \qquad (31.1)$$

where b is the unknown **complex amplitude**. The **range-finding radar signal model** is thus given by (31.1).

Signal Processing Theory

To complete a practical model for the received data, we add a sample function of a white, normal, complex, random sequence that models the thermal noise that is always present in radar data due to the material composition of the receiver and the viewed scene - the sky, for example. So the **range-finding radar data model** is thus given by (31.2):

$$z(t) = b \cdot f\left(t - \tau_o\right) + no(t) \qquad (31.2)$$

where the **pulse complex modulation** is

$$f(t) = f_m(t) \cdot e^{i \cdot \phi(t)} \qquad (31.3)$$

Our radar processing problem is twofold. First, we must decide if the signal is present in the data - this is the **detection problem**. If the signal is present then we must estimate the delay - this is the **estimation problem**.

What shall the radar processor be? There are several ways to arrive at the usual processor form, but we choose an intuitive argument. First, let us address the detection problem, assuming for the moment that the parameters (b, τ_o) are known and that $\tau_o = 0$ and $b = 1$. We know by now that a filter can partially eliminate the noise, so it is reasonable to take a linear filter with IR $h(t)$ as the first stage of the radar processor, forming the partially processed data

$$\int_{-\infty}^{\infty} z(s) \cdot h(t - s) \, ds$$

which we examine at $t=0$.

$$\int_{-\infty}^{\infty} z(s) \cdot h(-s) \, ds \qquad (31.4)$$

How shall we choose the IR h? The thermal noise has a spectral density uniform over frequency and it gives no preferable FR. So we consider the signal-dependent part of the form (31.4):

$$\int_{-\infty}^{\infty} f(s) \cdot h(-s) \, ds \qquad (31.5)$$

Regarding f(s) and h(-s) as vectors, the form is the scalar product of f(s) and conj[h(-s)], which is maximized over h by choosing conj[h(-s)] to be colinear with f(s). That is, we choose

$$h(t) = \alpha \cdot \overline{f(-t)} \qquad (31.6)$$

where α is a constant. This filter is famous in signal processing and was first discovered in the 1940s by D. O. North: it is called the **matched filter**.

EXERCISE 31.1 Show that the resulting maximum of (31.5), using (31.6), is real and that it is in fact the **energy**, the integral of the squared modulus, of the pulse complex modulation f(t). Show that the energy of the complex pulse modulation is twice the energy of the real pulse modulation. ¤

EXERCISE 31.2 The filter IR of (31.6) is complex. Show how this filtering may be realized with four filters with real IRs, given the real and imaginary parts of the complex radar data, which are obtained from the real narrowband radar data by using in-phase and quadrature local oscillators. ¤

Next, to decide whether the signal is present at t=0 with b=1, we compare the squared-magnitude

$$\left(\left|\int_{-\infty}^{\infty} z(s)\cdot\overline{f(s)}\; ds\right|\right)^{2} \tag{31.7}$$

with a real number tr called the **threshold**. The **decision rule** we choose is this: "Decide a signal is present if and only if the **test statistic** (31.7) exceeds tr."

Now we reexamine our processor choice when (b, τ_o) is not $(1,0)$; in particular, we examine it when the radar data is purely signal – that is, z(t) is replaced in (31.7) by $bf(t-\tau_o)$. Note that taking the magnitude in (31.7) means that b enters only as $|b|$: its unknown phase (of no interest to us anyway) does not enter the form.

EXERCISE 31.3 Referring to (31.7), show that if either the real or imaginary part is used instead of the magnitude, then the unknown phase would render the procedure worthless. ¤

If the delay is unknown, then our above reasoning leads us to compute a set of test statistics with $h(t;\tau_o)=conj[f[-(t-\tau_o)]]$ for a sufficiently dense set of possible τ_o. That is, we must compute the set of forms

$$\left(\left|\int_{-\infty}^{\infty} z(s)\cdot\overline{f\left[-\left(\tau_0 - s\right)\right]}\; ds\right|\right)^{2} \tag{31.8}$$

But all these computations can be realized in a fairly simple way. We perform a matched filtering of the radar data and examine its output over a set of times equal to the set of selected delays. If the maximum value exceeds the threshold, then we declare a signal present at the location of the maximum value.

Note that our processing scheme can, to a certain extent, handle the case of multiple objects with a modification of the decision rule. We decide an object present at every location whose output is above the threshold, assuming that signals are well separated, or resolved, with respect to the width of the IR.

Linear FM (Chirp) Pulse Modulation

A popular choice of radar pulse modulation has a phase modulation depending quadratically on time. The derivative of the phase, the frequency modulation, is therefore linear in time. At audible frequencies such a modulation like a chirp. This **linear FM**, or **chirp**, modulation is useful because its bandwidth can be independent of its time extent, which is determined by the pulse amplitude modulation. Thus, under a peak power restraint to prevent physical damage, a pulse amplitude modulation can be chosen of sufficient time extent so that the pulse modulation has the energy for good detection performance (recall Exercise 31.1) and has large bandwidth for location accuracy and resolution. We wish to illustrate these attributes of this signal.

We choose a magnitude for the linear FM pulse so that we can easily perform all the calculations with pencil and paper. Better, we employ the symbolic mathematics capability of Mathcad to good advantage - and leave the former efforts to problems as a check. For more practical magnitude models, the computations would likely be done numerically.

The linear FM pulse has a complex modulation modeled by

$$f(t) = \sqrt{\frac{E}{\sqrt{2 \cdot \pi \cdot T}}} \cdot \exp\left(-\frac{t^2}{4 \cdot T^2} - i \cdot k \cdot \frac{t^2}{2}\right) \tag{31.9}$$

where T is an indicator of the time extent of the modulation and k is the **linear FM rate**. The **energy** of f is

$$E_f = \int_{-\infty}^{\infty} \left(|f(t)|\right)^2 dt$$

 EXERCISE 31.4 Show that the energy E_f for f defined by (31.9) is E. ¤

This modulation has an unlimited time extent but falls off exponentially; it is not a bad model for practical signals whose precise extent is hard to define. It is useful to define the **time extent, T$_e$,** by the **radius of gyration measure**

$$T_e^2 = \frac{\displaystyle\int_{-\infty}^{\infty} t^2 \cdot (|f(t)|)^2 \, dt}{E}$$

  EXERCISE 31.5 Show that the time extent T$_e$ of f, defined by (31.9), is T. ¤

It is useful to define the **bandwidth parameter** Δ=kT, which is the extent of frequencies swept through in time T. Thus k=Δ/T. The **time-bandwidth product (TBP)**, of the linear FM waveform is defined to be TBP=ΔT. As we will see, it is a significant parameter of this modulation. With specific parameters convenient here, the complex modulation now takes the form

$$T := 5 \cdot 10^{-6} \quad \text{sec} \qquad \Delta := 2 \cdot \pi \cdot 10^6 \quad \text{rad/sec} \qquad E := 10^{-2} \quad \text{joule}$$

$$f(t) := \sqrt{\frac{E}{\sqrt{2 \cdot \pi \cdot T}}} \cdot \exp\left(-\frac{t^2}{4 \cdot T^2} - i \cdot \frac{\Delta}{T} \cdot \frac{t^2}{2}\right) \qquad (31.10)$$

We graph the linear FM modulation's magnitude and phase.

$$t := -5 \cdot T, -5 \cdot T + \frac{10 \cdot T}{128} \, .. \, 5 \cdot T$$

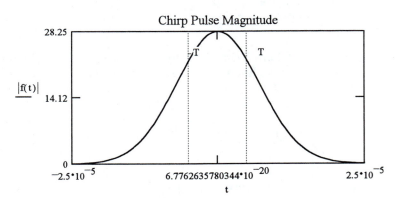

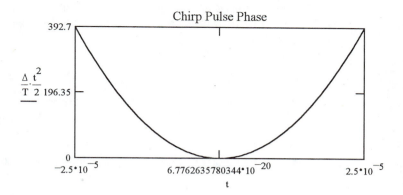

Chirp Pulse Phase

$\frac{\Delta}{T} \cdot \frac{t^2}{2}$

392.7

196.35

0

$-2.5 \cdot 10^{-5}$ $6.7762635780344 \cdot 10^{-20}$ $2.5 \cdot 10^{-5}$

t

Symbolic Computation of the Fourier Transform

We are interested in the FT of the chirp waveform. We compute it using the symbolic mathematics feature of Mathcad. It is convenient here to let ω be the frequency variable of the FT, which we usually have denoted by ν.

1. We isolate a copy of the right side of (31.10) and click on and enclose an instance of the t variable.

$$\sqrt{\frac{E}{\sqrt{2 \cdot \pi \cdot T}}} \cdot \exp\left(-\frac{t^2}{4 \cdot T^2} - i \cdot \frac{\Delta}{T} \cdot \frac{t^2}{2}\right)$$

2. Now we choose **Fourier Transform** from the **Symbolic** menu. The computation is placed below the form.

$$2^{\left(\frac{3}{4}\right)} \cdot \sqrt{E} \cdot \frac{\pi^{\left(\frac{1}{4}\right)}}{\left(\sqrt{T} \cdot \sqrt{1 + 2i \cdot \Delta \cdot T}\right)} \cdot T \cdot \exp\left[-\frac{1}{4} \cdot \frac{\omega^2}{\left[\frac{1}{(4 \cdot T^2)} + \frac{1}{2} \cdot i \cdot \frac{\Delta}{T}\right]}\right]$$

3. We enclose the exponent and then choose **Simplify** from the **Symbolic** menu. We repeat for the factor in front of the exponent.

$$2^{\left(\frac{3}{4}\right)} \cdot \sqrt{E \cdot \pi} \cdot \frac{\left(\frac{1}{4}\right)}{\sqrt{1 + 2i \cdot \Delta \cdot T}} \cdot \exp\left[-\omega^2 \cdot \frac{T^2}{(1 + 2i \cdot \Delta \cdot T)}\right]$$

We rationalize the complex fractions. For example, for 1/(a+ib) form (a-ib)/[(a+ib)*(a-ib)], select the bracketed expression and choose **Simplify** from the **Symbolic** menu.

$$2^{\left(\frac{3}{4}\right)} \cdot \sqrt{E \cdot \pi}^{\left(\frac{1}{4}\right)} \cdot \frac{\sqrt{T} \cdot \sqrt{1 - 2i \cdot \Delta \cdot T}}{\sqrt{\left(1 + 4 \cdot \Delta^2 \cdot T^2\right)}} \cdot \exp\left[-\omega^2 \cdot \frac{T^2 \cdot (1 - 2i \cdot \Delta \cdot T)}{\left(1 + 4 \cdot \Delta^2 \cdot T^2\right)}\right]$$

4. We now copy this result to a function declaration for the FT.

$$F(\omega) := 2^{\left(\frac{3}{4}\right)} \cdot \sqrt{E \cdot \pi}^{\left(\frac{1}{4}\right)} \cdot \frac{\sqrt{T} \cdot \sqrt{1 - 2i \cdot \Delta \cdot T}}{\sqrt{\left(1 + 4 \cdot \Delta^2 \cdot T^2\right)}} \cdot \exp\left[-\omega^2 \cdot \frac{T^2 \cdot (1 - 2i \cdot \Delta \cdot T)}{\left(1 + 4 \cdot \Delta^2 \cdot T^2\right)}\right] \quad (31.11)$$

Notice that the FT of this linear FM modulation itself has a quadratic phase and a Gaussian-shaped magnitude.

PROBLEM 31.1

Analytically compute the FT of the linear FM waveform. ‡

We can make a **radius of gyration definition of bandwidth** Δ_e analogous to that for time extent.

$$\Delta_e^2 := \frac{\displaystyle\int_{-\infty}^{\infty} \omega^2 \cdot \left(|F(\omega)|\right)^2 d\omega}{\displaystyle\int_{-\infty}^{\infty} \left(|F(\omega)|\right)^2 d\omega}$$

 EXERCISE 31.6 Show that, for the linear FM modulation,

$$\Delta_e := \sqrt{\frac{1 + (2 \cdot \Delta \cdot T)^2}{(2 \cdot T)^2}}$$

Show that when the TBP is large, the limiting form of Δ_e is Δ, *independently of the time extent T.* ¤

We now graph the magnitude of the FT of the chirp signal. The radius of gyration measure of bandwidth is Δ_e.

$$\omega := -5 \cdot \Delta_e, \left[-5 \cdot \Delta_e + \frac{2 \cdot (5 \cdot \Delta_e)}{128} \right] .. 5 \cdot \Delta_e$$

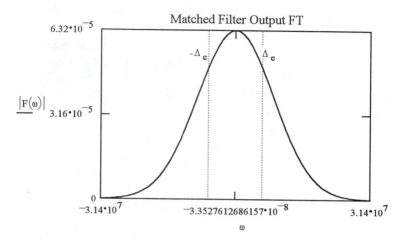

Symbolic Computation of Matched Filtering

We now compute the filter's output (in the absence of noise) using Mathcad's symbolic mathematics capability. We use the frequency domain method, which corresponds to the likely method used by a digital processor. The FT of the output signal's complex representation, Fo(ω), is the product of F(ω) and the frequency response of the matched filter, which is F(ω)*. So Fo(ω)=|F(ω)|².

5. We isolate a copy of the squared-magnitude of the right side of (31.11).

$$\left[\left| 2^{\left(\frac{3}{4}\right)} \cdot \sqrt{E} \cdot \pi^{\left(\frac{1}{4}\right)} \cdot \frac{\sqrt{T} \cdot \sqrt{1 - 2i \cdot \Delta \cdot T}}{\sqrt{\left(1 + 4 \cdot \Delta^2 \cdot T^2\right)}} \cdot \exp\left[-\omega^2 \cdot \frac{T^2 \cdot (1 - 2i \cdot \Delta \cdot T)}{\left(1 + 4 \cdot \Delta^2 \cdot T^2\right)} \right] \right| \right]^2$$

6. Now we click on and enclose the form and choose **Simplify** from the **Symbolic** menu.

$$2 \cdot \sqrt{2} \cdot |E| \cdot \sqrt{\pi} \cdot \frac{|T|}{\sqrt{1 + 4 \cdot \Delta^2 \cdot T^2}} \cdot \exp\left[-2 \cdot \omega^2 \cdot \frac{T^2}{\left(1 + 4 \cdot \Delta^2 \cdot T^2\right)} \right]$$

(31.12)

7. We now copy it to a function declaration defining the output signal's FT.

$$Fo(\omega) := 2 \cdot \sqrt{2} \cdot |E| \cdot \sqrt{\pi} \cdot \frac{|T|}{\sqrt{1 + 4 \cdot \Delta^2 \cdot T^2}} \cdot \exp\left[-2 \cdot \omega^2 \cdot \frac{T^2}{\left(1 + 4 \cdot \Delta^2 \cdot T^2\right)}\right]$$

8. We can now have Mathcad compute the IFT to find the output signal. We isolate a copy of the right side of (31.14) and click on and enclose an instance of the ω variable. Then we choose **Inverse Fourier Transform** and then **Simplify** from the **Symbolic** menu.

$$|E| \cdot \frac{|T|}{T} \cdot \exp\left[\frac{-1}{8} \cdot t^2 \cdot \frac{\left(1 + 4 \cdot \Delta^2 \cdot T^2\right)}{T^2}\right]$$

9. We now copy the result to a function declaration defining the output signal - with a little assistance as T and E are real and positive.

$$fo(t) := E \cdot \exp\left[\frac{-1}{8} \cdot t^2 \cdot \left(\frac{1 + 4 \cdot \Delta^2 \cdot T^2}{T^2}\right)\right] \tag{31.13}$$

This result is relatively simple. Note that the peak output value is the energy of the complex modulation, as predicted.

PROBLEM 31.2

Derive the matched filter output (31.13) analytically. ‡

EXERCISE 31.7 Show that the time extent, defined as the radius of gyration, of the output is

$$T_{oe} := 2 \cdot \frac{T}{\sqrt{1 + (2 \cdot \Delta \cdot T)^2}} \tag{31.14}$$

and that $T_{oe} = 1/\Delta_e$. Find the limiting form for large TBP and show that it is $1/\Delta$, *independently of T.* ¤

We plot the input and output signals, both normalized to unity maximum, to compare their time extents.

$$t := -3 \cdot T, \left[-3 \cdot T + \frac{2 \cdot (3 \cdot T)}{128} \right] .. 3 \cdot T$$

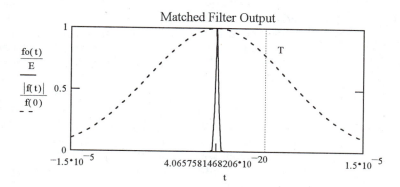

Matched Filter Output

We observe that the output signal has considerably less extent than the input signal. The **compression ratio**, **CR**, is the ratio of the extent of the input to the extent of the output, each measured by radius of gyration.

EXERCISE 31.8 Show that CR for the linear FM waveform is

$$CR := \frac{1}{2} \cdot \sqrt{1 + (2 \cdot \Delta \cdot T)^2} \qquad\qquad CR = 31.419905$$

Show that in the limit as the TBP=ΔT becomes large CR is TBP. ¤

Remark The intrinsic range estimation accuracy of the linear FM pulse, taken as the time extent of the output of its matched filter, is independent of the time extent of the pulse when the time-bandwidth product is large: TBP>>1. This makes it possible to transmit a long pulse, under a practical peak power restraint, with accumulation of large energy to enable good detection and estimation performance. In practice, radar systems employ TBPs as large as several thousand.

Digital Signal Processing

We have used symbolic mathematics to describe analog processing of a radar pulse with its matched filter. In practice, the processing is often done with a digital processor implementing a numerical algorithm. The received data is heterodyned with in-phase and quadrature mixers and sampled. This can introduce artifacts due to aliasing. The engineering design problem typically is to choose a sampling frequency sufficiently large that the artifacts are reduced to a tolerable level. We will see here that an artifact of aliasing can be the introduction of a false image. In a radar system, the received waveform from one transmitted pulse is relatively long and a fast convolution method (**Chapter 5**) may be used. Here we will be concerned with just one block of input data, of extent about that of the transmitted pulse, to reduce the computation to a feasible level. To reduce the required computation, we compute the digital filtering by the frequency domain method and use the DFT/FFT. Therefore, we arrange the samples in DFT order.

The linear FM pulse with a Gaussian magnitude is not limited in time or frequency. So sampling introduces both truncation and aliasing effects. To minimize the effects due to truncation, we choose the sample sequence of extent sufficient to include all but a negligible amount of signal energy. We will choose a sufficiently large sampling frequency by trial and error. We take the sampling frequency in the form $\phi\Delta$, where ϕ is a variable sampling factor . A ϕ no larger than 8 will be sufficient. Then a sample length of N=1024 includes all significant samples of f(t).

$$\phi := 6 \qquad \omega s := \phi \cdot \Delta \qquad \omega s = 3.769911 \cdot 10^7$$

$$Ts := \frac{2 \cdot \pi}{\omega s} \qquad\qquad Ts = 1.666667 \cdot 10^{-7}$$

$$N := 1024 \qquad n := 0 .. N - 1 \qquad fs_n := if\left[n \le \frac{N}{2}, f(n \cdot Ts), f((n - N) \cdot Ts) \right]$$

$$dft(v) := \sqrt{N} \cdot icfft(v) \qquad idft(v) := \left(\frac{1}{\sqrt{N}} \right) \cdot cfft(v) \qquad fsft := dft(fs)$$

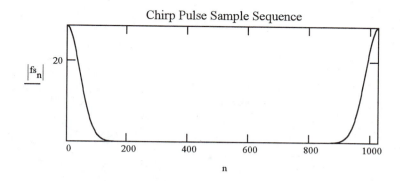

Chirp Pulse Sample Sequence

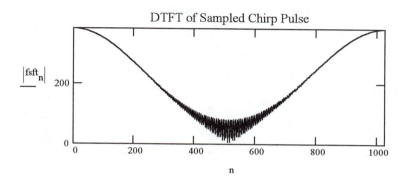

DTFT of Sampled Chirp Pulse

We can see $\phi=6$ results in a well-sampled signal with a slight indication of aliasing. For $\phi=5$, there is evident interference due to aliasing (**Chapter 15**).

EXERCISE 31.9 Vary f over a range of about 1 to 8 and note the aliasing effects in the DFT. Explain the interference pattern that is seen. Compute the percent energy of the waveform in the truncated section. ¤

The processing digital filter is defined as a sampling of the FR of the matched filter of the analog signal, which is the complex conjugate of the analog signal's FT. By defining the processing filter this way, we avoid aliasing artifacts in the FR of the processing filter. The sample spacing and the frequency samples, in DFT order, are

$$\delta\omega := \frac{2 \cdot \pi}{N} \cdot \frac{1}{Ts} \qquad Fs_n := if\left[n \leq \frac{N}{2}, F(n \cdot \delta\omega), F((n-N) \cdot \delta\omega) \right]$$

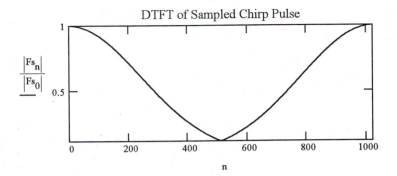

DTFT of Sampled Chirp Pulse

The envelope of the output of the digital filter is

$$Fos := \overrightarrow{(Fs \cdot fsft)} \qquad fo := idft(Fos) \qquad fom := \overrightarrow{|fo|}$$

$$mx := max(fom) \qquad fodb_n := 20 \cdot log\left(\frac{fom_n}{mx} + 10^{-5}\right)$$

Matched Filter Output

Examining the output, we note again that, relative to the input, the output is of a larger peak value and a very narrow time extent - in other words, of fine resolution. This is the great virtue of the linear FM signal. We see that the sampling procedure has introduced a **false image**, whose location and peak value depend on ϕ. By trial and error we find that, with $\phi=6.1$, these false images have a relative size of -45 db, perhaps sufficiently low to be ignored. However, radar signals can show a dynamic range of more than 70 db. That is, some weak signals of interest can be 70 db below the strongest signals.

EXERCISE 31.10 Vary ϕ and observe the location and height of the false images. For a -50 db specification on the false image level, what is the minimal ϕ? ¤

Project 31.1

 Extend the digital signal processing discussion by adding white Gaussian noise of variable level to the data. Study how the presence of this noise affects the detectability of the signal and the accuracy of the estimate of its position. Place a few signals of variable amplitudes in the data and study the resolution properties. Since the matched filter has an FR with a quadratic phase, it has a delay that depends linearly on frequency. Give a simple, even graphical, explanation for the compression phenomenon. A sample spacing adequate for processing may be too large for good accuracy. What can be done? ‡

Project 31.2

If an object is moving with a component v of its velocity **v** along its line of sight to the radar, then there will be a **Doppler shift** v in the frequency of the received pulse given by $v = (2v/c)v_c$. Thus, the radar can estimate this velocity by measuring the Doppler shift. The **range-Doppler-finding radar signal model** is now

$$b \cdot f\left(t, \tau_o, v\right) = b \cdot f_m\left(t - \tau_o\right) \cdot e^{i \cdot \phi\left(t - \tau_o\right)} \cdot e^{i \cdot v \cdot t}$$

All of the above discussion for the range-finding radar carries over with obvious modification. In particular, the squared-magnitude of output of the processing filter matched to this signal can be put in the form

$$q(\tau, \mu) = \left(\left| \int_{-\infty}^{\infty} f(t) \cdot f(t - \tau) \cdot e^{i \cdot \mu \cdot t} \, dt \right| \right)^2$$

where τ is the difference between the true delay and a test delay and μ is the difference between the true Doppler and a test Doppler. Thus we are interested in how $q(\tau, \mu)$ varies with changes in τ and μ. q is the famous **range-Doppler ambiguity function**. Its salient property is this: assuming that the energy of f has been normalized to unity,

$$\int_{-\infty}^{\infty} \int_{-\infty}^{\infty} q(\tau, \mu) \, d\tau \, d\mu = 2 \cdot \pi$$

Explain the significance of this result. Compute this ambiguity function for the linear FM pulse and make a surface plot for various choices of T and Δ. Make other choices of pulse modulation, for example, a finite sequence of pulses, with or without phase modulation. ‡

References

Srinath et al. (1996), Secs. 8.4-8.8
Woodward (1953)

32 Imaging Radar

The **Doppler** effect of relative motion on the frequency of waves is a commonly observed phenomenon. For example, as a train passes by, its whistle, a sound wave at a nearly pure frequency, will change to an apparently less shrill sound. This effect gives a measurement of the time that the train's position was at a known point on the track. The same phenomenon occurs with electromagnetic waves and can be cleverly exploited to yield a very important radar system, as we now discuss.

Imagine an airplane flying over a scene in a straight line at a constant altitude with uniform speed v. On the airplane we have a crude radar that radiates a sinusoidal, or **CW**, signal, of frequency v_c, through an antenna that confines the radiated signal to a narrow pattern directed abeam the airplane. Consider one small object on the terrain that reflects, or scatters, the signal back to the radar: the received CW signal will have a higher frequency (v_c+v_D) before it is passed by the airplane and a lower frequency (v_c-v_D) after it is passed. When the **Doppler shift** v_D is zero, the object is abeam the airplane and hence its relative position in the direction of the aircraft velocity vector **v** is thus known. We call this position the **azimuth** location.

▨ **EXERCISE 32.1** Show that the delay in the returned signal is

$$\tau(x)=\frac{2\cdot\sqrt{R_o^2+x^2}}{c}$$

where R_o is the (minimum) range when the object is abeam, x is its relative along-track position and c is the velocity of light. In the systems of interest to us here, the antenna pattern is very narrow and so R_o is much larger than any x of interest. Using the binomial expansion, show that now, to a good approximation,

$$\tau(x)=\frac{2\cdot R_o}{c}\cdot\left(1+\frac{x^2}{2\cdot R_o^2}\right) \qquad ¤ \qquad (32.1)$$

Since x=vt, we see that the returned signal will have a quadratic phase. The shape of its magnitude is determined by the antenna pattern, which gives it an approximately finite extent. The radar receiver employs in-phase and quadrature mixers and, in effect, we get a complex modulation that is the linear FM wave studied in **Chapter 31**. So, we already know how to choose and realize a good processor for this signal. The compression operation means here that the along-track resolution is much smaller than that afforded simply by the antenna: the system appears to have an antenna of much greater size, called the **synthetic aperture**.

A convenient parametrization of this Doppler-induced linear FM complex modulation is the following. The numerical values are selected to fit Mathcad.

azimuth resolution (m): $\rho a := 10$

azimuth bandwidth (rad/m): $\Delta := \dfrac{2 \cdot \pi}{\rho a}$ $\Delta = 0.628$

azimuth TBP: $TBPa := 10$

azimuth modulation extent (m): $X := TBPa \cdot \rho a$ $X = 100$

azimuth linear FM rate: $Ka := \dfrac{\Delta}{X}$ $Ka = 6.283 \cdot 10^{-3}$

azimuth antenna pattern shape: $b_m(x) := \exp\left(-\dfrac{x^2}{4 \cdot X^2}\right)$

azimuth complex modulation: $b(x) := b_m(x) \cdot \exp\left(i \cdot Ka \cdot \dfrac{x^2}{2}\right)$ (32.2)

Synthetic Aperture Radar

As we now have a way to determine the azimuth location of an object, we can pulse-modulate the RF to determine the range, thus locating the object in a plane called the **slant range plane**. By transmitting pulses rather than CW, we now sample the Doppler modulation. We also now understand the consequences of this in view of **Chapter 31**: in particular, we know that aliasing can generate false images. Note that the sampling is done by the actual analog system. In fact, for many years digital processors were not capable of processing this type of radar data. It was done by a type of analog processor, an optical processor. Such a radar system is called a **synthetic aperture radar**, **SAR**.

The most commonly chosen pulse modulation is linear FM. A convenient parametrization of this complex modulation follows. Again, the numerical values are selected to fit Mathcad. It is convenient to rescale the range coordinate from time to distance using c/2.

range resolution (m): $\qquad\qquad$ $\rho r := 10$

range bandwidth (rad/m): $\qquad$ $\Omega := \dfrac{2 \cdot \pi}{\rho a}$ $\qquad$ $\Omega = 0.628$

range TBP: $\qquad\qquad\qquad$ $TBPr := 10$

range modulation extent (m): $\qquad$ $Y := TBPr \cdot \rho r$ $\qquad$ $Y = 100$

range linear FM rate: $\qquad\qquad$ $Kr := \dfrac{\Omega}{Y}$ $\qquad$ $Kr = 6.283 \cdot 10^{-3}$

range pulse magnitude: $\qquad\qquad$ $f_m(y) := \exp\left(-\dfrac{y^2}{4 \cdot Y^2}\right)$

range complex modulation: $\qquad$ $f(y) := f_m(y) \cdot \exp\left(i \cdot Kr \cdot \dfrac{y^2}{2}\right)$ $\qquad$ (32.3)

Ignoring the aliasing effects due to sampling, the **SAR two-dimensional complex modulation** is

$$s(x,y) := f(y) \cdot b(x) \qquad\qquad s_m(x,y) := |f(y)| \cdot |b(x)| \qquad\qquad (32.4)$$

We plot this modulation's magnitude.

$M := 64 \qquad m := 0 .. M - 1 \qquad \delta x := \dfrac{6 \cdot X}{M} \qquad\qquad x_m := m \cdot \delta x - 3 \cdot X$

$N := 64 \qquad n := 0 .. N - 1 \qquad \delta y := \dfrac{6 \cdot Y}{N} \qquad\qquad y_n := n \cdot \delta y - 3 \cdot Y$

$smag_{m,n} := |s_m(x_m, y_n)|$

smag
SAR Complex Modulation (Magnitude)

The SAR Data

An actual scene such as the terrain has a very complex nature. It is often possible - and certainly very convenient - to describe the scene by a **reflectivity density**, g(x,y), the ratio of the reflected-to-incident electromagnetic fields at (x,y). In effect, the scene described by g(x,y) is scanned by the SAR system. The scanning in range is accomplished by electromagnetic propagation (at half the speed c of light) and the scanning in azimuth is accomplished by aircraft motion (at the much slower speed v). This scanning operation is described by the two-dimensional convolution

$$\mathrm{sf}(x,y) = \int_{-\infty}^{\infty} \int_{-\infty}^{\infty} s(x-\zeta, y-\eta) \cdot g(\zeta,\eta) \cdot e^{i \cdot 2 \cdot k_o \cdot \eta} \, d\zeta \, d\eta \qquad (32.5)$$

The phase factor $\exp(i2k_o\eta)$ accounts for the phase change $2k_o\eta = 2\pi(2\eta/\lambda)$ due to the round-trip ray path (2η) from the SAR antenna to the range η. Since s is a low-pass function, this phase factor results in g being sensed only in a band of spatial frequencies centered on the wavenumber $(0, 2k_o)$ and of width determined by s. Thus the SAR's image of a scene generally depends on its specific RF. This frequency diversity can be exploited in image processing.

Early SAR systems were feasible only because analog processing systems - in particular, analog optical processors - existed. These mimicked the signal generation - at optical frequencies, in effect scaling the processor to laboratory size! The signal sf(x,y) was actually recorded on film and called the signal film. It is an example of an **hologram**. We call sf(x,y) the **SAR complex data**.

The SAR Processor

To design a processor for the SAR, we may again consider one isolated object in the scene. To process this particular signal effectively, we may reason exactly as we did in **Chapter 31**. The theory outlined there applies equally well to the two-dimensional situation, and we conclude that the processor should again involve a (two-dimensional) matched filter. The appropriate matched filter is, then,

$$h(x,y)=\overline{s(-x,-y)} \qquad\qquad (32.6)$$

The SAR Image

The **SAR complex image** that results is then

$$i(x,y)=\int_{-\infty}^{\infty}\int_{-\infty}^{\infty} h(x-\zeta,y-\eta)\cdot sf(\zeta,\eta)\, d\zeta\, d\eta \qquad\qquad (32.7)$$

We therefore have a linear model for the SAR system that has the scene's reflectivity density as the input to a cascade of two two-dimensional, complex, linear, spatially invariant filters, one of IR s(x,y) and the other of IR h(x,y).

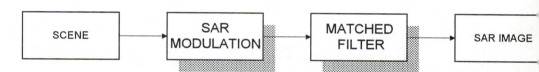

The SAR System IR

When the scene is simply a point scatterer, the SAR complex data is the SAR complex modulation and the image is then the two-dimensional convolution of the SAR complex modulation with the IR of the matched filter.

EXERCISE 32.2 Show that this two-dimensional convolution is expressible as the product of two one-dimensional convolutions. ¤

Then we can carry over the results of the symbolic calculation in **Chapter 31** to write down the **two-dimensional IR** of the SAR system. Within a complex scale, we have

$$h_{SARa}(x) := \exp\left[\frac{-1}{8} \cdot \frac{x^2}{X^2} \cdot \left(1 + 4 \cdot \Omega^2 \cdot X^2\right)\right]$$

$$h_{SARr}(y) := \exp\left[\frac{-1}{8} \cdot \frac{y^2}{Y^2} \cdot \left(1 + 4 \cdot \Delta^2 \cdot Y^2\right)\right]$$

$$h_{SAR}(x,y) := h_{SARa}(x) \cdot h_{SARr}(y) \tag{32.8}$$

EXERCISE 32.3 The TBP of an SAR system is typically several hundred to several thousand. Show that then the right side of (32.8) simplifies so that the radius of gyration definition of resolution is that consistent with the above parametrization of the two linear FM complex modulations. ¤

Digital Signal Processing and Simulation

If we are given the reflectivity density g(x,y) describing a scene, the SAR complex image of the scene is calculated by the convolution

$$i(x,y) = \int_{-\infty}^{\infty} \int_{-\infty}^{\infty} h_{SAR}(x - \zeta, y - \eta) \cdot g(\zeta, \eta) \cdot e^{i \cdot 2 \cdot k_o \cdot \eta} \, d\zeta \, d\eta \tag{32.9}$$

There is no need for the much more complicated calculation of the SAR complex data. Except for quite special examples, this convolution would be done numerically via the two-dimensional DFT/FFT. We have already discussed this in **Chapter 31** for the one-dimensional case, and we carry over that work here with the simple modifications needed for this two-dimensional, but factored, case.

$$h_{SARa_m} := \text{if}\left[m \leq \frac{M}{2}, h_{SARa}(m \cdot \delta x), h_{SARa}((m - M) \cdot \delta x)\right]$$

$$h_{SARr_n} := \text{if}\left[n \leq \frac{N}{2}, h_{SARr}(n \cdot \delta y), h_{SARr}((n - N) \cdot \delta y)\right]$$

Example 32.1

We assume a simple reflectivity density that can model a slightly rough area - for example, a locally breeze-ruffled sea surface that is otherwise glassy smooth.

$$g(x,y) = \text{if}\left[(x-X)^2 + (y-Y)^2 \leq X^2, 1, 0\right] \cdot \xi(x,y) \cdot e^{i \cdot 2 \cdot k_o \cdot y}$$

where $\xi(x,y)$ is uncorrelated over any scale of interest here. Then $\gamma(x,y)=\xi(x,y)\exp(i2k_o y)$ is uncorrelated over the bandwidth of the SAR, and we have the sampled model

$$\sigma_o := 5 \qquad \gamma^{<n>} := \text{rnorm}\left(M, 0, \sigma_o\right)$$

$$\gamma_{m,n} := \text{if}\left[(m \cdot \delta x - X)^2 + (n \cdot \delta y - Y)^2 \leq X^2, \gamma_{m,n}, 0\right]$$

We now compute the SAR image by the frequency domain method, taking advantage of the factored form of h_{SAR}.

$$H_{SARa} := \sqrt{M} \cdot \text{icfft}\left(h_{SARa}\right) \qquad\qquad H_{SARr} := \sqrt{N} \cdot \text{icfft}\left(h_{SARr}\right)$$

$$H_{SAR_{m,n}} := H_{SARa_m} \cdot H_{SARr_n} \qquad\qquad Hm_{m,n} := \left|H_{SAR_{m,n}}\right|$$

$$\Gamma := \sqrt{M \cdot N} \cdot \text{icfft}(\gamma) \qquad I := \overrightarrow{\left(H_{SAR} \cdot \Gamma\right)} \qquad i := \frac{1}{\sqrt{M \cdot N}} \cdot \text{cfft}(I)$$

$$\gamma m_{m,n} := \left|\gamma_{m,n}\right| \qquad\qquad im_{m,n} := \left|i_{m,n}\right|$$

γm
Object Reflectivity Density (Mag.)

im
SAR Image (Magnitude)

We see that the SAR image magnitude is a rather faithful reproduction of the object's reflectivity density magnitude, restricted to the SAR bandwidth. ‡

The SAR Image of a Two-Scale Scene

Models of the reflectivity density for types of interesting scenes can be found with techniques devised in electromagnetic scattering theory, a long-standing and sophisticated subject. One widely useful model is the **two-scale model**. This model applies to surfaces that are of high dielectric constant (e.g., good conductors) and that are the superposition of two height scales - a large-scale surface Ξ of radius of curvature large with respect to the RF wavelength λ and a surface ξ small relative to λ. It is convenient now to use a coordinate system fixed in the mean plane of the scene, called the **SAR ground range plane**.

One can show that this scene's reflectivity density is of the form

$$\beta = \frac{4 \cdot \pi \cdot \cos(\delta)}{\lambda} \qquad\qquad \alpha = \frac{4 \cdot \pi \cdot \sin(\delta)}{\lambda}$$

$$g(x,y) = g_0 \cdot \left(1 - i \cdot \beta \cdot \xi(x,y)\right) \cdot \exp(-i \cdot \beta \cdot \Xi(x,y)) \cdot \left(1 + \Xi_y(x,y) \cdot \tan(\delta)\right)$$

$$(32.10a)$$

Here δ is the incidence angle of the radar waves on the surface (generally an angle near $\pi/4$) and Ξ_y is the partial derivative of Ξ with respect to y. The fourth factor accounts for the tilt of the local surface away from the SAR direction. The phase factor of (32.9) now is $\exp(i\alpha y)$, as y is now ground range.

PROBLEM 32.1

Using a simple sketch of the geometry, compute the change C in ray path from the radar to the mean plane of the terrain and hence the phase change $2\pi(2C/\lambda)$. Then use the fact that $\beta\xi << 1$. This simple observation accounts for the first and second factors of (32.10). ‡

ξ is usually modeled as uncorrelated over any scale of interest here. Then, the sampled version of $\xi_c = \xi \exp(i\alpha y)$ is an uncorrelated set of random variables, easily generated in a simulation. One need not generate an impractically broadband ξ. This is an important observation for computational feasibility and leads us to break $\gamma = g\exp(i\alpha y)$ into a sum of two parts. The **specular** part is

$$\gamma_s(x,y) = g_0 \cdot (1) \cdot \exp(i \cdot \alpha \cdot y - i \cdot \beta \cdot \Xi(x,y)) \cdot (1 + \Xi y(x,y) \cdot \tan(\delta)) \qquad (32.10b)$$

and the **diffuse** part is

$$\gamma_d(x,y) = g_o \cdot \left(-i \cdot \beta \cdot \xi_c(x,y) \right) \cdot \exp(-i \cdot \beta \cdot \Xi(x,y)) \cdot (1 + \Xi y(x,y) \cdot \tan(\delta))$$

$$(32.10c)$$

Notice that γ_s contains the factor exp(iαy), which represents a very high spatial frequency. This renders the sampling of this factor difficult and hence the contribution to the SAR image of this term must be evaluated in a special way. At the intermediate incidence angles used in SAR systems (about $\pi/4$ rad), the specular contribution can be small.

Ξ is modeled as a narrowband random field whose highest wavenumber is well within the SAR passband. But note that Ξ also enters as exp(-i$\beta\Xi$), whose bandwidth is often greater than the bandwidth of Ξ and can even be greater than that of the SAR. (Recall that this is the form of phase modulation, which is typically bandwidth expanding - as in frequency modulation, FM.) It is this factor of g that may set the sample period that we use in a simulation. Thus the proper sample rate for γ=gexp(iαy) requires careful study.

PROBLEM 32.2

Study the required sample rate for exp(-i$\beta\Xi$). ‡

We can now write down the SAR complex image model (32.9) for the two-scale scene. For computational purposes, we must write it as a sum of two parts that result from the two terms of (1-i$\beta\xi$). The contribution corresponding to the "1" is the **specular** part:

$$i_s(x,y) = g_o \cdot \int_{-\infty}^{\infty} \int_{-\infty}^{\infty} h_{SAR}(x-\zeta, y-\eta) \cdot \gamma_s(\zeta,\eta) \, d\zeta \, d\eta$$

The contribution corresponding to the "-i$\beta\xi$" is the **diffuse** part

$$i_s(x,y) = g_o \cdot \int_{-\infty}^{\infty} \int_{-\infty}^{\infty} h_{SAR}(x-\zeta, y-\eta) \cdot \gamma_d(\zeta,\eta) \, d\zeta \, d\eta$$

Then the SAR complex image is

$$i(x,y) = i_s(x,y) + i_d(x,y)$$

$$(32.11)$$

Example 32.2

Suppose we assume that the large-scale Ξ is a sinusoid with a small frequency so that Ξ and also $\exp(-i\beta\Xi)$ have frequencies well within the SAR passband. Then, with an intermediate incidence angle, we can ignore the specular contribution.

$$\lambda := 10 \qquad \xi_c^{<n>} := \text{rnorm}(N, 0, \sigma_o)$$

$$\delta := \frac{\pi}{4} \qquad \beta := \frac{4\cdot\pi\cdot\cos(\delta)}{\lambda} \qquad\qquad \alpha := \frac{4\cdot\pi\cdot\sin(\delta)}{\lambda}$$

$$\beta = 0.889 \qquad\qquad \alpha = 0.889$$

$$\Xi_o := 10 \qquad k_x := 0.02 \qquad k_y := 0.02 \qquad \Xi_o\cdot\beta = 8.886$$

$$\Xi(x,y) := \Xi_o\cdot\cos(k_x\cdot x + k_y\cdot y) \qquad\qquad \Xi s_{m,n} := \Xi(m\cdot\delta x, n\cdot\delta y)$$

$$\Xi_y(x,y) := -\Xi_o\cdot k_y\cdot\sin(k_x\cdot x + k_y\cdot y) \qquad\qquad \Xi y s_{m,n} := \Xi_y(m\cdot\delta x, n\cdot\delta y)$$

The scene description's samples then are, for the diffuse part,

$$\gamma s\,d_{m,n} := \left(-i\cdot\beta\cdot\xi\,c_{m,n}\right)\cdot\exp\left(-i\cdot\beta\cdot\Xi s_{m,n}\right)\cdot\left(1 + \Xi y s_{m,n}\cdot\tan(\delta)\right)$$

We compute the SAR image.

$$\Gamma := \sqrt{M\cdot N}\cdot\text{icfft}(\gamma s\,d) \qquad\qquad I := \overrightarrow{\left(\Gamma\cdot H_{SAR}\right)}$$

$$i := \frac{1}{\sqrt{M\cdot N}}\cdot\text{cfft}(I) \qquad\qquad \text{imag} := \overrightarrow{(|i|)}$$

$\Xi s + \xi_c$
Surface Height: 2-Scale Scene

imag
SAR Image Magnitude: 2-Scale Scene

We see that the artifact of the long wave is just discernable in the SAR image. (It may be more evident if Color Shading is selected.) We chose an impractically long radar wavelength λ so that we would both satisfy the sampling requirement $2\pi/\delta x > 2(b\ \Xi_o + 1)k$ (Carson's rule)$_x$ and be able to see the wave artifact in the small image area that we are able to compute here. ‡

PROBLEM 32.3 Vary the parameters in the above SAR imaging model. For example, set to zero the variance of the small-scale height and note that there is then no image artifact attributable to the long wave. (You must carefully check for adequate sampling as parameters are varied - e.g., the height of the large scale.) It can happen that a two-scale scene as modeled appears to have one-half the wavelength of the large-scale structure: can you reproduce this phenomenon? ‡

Project 32.1

Simulate and study the SAR image of a scene that contains an object that is described by the specular part. (For example, you might model a large water storage tank as a sphere.) In practice, the presence of some types of objects in the scene is most readily determined by the presence of a "radar shadow". Extend the above model to include this effect. Another effect is "range inversion". For example, at intermediate incidence angles, the top of a tower is at a closer slant range than the base of the tower. Extend the above model to include this phenomenon. ‡

Reference

Harger (1970)

A Mathcad Tutorial

Here we will introduce you to many of the features in Mathcad or the Mathcad Engine that you will see used in this Electronic Book. Mathcad is a powerful tool and, as with any tool, practice makes perfect. Reading and experimenting in this chapter will provide you with the groundwork you may need to proceed with this Electronic Book. Remember, too, that you can always use the **Help** menu if you want help on particular Mathcad features. *This tutorial is meant to be interactive.* Try the examples given!

For working with the material of this chapter, it is convenient to have Mathcad in the automatic calculation mode. If you do not see "auto" in the lower margin of the screen, then select **Automatic Mode** from the **Math** menu. Now any changes you make to a variable, equation, etc., will automatically be updated. (This can cause inconvenient waiting so in all other parts of the book we suggest you do *not* use the automatic mode. Then, any time you want the document's computations updated, select **Calculate Worksheet** from the **Math** menu. A quick keystroke to do the same is **F9**.)

Regions

A Mathcad **document**, or **worksheet**, is composed of three types of **regions** and is stored in a single computer file with the extension .mcd. These region types are **text**, **mathematics** and **graphics**. Each band of text, each graphic and each mathematical expression stands alone as its own region.

To create a text region, place the red cursor in the document where the region is to be located, type **Shift "** and type the text. You try it in a blank region below.

To create a mathematics region, place the red cursor in the document where the region is to be located and enter the mathematical expression. We discuss this below, but for now try typing **x:7^2** in a blank region below.

To create a graphics region, specifically an x-y plot, place the red cursor in the document where the region is to be located and type **Shift@**. We discuss this further below, but for now try it in a blank region below.

A region, or set of regions, can be **selected** by clicking on a blank area of the screen and dragging the mouse across one or several regions. The selected regions are each enclosed in a dashed-line box, allowing you to move, copy, cut and paste them.

To cut, copy and paste regions, select them and then choose **Cut**, **Copy** or **Paste** from the **Edit** menu. Quick keystrokes for **cut** and **paste** are **F3** and **F4**, respectively.

To **move** regions, select them and then move the cursor within any of the regions. Notice that the arrow becomes a large, black crosshair. Hold down your mouse button and drag your mouse. The regions selected will move with it.

(If you are working in the Mathcad Engine, *you'll only be able to move and cut regions you create, not those that are part of the original book*.)

To deselect a region, click in an empty area of the document.

Text Regions

The ability to give clear explanations of accompanying mathematics and graphics is a powerful tool. A Mathcad document is itself then a complete report. Mathcad's text editor is fairly standard and you should not have any problems using it. Note that there is a spelling checker. Also, **F3** and **F4** can be used to cut and paste selected text.

To create a text region, place the cursor where the region is to be located and type **Shift@** and enter text.

Mathematics Regions

The ability of Mathcad to format mathematical expressions in a standard, familiar format and then to execute them is its heart and soul. Not unexpectedly, this will be the least familiar and will require the most effort to learn. Entering and editing mathematical expressions is a learned art. But the required skills are easily acquired with a little practice.

Calculation Order

Mathcad reads and computes regions from top to bottom, left to right. In other words, a Mathcad document's memory is to the left and upward. This implies that regions containing mathematics must be properly relatively located. To see an example of this, create a region that shows you the value of x, by typing $x =$. Move this new region, using the method described previously, to a location above the definition of x.

$$x := 3.3 \qquad\qquad x^2 = 10.89$$

If you do this, you'll find x is indicated as being undefined with reverse video. If you move your region below and/or to the right of the definition of x, Mathcad will be able to calculate the answer.

The Assignment Operator

To create a math region, click in any blank portion of the document and enter the expression or definition of your choosing. To define a variable or expression, you type the colon (:) character, which displays a :=. For example,

$$\text{age}_{\text{me}} := 22 \qquad\qquad \textbf{Type age . me : 22}$$

The := (said as colon-equals) is an **assignment operator**. To see the numerical result, use the =, as here:

$$\text{age}_{\text{me}} = 22 \qquad\qquad \textbf{Type age . me =}$$

Try clicking on the 22 in the definition of age_{me} above and backspacing over it to enter your own age. Once you hit enter, the displayed result of $\text{age}_{\text{me}} =$ will change as well. The subscript created with a period allows commonly used mathematical labeling.

If you are working in the Mathcad Engine, you will not be able to delete the : = in any math expression that is part of the original book, nor will you be able to modify text that is part of the original book. This is a safeguard, to keep you from destroying information unintentionally. You may want to try this now, to see what happens.

Operations

You can also perform operations within definitions. A list of the basic scalar operators and the keystrokes used to invoke them is shown here.

Operation	Keystroke	Example	
addition	+	$L_w := x + 4$	$L_w = 7.3$
subtraction	-	$t := x - 3.2$	$t = 0.1$
multiplication	*	$y := x \cdot - 0.8$	$y = -2.64$
division	/	$f := \dfrac{x}{x}$	$f = 1$
powers	^	$a := x^{1.2}$	$a = 4.19$
square root	\	$this := \sqrt{x}$	$this = 1.817$
integral	&	$i := \displaystyle\int_{0}^{10} x\, dx$	$i = 50$
derivative	?	$d := \dfrac{d}{dx} x$	$d = 1$

You will learn all of the operator keystrokes as you go along, but if you forget one for now, you can use the palettes. In some versions of Mathcad these palettes are at the left side of your screen. To scroll through different palettes, click on the uppermost, numbered palette button. In other versions of Mathcad these palettes are accessed by clicking on an icon in an array at the top left.

Editing

When you edit an expression, the space bar is used to determine the order of operations. For example

$(x + 1) \cdot x$ Type **x + 1 [hit the spacebar] * x**

If the spacebar had not been hit, you would have seen

$x + 1 \cdot x$

which is a completely different expression.

Certain operators, such as superscripts, subscripts, square roots and division, are called "sticky" operators because characters you type will stick to them until you specifically ask to get out by hitting the spacebar (or using your mouse).

For example

$$\left(x^2 + \frac{7}{3} \right) - y$$
Type **x ^ 2 [spacebar] + 7 / 3 [spacebar spacebar] - y**

Without hitting the spacebar, this would appear as

$$x^{2 + \dfrac{7}{3 - y}}$$

To change a variable or a number, click on it, backspace over it and reenter it. To change an operator, the following steps are necessary:

$$x^2 + x - y$$

To change the plus, click on it in the expression above. If you select more than just the first two variables, use the up or down arrow keys to put a blue box around just the x^2 and x, then hit the backspace key. This will delete the plus sign. Now type the correct operator, for instance, **/** for division, resulting in

$$\frac{x^2}{x} - y$$

If you had wanted to change the subtraction sign, you would have clicked on it instead of the addition sign as the first step.

Displaying Math

You can get **Mathcad** to display your calculated answers in different ways. For example, you can use either **j** or **i** to indicate complex numbers. Or, you can specify the number of digits of displayed precision on numbers. All of these choices are made through the **Numerical Format** dialogue box available under the **Math** menu.

Arrays

An **array** is an indexed set of numbers or variables. A **vector** has one index and will be used to store digital signals and digital filters. A **matrix** has two indices and will be used to store digital images and image filters. In Mathcad, the array indices are called **range variables** and are nonnegative integers. Because the arrays we use are relatively large, they are assigned values or variables most efficiently using range variables.

For example, to assign values to a vector we first define the range variable and then the values - usually in terms of the range variable.

number of values in vector:	$N := 32$	Type **N:32**
array index/ range variable:	$n := 0 .. N - 1$	Type **n:0;N-1**
assign values to vector v:	$v_n := n^2$	Type **v[n:n^2**

To examine the vector, we most often make a plot with n as the abscissa and v_n as the ordinate.

Functions

Defining your own functions is accomplished as follows:

$$f(x) := \sin(x)$$ Type **f (x) : sin (x)**

$$g(x,y) := x^2 - y$$ Type **g (x , y) : x ^ 2 [spacebar] - y**

Now these functions can be evaluated at specific values:

$$f(45 \cdot \deg) = 0.707$$ Type **f (45 * deg) =**

$$g(1,-1) = 2$$ Type **g (1 , - 1) =**

Symbolics

Symbolic expressions will appear in this book. They are written using the logical equals sign, which is formed using **Ctrl=**.

$$x^2 \cdot y = 2 \cdot b + \frac{x}{d} - 7$$

Type **x ^ 2 * y [Ctrl]= 2 * b [spacebar] + x / d [spacebar] - 7**

Most of the calculations we do in this book are numerical. But we will calculate expressions symbolically from time to time.

Symbolic expressions are also used in this book to state mathematical equations that will not actually be calculated. In this way we convey information best expressed mathematically.

Graphical Regions: Plots

Combining all of the techniques presented brings us to plotting. **Mathcad** has built-in plots with a number of formatting features available. A quick example of a simple x-y plot is

$$x := 0 .. 2 \cdot \pi$$ Type **x : 0 ; 2 * p [Ctrl]g**

$$f(x) := \sin(x)$$ Type **f (x) : sin (x)**

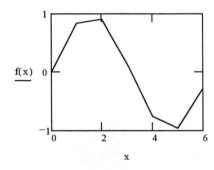

Type **f (x) @ x [Enter]**

The @ symbol created the plot region, giving you a plot of **sin(x)**. You may notice that the plot looks a little rough. This is because **x** is defined in intervals of **1** from **0** to **6.28**. To increase the intervals (and the smoothness of the plot), change the definition of **x** to read **0, 0.1 .. 2π**.

Anatomy of a Plot

If you click in a blank area of the screen and type **@**, you will see a plot with little black boxes called **placeholders** in which the variables should be typed. If you simply fill in the **x** and **y** arguments (the black boxes in the center of each axis) and hit **[Enter]**, the data limit placeholders will automatically be filled with the high (right and top) and low (left and bottom) values on the plot.

If you double-click on a graph, you'll get a dialogue box that allows you to change plot parameters, including plot markers (lines on the graph), line types and data markers (x's, boxes, etc. on a trace).

Formatting Plots

If you wish, you can enter numbers in the data limit placeholders to set the limits on the plot that are larger or smaller than your data set, or to create a marker on your plot.

Surface Plots

Mathcad also has surface plots and contour plots available for plotting matrices. For example

$$N := 20 \qquad i := 0..N \qquad j := 0..N$$

$$\text{Surface}_{i,j} := \left| \sin\left(3 \cdot \pi \cdot \frac{i}{N}\right) \right| + \left| \cos\left(2 \cdot \pi \cdot \frac{j}{N}\right) \right|$$

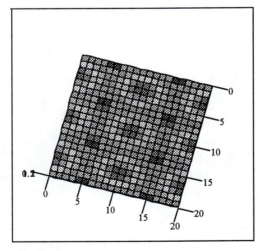

Surface

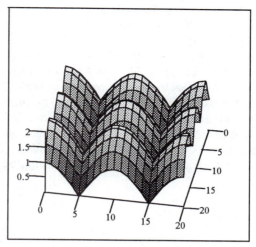

Surface

To create a surface plot, type **[Ctrl] 2** then enter the matrix name in the placeholder that appears in the lower-left corner of the box (where you see **Surface** above).

Again, double-clicking on the body of the plot will provide you with a **Plot Format** option box. Experimenting with these options using the surface plots above should make each option clearer. We suggest you try this now. (Notice that both of the above plots are of the same matrix at different rotations. Can you make them match?)

Programming

The most recent versions of Mathcad have an elegant function programming capability. These provide a powerful added capability but should not be used to routinely replace the built-in functions of Mathcad, which are likely to be more efficient. A particularly useful application here is to create vector and matrix functions, in effect making them of greater dimension. As Mathcad can directly define only vectors and matrices, of dimensions one and two, respectively, this is a powerful feature. We introduce this programming application now.

We show how to define a vector v(N) as a programmed function of its dimension N. Remember that such a vector is a sequence of length N. On the worksheet type v(N) and ":" in the usual way to declare a function and then click on the placeholder on the right side of the expression. Now click on the **programming icon** on the **Palette** to get the **programming palette**. Then click on **Add Line**: the expression's placeholder will be replaced by a vertical bar with two placeholders to be used to start to build the program. We want to construct a simple for loop: so click on the top placeholder and then click on **for** from the programming palette. We now have the following construct (which we have toggled off):

$$v(N) := \quad \left| \begin{array}{l} \text{for } \blacksquare \in \blacksquare \square \\[1em] \blacksquare \\[1em] \blacksquare \end{array} \right.$$

We next select the placeholders to declare the loop index - say n - and the limits of the for loop, which we take to be 0 and N-1. We now have the following (inactive) form.

$$v(N) := \quad \left| \begin{array}{l} \text{for } n \in 0.. \, N - 1 \square \\[1em] \blacksquare \\[1em] \blacksquare \end{array} \right.$$

We click on the placeholder in the second line and enter v_n, for which we will assign a simple form. Enclose v_n and then click on the assignment arrow on the programming palette. In the placeholder for the assignment, we type in simply n. Finally, in the last placeholder, we type in v, the vector we are defining.

$$v(N) := \quad \left| \begin{array}{l} \text{for } n \in 0.. \, N - 1 \\[1em] \quad v_n \leftarrow n \\[1em] v \end{array} \right.$$

To the right of the above form, type v(4)= and push F9. Try other values of N and verify that the for loop is correctly producing the vector v with $v_n = n$. You should use another definition for v_n and check the correctness of the program. ¤

More Help

The Mathcad window contains a **Palette**, a **Tool Bar** and a **Font Bar** that can be helpful. Run the mouse (no button depressed) over the icons and a message will disclose the function, or functions, that are accessed. Many of these functions are accessible other ways. When an electronic book is opened there is also a **Palette** of navigational controls for the book; this is discussed in the chapter about electronic books.

If you need any further assistance, please refer to **on-line Help** for more information by choosing from the **Help** menu. You can get context-sensitive help on any menu item, function or error message by typing **[Shift]-F1**, and then clicking on the item with which you'd like help. You'll know you're in the right mode because the cursor will change to a question mark. Exit context-sensitive help by pressing **[Esc]**.

That's a quick tour of the tools available in **Mathcad** or the **Mathcad Engine**. Don't be discouraged if you don't remember it all the first time. As you read through the sections in this Electronic Book, you'll gain experience with **Mathcad** as well.

Enjoy learning with this **Mathcad Electronic Book**! Click on the TOC icon to go back to the Table of Contents.

Bibliography

Books

Bateman, A., and W. Yates. *Digital Signal Processing Design*. Rockville, MD: Computer Science Press, 1989.

Crochiere, R. E., and L. R. Rabiner. *Multirate Digital Signal Processing*. Englewood Cliffs, NJ: Prentice-Hall, 1983.

Dudgeon, D. E., and R. M. Mersereau. *Multidimensional Digital Signal Processing*. Englewood Cliffs, NJ: Prentice-Hall, 1984.

Gibson, J. D. *Principles of Analog and Digital Communication*, 2nd Ed. New York: Macmillan, 1993.

Gold, B., and C. M. Rader. *Digital Processing of Signals*. New York: McGraw-Hill, 1969.

Harger, R. O. *Synthetic Aperture Radar Systems*. New York: Academic Press, 1970.

Hayes, M. *Statistical Digital Signal Processing and Modeling*. New York: Wiley, 1996.

Haykin, S. *Adaptive Filter Theory,* 2nd Ed. Englewood Cliffs, NJ: Prentice-Hall, 1991.

Ifeachor, E. C., and B. W. Jervis. *Digital Signal Processing*. Reading, MA: Addison-Wesley, 1993.

Jackson, L. B. *Digital Filters and Signal Processing,* 3rd Ed. New York: Kluwer Academic, 1996.

Jain, A. K. *Fundamentals of Digital Image Processing*. Englewood Cliffs, NJ: Prentice-Hall, 1989.

Kuo, F. F. and J. F. Kaiser (Eds.). *Systems Analysis by Digital Computer*. New York: Wiley, 1966.

Oppenheim, A. V., and R. W. Schafer. *Digital Signal Processing*. Englewood Cliffs, NJ: Prentice-Hall, 1975.

Oppenheim, A. V., and R. W. Schafer. *Discrete-Time Signal Processing*. Englewood Cliffs, NJ: Prentice-Hall, 1989.

Oppenheim, A. V., and A. S. Willsky. *Signals and Systems,* 2nd Ed. Englewood Cliffs, NJ: Prentice-Hall, 1997.

Press, W. H., B. P. Flannery, S. A. Teukolsky and W. T. Vetterling. *Numerical Recipes: The Art of Scientific Computing*. Cambridge: Cambridge University Press, 1986 (pp. 147-151).

Proakis, J. G., and D. G. Manolakis. *Digital Signal Processing*, 3rd Ed. Englewood Cliffs, NJ: Prentice-Hall, 1996.

Proakis, J. G., and M. Salehi. *Communication System Engineering*. Englewood Cliffs, NJ: Prentice-Hall, 1994.

Roberts, R. A., and C. T. Mullis. *Digital Signal Processing*. Reading, MA: Addison-Wesley, 1987.

Srinath, M. D., P. K. Rajasekaran and R. Viswanathan. *Introduction to Statistical Signal Processing with Applications*. Englewood Cliffs, NJ: Prentice-Hall, 1996.

Stearns, S. D., and D. R. Hush. *Digital Signal Analysis,* 2nd Ed. Englewood Cliffs, NJ: Prentice-Hall, 1990.

Woodward, P. M. *Probability and Information Theory, with Applications to Radar*. London: Pergamon Press, 1953.

Articles

Barbosa, L. C., "A maximum-energy-concentration spectral window," *IBM Jo. Res. Develop.* **30**, pp. 321-325, May 1986.

Meng, T. H., B. M. Gordon, E. K. Tsern and A. C. Hung, "Portable video-on-demand in wireless communication," *Proc. IEEE* **83**, pp. 659-680, April 1995.

Widrow, B., and R. Winter, "Neural nets for adaptive filtering and adaptive pattern recognition," *IEEE Computer Mag.*, pp. 25-39, March 1988.

Index

The items are referenced by chapter and page. For example, 29-1 refers to Chapter 29, page 1. The page numbers may be approximate because the way the electronic book is displayed depends on your computer.

The reader is reminded of the **Search Book** facility, accessed under the **Books** menu item, of the Electronic Book.

matched filter, 5-5, 31-3
    symbolic calculation, 31-7
moving average (MA) filter, 2-1, 18-**2**
    simple, 2-1, 2-15, 3-12, 4-11, 7-4, 18-2
multi-rate systems, 17-10

narrowband signal, 31-1
noise cancellation, 29-8
normal equations, 30-4
    LMS algorithm, 30-7
notch filter, 20-6
Nyquist condition, 15-5, 17-4

overlap-add method, 5-7
overlap-save method, 5-10

passband, 21-10
periodic
    convolution, 2-10
    extension, 1-14
    image, 27-2
    signal, 1-5
periodogram, 26-1
    modified, 26-7
phase
    for causality, 10-3
phase unwrapping algorithm, 3-11
pixel, 27-1
pod function, 1-13
pole-zero plot
    definition, 6-5, 9, 19-2
    FIR filters, 8-11, 9-1
    IIR filters, 19-2
pulse
    amplitude modulation, PAM, 30-1
    radar, 31-1

quadratic resonator, 18-7, 19-6, 22-4

spectral density
    definition, 24-11
    estimation
        modified periodogram, 26-7
        periodogram, 26-1
        optimal window, 26-9
    properties, 24-13
spectral (FT) estimation, 7-9, 15-8
stability, 18-5
stopband, 21-12
symbolic computation
    DFT, 3-13
    DTFT, 6-9, 6-16
    FT, 31-6
    LDE, 18-12
    matched filtering, 31-8
    ZT, 6-9, 6-16
synthetic aperture radar, 32-2
    complex data, 32-4
    complex image, 32-5
    complex modulation, 32-3
    impulse response, 32-4
    simulation, 32-6
system function, 6-4
system identification, 29-1

test statistic, 31-4
threshold, 31-4
time-bandwidth product (TBP), 13-14, 31-5
time invariance, 2-7, 2-15, 18-2
transfer function: see system function
transition band, 10-6, 21-10
truncation, 7-9, 15-10
two-scale model, 32-8

unit impulse, 1-3
unity gain resonator, 19-6